CONTESTING THE STATE

First published in 2012
Paperback edition published in 2014
Sean Kingston Publishing
www.seankingston.co.uk
Canon Pyon

In association with
The Centro Incontri Umani, Ascona

British Library Cataloguing in Publication Data
A catalogue record for this book is available from the British Library.

The moral rights of the authors and editors have been asserted.

Printed by Lightning Source

ISBN 978-1-907774-35-5

Contesting the State

The Dynamics of Resistance and Control

Edited by Angela Hobart and Bruce Kapferer

SK
ublishing
Sean Kingston Publishing
www.seankingston.co.uk
Canon Pyon

In association with
The Centro Incontri Umani,
Ascona

ACKNOWLEDGEMENTS

The conference 'Contesting the State: the Dynamics of Order and Resistance' was hosted at the Centro Incontri Umani (cross-cultural centre) Ascona. The Centre supports projects that assist in the pursuit of human dignity and human diversity. The fragility of the quest for human dignity and 'freedom' is epitomized by this volume, which discusses diverse socio-political processes across the globe, ranging from Africa and the Middle East, to Europe, Asia and South America. The book went through a number of transformations. Sadly, Professor Keith Hopkins died soon after the conference in Ascona. We still remember with delight his pleasure eating spaghetti in the piazza, while gazing at small Ticino boats gliding through the calm blue waters of Lake Maggiore, aglow with the last rays of the descending sun. We want to express our gratitude to all the participants whose probing chapters make up this book. We would like to thank Sean Kingston especially for his patience, competence and meticulousness in bringing the book to publication.

Saddam Hussein presented himself as descended from Nebuchadnezzar, the founder of the Neo-Babylonian empire (see Dawod's chapter), a figure that William Blake brings to life in his etching (on the cover). Is Nebuchadnezzar a tyrant, a boundless despot, a figure who shows that in political life no sharp division can be made between 'virtue' and 'vice'? Machiavelli's prince is half man, half beast, *mezzo uomo e mezzo bestia*, who in political games follows the patterns of the lion and the fox. Focusing on the Machiavellian aspects of power politics inherent in formal institutions of control and order ignores their transformational potency; it also fails to capture the dignity, modesty, anguish, wisdom, laughter and aesthetics of the people at the grass-roots level. There are local kinds of dynamics of power and relevant cosmologies that may interpenetrate contemporary settings. That is a theme picked up in many of the chapters in this book that explores alternative imaginings of the state, of power configurations, and of global processes. As Ernest Cassirer said in *The Philosophy of Symbolic Forms* (1996:111):

> Man is not limited by this immanent boundary in his perception and action, but ventures to fly beyond them. So man comes to share in a new heaven and earth.

Angela Hobart
Bruce Kapferer

CONTENTS

CONTRIBUTORS

Hosham Dawod is Head of Institut Français du Proche-Orient in Iraq (IFPO), and a researcher in social anthropology at the Centre National de la Recherche Scientifique (CNRS) in France.

T.M.S. Evens is Professor of Anthropology at the University of North Carolina at Chapel Hill, USA.

Jonathan Friedman is Directeur d'études, l'École des Hautes Études en Sciences Sociales (EHESS), Paris, France and Distinguished Professor of Anthropology, University of California, San Diego, USA.

Laurie Kain Hart is Edmund and Margiana Stinnes Professor of Global Studies and Professor of Anthropology, Department of Anthropology, Haverford College, USA.

Angela Hobart is Director of the Centro Incontri Umani, Ascona, Switzerland, and a Research Fellow, Medical Anthropology Department, University College London, UK.

Bruce Kapferer is Professor in the Department of Social Anthropology at Bergen University, Norway, Adjunct Professor at James Cook University, Australia and Honorary Professor at University College London, UK.

Joanna Overing is Professor Emeritus, Department of Social Anthropology and Researcher within the Centre for Amerindian, Latin American and Caribbean Studies (CAS), University of St Andrews, Scotland.

Bal Gopal Shrestha is a Research Fellow at the Institute of Social and Cultural Anthropology, University of Oxford, UK.

Christopher Taylor is an independent scholar.

Roshan de Silva Wijeyeratne is a Lecturer in Law at Griffith Law School, Griffith University, Brisbane, Australia.

INTRODUCTION

Forces in the production of the state

BRUCE KAPFERER AND CHRISTOPHER C. TAYLOR

The state is frequently conceived as a universal, although one apparently extraordinarily difficult to define. It often appears in academic discourse and, especially, in the popular imaginary as an abstraction, usually nebulous, grasped as pervasive – a spectre to be feared. Indeed much of the potency of *the state* is in the imagination of it. Conventionally, the concept of the state typically refers to a largely bureaucratically coordinated system of institutions of governing control over a defined territorial expanse. It was broadly for this reason that Radcliffe-Brown (1970) indicated that the term government should be used instead of the state, a position that Abrams (1988) and others such as Trouillot (2001) have followed. The question of the state once received major attention in anthropology, which then seemed to recede, only to achieve a revival in recent years, if mainly along different lines. Here we comment that in the years between the World Wars and soon after the Second World War there were in fact highly influential works in anthropology on the state. Robert Lowie (1948), M.G. Smith (1975), S.F. Nadel (1942), Lloyd Fallers (1940), Max Gluckman (2006) and more recently Stanley Tambiah (1976), Louis Dumont (1980), Eric Wolf (1973) and Clifford Geertz (1980) are a few of the most outstanding authors. They took a predominantly institutional and ideological view in which the classic studies of de Tocqueville (2001), Maine (1917), Durkheim (1976), Marx (1967) and Max Weber were influential. Their thought was thoroughly grounded in European historical and philosophical work, but there was considerable effort to search for the distinctions that state systems outside the European expansion might manifest. Of considerable significance in this regard is the path-breaking work by Edmund Leach (1965, and see Jonathan Friedman's 1998 important critique), who took a less formal institutional and more dynamic approach. Leach in effect opened the question of the presence of inherent state-like (hierarchical) generative and counter-state (egalitarian) processes within social relations. Leach wrote effectively about the lability of institutional orders, their transformational processes and, most significantly for our discussion, the emergence of state-like orders and potencies from avowedly anti-state dynamics and vice versa. Leach (and other anthropological authors, some of them mentioned above) is an important reference for the dynamic approach to state and other socio-political process taken by Deleuze and Guattari that we discuss later. For the present, we note that Leach (and to a large extent Deleuze and Guattari) explores the potentials for the emergence of state institutional orders and their effects in the structural dynamics of a variety of relations. Power is not the immediate focus of analysis, but rather the processes from within which power is emergent, becomes formed and is supported, as well as being made intensely vulnerable.

Here we note the dominance of the work of Michel Foucault in much recent anthropology of the state. This has informed important anthropological approaches, especially those concerned with a critical deconstruction of colonial and imperial forces that, to a major extent, were and continue to be influential in constituting the orders and lives of the peoples who anthropologists predominantly worked with. The approach of Foucault has possibly achieved a growing significance in the contemporary circumstances of globalization, and in what Foucault would discern to be the manifold technologies of power – many of which do not immediately appear to be directly involved with power, such as the family, education, a variety of knowledge practices (including science and anthropology for that matter) – that have effects which support and influence formal state, or government, institutions. Foucault's notions, especially of bio-power and the hegemonic embodiment of state forms of control in the body and the self, take power as a general force infusing all practice. Power, as the key dimension of the state, is immanent in all processes of modernity. The state is submerged in society (as governmentality) and is no longer the transcendent entity producing the order of society described by Hobbes. Effectively, a Foucauldian perspective sees little outside the processes of power and the state. Although not a Weberian perspective, there seems, in a Foucauldian approach, to be nothing outside the iron cage of power.

While a Foucauldian perspective is undoubtedly important and highly influential in the social sciences, in our opinion it is strongly European and North American centred. Foucault himself conceived his approach through a consideration of European and, critically, mainly French history. The thorough emphasis on power as distributed throughout the reaches of the social, as no doubt Foucault himself would have accepted, is the situation of modernity, and a particular modernity at that. The anthropologist Louis Dumont argues that the primacy of power (and also the economic) in largely Western social-science analyses is connected to the individualism (the individual as a value) that underpins conceptions concerning the structuring of society and social relations, both in practice and in theoretical conceptions (especially in the dominant disciplines of economics, psychology and political science). Foucault, we would interpret, gives an account of how a focus on the individual and power arose in Europe through the transformations into the modern state. But we would suggest that his approach is nonetheless bound within the very individualist and power-centred terms of his analysis, as are many of the postmodern orientations of many anthropologists who are in the main Foucauldians (see Sahlins 2000).

In our opinion an anthropological conception that is based in diverse ethnographic contexts outside, or at least marginal to, Europe and North America, if not beyond their controlling influence in globalizing realities, concentrates not only on different kinds of complexes of power – the institutional and other dimensions – but also upon processes that are external to power and often against it, as Pierre Clastres (1974, 1987) has famously argued.

What we are saying does not exclude the importance of Foucault's approach (and it is certainly relevant to the arguments in some of the essays in this volume), but we are also indicating an anthropological perspective that is concerned to look at various different kinds of social and political articulations and organizations that cannot be reduced to a discourse of power or its technologies. As Foucault himself stressed, power generates its resistances, which in this sense are products of power; but the resistance to power can already be integral to social dynamics that may inherently reject power and its hierarchies quite independently of the presence of formal frameworks of power, as both Leach and Clastres argue on the basis of their ethnographic evidence. Indeed, Clastres's important critique of many anthropological works, for example on so-called segmentary lineage and stateless societies, is that anthropologists conceived of their dynamic as always in the shadow of the state and complicated by a Eurocentric obsession with the state and its necessity for the ordering of society. Thus anthropologists tended to see clearly non-state institutions, even anti-state forms, as equivalents of state apparatuses or as forerunners of the state. The problematic aspect of this is driven home in Scott's (2009) recent work that discusses the various strategies that societies in Southeast Asia, particularly, engage to avoid the state.

Although we share with Foucault a concern to shift the focus away from the formal orders of power, our position is directed to the dynamics which underpin the emergence of different kinds of power regimes or state (inclusive of the formal apparatuses of government) and the kinds of effect they have on human experience. We are also concerned with dynamics that cannot be reduced to power or statist terms, a potential paradox in Foucault's approach. As anthropologists, we and the other contributors to the volume are also concerned with socio-political processes as they are culturally conceived, imbued with particular meanings and symbolically presented. In this we stress not only an anthropological interest in different structures of institutional power, but the persistence or transmutation of particular kinds of power and their relevant cosmologies into current forms and dynamics. As both Kapferer (1988) and Taylor (1999) have shown, cosmologies relating to states and their potency in particular historical contexts can be ideologically continued into present circumstances and have particular effects for social action. This, we add, is not to be seen as the continuity of the traditional into the modern, but as a particular innovative kind of modernity, a reconfiguring in an ongoing present that has effects that cannot be reduced to over-generalized and often intensely Eurocentric concepts of power and the kinds of subjects or subjectivities that are realized by them.

Our aim in this introduction is to outline an approach to socio-political processes that may centre on the state as an apparatus of control and order, but not exclusively so. We concentrate not so much on the formal properties of state authority and power, as on the kinds of dynamics that may underpin their formation. As we have said, the approach is not about power as some kind of stable force or an essentialized ground of understanding, but focuses upon the structuring dynamics upon which what are seen as the institutions and practices of power (including war and violence) take form or are subverted. Coupled with this, we briefly set out dimensions of the larger global political economic context in which there appears to be major shifts in the structuring of socio-political orders and/or processes that are having effects on state or other practices of control.

Much of political anthropology, especially that relating to the state, was developed in the era of the nation-state. Indeed, the so-called problem of order that is the question that informed both Durkheimian and Weberian approaches in sociology and anthropology (apparent in analytical categories and an emphasis on formal institutions) is a question asked from the position of the nation-state. While obviously nation-states persist and the problem of order continues, reconfigurations of the state, as a formal institutional apparatus and what may conceived of as technologies of power (e.g. international aid, patterns of surveillance), are occurring. Related to such reconfigurations are other problematics connected, for example, to matters of sovereignty and territoriality. The terrain of the nation-state and the character of the interrelations between such states is being thoroughly problematized in a global context in which organizations of control other than those of the state are emergent and might be seen as overcoming, and certainly competing with, orders once tied to the nation-state. The recent crisis in the global market economy gives a strong sense of some of the changes and tensions that are taking shape. In this context our discussion of a dynamic approach to the state and other orders and structures of control in the erstwhile realms of the state is designed to address the kinds of forces involved, which we connect to a shift beyond the nation-state to that of the corporate state, a newly emerging global formation or assemblage.

State and war-machine dynamics

We conceive of 'the state' in general, non-specific terms as a self-reproducing, totalizing constellation of forces whose collective dynamics might be conceptualized as a politics machine directed toward creating and shaping relations in socio-cultural fields that are relevant to the reproduction of state power. Moreover, the dynamics of the state are oriented to achieving an exclusive and overarching determining potency in the diverse sets of social relations in which the state is situated. State agents and agencies achieve this through numerous procedures, among them the incorporation, regulation, exclusion, marginalization or suppression of communities, organizations, or other kinds of socio-political orders (including competing state entities) that may be present in the environment of the state. Some of the typical political techniques that the state, its agents and its agencies use to ensure these outcomes are, first, territorialization (not necessarily geographical but the bounding and controlling of regions or spaces of interest); second, social coding and redifferentiation, usually of a bureaucratic kind; and, third, control of subjectivities, as well as their capture and production, relative to the hegemonic interest of those in command of state agencies.

   In the foregoing, we follow Deleuze and Guattari (2004a and b), who suggest that such dynamics are intrinsic or immanent in all social and political assemblages, regardless of whether or not an actual formal state order exists. In their view, the state dynamic is counteracted by that of the 'war machine': each dynamic is bound to and implicit in the other, but with its own distinct (violent) potential. Altogether different in principle, the war-machine dynamic is rhizomic and open ended, characterized by a relational and structuring process that spreads out laterally in all directions. Both dynamics are apparent in most social processes, although they will manifest in diverse ways relative to the historical, cultural and other contingencies of a particular context or situation. These kinds of dynamics draw their conceptual distinction through contrast. Thus, the state dynamic is hierarchical (an apical tree-like process), vertical and bordering (territorializing); whereas the war machine is thoroughly ahierarchical (radiating across a number of nodal points, often unconnected), acentered and relatively non-systemic or counter-systemic in a closed or bounded sense. The relations and structuring of the war machine create and generate the flow of its socially forming energy along spreading networks, blurring or overrunning bounded, territorialized or categorized entities. The war machine is a deterritorializing dynamic when brought into relation with state tree-like processes.

In Deleuze and Guattari's approach, these dynamics co-exist, perdure and are intertwined, but not in the dialectical sense of a Hegelian or Marxist perspective, which Deleuze and Guattari seek to avoid. Thus, the two dynamics are irreducible to each other; and are neither dissolvable nor capable of being synthesized, in a Hegelian sense, into a third term that is either their singular base or ultimate resolution. One of Deleuze and Guattari's central arguments is that these processes are potentially mutually annihilating and, in their full emergence in the context of each other, realize thoroughgoing destruction. This clash is of the nature of the neutralizing effect caused by the coming together of two forces that have similar strengths but incompatible polarities. What Deleuze and Guattari conceptualize as the dynamics of the state and the war machine, we regard as key aspects of the structuring logics involved in contemporary empirical contexts of globalizing and state processes. The dynamics, of course, assume varied accents and significance in the particular cultural and social constructions and situational contingencies that make up the flux of history. It is our concern here to outline dimensions of the logics of the state and war-machine dynamics as these may be contemporarily apparent.

We should emphasize that the approach to the state that we are articulating is one that stresses dynamics over form. Furthermore, they are dynamics that should be distinguished from the institutional orders of actual states and from those political or social phenomena that may be seen as antagonistic or resistant to actual state controls. Thus, the concepts of state and war machine are not concrete oppositional terms. They refer to dynamics that can appear together and in a diversity of mixtures in any realized political practice, whether that of the bureaucratic governing apparatuses of the state or of resistance organizations that challenge state orders. Actual historical states may give greater prominence to the dynamics of the war machine (and not just in military enterprises or in processes of conquest) at specific moments of (re)formation or at particular sites of their extension. Examples from the past might be Ottoman Turkey or China after the decades-long Mongol invasion. In the case of Ottoman Turkey, the imagination or mythos of the state has many of the features of what Deleuze and Guattari would describe as the dynamics of the war machine.

The dynamics of the war machine are very much a part of what we will describe as the shape of the practice of emerging corporate states. We suggest that a feature of corporate states is that the rhizomic dynamic moves from a position that is more external or peripheral to state processes, to one that is closer to the heart of the state, as well as having more overt state-like ordering effects throughout national territories. Moreover, in many ways the hegemonic forces of control that are both directly and indirectly associated with state power become intensified in this process, if often more hidden. In the emergence of corporate states, there is a reterritorialization of the orders created in autocratic or nation-state formation in order to align them with the ideological objectives of corporate states. This results in a greater flexibility and openness, which drives a particular crisis of control reflected in the use of borders as filtering mechanisms (e.g. acting in response to the shifting corporatizing demands of changing state-ratified interests) and an increasing obsession with security.

Violence, whose monopolization was once said to be a centrally defining characteristic of the classic state, becomes increasingly corporatized and privatized in nation-states as they move to becoming corporate states. Possibly the oldest form of this is the mercenary army, which was once peripheralized and subordinated to citizen authority. Today, most states employ mercenaries and quasi-mercenaries, but even among the armies that can justifiably be called 'citizen armies', many have progressively allocated the bulk of their tasks, be these in combatant or non-combatant roles, to private companies whose interests are rhizomic (primarily, profit and capital accumulation) and not necessarily those of the state. It is interesting to note in this regard that when the United States leaves Iraq, it will be leaving mercenaries, who once were US military personnel, in charge of security operations there, and that their salaries will, of course, be considerably higher. Overall, our argument is not for or against the state per se in relation to issues such as violence and war. Neither is it directed to ascertaining some kind of idealistic hierarchy of socio-political forms defined in terms of their propensity to inflict the suffering and devastation of violence and war. In our opinion, autocracies (and highly centralized autocratic nation-states) are more likely to engender harm than democratic nation-states, although this is by no means a given. Democratic populisms are vulnerable to a slide into autocracy, a potential that de Tocqueville (2001) indicated for the United States. The totalitarianism of socialist and populist European states in the twentieth century achieved the peak, so far, of human devastation. The colonial states and the violence with which they subdued the majority of their subjects are also stark examples of this potential for human destructiveness. The Athenian democracy wreaked extreme destruction upon the states and societies in its environment, a fact that Thucydides observed at the time. Sahlins (2004), in an analysis of the factors leading to the defeat of the Athenian democracy in the Peloponnesian wars, offers an ironic commentary on the current democracy-inspired adventure of the US and Britain in Iraq. Most recently, John Gray (2007) has attacked utopian idealisms of human liberation and peace, mainly of the doctrinal sort (present day Libya would be an example), as themselves leading to annihilating consequences, a view also expressed by Adorno (1973) regarding idealisms in general. In our perspective, what is conceived of as 'the state' has innumerable potentialities, whose realization for the benefit or destruction of human populations is empirically contingent.

Newly emerging ontologies

For any state to arise, sociality itself, as well as notions of moral personhood, must be modified in facilitating the hegemony of the state order. As Clastres demonstrated, however, this process is not a given. To refuse the state, conscious opposition to it and its ontological foundations are required. In the case of the lineage-based Amazonian peoples discussed by Clastres, this meant either emigrating from areas under the state's purview or armed opposition to it (but see Overing this volume, also Scott 2009). This is less possible in the late-modern world, there being few who do not come under the aegis of a state. The modern nation-state, its agents and its institutions have become ubiquitous, and are consciously oriented to the creation of the very society in which state sovereignty is defined. Furthermore, the modern state engages its citizenry to reproduce the society of the state through a variety of discursive practices. Power and control became effects of social production in line with state interests. This applies as much to autocratic states as it does to democratic nation-states. In other words, the activity of the agents and agencies of the state in social production and the creation of its moral order – and in varying degrees the involvement of the citizenry – can be seen as a major strategy for addressing forces that might challenge or resist the state.

Deriving from this, the violent power at the heart of the authority of the state is distributed through a variety of state and non-state disciplinary practices involving, but not limited to, education, the family and work. Not only are such practices supported by the ultimately violent power of the state, they also reinforce the state's overall authority, further allowing it to become the central force in the production of the social and of society. The very notion of the social contract between the state and society, so vital in the legitimation of state power, is further grounded in such processes and is itself a major ideological instrument for the production of the society of the state, whereby the crisis of power at the heart of the state may be averted or reduced.

It should be noted that while the violent, physical power at the centre of the state is concealed or suppressed in less forceful disciplinary practices, it is nonetheless an ever-present capacity underpinning state order. Its enactment is never simply a last resort. This aspect has led Agamben (2005: 40) to argue for the centrality of the 'state of exception' in analyzing the nature and practise of state power, the state of exception marking 'a threshold at which logic and praxis blur with each other and a pure violence without *logos* claims to realize an enunciation without any real reference'. Recent examples of this include Yugoslavia, Rwanda, and Sri Lanka; a present example might be Libya. However, through the establishment of state agencies, institutions and practices (including state-supported ideologies) of social production, the state's controlling and ordering function is often augmented and dissipated, as well as transmuted, into what Bourdieu (1992:190–7) has called a 'symbolic violence'.

Modern nation-states have commanded and directed social production through bureaucratic institutions and related practices of cultural (re)invention. Both accentuate what we have referred to as a state dynamic, especially when applied in conjunction. The modern state took its current form largely through the development of a rational bureaucratic system. Its logic – what Handelman (2004) describes as a bureaucratic logic – principally involves a process of coding.

In effect it is human subjects who must embody the codes and occupy the places and functions within the bureaucratic apparatus. This means that the system's rationality must concur, at least operationally, with that of those who man it. Bureaucratic processes assume particular force in the social assembly and regulative dynamics of modern states and, indeed, can inhabit the conventional thought processes of the citizenry (a 'thinking' as much as a 'seeing' like a state), thus giving form to state violence as was witnessed in Sri Lanka, where government forces rooted out insurgents by using the logic of bureaucratic categories or social indicators (e.g. age, caste, village) to identify potential threats; and in Rwanda, where soldiers and militia members sought those who bore the wrong ethnic description on their national identity cards. This magnified the extent of the human destruction and defined the nature of state terror. The bodies of victims were often dumped on the margins of human habitation or in latrines, an action that symbolized simultaneously their exclusion from the social order commanded by the state (indicating their threat to it as well) and the reterritorializing discourse of state violence (see Kapferer 1997). Variations on these examples are common worldwide.

While the efforts of modernist states and especially nation-states to create those forms of sociality and personhood which promote them are relatively visible, this is less the case with corporate states. However, a frequent

observation underlying state formation in modernist and postmodern times
is the emphasis on individualism linked to a growing economic determinism.
Polanyi (and numerous others, notably Louis Dumont in anthropology)
pursued this point. This certainly seems to be so in the context of the
emergence of the corporate state, whose commanding rhetoric associated
with business and management – such as efficiency, strategy, negotiation,
targets – and a choice/consumerist focus lend support to the identification.
In this, and in the circumstances of the corporate state, the conception
of the social and its structural process is becoming thoroughly grasped in
terms of an individualism that frequently asserts essentialisms of a biological
and psychological nature gathered together in an overarching economistic
discourse. The economic is the most inclusive discourse in the sense that its
dynamics are vital across hitherto different or relatively distinct registers of
human-related action. Economic and business-management metaphors are
in a commanding position. Furthermore, they have been naturalized; that is,
they have achieved a truth level more thoroughgoing than mere assumptions.
Even more, there has been a subtle (or not so subtle, depending on one's
perspective) shift wherein the economic is not at the root of the social, but is
the social. It is the lens through which social action is to be comprehended,
both by scholars and, we contend, among the lay public. Strangely, the
principles of the economic are not conceived of as economic, but as the
veritable ontological ground of being.

Polanyi (2001) argued that in the context of the great transformation
and the development of nation-states, the idea of the economic was socially
disembedded. Gudeman (2009) has observed that this is so only up to a
point, for the contemporary context concerns the re-embedding of the idea
of the economic. He notes (as does Steiner 2009) that much sociological/
anthropological theorizing embeds economic assumptions in the very
production of ethnographic description. In this way, evidence is thoroughly
constructed (often in ways to which analysts are oblivious) to support the
veracity of economistic concepts – their confirmation presented as universally
intrinsic to the social. What Friedman has called 'vulgar materialism' comes
very close to this kind of reasoning, a criticism that has also been offered
by anthropologists such as Dumont and Sahlins. The extension we would
make here is that the economic is not re-embedded in the social so much
as the idea of the social and sociological understanding has been thoroughly
reconfigured into economistic terms. This has happened elsewhere, notably
in biology, where varieties of economic argument have become intrinsic to
the description and understanding of biological – and these days genetic –
processes (see Prindle 2009). The ideology of economism is so deeply layered
that it is not seen as such. Insofar as it is constituted in the circumstance of

a corporate state assemblage, a society of the state is thoroughly economic, even though it is conceived as being thoroughly sociological. This is not a re-embedding of the economic in society, as Gudeman suggests, but rather an embedding of the social within the economic. It is an intensification of what Polanyi was observing, a dissolving of the economic so as to become the social.

Concluding comments

The assemblage of the corporate state is emerging from within the context of the nation-state and, depending on local contingencies, is likely to take different shapes. This present discussion has been informed by North American and European experience, and there is reason to believe that some of the dimensions we have outlined are likely to be different elsewhere (e.g. with regard to China, see Arrighi 2009). One feature of the emergence of the corporate state in the West is the break from Hobbesian notions of the state, or ideas concerning its social contract, whereby the state gained legitimacy either through its institution of society or its contract to safeguard the social. By and large, these projects are being abandoned, although traces remain, for example, of the role of the state as a guardian of social morality. However, even this is being deflected onto international bodies that are relatively impotent, freeing those in command of the state to pursue a more egregious pragmatism. Two examples include Rwanda and Sri Lanka, where the impotence of UN humanitarian intervention was displayed in the largely state-mediated abuses against unarmed civilian populations. In some respects, the state and its various machineries are oriented to erecting protective barriers around the instruments of state/corporate power, thus forcing a growing division between state-corporate-oligarchic potencies and instruments, on the one side; and society or the social masses, on the other. The latter are in effect becoming more disenfranchised (even as they are declared more democratized), their protests and electoral actions achieving little to modify the political and oligarchic course of those in control of state machinery.

There are of course considerable variations across the globe within which the dynamic assemblage that we refer to as the corporate state along with its economistic ontologies have developed. The market socialism that Arrighi (2009) describes for China might be a case in point. Outside Europe and North America all signs seem to point, despite the persistence of the nation-state, to their reconfiguration along corporate-state lines. The common reference to the kinds of processes that we are discussing – neo-liberal is in frequent usage – fail to capture the sense of the new dynamic ordering of global politics that are taking place. The effects we suggest are apparent in the emergence of a new problematics in the nature of sovereignty – for example, its separation from a link with a defined territory pertinent to the nation-state;

and its investiture in other kinds of organizations with increasing political effects such as business and industrial corporations. Within the new horizons of the corporate or corporatizing state the dynamics of the rhizome or war machine and that of the hierarchializing state may achieve a new integration while opening novel possibilities of contestation and control, as well as of exclusion and war.

Essays on power, the state, and global processes at the margins

The volume begins with the essays of Evens and Overing. These are each, in their separate ways, a tour de force, for they raise through close ethnographic investigation (of the Nuer for Evens and the Amazonian Piaroa for Overing) many of the key anthropological and philosophical questions that arise in the context of the state, such as power, its tyrannical and totalitarian forms, the dimensions of hierarchy and the nature of the individualism that may oppose the state and power, or else give it sustenance as in the individual loneliness of mass society. The two essays are critical, because in the best of anthropological traditions they explore the problematics underlying some of the key analytical concepts that are engaged in the analysis of political processes and the social relations involved.

Both essays open with a consideration of Clastres's important work. Evens indicates that Clastres could have made a deeper consideration of Evans-Pritchard's Nuer material, which not only extends Clastres points (and well before he had written his work), but reveals many other aspects of a non-state configured reality that militate against the state. Evens attacks the dualisms that underpin largely European statist orientations and then proceeds to a consideration of non-dualist systems – from the Nuer to hierarchical India – which reveal, among many other matters, the gross inadequacies of European- and North-American-centred assumptions concerning socio-political orders and processes. From a reconsideration of Clastres, Evens expands his compass to major questions: from the nature of totalitarianism, and Hannah Arendt's seminal arguments, to the different shapes of egalitarianism – the distinction between the powerful affirmations of the Nuer and those in an Israeli kibbutz. The Nuer egalitarian form is not, as we might expect, reducible to the Israeli sense, nor that of anywhere else in the West. Indeed, there is a strong suggestion in Evens's chapter that the egalitarianism that is valued in the West harbours a deeply statist possibility that is absent in the affirmations and practices of the Nuer.

Overing's opening tack is to modify aspects of Clastres' argument so as to be relevant to a situation in which it is not so much 'Society against the State' as 'Society against the Tyrant'. The essay is no less wide-ranging than Evens's. She addresses other major anthropological arguments also, presenting a critique of

Sahlins' important work and, perhaps, the European statist assertions that may underpin it. Overing addresses Sahlins' more evolutionist phase culminating in *Stone Age Economics*, his most strongly Marxist influenced work. There is the suggestion in this work that some societies have achieved the kind of ideal that Marx and Engels refer to in *The Communist Manifesto* – a society without the state, but which is destroyed through the forces of Capital. This then is an anti-evolutionist position, within which the development of modern consumerist realities in which work and money are necessities is not the development of a higher form. It can instead be conceived as a devolution rather than an evolution, with the emergence of institutional forms chaining and imprisoning human being, as Rousseau and also Nietzsche recognized, and as is central to Sahlins' point. This is also Clastres' observation, which is perhaps stronger because he makes it clear that Western systems cannot be seen on the same linear evolutionary (or devolutionary) scale as those of Amazonia, for example, a dangerous conflation. Overing makes it apparent that concepts such as power cannot be universalized, stressing that the Piaroa recognize its importance and even desire it, but that the very idea of power and its expression has distinct dimensions from those conventionally grasped in contemporary contexts. She refers to the significance of rhetoric, the poetic and the aesthetic, a vital manifestation of individual and female power among the Piaroa as in many societies outside the conventional grasp of much modernity – including the ancient Greeks. Overing's ethnographically rich argument aligns with Evens's, indicating a very different orientation to the individual as value, in Louis Dumont's sense, that underpins contemporary discourses; for example, relating to the force of many current states, their dictatorships or democracies, or to the energy required to promote individual freedom and liberation.

Evens and Overing explore largely Western conceptions of power and dynamics of state orders through the critical prism provided by anthropological ethnography that is largely outside Occidental history. It is an approach that, as exemplified in many postmodern critiques in anthropology and outside, has fallen foul of the criticism of Orientalism (see Said 1978, but also Clifford and Marcus 1986). Dawod's essay on contemporary Iraq and the socio-political formations around which Saddam Hussein built his state whose dynamics are integral to the post-US/UK invasion brings the reader sharply into current realities.

Dawod attacks certain aspects of the postmodern, anti-Orientalist critique of anthropology, forcefully arguing that not everything can be put down to modernity. That is, processes that are major factors in the tragedy which is modern Iraq (see Sahlins 2011) are no less than contemporary, but are articulated through structural dynamics that have an extensive history reaching into periods pre-existing the modernity that Europe and America have largely defined. Aspects of the Occidentalist critique have been vital to the ignoring of processes that are not to be reduced to the kinds of trivializations of Huntington's 'clash of civilizations' kind (a conception very much fuelled by modernity and of the Orientalist prejudices it has encouraged). We remark, following Dawod, that anthropology, at least the kind we advocate, has by and large been concerned not to engage in an Orientalizing exoticism, often of an intensely romantic kind, but rather to explore differences, no less part of the present, crucial to understanding contemporary processes. The Iraq state was not built upon the foundations of the bureaucratic kind common in northern Europe; and its dictatorship, while centred on the person of Saddam, was not a mere cult of the individual but was rooted in dynamics of a partly tribal kind that are largely foreign to conventional Western understandings. Dawod explores the complexity of Iraqi social relations, among them tribal affiliations, but does so in a way that largely rejects Western stereotypes and simplistic dualisms (e.g. Sunni versus Shi'ite) that have conditioned both commentary and policy. He shows how certain aspects of tribal resurgence were indeed a direct response to post-invasion policy and strategic interests. We consider Dawod's essay to be a major contribution to the understanding of what many might see as the current debacle in Iraq (and as we write this, seems perhaps tragically relevant to Libya), and that it thoroughly supports the anthropological project that directs the essays in this volume.

Taylor's essay concentrates on the discourse surrounding the death of President Habyarimana of Rwanda, whose plane was shot down, an event that precipitated the Rwanda genocide. He examines the cosmological metaphors in terms of which Habyarimana's presidency was understood, and which combined the wild and domesticating dimensions of royal power. These were integral within the modern, post-colonial, democratic state, and in fact were dynamics supporting its practices. One of Taylor's points is that, contra some of the discussions of modernity, this does not create a modernity that is opposed to or generative of tradition. In effect, the concepts of modern and tradition are thoroughly embedded in Western dualistic thinking. All contemporary societies are modern, if in different ways, and the cosmological/ ontological orientations of Rwandan kingship, as Taylor demonstrates here and in other publications, are vital within a diversity of existential concerns that stretch from personal embodied processes (often to deal with health) through to collective concerns. These, Taylor argues, are not all to do with power per se (with the invasion of the state into the being of the person – as Foucault importantly argues for Northern Europe), but are to do with processes upon which the institutional dynamics of power build. Such a cosmological orientation is continually realizing itself anew, not as a repetition of the past, but as a dynamic of becoming (to put the argument in the terms of Deleuze) in which the original possibilities of such a cosmology are constantly being realized. One was the identification of Habiyarimana as endangering Rwanda society and Hutu interests – interpretations of experiences made dangerously possible within the cosmological orientations of Rwandan kingship, and which were to have devastating consequence. There is no suggestion that it was a cause of the tragic occurrences, but rather that it is a ground for understanding their significance and gave them shape.

Kapferer and Wijeyeratne develop a similar position to that of Taylor, but in the context of Sri Lanka following the end of the civil war. In Sri Lanka the cosmology of ancient kingship has played a role in modern nationalism. Engaged in the political rhetoric of Sinhalese hegemony, it became instrumental as a technology of power in Foucault's sense. This continues into post-conflict Sri Lanka and is integral to state restructuring, which has strong resonances of an emergence to dictatorial power. The re-structuring is taking place in the circumstances of increasingly embracing global forces – of a corporate state dynamic kind – that reflect shifts in the organization of global imperial power (from the West to the East). While ancient mythology is effectively reinvented in its meaningful significance as a contemporary technology of state power, it has potential in excess of powerful interests. That is, it generates circumstances that have effects beyond narrow individual or state instrumentality, creating potentialities for the continuation of practices that may re-generate the kinds of socio-economic realities, including that of ethnic humiliation, which gave birth to the very kind of processes which the end of the civil war ostensibly concluded.

Ancient mythologies are also the theme of Angela Hobart's discussion, but in a more metaphorical sense than in the previous two essays. Hobart shows the legitimating function of mythologies, both as frameworks for the interpretation of contemporary events and as means through which to communicate with populations dealing with the shadows of Indonesia's violent past, and the aftermath of local disasters such as the Bali bombing. A major contribution of Hobart's essay is the discerning presentation of the range of everyday cultural practices – from theatre, ritual and local medicine – in which mythological reasoning is apparent. It helps to underline a key theme of the volume, that apparently ancient myths in realities outside those of North America and much of industrialized Europe, what Ricoeur (1991) has described as the largely demythologized realities of the West, are part of living practices of great diversity. Although they are utilized to political effect, they are also vital aspects of everyday life in a much broader degree. They are not traditional survivals (as presented in the discourse of much tourism, especially as directed to foreign travellers), but are integral to the always-becoming modern (in Latour's (2005) sense, drawing from Deleuze). Moreover, they comprise a type of 'symbolic capital' (Evans-Pritchard 1940, Bourdieu 1992) in relation to which the populations in Java and Bali discussed by Hobart can continually orient themselves in changing realities.

Bal Gopal Shrestha traces the transition of Nepal from an autocratic state centred around the idea of Hindu cosmic kingship to that of a republican democracy. The history of Nepal would indicate the development of an uneasy relation between power (the kingship) and the notion of the king as also a god (Visnu). This would seem to be quite distinct from Western notions of kingship (the idea of the king's two bodies – see Kantorowicz 1957), and more appropriate to Dumont's hierarchical notion, whereby in the Nepal case the King would be a combination of Brahmin and Kshatriya (warrior). This, of course, is open to major scholarly dispute, although Shrestha's analysis indicates an irresolvable tension of a Dumontian sort (present in the impossibility of the combination) which could result in an intensification of autocratic power to effect the otherwise impossible unity. However, quite apart from such an argument, it is clear in Shrestha's discussion that the autocracy of the king was forged in a process of democratization (and secularization) that starts apace in the 1950s and which opens a complexity of irresolvable fractures in Nepalese socio-political processes. These involve groups that are religiously external to Hindu orientations (e.g. the substantial Buddhist communities), and the increased pressures from low-caste and outcaste groups to break out of a system that attempted to enforce Hindu hierarchical value. This is particularly interesting in the Nepal situation, where it can be argued that the Gorkha military conquest that established Nepal is a classic instance of the engagement of Hindu religious ideas as a technology for the institution of, in some respects, an externally imposed power. The transition that Shrestha describes to republican democratic rule via Maoist insurrection appears to manifest the complexities alluded to here and which continue to extend towards new possibilities.

The two final essays in the volume, that of Hart and Friedman, examine dimensions of state formation and reactions to it in historical perspective. Hart's chapter concentrates on personal experience and memory of global and state forces, with an emphasis on the situation of the exile. The focus on the personal reflection on the effects of global and state processes in the course of a life dramatically points up the experiential dimensions of forces too easily lost in the stressing of structural change and transformation. She presents a powerful insight into individual anxieties and the generation of a contemporary cynicism that is apparent at the grassroots in Europe as elsewhere.

Hart's essay dovetails with Friedman's more macro considerations. He concentrates on the ways in which state and global processes are thought about as well as realized. Of major significance in his argument is the evolutionism that haunts present conceptions of the global and state formation within them. He crucially shows how dominant positions often have more import as intellectual illusions (largely Western) and glib epithets, than as realizations on the ground. He underscores the importance of grassroots ethnography of the kind that Hart presents. One of the major points that Friedman develops is the repetition of cycles of global expansion and then retraction. The historical contexts upon which Hart's essay reflects show how recent state formations grew out of the collapse of imperial cosmopolitan orders to now, once again, be threatened by the emergence of new imperializations and global assemblages – indeed, along the lines of corporate-state orders that we have discussed earlier in this Introduction.

REFERENCES

Abrams, Philip, 1988, 'Notes on the difficulty of studying the state', *Journal of Historical Sociology* 1(1):58–89.

Adorno, Theodor W., 1973, *Negative Dialectics*, trans. E.B. Ashton. London: Routledge & Kegan Paul.

Agamben, Giorgio, 1998, *Homo Sacer: Sovereign Power and Bare Life*, trans. Daniel Heller-Roazen. Stanford: Stanford University Press.

——— 2005, *State of Exception*, trans. K. Attell. Chicago, IL: University of Chicago Press.

Arrighi, Giovanni, 2009, *Adam Smith in Beijing: Lineages of the Twenty-first Century*. London: Verso.

Bourdieu, Pierre, 1992 [1977], *Outline of a Theory of Practice*, trans. Richard Nice. Cambridge: Cambridge Univeristy Press.

Clastres, Pierre, 1974, 'De l'ethnocide', *L'Homme* 14(3–4):101–10.

——— 1987 [1974], *Society Against the State: Essays in Political Anthropology*, trans. Robert Hurley with Abe Stein. New York: Zone Books.

Clifford, James and George E. Marcus, 1986, *Writing Culture: The Poetics and Politics of Ethnography*. Berkeley: University of California Press.

Deleuze, Gilles, 1992, 'Postscript on the societies of control', *October* 59 (Winter):3–7.

Deleuze, Gilles and Felix Guattari, 2004a [1972], *Anti-Oedipus: Capitalism and Schizophrenia*, trans. Robert Hurley, Mark Seem and Helen R. Lane. London: Continuum.

——— 2004b [1980], *A Thousand Plateaus: Capitalism and Schizophrenia*, trans. Brian Massumi. London: Continuum.

Dumont, Louis, 1980, *Homo Hierarchicus: The Caste System and its Implications.* Chicago: University of Chicago Press.

Durkheim, Emile, 1976 [1915], *The Elementary Forms of the Religious Life.* London: Allen and Unwin.

Evans-Pritchard, Edward, 1940, *The Nuer.* Oxford: Clarendon Press.

Fallers, Lloyd, 1940, *Bantu Bureaucracy: A Century of Political Evolution among the Basoga of Uganda.* Chicago: University of Chicago Press.

Foucault, Michel, 1977, *Discipline and Punish: The Birth of the Prison.* New York: Vintage Books.

——— 1991, 'Governmentality'. In *The Foucault Effect: Studies in Governmentality,* ed. Graham Burchell, Colin Gordon, and Peter Miller. London: Harvester Press.

Friedman, Jonathan, 1998, *System, Structure and Contradiction: The Evolution of 'Asiatic' Social Formations.* Berkeley, CA: AltaMira Press.

Geertz, Clifford, 1980, *Negara: The Theatre State in Nineteenth Century Bali.* Princeton, New Jersey: Princeton University Press,

Gluckman, Max, 2006, *Politics, Law and Ritual in Tribal Society.* Oxford: Basil Blackwell.

Gray, John, 2007, *Black Mass and the Death of Utopia.* New York: Farrar, Straus and Giroux.

Gudeman, Stephen, 2009, 'Necessity or contingency: mutuality and market'. In *Market and Society: The Great Transformation Today,* eds. C. Hann and K. Hart. Cambridge: Cambridge University Press.

Handelman, Don, 2004, *Nationalism and the Israeli State: Bureaucratic Logic in Public Events.* Oxford: Berg Press.

Hobbes, Thomas, 1991 [1651]. *Leviathan.* Cambridge: Cambridge University Press.

Kantorowicz, Ernst, 1957, *The King's Two Bodies: A Study in Mediaeval Political Theology.* Princeton, NJ: Princeton University Press.

Kapferer, Bruce, 1988, *Legends of People, Myths of State.* Washington (DC): Smithsonian Institution Press.

——— 1997, *The Feast of the Sorcerer: Practices of Consciousness and Power.* Chicago, IL: University of Chicago Press.

Latour, Bruno, 2005, *Reassembling the Social: An Introduction to Actor-Network Theory.* Oxford: Oxford University Press.

Leach, Edmund, 1965, *Political Systems of Highland Burma: A Study of Kachin Social Structure.* Boston: Beacon Press.

Lowie, Robert, 1948, *Social Organization.* New York: Holt, Rinehart, and Winston.

Maine, Henry, 1917, *Ancient Law.* London: J.M. Dent and Sons.

Marx, Karl, 1967, *Capital: A Critique of Political Economy.* New York: International Publishers.

Nadel, S.F., 1942, *A Black Byzantium: The Kingdom of Nupe in Nigeria*. London:
    Oxford University Press.

Polanyi, Karl, 2001 [1944], *The Great Transformation: The Political and Economic
    Origins of Our Time*. Boston, MA: Beacon Press.

Prindle, David F., 2009, *Stephen Jay Gould and the Politics of Evolution*. Amherst, NY:
    Prometheus Books.

Radcliffe-Brown, A.R., 1970 [1940], 'Preface'. In *African Political Systems*, eds. M.
    Fortes and E.E. Evans-Pritchard. London: Oxford University Press.

Ricoeur, Paul, 1991, *From Text to Action*. Evanston: Northwestern University Press.

Sahlins, Marshall, 2000, 'The sadness of sweetness; or, the native anthropology of
    Western cosmology'. In *Culture in Practice*. New York: Zone Books.

——— 2004. *Apologies to Thucydides: Understanding History as Culture and Vice
    Versa*. Chicago, IL: University of Chicago Press.

——— 2011, 'Iraq: the state-of-nature effect', *Anthropology Today* 27(3):26–31.

Said, Edward W., 1978, *Orientalism: Western Conceptions of the Orient*. London:
    Routledge & Kegan Paul.

Scott, James C., 2009, *The Art of Not Being Governed: An Anarchist History of Upland
    Southest Asia*. New Haven, CT: Yale University Press.

Smith, M.G., 1975, *Corporations and Society: The Social Anthropology of Collective
    Action*. Chicago: Aldine Press.

Steiner, Philippe, 2009, 'The critique of the economic point of view: Karl Polanyi and
    the Durkheimians'. In *Market and Society: The Great Transformation Today*,
    eds. C. Hann and K. Hart. Cambridge: Cambridge University Press.

Tambiah, Stanley,1976, *World Conqueror and World Renouncer: A Study of Buddhism
    and Polity in Thailand against a Historical Background*. Cambridge:
    Cambridge University Press.

Taylor, Christopher, 1999, *Sacrifice as Terror*. Oxford: Berg.

Tocqueville, Alexis de, 2001, *The Old Regime and the Revolution*, ed. Francois Furet
    and Francoise Melonio, trans. Alan S. Kahan. Chicago, IL: University of
    Chicago Press.

Trouillot, M-R., 2001, 'The anthropology of the state in the age of globalization',
    Current Anthropology 42(1):1–24.

Wolf, Eric, 1973, *Peasant Wars of the Twentieth Century*. New York: Harper and Row.

CHAPTER 1

The phenomenology of a stateless society

Non-dualism, identity and hierarchical anarchy among the Nuer

T.M.S. Evens

In memory of M.G. Smith

Only kings, presidents, editors, and people with tapeworms have the right to
use the editorial 'we'. — Mark Twain

We must avoid both egoism and nosism in order to realize the glory of
humanity. — H. Odera Oruka, *Philosophy, Humanity and Ecology*

Introduction
The question of power and value
In a phenomenological tour de force, Pierre Clastres' *Society Against the State*
(1987) throws open to question the Western presumption of the state as the
master key to any political order among men.[1] In light of his finding of a social
order (certain South American Indian peoples) that not only lacks a state but
actually works to prevent the formation of one, Clastres is given to wonder
why humans would ever willingly subject themselves to an institutional
division between ruler and ruled. In their brief tribute to his memory, Deleuze
and Guattari (1987:357–61), conceiving of the state as a matter of sovereign
power, take Clastres to task for depicting as clean the break between state
and counter-state societies (and thus for implicating an evolutionary schema
despite himself). As I read them, they argue, conversely and non-dualistically,
that, as an impulsion to unity and rigidity, the state has always been ubiquitous
in human social order at large, such that each, state and stateless societies,
supposes the existence of the other.

Clastres begins his argument by distinguishing between two kinds of power: coercive and non-coercive. His task is to clarify the nature of the latter kind and to identify the mechanisms by which 'societies against the state' prevent the growth of the former. Among the Guarani Indians a chief has no power to impose his will by force, and he can be replaced whenever the group sees fit. In describing the figure of the Guarani chief, Clastres draws on Robert Lowie's determination of 'the three essential traits' of the (North and South) American Indian leader: he must be an effective peacemaker, a generous provider of his goods and talented orator. To this list of traits Clastres adds a fourth, one that characterizes the (South American Indian) chiefs in particular, namely polygyny. It is usual, he finds, that this form of marriage is the chief's exclusive prerogative, and with this feature he turns to the question of the means by which these social formations take a stand against the emergence of the state. He contends that, although one might expect the chief's more or less exclusive right to women is granted in exchange for his goods and oratorical services, this is precisely not the case. The chief has no way to amass sufficient goods to meet his followers' demands on him, which are excessive, and his oratorical function is, rather than his to give, a duty imposed on him by the group. In Clastres' finding that the relationship between the chief's privileged possession of the women and his disposition of goods and words is not a matter of exchange at all, he locates his answer to the powerless power of the chieftainship and the preclusion of the state. With exceptional insight, playing off Lévi-Strauss' structural equation between society and the reciprocal exchange of 'signs', Clastres argues that by founding the relationship between the group and the chieftainship outside the principle of exchange, the group manages to effect a leader and at one and the same time contest and contain any coercive power he may contemplate. Since the principle of reciprocal exchange defines the group as such, instituting the chieftainship by transcending this principle alienates from the group the very power it allows to emerge within itself. Put differently, the act of transcendence converts power into value. Clastres puts it this way (1987:41–2):

> ...this triple movement [of women, goods, and words] manifests a common
> negative dimension which assigns these three types of 'signs' an identical
> fate: they no longer appear as exchange values, reciprocity ceases to regulate
> their circulation, and each of them falls, therefore, outside the province of
> communication. Hence a new relationship between the domain of power
> and the essence of the group now comes to light: power enjoys a privileged
> relationship toward those elements whose reciprocal movement founds the
> very structure of society. But this relationship, by denying these elements
> an exchange value at the group level, institutes the political sphere not only

as external to the structure of the group, but further still, as negating that structure: power is contrary to the group, and the rejection of reciprocity, as the ontological dimension of society, is the rejection of society itself.

In this chapter, in accord with Deleuze and Guattari's non-dualist position[2] on statelessness and the state, and reverting to the classic ethnography of the Nuer as my working example, I want to expand on the general question of the ontological nature of sovereignty as a principle of human behavior. The Nuer material, pertaining to the socio-political organization of this East African tribal people *as they were in the 1930s*, when the British social anthropologist E.E. Evans-Pritchard did intensive fieldwork among them, is at once luminously descriptive of a non-state social formation while also somewhat involved when it comes to hierarchy and the play of power. My argument is directed to exploring Clastres' implicit distinction between two kinds of sovereignty further, and to understanding, in terms of phenomenology and ontological difference, the continuity and discontinuity between them. To these ends, I first take up Nuer statelessness, examining the ontological conditions of its diagnostic an-authoritarianism and egalitarianism. These conditions bear especially on the radically non-dualistic way in which Nuer perceive and experience the relation of individual, self and society, as well as that between exchange and power. The question of Nuer selfhood in relation to their socio-political dynamic is decisive in this connection. Given the analysis of the Nuer, I then proceed to discuss the matter of sovereignty in the broader comparative context of modernity and Western political thought, appealing to certain phenomenological notions due to Hannah Arendt and Giorgio Agamben, notions bearing on the ontology of identity and the individual.

The Nuer
Acephalous democracy and hierarchy

Given his central concerns, it seems strange that Clastres failed to cite Fortes and Evans-Pritchard's (1940) classic edited collection on *African Political Systems*, which appeared more than three decades before *Societies against the State*, and in the introduction to which the two British anthropologists elaborate, eminently, the analytic distinction between state and stateless societies. Indeed, Evans-Pritchard's analysis of the Nuer political system became a veritable model for the discipline.[3]

What impressed Evans-Pritchard most about the Nuer political life were its radically acephalous organization and its deeply democratic tenor (1940a:181; see also 1940b:296):

The lack of governmental organs among the Nuer, the absence of legal
institutions, of developed leadership, and, generally, of organized political
life is remarkable. Their state is an acephalous kinship state ... The ordered
anarchy in which they live accords well with their character, for it is
impossible to live among the Nuer and conceive of rulers and ruling over
them.

As well as talking of 'ordered anarchy', Evans-Pritchard also spoke of this
system as 'order without government' and explained it as a 'kinship state' in
which order was maintained by virtue of 'self-help'. Structurally, as Evans-
Pritchard saw it, the system described two organizations. One was territorial
and comprised of residential groups, recruitment to which proceeded on a
variety of principles, including especially interpersonal kinship (on both the
mother's and father's side), relations by marriage and adoption. The other was
constituted by agnatic lineages, that is, unilineal descent groups comprising
all persons who can trace their descent to a common male ancestor. The latter
organization was genealogical, not residential. Famously, Evans-Pritchard
analyzed it as a segmentary system, by which he had in mind a lineal whole
that is bifurcated into collateral segments, each of which is itself bifurcated,
and so on, following certain lines of cleavage that emerge naturally between
agnates.[4] What is especially important for present purposes is that these two
organizations, the territorial and the agnatic, critically informed each other.
According to Evans-Pritchard, whereas the agnatic provided the territorial
system with structure, the territorial system gave the agnatic one corporate
substance.

Nuer political life seems to turn strictly on a value of equality (Evans-
Pritchard 1940a:181–2).

The Nuer is a product of hard and egalitarian upbringing, is deeply
democratic, and is easily roused to violence. His turbulent spirit finds any
restraint irksome and no man recognizes a superior. Wealth makes no
difference... Birth makes no difference...

That every Nuer considers himself as good as his neighbour is evident
in their every movement. They strut about like lords of the earth, which,
indeed, they consider themselves to be. There is no master and no servant
in their society, but only equals who regard themselves as God's noblest
creation...

Indeed, if the notion of social stratification is taken in its most concrete
sense, as referring to a distribution of advantages and benefits that determines
an evaluative ranking of separate and distinct social groups, then Nuer

society largely went unstratified.[5] This is the case for the Nuer with respect to political authority as well as material benefits. It is true that the Nuer acknowledge some such graded relations by reference to the principles of age, gender, agnatic primordiality ('first occupants' of a particular locality), tribal provenance (many Nuer are of Dinka descent) and ritual distinction. But over time the authority based on age falls to every man, and, as far as one can tell from the ethnography, that based on gender, although ideologically plain, has little significance in the micro-political course of everyday interaction between men and women.[6] As regards agnatic primordiality, ritual distinction and even tribal provenance, these advantages could only grant influence rather than power.

It is all the more striking, then, that this manifestly acephalous and fiercely egalitarian socio-political order is also critically hierarchical. In fundamental respects, the key to the system's marked statelessness rests precisely with a principle of hierarchy. The relevant concept of hierarchy is due to Louis Dumont (1970). It features relations of encompassment rather than layered detachment between graded groups or categories. The higher is not only superior to the lower, but also includes it. In other words, by glaring contrast to received usage, Dumont's concept of hierarchy describes a zone of relative indistinction between subordinate and superordinate, even as it differentiates the two. This logically scandalous picture, whereby the inside consists of the outside, was Dumont's answer to the problem of the relations between status and power in the Indian caste system. In that system, on Dumont's reading, the priest or Brahman constitutes the apex of the status hierarchy and accordingly enjoys spiritual supremacy over the king or Kshatriya, but cannot possess the benefit of temporal prepotency. Were he to have the upper hand politically, it would be implicit that power and status are on an equal footing. This, in turn, would spell the effective destruction of the hierarchy, by making spiritual authority reducible to political power. In effect, the two principles remain absolutely distinct, even within the formal hierarchical interdependence created by the encompassment of power by status.

Now, the categorically acephalous organization of Nuer political life scarcely amounts to a caste system. Yet, as the segmentary order was described just above (formally and *in the abstract*, as a system comprised of unilineal descent groups and organized, on the basis of genealogy, in a series of segments or boxes within boxes, such that social distance is measured according to the degree of collateral kinship), it is hierarchical in shape, and the paradoxical way in which it turns on its key organizing principles is formidably evocative of the relationship between status and power as described by Dumont for India.[7] The relevant Nuer principles are, as we have seen, territory and agnatic descent. It is readily apparent that descent may be understood as a principle of status whereas territory, as has been the standard interpretation in Western political theory, is a cipher of political power and statism.

Fundamental ambiguity

Even in his earliest efforts to treat the Nuer materials, Evans-Pritchard found the connection between the Nuer territorial system and their system of agnatic descent groups sorely vexing. He wrote that 'It is very difficult to analyze Nuer society without repetition because when we speak of the tribe we are also speaking of political aggregates which crystallize around some clans,' and in light of this difficulty he concluded that 'it is imperative to keep these two groups, the tribe and the clan, distinct if endless confusion is to be avoided' (1933:24 and 22–3, 28–9, 36; see also 1934:6, 32). Adducing the standard theoretical association between polity and territory, he clearly identified the Nuer political system as consisting of the relations between the territorial rather than the descent groups. He also laid ultimate stress on the regulation of the agnatic by the territorial principle (1940a:265; see also 203–5, 240ff., and 1940b:287), asserting that 'the territorial system of the Nuer is always the dominant variable...'. In effect, Evans-Pritchard portrayed the Nuer principles of territory and agnation as asymmetrical and as absolutely distinct, in much the same way that Dumont pictured power and status in the caste system. Except that, for the Nuer, in Evans-Pritchard's account, it is the political rather than the moral or principled principle that enjoys formative primacy.

In my view, however, notwithstanding the determining force of territory, the constituting principle is in fact agnation. I also submit that the two systems glossed by these principles, although significantly independent of each other, are, Evans-Pritchard's caution notwithstanding, endlessly confused in fact. If this is true, then the system is fundamentally paradoxical. Each of the defining principles is, logically speaking, the antithesis of the other. Whereas territory describes organization as based on expedience and power, agnation makes it out as proceeding according to principle, that is, value; the one betokens material needs and satisfactions, the other ideal conduct. Insofar as the two principles together define a single system, they define each other, in which case each is being defined in terms of what it is not. With all due respect to Evans-Pritchard, then, the fruitful question is not how to resolve the paradox, but rather how the Nuer manage to live it.

The primacy of agnation

Despite his interpretation of territory as the 'dominant variable', Evans-Pritchard was in no doubt that the *normative* axis, and in this limited sense the first principle and value, of Nuer social life is agnatic descent. Agnation, he said (1945:64), is 'the fundamental principle that gives structural uniformity' to

Nuer social organization, and the principle by virtue of which 'a man becomes a social being' among the Nuer (1945:64). It is thus a principle of social identity or social wholeness. The Nuer use the word for agnation, *buth*, to describe not interpersonal relations, but kinship between groups – it applies to individuals only in virtue of their membership in these groups (1951:6). Kinship between individuals as such is called *mar*, meaning cognatic kinship, but particularly through the mother. By Nuer definitions, uterine kinship cuts agnation; it opposes interpersonal relationships by blood or marriage to kinship between groups, that is, it opposes the individual to the social whole. The Nuer associate cognation with common residence, and cognatic kinship lies at the bottom of the formation of the territorial group (*cieng*), what Evans-Pritchard called the 'community of living' (1933:46; 1940a:228).

But, although Evans-Pritchard failed to see this, Nuer agnation *in its own right* implicates difference and material extension. That is, the normatively superior principle contains within itself its own compromise. *Buth* refers to the 'people who share in the flesh of sacrifices', but it also means 'first' as in, say, 'first-born' (Evans-Pritchard 1956:287; see also Crazzolara 1953:26).[8] It thus combines the meanings of one flesh or one blood with primordiality. But flesh and blood are (although for the Nuer not, I think, only this) matters of substance, and in this sense, territorial. Moreover, as an ordinal number, 'first' entails 'second' and 'third' etc. – the meat of sacrifices is, after all, distributed according to an order of precedence (Evans-Pritchard 1956:287ff.; Crazzolara 1953:24n.1). In other words, *buth* always already insinuates division, a shift from oneness to manyness, from the agnatic whole to the territorial part. Put another way, Nuer agnation is territory.

Still, this indispensable compromise of *buth*'s holism is, in the nature of the case, always contained. That is, the shift from the one to the many never fails to reverse course. Agnation describes temporal and substantive extension from a first male ancestor. If the latter is conceived of as an absolute source, then this extension is innately hierarchical in the Dumontian sense. A primordial ancestor of this kind is creative rather than merely procreative, producing absolutely, as a plenum unfolds. The Nuer word for this kind of creativity or engenderment is *cak*, meaning 'creation by thought or imagination' as well as 'creation from nothing'. The ethnography leaves no doubt that the Nuer do indeed presume such a profoundly creative first ancestor: the opening sentence of the opening chapter of *Nuer Religion* reads, 'The Nuer word we translate "God" is *kwoth*, Spirit' (1956:1, 4–9), and shortly thereafter (ibid.:4–9) the author writes that for the Nuer *kwoth* 'is the father of men'.

Although Evans-Pritchard concluded that this sort of talk (depicting *kwoth* in terms of kinship) was merely allegorical, he also observed that the Nuer 'think of conception as a product of [the] combination of human and divine action' (1956:156). In which case, it stands to reason that the Nuer must mean it in some ordinary sense when they trace their descent to *kwoth* and speak of him as their father.

Metalogical hierarchy and axiological reversal

Given this primordial figure of engenderment, the hierarchy of descent determined by Nuer agnation is 'metalogical' in structure. The metalogical makeup of this hierarchy describes the structural aspect of what Evans-Pritchard distinguished in terms of segmentation: the widest organizational unit is divided into coordinate segments, each of which 'is itself segmented and there is opposition between its parts', but being always referred to and contained by the next higher generational plane – that is, the immediate meta-level – of the hierarchy, and ultimately by the primordial plane (the first ancestor or *kwoth*), the segmental opposition is forever structurally mediated (1940a:142, 197–8). What is more, because by virtue of its metalogical nature the defining principle of agnation, Spirit (*kwoth*), necessarily enfolds its own antithesis, the tellurian domain, it may be seen to determine both of the Nuer hierarchical organizations, descent and territory. Indeed, given the hierarchical relation between these two organizations, the principle determines them as one and two at the same time (Evans-Pritchard 1940b:286):

> There is a straight relation between political structure and the clan system,
> for a clan, or a maximal lineage, is associated with each tribe, in which it
> occupies a dominant position among other agnatic groups. Moreover, each
> of its segments tends to be associated with a segment of the tribe in such
> a way that there is a correspondence, and often a linguistic identification,
> between the parts of a clan and the parts of a tribe.

Logically, the condition of the two hierarchies being one pivots on the Nuer distinction between 'strangers' (*rul*) and 'first occupants' (*diel*). The unilineal descent group to which the first occupants belong is peculiarly identified with and often gives its name to the area of occupation, converting the territorial hierarchy into the agnatic one (Evans-Pritchard 1940a:212ff.). Although Evans-Pritchard used 'aristocrat' interchangeably with 'first occupant', as we shall see, the distinction between 'first occupants' and 'strangers' simply reproduces that between 'agnation' and 'territory', and, accordingly, entails hierarchy in terms of encompassment rather than political power proper.

In the Indian caste system, as Dumont saw it, while power is encompassed by status, the distinction between the two principles is, in a critical sense, absolute. Because of its dualist nature, the distinction can lead to situations that are defined as hierarchically inferior, thereby allowing power to take precedence over status, without, however, impugning the axiological supremacy of status. Once power is perfectly differentiated from status, it becomes possible to resolve some situations as purely a matter of power rather than status.

By substantial contrast, while Nuer territory is encompassed by agnation, at no point in the resulting hierarchical order is the former principle ever strictly distinguished from the latter. No situation can be defined as simply a matter of territory, and, therefore, of power. Although axiological reversal is a requirement of the system, it is never made explicit. Instead, the conflict between the two defining principles takes the form of an existential dilemma that contains within itself the mediatory wherewithal to avoid an antinomical outcome and reinstate the normative reality. In other words, the reversal, while it can be known by its empirical consequences and is given on the ground by virtue of the territorial unit (the *cieng* or Evans-Pritchard's 'community of living'), never really enjoys outright recognition. Instead of situations in which territory is rendered autonomous, there are situations in which a *de facto* territorial determinacy is restrained by its apperception in terms of agnatic reality.

In effect, territorial interference with agnation, whether it results in residential dispersion, blood-feud or even permanent fission, is always mitigated by the giving of the name or identity of agnation to these results. This sort of mediatory translation is and appears fraudulent or manipulative only if implemented and viewed from the perspective of dualism, a perspective the system itself does not afford. For a Nuer a name is not simply nominal, but somehow realizes and participates in what it names. What counts is the name not as a mere word, but in its naming what it names, and in the latter's being distinguished by that name.[9] In point of fact, the ontological authority of the name may be seen to present a paradigm of the hierarchical encompassment relation I am claiming for the Nuer socio-political order.[10] The translation of territory into descent follows from the structural correspondence between the two hierarchies, a correspondence that betrays, as I have argued, a basically ambiguous ontology, not a dualistic one.[11] As a worldly principle, agnation is essentially equivocal as between its identity as a body of principles and territorial or material embodiment, and among the Nuer this condition takes the form of encompassment, whereby territory is contained by agnation as its mirror image. This chiastic relationship describes the fundamental ambiguity of what's in a name.

Segmentary self-identity and the individual-as-other

The difference in the degree to which each of the two socio-political systems, the Nuer and the Indian, distinguishes between its defining principles is of

great significance. On it turns the most conspicuous difference between these
two hierarchical orders: whereas the caste system admits of formal relations
of political authority between men, Nuer hierarchy does not. 'There is no
hierarchy without authority', according to Hannah Arendt (1973:404). The
Nuer hierarchy is no exception. It is just that in its case the authority does not
obtain between one individual and another.

The movement from the apex to the base of the Nuer hierarchy entails a
corresponding swing, in the focus of the self's identification, from the moral
to the substantival. But the process does not conclude in the figure of the
individual as such. As keyed by agnatic descent, Nuer reality may be said to
begin with the whole rather than the part, by which I mean that it presumes
an ultimate integrity between one thing and another. In such a reality, the
particular can be defined only relative to the whole and never as ultimately
identical to itself. This reality assumes self-identity only to the degree to which
such identity presents the whole, in which case, the concrete individual makes
a troubling candidate. In a plain sense, the figure of the individual emulates the
whole; but in doing so, precisely because of its hermetic determinacy, it denies
the whole's allness. The agnatic set of full brothers, though, because it is both
plural and singular at the same time, best represents the whole for the Nuer.[12]

Being Nuer comprises two key sorts of self-identity. On the one hand,
there is the identity that follows from apprehending oneself directly in relation
to the apogee of the hierarchy, that is, to *kwoth*. This sort of identity is secured
especially by sacrifice, and by the boys' initiation ceremony, known as *gar*. In
identifying the Nuer with their cattle, *gar* sanctions the substitution of beast
for man in sacrifice (the boys have their foreheads severely scarified, from ear
to ear, on the pattern of the horns of cattle). The mark of *gar* is the diagnostic
mark of Nuerhood, since through sacrifice the Nuer identifies himself as God's
special creature, and in this sense with every Nuer. Clearly, this sort of identity
is holistic: instead of distinguishing one Nuer from another, it marks each as
the same sort of being, an exemplar. On the other hand, there is the identity
that issues not from defining oneself directly in relation to one's creator,
but from doing so as against one's fellow creatures. This sort of identity is
occasioned by competition over, rather than sacrifice of, self, and accordingly
serves to differentiate one Nuer from another. However, given the segmentary
hierarchy, in thus distinguishing himself from some Nuer laterally, he
necessarily identifies himself with them lineally, on the hierarchical ascendant.
For, the object of his competition is precisely his Nuerness, in which case his
success can only reinforce his identity with the agnatic whole. Put differently,
in this society, individualistic self-enhancement is curtailed in the nature of
the case, since the result is always re-appropriated by the order of the general
other.

If from the descending perspective individuation is arrested before it can reach the individual as such, from the ascending aspect the figure of the individual becomes progressively more indistinct. In fact, the individual is indistinct enough that throughout the hierarchy, and increasingly as one ascends it, it does not make sense exactly to speak of individuals and their interrelationships. Such as they are, these individuals exist between themselves before they do within themselves; their self-identity in their capacity as lineage members enjoys ultimate ontological priority over their self-identity in their capacity as individuals. Hence, as absurd as it may seem to say so, it is necessary to speak here, not of the individual-as-such, but of the individual-as-other. This understanding puts Evans-Pritchard's interpretation of *buth* as 'group kinship' in a light our ordinary acceptation of 'group' cannot discern and our received ontology does not admit.

Leaderless but effective governance

If the individual-as-such is not a significant categorical component of the hierarchy and in fact becomes by degrees, as one scans upward, the individual-as-other, then the positions of superiority constituting the hierarchy cannot be open to the individual-as-such but only – and this in a graduated fashion that progresses directly with the steadily increasing diffusion of the individual – to the individual-as-other. In other words, remarkably, the assumption by an individual of a position of authority always amounts to the subordination of his more exclusive to his more inclusive self, but never to his elevation over other Nuer. By virtue of the ontological primacy of holistic identity, which by degrees transforms each Nuer into every Nuer, each, without exception, enjoys every hierarchical position. The hierarchical relations, then, do not obtain between individuals-as-such but within the individual-as-other. Put another way, among Nuer selfhood is segmentary, and is organized in much the same way as their social structure.

The lack of political authority notwithstanding, in fact the segmentary hierarchy functions to organize and manage affairs on every plane of Nuer public life (with the capacity to settle feuds, arrange rituals, strike camp, etc.). For this reason, to make use of M.G. Smith's comparative political theory (1960:ch.2), the Nuer hierarchy may be said to discharge the functions of an administrative order. In connection with Nuer 'administration', though, it is futile and misguided to search for the sort of authority that entails institutionalized differential advantage between men. The authority that in fact obtains is of a different sort. In this kind of administrative hierarchy the unequal orders of group, meta-group, meta-meta-group etc. do indeed distinguish correspondingly different categories of men, but all the categories are allocated at all times to every man. Therefore, insofar as each man enjoys authority, he does so always over himself as a member of a group. In result, each man remains his own governor, and, although his person (which, recall is not confined to or even centred on his concrete individuality) is internally differentiated by virtue of authority, he remains undifferentiated from other men in the same regard. In an exact sense, then, the constituted authority of this kind of 'administrative' hierarchy is not authority at all.

To detect just how different this kind of administrative authority is from the received Western sense, it is edifying to consider that the Nuer political system is for all practical purposes even less authoritarian or statist then, say, an out-and-out collectivist and 'alternative' social order such as the Israeli kibbutz. Dedicated to direct democracy, the kibbutz has as its sovereign 'the people', who meet often, regularly, and as a whole – constituting a General Assembly – to devise and initiate all manner of public decisions. In addition to this axial institution, kibbutz government is also characterized by a multitude of functionally specific administrative committees and positions, the incumbents of which are rotated fairly rapidly. Through these technical organizational means, the kibbutz seeks to minimize the development of differential authority. Nevertheless, sovereignty remains here a matter of ruler–ruled relationships. It is just that the kibbutz does its institutional best to distribute these relationships as equally as possible among the individual members of the community, by contriving to reverse the roles of ruler and ruled as often as is feasible given the need for effective governance. But even the General Assembly, the pivotal organ of this direct democracy, retains the received meaning of authority. The operation of this institution is predicated on the Rousseauian ideal of the subjugation of the 'particular' to the 'general' will, which is nothing but the ruler–ruled relationship, but instead of being between one individual and another it is between society and the individual.[13] The idea is for the members to preserve their individual autonomy and constitute the social whole at one and the same time, by choosing *freely* for the interest of the latter. It is crucial to see that this idea, one of Rousseau's answers to the problem of freedom posed by (what he saw as) the imposition of society on the individual, makes sense only if one's thinking begins with the predication of the absolute or autonomous individual. We have already seen, though, that this figure of the individual, so intensely sculpted in the philosophies of Descartes and Kant, is not a basic feature of Nuer phenomenology.[14] But in the absence of this figure, a ruler–ruled relationship, whether between individuals or between the individual and society, cannot sensibly appear. Given a non-dualist purchase on reality, wherein the individual is perceived as basically ambiguous as between self and other, authority cannot obtain between one self and another but only *within* the self-as-other. In result, authority materializes as encompassment, such that the self instead of being simply subject-ed, as in a ruler–ruled relationship, is generated paradoxically as a kind of integral – the relatively autonomous kind – of what it is not or what is other to it. That is to say, the self manifests itself as, in sharp contrast to a thing-in-itself, something between itself and its other, and in virtue of this chronic indeterminateness, as a creative process of becoming. This process describes the self as a dynamic of continuous but transformative renewal: by *giving way* to what it both is and is not, that is, to its own encompassing otherness, the self makes room for incessant self-generation. Under this kind of 'sacrificial' regime, authority manifests itself more as a matter of creation than of coercion.

Power and competition over equal place

It would, however, be mistaken to conclude from this picture of Nuer political life that differential advantage, that is, power, does not in fact exist among them. Their agnatic principle virtually guarantees, even demands, the operation of differential advantage. As we have seen, Nuer practice entails the territorialization of agnation, and thus the opening of the principled universe to the world of difference. Just as the value of agnation normatively defines the nature of advantage, so the practice of this value makes such advantage unequally available according to the contingent circumstances of worldly existence. Whatever the normative intentionality of agnation, a Nuer can in fact distinguish himself from his fellows by means of a variety of advantages, including, most notably, cattle, women and land. But the normative order's refusal to found and sanction positions of differential advantage means that such advantage as the system affords cannot be converted into rank as such. In this system, to endeavour to employ advantage to the end of differentiating oneself by reference to superior rank is pointless, for it can serve only to project oneself onto the next higher plane of the hierarchy, and thus to merge one's identity with those over whom one aims to gain ascendancy. The Nuer cannot contrapose himself to other Nuer in terms of a relation of ascendancy, since such contraposition entails his own subsumption, on the ascending plane, through his identification with the selfsame others.

As explained earlier, the segmentary and metalogical organization of the Nuer social system also describes the Nuer's person, featuring two kinds of self-identity: its relative opposition to collateral others determines the one, whereas the other kind is holistic, referring itself to the apogee of the hierarchy. Despite its holism, however, since it is divided according to the planar steps of the lineal hierarchy, the latter sort of self registers the segmentary principle too. As the hierarchical planes ascend metalogically, such that the next higher one not only outranks but also encompasses the one below it, so the corresponding Nuer self is riven into segments of greater and greater inclusiveness. What is from a modern perspective downright strange in this is that the more inclusive a Nuer's self becomes, that is, the nearer it finds itself to the apex of the hierarchy, the more it grows to be, rather than self-contained and individuated, indistinguishable from other Nuer. Indeed, at its most inclusive, the Nuer self becomes acutely other to itself. This is because the kind of whole that defines this sort of self-identity, the kind Nuer address and refer to as *kwoth*, is in the first place arrived at on the principle of allness or openness rather than oneness.

Hence, in the Nuer's world, a man's self-identity is located at all times on every plane of the metalogical order. In this formal and, for Nuer, concrete sense, any immediate difference between him and another, however materially consequential, is always already mediated. This is because the hierarchy is metalogical and functions as the final horizon of every situation, that is, as the phenomenological scaffold to which the reality and meaning of any situation is ultimately referred. In view of the manner in which the Nuer's self, with its stepwise distribution in the lineal hierarchy, becomes increasingly other to itself, it not simply *represents* but veritably *presents* Everyman. When the queen of England refers to herself as 'we' (as in 'We are not amused'), she draws on, in consideration of her monarchical role, a symbolical and irregular usage (the 'royal we'). But the Nuer, *simply by virtue of being Nuer*, wordlessly refers to himself as, in a perfectly ordinary meaning, 'we', for he counts as every Nuer in a sense that is irreducible to a trope, an authentic, substantive sense to which Western ontology is constitutionally blind. And this overriding, 'holistic' sense of self is why he cannot convert into formal ascendancy any differential advantage he, in his individuality, may enjoy over others.

The only way, then, the Nuer can transform advantage into differential advantage is to employ it in the interest of his contraposition to coequals and coevals. Horizontal opposition is the principal structure provided by the agnatic precept for the development of a Nuer's exclusive identity. In effect, strikingly, the Nuer's efforts to acquire advantage take the form of competition over, not unequal, but equal place.[15] It seems odd that the Nuer must compete over parity, since the system already bestows it on him. But no more than any other social order can this system guarantee in practice what it confers in principle. While it grants to no man authority over another, and equal place to every man, owing to agnation's need to subject itself to the uncertainties of worldly existence, any man is liable to lose his given place. Because of contingent circumstances, from plague and pestilence to impotence, birth-order and natural endowment, a man cannot be absolutely secure about his given place in the system and must be prepared to struggle to preserve it.

Nuer are most tenacious of their rights and possessions. They take easily but give with difficulty. This selfishness arises from their education and

from the nature of kinship obligations. A child soon learns that to maintain
his equality with his peers he must stand up for himself against any
encroachment on his person and property. This means that he must always
be prepared to fight, and his willingness and ability to do so are the only
protection of his integrity as a free and independent person against the
avarice and bullying of his kinsmen.

(Evans-Pritchard 1940a:184)

Indeed, the Nuer who fails to retrieve what he loses to misfortune, or to
defend himself against those who lay claim to his advantages, will find himself
short of life chances, or opportunities to produce, either naturally or by proxy,
offspring to himself. In effect, he will lack the wherewithal to carry on his
name (Evans-Pritchard 1940:198–9):

> In theory every man is a potential founder of a lineage, but, in fact, lineages
> spring from very few names. The others, for one reason or another, drop
> out, so that only certain lines of descent are remembered. Also, in those
> lines that persist names drop out of the steps in ascent to the founder of the
> clan . . .

Thus the Nuer's failure to effectively maintain his equal place portends
his death in the sense of failure to realize the line of descent of which he is a
potential founder. It is as if he never lived. Given that the ontology implicit
in the Nuer form of life neither begins nor ends with the individual per
se, it stands to reason that the Nuer contemplates death of this peculiarly
human kind with more gravity and apprehension than ever he does death
defined simply by the end of his individual existence. Thus a singularly
vital competitive premium is put on the disposal of the material resources
underlying the maintenance of equal place.

Exchange, transcendence and sacrifice

For the Nuer neither property nor the power to dispose it are ends in
themselves. In this system competition over material wherewithal is induced
by a man's need to preserve his equality with all other Nuer in the face of
uncertain and even contrary conditions. Needless to say, however, there is no
evidence that Nuer concern themselves with a doctrine of equality, and I am
not claiming they are moved by an ideal as such. Rather, as just mentioned, it
is ethnographically unmistakable that a Nuer's failure to defend his interests
is conventionally experienced by the concerned parties in terms of a vital
threat to his person. By its very nature, the segmentary hierarchy confounds
property and person so inextricably that it is impossible to compete over the

former without having the latter in contention. In fact, although differential control over land, women and cattle can give to the Nuer little in the way of special privilege and rank, these 'goods' do constitute a crucial medium of his person. In the case of women and cattle, the Nuer chiefly want them as media of exchange – they are exchanged for each other. But this sort of exchange is only part of a network of forms of exchange. Given that in this context of the reciprocal transmission of goods the fundamental role of women is that of procreative medium, in giving his sisters in exchange for cattle, and in turn his cattle for someone else's sisters, the Nuer expects ultimately to receive children in return. He is, in effect, exchanging both women and cattle for children, that is, for the perpetuity of his agnatic self. The equivalence thus created between cattle and children conditions a further kind of exchange, that of sacrifice to *kwoth*, in which the Nuer gives up his children, in surrogate (cattle) form, to ensure their receipt to him in their own form. Land is used in reciprocal exchange to create resident allies, strengthening the local elements of descent groups and realizing the territorial units as corporate groups, and also incorporating them into the lineage system. In effect, then, all three – land, women and cattle – are used in exchange to ensure the generational continuity of the particular Nuer's personhood in its relation to the supreme value of being Nuer. In which case, though, as among Clastres' Guarani, exchange as such has been transcended by value as such.

The key to this kind of transcendence is the practice of sacrifice. Thus while cattle are sacrificed to *kwoth* on behalf of self-perpetuation, they, women and land are sacrificed to other men to the same end. In each case something internal, an element of the self, is alienated, and something external, an element of the other, is incorporated in order to promote the self's continuation. Thus the self reconstitutes itself not simply through, but veritably with, the stuff of the other. It is crucial to see, though, that with the shift from exchange between men to exchange between man and *kwoth*, the meaning of exchange is profoundly altered. For whereas the former kind of exchange is indeed intended as equal, the latter sort, between man and *kwoth*, cannot be conceived of in terms of reciprocity at all. Since *kwoth* is for the Nuer the ultimate source of everything, it is not possible to redeem one's debt to him. The sacrifice of cattle then to *kwoth* cannot be offered in exchange. Instead, given that the cattle are identifiable with the Nuer themselves, in a concrete sense logically outlandish in Western discourse, in sacrificing cattle to *kwoth* the Nuer are in effect giving of themselves. In other words, it is not an exchange so much as a gift. To be sure, the Nuer perform sacrifice with the expectation that they will be revitalized as a result. But precisely because it is *life* at issue, something *kwoth* alone can secure, they know that their gift cannot bind him and that their expectation is a matter of trust and not barter. Moreover, because this act of giving is the pinnacle of the system of exchange in its entirety, all exchanges among this people, including those sharply characterized by haggling and negotiation, are ultimately informed by sacrifice. All of them constitute links in a sacrificial chain the end of which is *being*, in the sense of continuing agnatic vitality.

Sovereignty and identity
Exchange and value

With respect to the problem of powerless but effective governance, the Nuer order is thus remarkable. It is useful now to recall Clastres' insight about how the Guarani founded the relationship between the group and the chieftainship: by exceeding the principle of exchange, to the point of prestation, they made the chief their hostage rather than ruler. When Jesus admonishes 'whosoever shall smite thee on thy right cheek, turn to him the other also', he is eschewing reciprocation in favour of an offering. The idea is to engender value as such, that is, value that does not reduce to utility and economic worth, and entails an indebtedness that can never be redeemed. In the nature of the case, indebtedness of this kind obtains on the other side of power, for, having resulted from the voluntary forfeit of payback (in political terms, revenge), it realizes a relationship based on value rather than power. So too with Clastres' Indians: they have generated the chieftainship on the basis of value creation rather than reciprocity. But Clastres, like Matthew in his Gospel and Lévi-Strauss in his, seems to presume that society has its beginning in exchange and power, and therefore must seek, if only unconsciously, a means to transcend itself.

For the Nuer, however, the world, including the social world, does not begin with reciprocity, but with primordial value. I have spoken throughout of *buth* or Nuer agnation as a first principle. By 'principle', it is sociologically usual to have in mind an analytical abstraction that essentializes a social process or organization. But *buth* is not an analytical abstraction of this kind. Nor is it a rule according to which Nuer can agree (or not) to conduct themselves – as if they existed, as Nuer, apart from it. Rather, *buth* is an existential principle or, as the philosophers might say, a synthetic a priori. Under ordinary circumstances, a gap between it and practice cannot emerge, since, by virtue of its hegemonic purchase, it operates as a practice rather than an institution. It is a convention, but one that functions as a given, as does for us, say, the principle of subjectivity. What is more, this particular given is so perfectly round, it serves to compose a world: it stands firm for the Nuer because, instead of being a single principle, it constitutes an axis around which turns *everything* that is. Therefore, it is not open to question, for to question it would not be to test its veracity but to threaten the world with annihilation.[16]

The Nuer, then, have no need to engineer a mechanism to prevent the emergence of power, since their very reality begins and ends with a value that, non-dualistically, depends on and allows for power while it contains it. As a result, to take a routine instance, the Nuer who finds it in his interest to take up residence with his cognatic relatives undermines agnation on one count, only, however, since his cognates too are identifiable with an agnatic group, to reinforce it on another.

Loneliness and absolute identity

The agnatic whole that non-dualism describes is, as against all logic, open. The commonplace conception of a whole in terms of absolute closure springs from ontological individualism. When, as in Hobbes, it is conceived of with the idea of the self-contained individual, the whole signifies fixity and impregnability. But the idea of the hermetic individual presupposes philosophical dualism, which renders immaculate boundaries as it determines mutual exclusivity. This is what the Guarani speak of as the evil of the One (Clastres 1987:169–75), distinguishing the One from the All. The One denotes the finitude or closure of things, and thus implicates the physical principle of death and the metaphysical one of identity. The All, however, signifies the plurality or betweenness of any entity, its essential connection to what is other to itself, and hence intimates infinity and ongoing vitality. In this connection, Clastres submits that the Guarani's explicit refusal of the One amounts also to the tacit refusal of the state, whose essence, he holds, may be defined in terms of the One (1987:216–17).

In her magisterial study of the origins of totalitarianism, Hannah Arendt (1973:474ff.) inquires into the 'basic human experience' from which arises the possibility of totalitarian governance, and finds her answer in a phenomenological notion of 'loneliness.' 'Loneliness' describes a state of being wherein, even in the midst of others, one has lost contact with oneself, to the point of thoughtlessness, and, correspondingly, with the world. It is the experience of total abandonment, such that the presupposed human world on which one relies for routine living vaporizes beneath one's feet. Although her immediate focus is totalitarian regimes and their ironclad logicality, it is plain from her overall work that she intends her critique as a more sweeping condemnation (e.g. 1958:58). As she sees it, with the rise of modern mass society, loneliness has become, instead of a 'borderline' experience, routine – even the rule. As the axial organization of every modern nation state, bureaucracy, with its geometrically insensible, wheel-like order, in which everybody is reducible to a cog, is for her representative of this experiential state of being. Politically, Arendt associates this experience with a form of reflective isolation, by virtue of which humans lose their ability to act together to create a world in common, but one that is also open to the unique perspective of each of its creators. In other words, loneliness devastates the human capacity for creativity, a capacity she calls 'freedom' and thinks of – notably along the lines of the kind of engenderment Nuer ascribe to *kwoth* – as 'thinking', in the sense of 'beginning' or 'originating' (1973:473). What is important to see here, though, is that the propagation of the human experience Arendt sees as mutually implicated with totalitarian governance is a likely effect of any regime keyed to ontological individualism and the principle of absolute identity.

Arendt's argument may be broadly assimilated to the Guarani's cutting mythological account of the One and the All. The 'sameness in utter diversity' she extols as the defining human condition catches the spirit of the Guarani 'All', whereas the state of social affairs she censures, although a condition of mass society, is akin to the evil that Guarani call the One. There is a logical consistency between Arendt's ideas of loneliness and isolation and the Guarani conception of the One; and the relationship between the Guarani group and its chieftainship, although far from Arendt's empirical materials, seems in a broad but informative way to describe her ideal of a political order keyed to commonality and plurality at the same time. It is reasonable to expect, then, that Arendt's phenomenological thesis about loneliness, coupled with the ontological one about the principle of identity, can throw light on Clastres' question of why humans would ever give way to a ruler–ruled relationship.

Perceptual alternation and the emergence of the state

If 'loneliness' is a basic human condition, then it cannot be alien to the Nuer. But insofar as they do not adhere to the identity principle on which this experience can feed excessively, it is difficult to imagine loneliness obtaining as the rule among them. In which case, the kind of dehumanizing sovereign power that critically defines the modern state is given no place to appear to the Nuer mind's eye. There does seem to be at least one chink, though, in this system's armour against the absolute differentiation of power from within. Among the Nuer, all of the social distinctions that might suggest differential authority – including that of male over female, man over boy, first occupant (*dil*) over stranger (*rul*), Nuer over adopted Dinka (*jaang*), as well as the so-called leopard-skin chief – operate according to the common model of power in this system, such that the 'power' in question is always a matter of generative influence rather than political might.[17] The Nuer prophet, however, presents a critical difference of kind. Although his figure too is tied to the power of the whole, he appears to represent that power, not so much as an integral of the whole, but precisely in his individuality. That is to say, with the figure of the prophet it would seem that the power that is *kwoth* enters into the body of one man in that man's singularity, thus bringing to individuality among this people essential rather than idiosyncratic definition. The ethnographic picture of the prophets as uniquely charismatic figures as well as, from the point of view of the colonial administrators, distinct political threats certainly lends support to this conjecture.[18] If the conjecture is sound, then the figure of the prophet intimates the principle of absolute identity, and therewith promises the possibility of conclusive territorialization. In the event, the hierarchy of agnation and territory would be inverted once and for all, transforming it into the kind of hierarchy characterizing states in the proper sense.

As part of his effort to address the problem of why peoples would ever agree to subject themselves to state power, Clastres, too, speculated that with the historical emergence of prophetic types among the Tupi-Guarani, there appeared the possibility of a leader–follower relationship in the modern sense.[19] What I want to emphasize in the analysis of the Nuer, though, is that the change implicating concession to proper political authority is not so much a question of will, even if unconscious, but of perception. The Nuer ambiguity of territory and agnation may be regarded in terms of a gestalt switch, but one in which the conditions for the alternation of perception are so phenomenologically weighted in favour of descent, that a well-differentiated appearance of the territorial image is ordinarily precluded. With the emergence of a figure whose physical contours serve to confine the spiritual power of the whole, however, these conditions themselves become subject to change. They open themselves to redefinition in terms of an unmitigated principle of identity, which in turn makes all the difference in the world to the gestalt switch in question. By presenting the possibility of the complete incarnation (which is to say, territorialization) of spiritual power, the change enables an inversion of the encompassment relation, insinuating an absolute distinction between a reality keyed to basic ambiguity (Nuer descent), on the one hand, and a reality centred in decisive boundaries (Nuer territory), on the other. This ontological difference brings with it differences that make the difference between the modern world and societies like the Guarani and the Nuer. One such huge, but still relative, difference lies in the authorized relationships of political inequality and, correlatively, the institution of the state. Thus the dynamic logic of the figure of the prophet makes clear the essential continuity between non-dualism and dualism. Because the order of descent included as a vital component its counter principle, namely territory, its own framing entailed hierarchical inversion, but only in limited terms. With the appearance of the prophet, however, who embodies in his singularity the power of the whole, the hierarchy was opened to inversion in absolute terms. Such a total inversion amounts to more than a simple exchange of locations, whereby territory takes the place of descent. The incorporation of the generative principle by the territorial one does not simply turn the hierarchy on its head;

it transforms it in a way so radical that what is hierarchic about it becomes, apparently, something else entirely. Differentiated as a stuff in its own right, territory determines absolute rather than relative boundaries. In other words, the inversion applies also to the kinds of boundary at stake, bringing into view ones that serve solely to detach and exclude. As a result, the inversion stands to close the whole, defining things in themselves and reconstituting the hierarchy as a ladder instead of a segmentary set of boxes graduated in size so that each fits in the next larger one.

What is highly striking, and epoch forming, about this move from non-dualism to dualism, is that once dualism is in place, standing on its own two feet, as it were, the continuity between these two sorts of reality is made to disappear: given boundaries that present themselves as impermeable, the continuity is hidden from view. Ironically, the condition that conceals the link is the same condition that enlarges self-consciousness, namely, absolute rather than relative boundaries. With this eclipse of perspective, we have, I suggest, a crucial phenomenological condition of modernity, including the disciplinary inquiry of modern anthropology (in as much as the inception of this field of study was predicated on 'other' cultures, that is, on what appeared to be unfathomable otherness). But the immediately salient point is that complete inversion of the hierarchy makes ambiguity intolerable, banishing it and fostering, to use the Guarani distinction, the One rather than the All, which is to say, the state and the kind of sovereignty it entails.[20]

Two kinds of sovereignty

What kind of sovereignty does the state entail? Giorgio Agamben makes the case that sovereignty in Western political theory and practice, totalitarian and democratic governments alike, is predicated on the idea of absolute power. The sovereign stands for both the constituted and the constituting power of the state, and therefore is lawfully unbound by the law. What ultimately defines sovereignty in this tradition, according to Agamben, is absolute right over life and death. A capital decision becomes an expression not of any prior general power (including specifically human or divine law), but of the unqualified autonomy of the sovereign. As a result, sovereignty logically entails a kind of life not subject to ritual sacrifice (i.e., divine law), but open to killing with legal impunity. Agamben calls this kind of life 'bare life', and he writes: 'the production of bare life is the originary activity of sovereignty' (1998:83). In effect, the concept of bare life denotes a category of, so to speak, existence in death, and therewith attributes to the sovereign's control over life and death not only the possibility of killing but also of making the dead live – that is, in a sense, the possibility of resurrection. This sovereign power, although even today everywhere on display, was given representative expression in the

Nazi concentration camps, in which the idea of 'the living dead' was realized consummately (cf. Levi 1993:88–9).

The concept of 'bare life' (which Agamben takes from Arendt) is intimately tied to Arendt's notion of loneliness. Both notions picture a living death of human beings who, to quote Agamben's description of the death camp inmates (1999:43), 'became indifferent to everything happening around them' and 'excluded themselves from all relations to their environment'. In essence, this description matches the political scenario Arendt draws from the condition of generalized loneliness: a consequential thoughtlessness and inability to act with others in virtue of one's uniquely human nature, that nature distinguished by its manifest capacity to fashion itself. The importance of Arendt's notion of loneliness for my argument is that it conveys the critical link between bare life and the ontological principle of absolute identity. Given the normative and phenomenological dominion of this principle in modern life, its intimate connection with 'bare life' enables us to see not only why Agamben feels free to speak of the whole modern world as having its logical conclusion in the concentration camp, but also how the principle of identity underlies the kind of sovereignty defined by the modern state. Arendt herself initiates the case when she ties the Western idea of a good leader to 'Platonic rulership', the legitimacy of which 'rested upon the domination of the self' and 'draws its guiding principles – those which at the same time justify and limit power over others – from a relationship established between me and myself' (1958:237–8). Arguably, the implications of this principle of leadership, implications for the development of absolute power and the objectivization of self and other, have been brought into focused relief in Foucault's oeuvre.[21]

If 'sovereignty' is taken more broadly, though, to mean, instead of the domination of the self, the freedom to govern the self, in the sense of being self-responsible, then in an elementary way the Nuer enjoy sovereignty. Their anarchical system of self-help exhibits pointedly such freedom from the control of other individual Nuer, at the same time as it discharges the various functions of governmental order. But their system does not reduce to the individual qua individual, and is based on anything but a principle of absolute identity. Instead it begins and ends with a value that, by never allowing the self to conceive of itself as identical to itself, curtails the development of the individual as such.

To come to terms with the kind of sovereignty that results from such a value, it helps, I think, to appeal also to paradigmatic ideas other than the Graeco-Roman, but Western nonetheless. Agamben's description of the sovereign in terms of absolute power, although tied especially to 'an obscure figure of archaic Roman law' (*homo sacer*) (1998:8), resonates also with an elemental Hebrew biblical tradition concerning a desire on the part of man to assume godly powers, especially the power over life and death. This tradition can be traced back to the second and third chapters of Genesis itself, where once man appropriates the fruit of the Tree of Knowledge, God quickly acts to eject him from the Garden of Eden, to ensure that the other great tree placed there, the Tree of Life, remains out of his reach. But in the biblical tradition, this bid for sovereign power is conceived of in terms of temptation, a notion that plainly comports with political ambition, but issues from an experience of a wondrously different kind. To tempt is to test, implying agency in the sense of a capacity (the fruit of the Tree of Knowledge) to always do otherwise.

Now, the biblical story pictures man's selfhood as a creation of his Other. Ironically, though, selfhood tends to implicate the Other, and, more generally, the other, as already eclipsed or forgotten. For, with each advance in the development of self-consciousness, man is given to feel more secure in the promise of his own empirical being, and, correspondingly, less watchful of his own otherness, the vital condition of his self. In effect, man's self-consciousness – his agency or power of choice – moves in a reflexive arc to increase his desire for self-closure. Indeed, even should he choose in favour of his other, the fact that *he* has chosen, tends to reinforce his sense of self. Selfhood, then, is always already temptation, the temptation to shake off the encumbrance of otherness, displacing the other with the self. When this temptation is given into finally, the result is onto-epistemological dualism, the metaphysical platform according to which sovereignty in the Western sense of the term, the Platonic and the Hobbesian sense, arose. For, it is this dualism that furnishes the idea of boundaries so perfectly exclusive as to yield the sovereign individual, the legitimating figure of subjection to the state. Here, then, we have the basic human experience – selfhood itself – that promotes the kind of sovereignty associated with the state.

I have introduced the story of Genesis on behalf of the distinction between two kinds of sovereignty. In the biblical description, the desire to assume godly powers is, before it is a struggle over power, an ethical event. That is to say, rendered in terms of a choice between power and not-power, sovereignty's nature as power-driven is trumped by a question of value. The value inheres in the implicit understanding that such power as man enjoys ultimately issues from and stands in the service of a higher, encompassing power. In its received meaning, though, the latter transcends power as such, for it rules, at least ultimately, by virtue of generation rather than compulsion or imposition. Accordingly, this kind of rulership, even in the case of, say, sacral kings and prophets, where power as such might be said to lurk just around the corner, does not draw its legitimacy from the individual's relationship to himself, but rather from his intimate relationship with a supreme and limiting value, although one that is constitutionally open to its own counterpart. In other words, sovereignty of this kind betrays a selfhood that not only acknowledges but also accepts, as a condition of its own constituting agency, its own otherness.

I have argued that Nuer selfhood is just so, a construction on the self-as-other. As such, it appears to be systematically ambiguous, unconstrained by immaculate division and essential identity. It is neither universal nor particular. This picture of selfhood approaches Agamben's notion of 'whatever being', that being which is always beside it*self*, neither individual nor generic, and therefore the exemplar of what Agamben calls the 'coming community'. This represents the idea of a community in which, although one belongs, there is no condition for belonging, and therefore no possibility for the establishment of community as we know it, in particular a state. Such a community is always in the in-between, in the sense of be-coming or coming to be, and therefore uncircumscribable.

Perfectibilism in question

But, as in Clastres' case, it is too easy to get carried away with such a grand claim about a social order like the Nuer's. While Nuer selfhood is positively ambiguous between self and other, it is after all keyed to an overriding condition of belonging, namely, agnation – even if this value does admit of its counterpart in measured doses. Among the Nuer as well as in the Hebrew biblical tradition, the representative relationship of the kind of sovereignty at issue here, generative rather than absolute, happens to be between father and son.[22] And that relationship can scarcely be construed as politically benign. It is not for nothing that for Nuer, despite the utterly explicit status of agnation as the supreme value of their social life, the question of whether or not agnatic identity issues primarily from the father or from the mother remains ever implicit. In view of the fact that children of the same father but different mothers mark the representative fault lines along which a lineage is expected to split, it is an unwanted but ever present implication of the system that the defining axis of agnatic solidarity is actually the feminine principle. In a critical sense, it is the difference the mother makes that makes the difference for agnation ('for brothers are a corporate group,' avers Evans-Pritchard [1940a:210], 'and, especially if they are sons of one mother, stick together'). Similarly, as I have essayed elsewhere (1997), notwithstanding the transparent patriarchalism of Genesis, one of the deepest secrets the story contrives to keep is that it tells of a profound identification of the figure of God with the feminine principle. Thus, as these two examples of the suppression of the feminine as an originating value intimate, power is not only agreed to in these systems, as an opposing yet complementary principle, but is also exercised, in the nature of the case, by the ruling value itself.

This circumstance means, I suggest, not that sovereignty keyed to engenderment rather than power is bogus, but rather that any particular value, even if non-dualistic, although it is enough to differentiate sovereignty of a different kind, is not enough to present it in any form but an imperfect one. And since, by reason of life on this earth, every value is particular, we should neither expect nor hope for this sovereignty in anything but an imperfect form. The fact is that were this kind of sovereignty to attain perfection, it would then define absolute boundaries, in which case it would simply have become the other kind of sovereignty. Ironically, as Rousseau surmised (1992: 25–6), the faculty of perfectibility, although it is the springboard of our second nature, that is, the nature we engender in or give to ourselves, might well be thought of 'as the source of all man's misfortunes' and is what 'eventually makes him a tyrant over himself and nature'. Surely, this thesis is born out (to cite what may well stand as the most inexcusable example from the opening moments of the twenty-first century) by the power-driven war that was waged by the gang of true-believers that, from 2001 to 2009, ran the government of the United States of America. In connection with this example and Rousseau's thesis, one need merely bring to mind the titular head of that gang (a virtual sovereign in a regime that presents itself as the universal model of democracy), to realize that the good Jean-Jacques was misguided only in thinking that man must wait for his dotage, when time will have eroded the second nature his perfectibility 'enabled him to acquire', to become 'an imbecile'.

Dualism, absolute identity, and the state are of a piece, and may be regarded as manifestations of perfectibilism. Non-dualistic values too, though, wield power qua power. In particular, they do so by virtue of the kind of hegemonic rule that promotes substantial naiveté. For this reason, even sophisticated rationalists the likes of Robin Horton and Jurgen Habermas speak of such 'pre-modern' systems as closed. But of course this appraisal constitutes an ironic conceit, for the manner in which rationalism prevails in modernity is, as postmodernism and critical theory before it have shown, while significantly enlightening in one way, deeply benighting in another. In particular, rationalism, in as much as it remains tied to the canonical laws of classical logic (identity, non-contradiction and the excluded middle), makes it ultimately impossible to understand and tolerate ambiguity. In light of this consideration, a system such as the Nuer's is as instructively open as it is closed, for it is attuned precisely to the essential ambiguity of things. As a desirable result, it can yield a 'non-political' political order, an order in which there are no ruler-subject relationships to speak of.

I suggest, then, that the fact that this kind of system also wields power qua power does not invalidate the truth of the special kind of sovereignty at issue here. Instead, it implies that any particular value must be prepared not only to admit of its complement but also, as against the grain of the very idea of institutionalization, to entertain the possibility of its own displacement by other such values, ones given no less essentially to engenderment, that is, to coming community. Of course, as Deleuze and Guattari's supposition (mentioned above, in the Introduction) about the ubiquitous presence of the state and sovereign power might suggest, truly constructive values too are bound to be imperfect. In light of such reliable imperfection, can we, then, conceive of a state that has institutionalized its own deinstitutionalization on, if not a daily basis, at least an earnest one?

ACKNOWLEDGEMENTS

I'm extremely grateful to Bruce Kapferer and Angela Hobart for their invitation to participate in the conference for which this paper was prepared. Aden Evens, a philosopher by trade, read an early draft of this paper and his suggestions and insights helped me considerably to organize and strengthen my argument. In addition, I'm indebted to the members (outstanding students all) of my Spring 2003 graduate seminar in phenomenological anthropology – Annie Blakeney-Glazer, Christina Foust, Kit Leckerling, Kyungmook Lee, Kacie Martin, Chris Roberts and Luke Roberts – who allowed me to present the paper to them as a trial run. The discussion that followed yielded a number of useful recommendations for clarification and improvement.

NOTES

1   Hannah Arendt (1958:222):

> Escape from the frailty of human affairs into the solidity of quiet and order has in
> fact so much to recommend it that the greater part of political philosophy since
> Plato could easily be interpreted as various attempts to find theoretical foundations
> and practical ways for an escape from politics altogether. The hallmark of all
> such escapes is the concept of rule, that is, the notion that men can lawfully and
> politically live together only when some are entitled to command and others
> forced to obey. The commonplace notion already to be found in Plato and Aristotle
> that every political community consists of those who rule and those who are
> ruled (on which assumption in turn are based the current definitions of forms of
> government—rule by one or monarchy, rule by few or oligarchy, rule by many or
> democracy)...

2   By 'non-dualism' I intend a relationship of basic ambiguity rather than one of either mutual exclusion ('dualism') or of absolute inclusion ('monism'). By the same token, most tellingly, non-dualism predicates boundaries that not only separate but also connect. In *Anthropology as Ethics: Nondualism and the Conduct of*

Sacrifice (Evens 2008), I have expanded on the anthropological, phenomenological and ontological force of this paradoxical concept.

3   It is true that whereas Clastres is keen to draw on political philosophy in his study, Evans-Pritchard and Fortes, exercising the scientific enthusiasm characteristic of the beginning stages of modern social anthropology, eschewed 'the theories of political philosophers', on the grounds that these theories concerned themselves more with the 'ought' than the 'is' of political life (Fortes and Evans-Pritchard 1940:4). In addition, of course, Clastres was no structural functionalist. Nevertheless, there can be no question that Evans-Pritchard and Fortes no more wished to entertain evolutionism and ethnocentrism than did Clastres, and that their empirically informed analyses of stateless societies were exceptionally illuminating, precisely in ways relevant to Clastres' project.

4   Radcliffe-Brown identified the principles on which this system is based as the unity of the sibling group and the equivalence of same-sex siblings (1952:64ff.; cf. also Fortes 1953 and Smith 1956). Of greater interest here, though, is Durkheim's description of what he called 'segmental societies with a clan-base' (1933:174ff.):

> We say of these societies that they are segmental in order to indicate their formation by the repetition of like aggregates in them, analogous to the rings of an earth worm, and we say of this elementary aggregate that it is a clan, because this word well expresses its mixed nature, at once familial and political. It is a family in the sense that all the members who compose it are considered as kind of one another, and they are, in fact, for the most part consanguineous. ... But, on the other hand, it is not a family in the proper sense of the word, for, in order to partake of it, it is not necessary to have any definite relationship of consanguinity with other members of the clan. ... Thus, the clan contains a great many strangers, and this permits it to attain dimensions such as a family, properly speaking, never has. It often comprises several thousand persons. Moreover, it is the fundamental political unity; the heads of clans are the only social authorities.
>
> We can thus qualify this organization as politico-familial. Not only has the clan consanguinity as its basis, but different clans of the same people are often considered as kin to one another.... Among the Jews, who present ... the most characteristic traits of the same social organization, the ancestor of each of the clans which compose the tribe is believed to be descended from the tribal founder, who is himself regarded as one of the sons of the father of the race...

Especially striking in the present connection is Durkheim's attention to this kind of system's 'mixed nature' as 'politico-familial', for this is the very nature that so challenged Evans-Pritchard's powers of analysis in his study of the Nuer polity, given this polity's systematic organizational ambiguity as between territory and agnation.

I should add here that, as regards their social and political organization, it's likely that the Nuer differed significantly from one part of Nuerland to another. In raising the question of the link between the Nuer and the Dinka, Evans-Pritchard himself perhaps implied as much (1940a:3). Still, in his well-known article on the segmentary lineage system, Sahlins argued (1961), as against the brunt of Evans-Pritchard's analysis, that it is necessary to grasp the segmentary lineage system as a matter of ecological adaption and social evolutionary development, rather than as a function of a certain principle of social structure (the 'segmentary principle'). If we put aside its broad evolutionism, Sahlins's argument (1961:323) – that 'a segmentary lineage system is a social means of intrusion and competition in an already occupied ecological niche' and that it is 'a successful predatory organization in conflicts with other tribes' – would imply that the Nuer polity and segmentary principle should vary with the particular social, geographical and historical locale in which they find themselves. But my concern in this essay is with neither the segmentary lineage system in itself nor the range of variation of Nuer political order. Rather I want to explore the phenomenology of the stateless nature of the Nuer polity as Evans-Pritchard found and ethnographically described this polity *among the Nuer with whom he worked.* My aim is to draw out the experiential fibre and advance towards the feel of the statelessness of that order.

5   The critical study in this respect is M.G. Smith's luminous 'Pre-industrial stratification systems' (1966), a commanding critique, from the empirical perspective of comparative ethnography, of the one-time prevailing sociological thesis that stratification is a functional prerequisite of any social order. The particulars of the critique follow from Smith's powerful comparative and dynamist theory of government and society, Weberian in spirit and ethnographically intensive in scope (e.g. 1956, 1960). Like Fortes and Evans-Pritchard's work on stateless societies, Smith's essay on stratification as well as his theory of government tends to open to question the routine Western presumption of ruler–ruled relations. What is more, it does so while embracing the ubiquity of power and political competition. However, Smith's essay, published in an edited sociology collection, was hardly perused by his anthropological colleagues to the same extent as was Fortes and Evans-Pritchard's classic collection on African political systems, and there is no reason to think that Clastres read it by the time his own book was finally published (his book was, I believe, completed well before it appeared in print), if, indeed, he ever even saw it.

6   The authority of Nuer men over women is pronounced and runs deep, and yet Evans-Pritchard's observations suggest that women hold their own in everyday life (1951:134, 132–3):

With rare exceptions, I found Nuer women well content with their station and that their husbands and other men treated them with respect. In saying that their status in society is high I am judging not so much by the fact that the same number of cattle have to be paid for the homicide of a woman as of a man … but by the part women take in the daily life of the community. They mix freely and with easy assurance with the men, and they do not hesitate to argue with them about matters in which they are interested as women. They have as intimate relations as the men with the cherished cattle, share with them the life of the kraal, and enter the byres when they wish to do so.

I take it that this character of the relations between the sexes reflects the fact that, even though social difference is significant and acknowledged, the value of equality remains general and is simply taken for granted in Nuer society.

7   Focusing on the principle of segmentation, Dumont himself drew the parallel between the caste system and the Nuer political order (1970:41–2).

8   It means 'leader' or 'guide' as well (Kiggen 1948; Stigand 1923). For an interpretation of how these meanings hang together with the others, see Evens 1984:323–5.

9   I have paraphrased Agamben here (1993:72), who tells us that the fact that one never mistakes the term 'shoe' for a shoe is not a worthwhile objection to the relevant idea, for 'What is in question is not the word "shoe" in its acoustic or graphic form (the *suppositio materialis* of medieval logicians), but the word "shoe" precisely in its signifying the shoe (or, *a parte objecti*, the shoe in its being signified by the term "shoe").'

10   This point helps explain the importance of oratorical skill as an attribute of Clastres' Indian chief (1987:31): 'the Indians place a high value on [the chief's] words: talent as a speaker is both a condition and instrument of political power.' Perhaps oratory as a necessary condition for this kind of leaderless leadership reflects the ontological authority of the name, an authority that is a matter of encompassment rather than coercion. The figure of the Nuer 'leopard-skin chief' is another case in point here (Evans-Pritchard 1940: e.g. 5, 152–5, 163–4). His office lacks the power of coercion, and instead represents the possibility of the peace in the feud, by virtue of settlement through word rather than deed or blood revenge. B.A. Lewis, a one time district commissioner among the Nuer, found that 'practically all' Nuer who were regarded as 'spokesmen' or *ruic* were also leopard-skin chiefs (1951:32, 77–84), and wrote that 'the word *ruic* is derived from the same root as *ruac* meaning "speech" or "talk", and a *ruic* is said to have *ruec*, which is perhaps best translated as "influence", for "authority" would be too strong a word for the very limited control these leaders were able to wield over their turbulent, independent tribesmen.' However, as we shall see below, in the case of the so-called prophet among both the Guarani and the Nuer, this kind of 'logological' authority, notwithstanding its nature as encompassment, can be turned to the advantage of coercive power.

11   Evans-Pritchard clearly projected the correspondence between the two systems,
      but, held fast by a dualistic presumption of the relation between territory and
      agnation, he failed to see that the correspondence is not merely nominal but
      follows in the nature of the case.

12   Apart from twins, whose plurality and singularity are utterly confounded, and
      who, as Evans-Pritchard made plain in his famous discussion of the Nuer assertion
      that 'twins are birds', enjoy a very special status among this people. Indeed, it
      would appear that for Nuer the perfect way twins are both one and two at the
      same time distinguishes them as both a representation of, and a threat to, the
      agnatic whole. For as a plurality the wholeness of which is somehow complete,
      twins portend the possibility of displacing rather than perpetuating the whole in
      its current form. No wonder, then, as Evans-Pritchard observed (1936:230–1; cf.
      also Littlejohn 1970:101–4), Nuer regard twins as parent-killers.

13   Hence, in his classic interpretation (1970), J.L. Talmon sees Rousseau as the
      philosopher of 'totalitarian democracy'. Of course, in light of the established
      murkiness of Rousseau's notion of 'general will', many interpreters of the great
      French thinker have argued otherwise.

14   Cf. here Kenneth Read's superbly insightful essay on the Gahuku Gama, in which
      he demonstrates, ethnographically, the relative nature of the Kantian individual
      (1955).

15   Evans-Pritchard's (1940a:158f.) and Howell's (1954:221–4) functionalist accounts
      of Nuer justice as being based on retaliation and directed to 'the restoration of
      equilibrium' display a distinct phenomenological acuity when they are seen in
      connection with the thesis that the motivational axis of Nuer competition is
      egalitarian.

16   I have developed this notion of principle in at least two other places (1984 and
      1989), both being reinterpretations of the Nuer.

17   For instance, although Evans-Pritchard called first occupants, or *diel*, 'aristocrats',
      he also observed that they 'have prestige rather than rank and influence rather
      than power' (1940:215).

18   See Evans-Pritchard's brief but, in my view, very insightful discussion of the
      significance and rise of the Nuer prophets (1940:189; also 185ff.):

> For the first time a single person symbolized, if only to a moderate degree and in a
> mainly spiritual and uninstitutionalized form, the unity of a tribe, for prophets are
> tribal figures. But they have a further significance, for their influence extended over
> tribal boundaries. ... They were not a mechanism of tribal structure like leopard-
> skin chiefs, but were pivots of federation between adjacent tribes and personified
> the unity and homogeneity of Nuer against foreigners. Probably, the coalition of
> tribes and the organization of joint raids is very largely their achievement ... and
> has made them important and powerful figures in Nuerland. This interpretation

explains how it is that prophets began half a century ago, or at any rate came to the fore then. Certain structural changes were taking place in response to changed conditions: the development of functions that were more purely political than any exercised by individuals before and of a greater degree of unity among neighbouring tribes than there had been hitherto. ... As we understand the situation, the prophets were inevitably opposed to the Government because it was this opposition among the people which led to their emergence and was personified in them.

Cf. also Douglas Johnson's extremely useful and substantial history of these figures (1994). Johnson seriously questions Evans-Pritchard's political interpretation of the Nuer prophet. Elsewhere (Evens 1996), I have suggested that in this particular respect Johnson's argument is doubtful.

19 Clastres argues (1987:205ff.) that the only element escaping 'primitive society's' ability to 'reproduce itself perpetually without anything affecting it throughout time' is demography. These societies centre on economic autarchy and radical political independence and therefore rest on, he concludes, relatively small size. In this connection, Clastres paints a picture of the Tupi-Guarani, at the time they happened to be discovered by Europeans (the fifteenth century), as characterized by relatively powerful chieftainships, and points out that this circumstance, which was anomalous for the culture area, correlated with an abnormal demographic expansion of this people and, correspondingly, a rise in outsized local groups. In reaction to this demographically kindled threat to its stateless integrity, Tupi-Guarani society threw up prophets to preach against the evil of 'the One', which is to say, sovereign power or the state. Ironically, though, in their insurrectionist quest, the prophets managed to mobilize, by means of their Word, tremendous followings, thus themselves creating the possibility of the emergence of the state.

20 For this reason, though the exceptional anthropological value of Dumont's thesis cannot be gainsaid, his critics from the left had something important to say. Despite the continuing normative supremacy of status, given the total differentiation of power from status, the Indian caste system lent itself, in a substantially perverse way largely unthinkable among the Nuer, to the execution of power in the name of value.

21 Or so one might think, despite the fact that Foucault embraced, in his last years and in the spirit of Nietzsche, the very Greek ideal of self and leadership that so troubled Arendt (Fornet-Betancourt *et al.* 1987).

22 The Roman figure of *homo sacer* is also intimately tied to the father-son relationship. Agamben observes (1998:87–8) that the first time the right over life and death is encountered in the history of Roman law is in regard to the father's unconditional authority over his son, 'a power that follows immediately from the father-son relation'. But on Agamben's account there's no reason to see in

this power the kind of (positive or creative) sovereignty I suggest attaches to the Hebrew example. In this connection, it's telling to compare the *Akedah*, the story of Abraham's 'binding' of Isaac (Chapter 22 of *Genesis*), to Agamben's example of how the father-son relation becomes politicized. In the Hebrew biblical tale, God commands Abraham (a.k.a. 'Father Abraham') to sacrifice his beloved son Isaac, but at the critical moment Abraham, knife in hand, is held in check by God, who thus ensures the life of the Jewish *people*. By contrast, here is Agamben's example (1998:88–9):

> when we read in a late source that in having his sons put to death, Brutus 'had adopted the Roman people in their place,' it is the same power of death that is now transferred, through the image of adoption, to the entire people. The hagiographic epithet 'father of the people,' which is reserved in every age to the leaders invested with sovereign authority, thus once again acquires its originary, sinister meaning.

The sinister meaning of which Agamben speaks is, in my view, also present in the Akedah. But the fact that in this biblical story the continuity between the son's life and that of the people as whole depends finally on the father's *willingness* to put the son to death, rather than on the murderous act itself, complicates matters and introduces a value that looks beyond the malevolent.

REFERENCES

Agamben, Giorgio, 1993, *The Coming Community*, trans. Michael Hardt. Minneapolis: University of Minnesota Press.
——— 1998, *Homo Sacer: Sovereign Power and Bare Life*, trans. Daniel Heller-Roazen. Stanford: Stanford University Press.
——— 1999, *Remnants of Auschwitz: the Witness and the Archive*, trans. Daniel Heller-Roazen. New York: Zone Books.
Arendt, Hannah, 1958, *The Human Condition*. Chicago: University of Chicago Press.
——— 1973 (1953), *The Origins of Totalitarianism*. San Diego: Harcourt Brace & Company.
Clastres, Pierre, 1987, *Society Against the State: Essays in Political Anthropology*, trans. Robert Hurley with Abe Stein. New York: Zone Books.
Crazzolara, J.P., 1953, *Zur Gesellschaft und Religion der Nueer* (Stud. Inst. Anthropos. 5). Modeling bei Wien: Institut. Anthropos.
Deleuze, Gilles and Felix Guattari, 1987, *A Thousand Plateaus: Capitalism and Schizophrenia*, trans. Brian Massumi. Minneapolis: University of Minnesota Press.
Dumont, Louis, 1970, *Homo Hierarchicus: An Essay on the Caste System*, trans. Mark Sainsbury. Chicago: University of Chicago Press.

Durkheim, Emile 1933 *The Division of Labor in Society*, trans. George Simpson. Glencoe: The Free Press.

Evans-Pritchard, E.E., 1933 and 1934, 'The Nuer: tribe and clan', *Sudan Notes and Records* XVI (1933):1–53; XVII (1934):1–57.

——— 1936, 'Customs and beliefs relating to twins among the Nilotic Nuer', *Uganda Journal* III, No. 3 (Jan.):230–8.

——— 1940a, *The Nuer: A Description of the Modes of Livelihood and Political Institutions of a Nilotic People*. Oxford: Clarendon Press.

——— 1940b, 'The Nuer of the Southern Sudan'. In *African Political Systems*, eds. M. Fortes and E.E. Evans-Pritchard. Oxford: Oxford University Press.

——— 1951, *Kinship and Marriage among the Nuer*. Oxford: Clarendon Press.

——— 1956, *Nuer Religion*. Oxford: Clarendon Press.

Evens, T.M.S., 1984, 'Nuer hierarchy'. In *Differences, Valeurs, Hierarchie* (Festschrift for Louis Dumont), ed. J.C. Galey. Paris: Editions de l'EHESS.

——— 1989, 'An illusory illusion: Nuer agnation and first principles'. In *Culture*, ed. Craig Calhoun, *Comparative Social Research* 11:301–18. Greenwich, Connecticut: JAI Press Inc.

——— 1996, Review of *Nuer Prophets* by Douglas H. Johnson, *Current Anthropology* 37 (3):571–4.

——— 1997, 'Eve: ethics and the feminine principle in the second and third chapters of Genesis'. In *The Ethnography of Moralities*, ed. Signe Howell. London: Routledge.

——— 2008, *Anthropology as Ethics: Nondualism and the Conduct of Sacrifice*. New York & Oxford: Berghahn Books.

Fornet-Betancourt, Raúl, Helmut Becker, Alfredo Gomez-Müller, and J.D. Gauthier, 1987, 'The ethic of care for the self as a practice of freedom: an interview with Michel Foucault on January 20, 1984', *Philosophy & Social Criticism*, 12(July):112–31.

Fortes, M., 1953, 'The structure of unilineal descent groups', *American Anthropologist* 55:17–41.

Fortes, M. and E.E. Evans-Pritchard (eds), 1940, *African Political Systems*. Oxford: Oxford University Press.

Howell, P.P., 1954, *A Manual of Nuer Law*. London: Oxford University Press.

Johnson, Douglas H., 1994, *Nuer Prophets: A History of Prophecy from the Upper Nile in the Nineteenth and Twentieth Centuries*. Oxford: Clarendon Press.

Kiggen, J., 1948, *Nuer-English Dictionary*. Mill Hill, London: St Joseph's Society for Foreign Missions.

Levi, P., 1993, *Survival in Auschwitz*, trans. Stuart Woolf. New York: Collier Books Trade Edition.

Lewis, B.A., 1951, 'Nuer spokesmen: a note on the institution of the *Ruic*', *Sudan Notes and Records* 32:77–84.

Littlejohn, James, 1970, 'Twins, birds, etc.' *Bijdragen tot de Tall -, Land- en Volkenkunde* 126:91–108.

Radcliffe-Brown, A.R., 1952, *Structure and Function in Primitive Society*. Glencoe: The Free Press.

Read, K.E., 1955, 'Morality and the concept of the person among the Gahuku-Gama', *Oceania* 25 (4), 233–82.

Rousseau, Jean-Jacques, 1992 (1755), *Discourse on the Origin of Inequality*, trans. Donald A. Cress. Indianapolis: Hackett Publishing Company.

Sahlins, Marshall D., 1961, 'The segmentary lineage: an organization of predatory expansion', *American Anthropologist*, 63:322–43.

Smith, M.G., 1956, 'On segmentary lineage systems' (Curl Bequest Prize Essay, 1955), *JRAI* 86 (2):39–80.

——— 1960, *Government in Zazzau 1800–1950*. Oxford: Oxford University Press for the International African Institute.

——— 1966, 'Pre-industrial stratification systems'. In *Social Structure and Mobility in Economic Development*, eds Neil J. Smelser and Seymour Martin Lipset. Chicago: Aldine Publishing Company.

Stigand, C.H., 1923, *A Nuer-English Vocabulary*. Cambridge: Cambridge University Press.

Talmon, J.L., 1970 (1952), *The Origins of Totalitarian Democracy*. London: Sphere Books.

CHAPTER 2

The spectre of the tyrant

Power, violence and the poetics of an
Amazonian egalitarianism

✦

JOANNA OVERING

It has now been over half a century that the egalitarian polities of Amazonian indigenous peoples have been recognized by anthropologists as a 'sociological' puzzle, and as such, ground for continual and passionate debate. How do we interpret the disdain displayed by peoples of the Amazon rainforest for rules and regulations, their rejection of relations of command, and their insistence upon personal freedom and disregard of formal social groupings – a cluster of values attached at the same time to a strong commitment to the aesthetics of their informal, convivial relations and practices of community life (e.g. Overing 1989, 1993a; Overing and Passes 2000a, 2000b)? Amazonian understandings of sociality, society and polity have appeared to be truly untranslatable – at least through our own sociological and cultural understandings of power, polity, and society.

As Rivière notes (1984) of the indigenous peoples of the Guianas, 'the social and political organization of these societies is so unformalized that it has often been difficult to understand how they work at all'. With dismay, he notes that the literature continues to complain that these are peoples who are 'lacking': their leaders have no power (of command or coercion) and their communities no clearly structured corporate groups. They are 'lacking' because they have no stable hierarchy through which to sustain 'societal order'. Rivière concludes that it is because Amazonian peoples have been defined by such negatives – by what they do not have, rather than by what they have, that they have been absurdly perceived as not only short of polity, but of society as well (see also Clastres 1977:12). He suggests that if we cannot identify for Amazonian peoples a polity, we have been looking for the wrong thing, or at the wrong place.

It is Rivière's suggestion (ibid.) – which is also the main point of this paper – that the Amazonian rejection of formal institutions must therefore be viewed as a positive attribute, highly relevant to their, but not our, understanding of egalitarianism. In other words, doctrines and practices of egalitarianism are both locally and historically situated (as is the case for all political ways of thinking and doing), and thus there is no good reason to expect an Amazonian egalitarianism to be a mirror image of our own. Once we recognize that we are dealing with translating local theories (both theirs and ours), we need to know why they lack what we have; and just as importantly, *why we lack what they have*: Amazonia 'lacking', modernist West 'lacking'. How do we achieve interesting conversations between the two? This is a goal worth pursuing.

We at long last are recognizing that any 'fault' lies, not with the political and social acuity of Amazonian peoples, but with the Eurocentric vision of mainstream sociological thought: its interests and lack of imagination. It is wise to remember that our academic sociological narratives of 'society' and 'polity' emerged within a particular historical context. It was not until the eighteenth century, in the wake of the rise of the nation-state (Williams 1983:293; see also Rapport and Overing 2000, 2007), that the construct of 'society', which until then denoted sociability and face-to-face relationships within a community, began to be used in the modernist, general, abstract sense to denote particular 'social orders', with prevailing notions of both society and polity becoming mimetic of the nation-state's hierarchical and hegemonic institutions of control (Williams 1983:291–2).

Amazonian peoples would abhor such structures of domination and subordination. For them, the very idea of society being based upon juridical foundations, and built through legislative, juridical and bureaucratic procedures, would be too dangerous, too repellent, too violent – and indeed, not thinkable. This is an attitude that is general to Amazonian points of view, for, as Rivière (1984) and others have observed (e.g. Overing 1975, 1985a; Ales 2000; Londono Sulkin 2000; Belaunde 2000), in Amazonia power usually pertains not to the group but to the individual – each in relationship to other individuals. The person has power, not the institution. It is the individual, not the group, who is ultimately responsible for mastering his or her own power. Among Piaroa people of the Orinoco River region, with whom I worked, one's own autonomy is dependent upon the autonomy of others, and vice versa. Personal freedom is rarely abused in Piaroa society only because of the practice of recognizing each other's right to personal autonomy (also see Thomas 1982 on the Pemon). Within such non-contractual societies, the only undertaking is this imperative, which in fact can only be backed by personal judgements of trust (Overing 2003).

The danger to society is an individual who becomes unable to master his or her own power, especially if the culprit is a powerful shaman leader. It is the Tyrant they watch out for: he who might wish to impose violence on his own kinspeople, and who, through madness and hubris, desires to subjugate, command and generally mistreat them (Overing 1985a, 2006b). The notion that the 'group' be identified with 'power' would be an oxymoron. It is only through individuals that society can be created, and through individuals that it can be destroyed. Given their highly realistic view of the negative, coercive, and indeed absurd, side of power, the Piaroa have quite rightly decided that the weighty (hierarchical) institution would be far too dangerous for them as a means for harnessing and channelling it (see Overing 1993a, 1993b, 2003).

In contrast to Clastres (1977), who speaks of Amazonian societies as 'against the State', I shall speak, instead of 'Societies against the Tyrant' – or, indeed, of 'Individuals against the Tyrant'. The question remains of how to translate the sociologies of Amazonian peoples. How can we do justice to their rich political and social philosophies (Overing 2004, 2006a, 2006b; Graeber 2004)? To do so, we must contemplate subjects that ill fit our present sociological narratives, such as the humour, aesthetics, poetics, the life of the senses, and mythscapes (or cosmogony) of everyday knowledge practices.[1] We must capture fractal universes of meaning to begin to understand the delicacy of Amerindian ways of thinking about society. We must also speak of virtues and the passions, and not law and contract (cf. Graeber 2004).

On the other hand, we can also explore pathways of conversation through which we might disclose a *similarity* of concerns within Western and Amazonian thinking, for instance with regard to power, and its violence. What is the proper way of handling it that allows for a human sort of life, a safe life? I will be comparing material from ancient Thebes, and from the modernist West, in order to consider a comparison of understandings of the relation of power to the creation of 'proper' society. 'Egalitarian societies' do differ from one another, yet at the same time they can be interestingly compared, certainly on the level of 'key concerns'. We shall find that while concerns may be similar, solutions can vary considerably.

Society, polity, and the question of the violence of power: an anthropological conundrum
Sahlins on 'society' and the tyrant
As already stressed, the largest barrier to successful translation in our anthropological endeavours has been the immense baggage of the nation-state that dwells within our sociological narratives. (see Overing 1985b, Rapport and Overing 2000, 2007, Passes forthcoming). For instance, there is the idea that 'society' must be built upon a *particular kind of violence and institutional*

rigour, which leads to the conclusion that if there's no command and coercion, and no firm hierarchical arrangements, then there's no 'society' or 'polity', or perhaps not much of either. We are then confronted with the highly dubious notion prevalent in social evolutionary theory that assumes that through history societies have increasingly achieved greater 'degrees of society' and 'degrees of polity'.

A very powerful example of such neo-evolutionary 'wisdom' can be found in Marshall Sahlin's 1972 volume, *Stone Age Economics*. What is frustrating is that Sahlins in his first chapter displays good insight into the values of autonomy and the desire for the comfortable life typical of societies such as we find in Amazonia (e.g. Rivière 1984; Overing 1993a, 2003; Overing and Passes 2000a, 2000b). He understands their value of 'leisure' and praises their 'affluence' (their abundance in food). But then, he *passes judgement*. For him, 'society' can be built only on a particular kind of political and institutional violence that should (originally) be in the hands of the despotic chief: one who commands and coerces people to work hard for him, as he builds ever wider networks of power and control. He notes that because these are peoples who dwell instead within a state of 'domesticity', and thus detest structures of command and coercion, they refuse – for the sake of selfish, asocial comfort – the introduction of such hierarchical and institutionalized violence.[2] They therefore have achieved neither polity nor society. They lack both, from Sahlins' point of view. These remain undeveloped because they are peoples who have not yet overcome their particular values of autonomy, equality and a convivial quality of life. They are neglectful of institutional rigour because they refuse the coercive demands of the tyrant.

Sahlins' understanding of what would definitely equate to an Amazonian set of values is in itself an important insight, and one I wish to develop further – but with a very different message and conclusion. Amazonian peoples *do* demand personal freedom and the right to not obey (e.g. see Clastres 1977; Lévi-Strauss 1967; Overing 1975; Rivière 1984; Thomas 1982). They *do* refuse the despot. It is Sahlins' assessment of such values that is depressing. What most Amazonian peoples understand to be the achievement of healthy society is for Sahlins but an 'anarchy of nature'. While he, himself, reduces the very emergence of 'society' to the *political and economic progress of the tyrant*, Amazonian people, on the other hand, would understand that it is precisely the emergence of such a tyrant that could destroy all possibility for society (Overing 1985a, 2006b). Such sociological narratives of the social and the political as Sahlins presents us exclude much of what many indigenous people, certainly of Amazonia, most value in life, namely, their aesthetics, poetics and conviviality. These are peoples who have their own strong local views about proper human sociality, and who have deliberately *chosen* – for political reasons – to live as they do (also see Thomas 1982; Overing and Passes 2000; Gow 2000; Overing 2003, 2006a; Oliveira 2003; Lagrou 2007). Nevertheless, it is apparent that if we universally define either 'society' or 'polity' in terms of institutions of hierarchy and coercion, many indigenous peoples do not have much of it, nor do they desire it (Diamond 1974; Clastres 1977; Overing 1975, 1993a; Overing and Passes 2000, Graeber 2004).

Clastres and the riddle of 'powerless' power

The Amazonian specialist Pierre Clastres, in his book of essays, *Society against the State* (1977), argues, in contrast to Sahlins, that peoples of Amazonia are not only strongly social, but also political.[3] He sets out to rethink the sociological treatment of 'power' in order to include Amazonian peoples into the discussion of 'society' and 'polity' in a more sensible way. He proposes that there is no such thing as a non-political society (Clastres 1977:14). What Amazonian societies do not have is 'the State'. This is not to be understood as a lack, but as a desire: a brave conclusion at the time of his writing. Many Amazonian peoples refuse hierarchy and coercion. They also refuse a political economy. It is therefore not possible for the State to arise from *within* the context of an Amazonian society (ibid.:181). He argues that the profile of the Amazonian leader in no way foreshadows that of a future despot (ibid.:175). There is nothing about the 'chieftainship' to suggest that State apparatus can be derived from it. The chief is not a chief of State. He has no power of coercion, no means of giving an order. He is not a commander: his people are under no obligations to obey. He serves the people, but does not rule them. The leader cannot reverse that relationship for his own ends, to put society in his service, to exercise what is termed power *over* the people. The people of an Amazonian society would not tolerate a leader who attempted to transform himself into a despot. They would watch him carefully to prevent the emergence of such despotic characteristics (ibid.:175). He goes on to note, quite rightly, that the understanding of 'political power' as coercion should not be the model of 'true power', but only a particular case.

Clastres argues that for Amazonia it is society, and not the chief, that possesses power. A power which, moreover, says Clastres, must be expelled from society, for society's own sake. It is the people of the community who exercise authority over the chief (ibid.:174). Society, which – in his narrative – is based on a structure of reciprocity, refuses a reciprocal relation with the chief, thereby leaving him within society as a person with no power. And that in itself, Clastres argues, must be understood as a political act. Political power – as violence – has been ousted from society into the domain of 'nature' (ibid.:34–5). Power remains as a negativity, and thus stripped of any real might (ibid.:34–5). Although the 'political' as experienced by Amazonian people appears to be the negation of that experienced by people of the West, such negation does not signify 'nothingness' (ibid.:13).

This business of 'power' must be re-evaluated. Present day ethnographers would agree whole heartedly with many of Clastres' observations: in particular, the ubiquitous Amazonian allergic reaction to rules and regulations, and indeed any power they perceive as coercive and controlling of the person. He has not, however, solved the crucial riddle of power. Although he argues passionately for the recognition of both coercive and non-coercive understandings of 'power', he falls into the reductive trap of retaining its definition as the infliction of violence (ibid.:14). While we may well argue that Amazonian societies work to expel the violence of power from society, it is another matter to say that they have ejected power out of society and into the domain of something called 'nature', although we can well agree that it *is* a political act for people to work towards excluding the violence of power from society. It is also questionable to then assume that the Amazonian chief has no power because political violence is not allowed. Power has its positive side, as well as its negative – and this is the point upon which I shall dwell. It is confusing the issue to suggest that 'power' in Amazonia appears only as a negativity, and as no more than the furtive manifestation of 'nature' ever to remain out of society (Clastres 1977:35). I daresay that without the positive side of 'power' neither society nor polity could be created: certainly from an Amazonian point of view (e.g. see Alès 2000 on the Yanamami).

There is also the unfortunate twist to Clastres' admission (ibid.:33) that the means by which Amazonian peoples chase power out of society (i.e. their 'social structures' based on the reciprocal exchange of women, words and goods) exists only on the level of the unconscious. At the level of intellect it would seem, then, that Amazonian peoples understand neither their own sociality nor their own polity! Are they not reflective about their own social and political practices? When it comes to the topic of 'power', it appears that Clastres has embedded potentially fascinating issues within a structuralist narrative that reduces Amazonian 'society' to a narrowly conceived and unconscious structure of reciprocity, and 'power' to a language of 'nature' and 'culture'.

Thus, in reading Clastres, we realize that the tantalizing problem of power has not yet been resolved, for the 'package' that he presents is frustratingly flawed. His conclusions emerge from the high theory of structuralism, not rich ethnography. This leads him to degrade the role of leader, as one with no power. In Amazonian ethnography we often find that a good leader is considered to be extraordinarily powerful – yet neither violent nor coercive – at least within society. *It is this positive side of power, and not only the negative, that we must unfold.* To do so we need to deepen our conversations with the peoples of the Amazon, particularly on the topic of the violence of power, about which we are both concerned. Why is the vision of power so different in Amazonia? Is it a matter of history? values? cosmology? Do god-given rights differ? Through ethnography we are beginning to ask better questions. Thus, we must continue to rethink this Amazonian riddle of power. Let us begin by introducing ethnography.

Some early ethnography on Piaroa of the Orinoco basin: the consciousness of the relation of power to daily practices[4]

It is through the insights gained in the first months of their research that the ethnographer can begin to recognize shadows of meaning[5] that are of central importance to the understanding of another society, one that is so different from one's own. Much that I learned in 1968 during my first fieldwork within a Piaroa community has remained of critical concern for me over the years. Much was puzzling during this period of research – at least in the face of received anthropological wisdom of the 1960s with regard to 'social order'. At that time, the literature spoke of 'reciprocal networks of exchange', of men exchanging women. It spoke of corporate groups, rules and regulations, and the power of the elders. Needless to say, being in Amazonia, I found little of any of this. There were no corporate 'groups of elders', or of men. If I asked about 'rules', such as the 'rule' of residence after marriage, the emphatic answer was that it was the 'choice' of the bride and groom that determined residence, not a rule. And so it went with most of my early questions. However, what I did find, if not rules and regulations, were people living in a community who related to each other as individuals: where no one could be the voice for another. The message that became loud and clear, if not finally understood, is that their practices – on the *conscious* level of both daily speech and action – deliberately and systematically denied the worth of all the ways to social order envisioned by our sociological narratives of society. I came to realize that it was through this very act of denial that they understood that they could work toward preventing the intrusion of violence into their own social setting. For them, all such practices were *political* acts, and as such the responsibility of each adult individual, whether female or male. As I shall continue to unfold, power was personal, and it was only through the *personal power of each adult* that the community could be created and re-created on a daily basis. Such personal power was always to be considered as relational, that is, taking others into consideration in its enactment.

On the other hand, there is the fact that their shaman leaders (*ruwatu*) were considered by Piaroa people as having immense personal power. We are confronted here with the very interesting riddle of a leader with immense power, but no authority of coercion within society. Piaroa leaders were

Figure 1   A *Piaroa* ruwahu, *who was the wife of a Piaroa shaman (ruwa). Note her 'beads of knowledge', which display her mighty powers of fertility.*

described as people of extraordinary power and wisdom. The shaman leader was first and foremost a person of knowledge. The people had strong respect for this knowledge. Without a shaman leader, people would have been unable to create a viable and healthy community of relationships. As an intellectual, the shaman leader had deep knowledge of cosmological circumstances, and their possible effects upon the members of his community. Where I resided, the shaman leader presented a powerful display each night of his knowledge of the cosmic past through lengthy chanting sessions to enable the health of the members his community. Through the powerful words of his chant, he both cured illness and prevented it. He also was responsible for making

Figure 2   A Piaroa (ruwa), who was husband of the powerful Piaroa ruwahu. Note his 'beads of knowledge', which display his mighty shamanic powers .

fertile their resources of land and water. Each ritual he performed – whether curing, first menstruation, or the endowment of hunting, fishing, or shamanic skills – was also a rite of fertility. The richer the chanting, the more powerful the shaman was perceived. Each morning, the members of the community *drank* the *words* of his nightly chants, which he had blown into containers of water or honey, to enable them to carry out *safely* their tasks of hunting, cooking, working in the gardens, and other everyday activities (see Overing 1975, 2006b). Thus, against the thesis of Clastres that the words of the leader in the Amazon are neither heard nor heeded, and thus they are powerless, shamanic words in Piaroaland were taken very seriously – and also deeply enjoyed. Moreover, without them, a person would not be safe. Without them, you probably would die. The leader partook of the powers of the cosmos, and instilled them within the bodies of the members of his community. It was he who travelled to the homes of the celestial gods and through the dangerous world of cosmic time in order to explore the cosmic origins of life on earth that both allowed and worked against the safety and health of members of his community. For this reason, and others, his power was considered to be a necessary ingredient of the very possibility for the ongoing safe, fertile and comfortable existence of the peoples and communities he served. His actions were recognized and constantly talked about: for his power was great and his intelligence impressive. People depended upon their shaman leader. He was a skilled wizard, an outer-space warrior, a doctor, psychologist, pedagogue, kindergarten teacher, professor, philosopher, cosmologist, comedian, poet laureate, hunter and agronomist (e.g. see Overing 1990; 2006a, 2006b). He taught five-year-old children about social propriety, and endowed teenage boys with their powers to hunt and to fish, and girls the power to garden and not only give birth, but also to be responsible for this process.

At the same time, in everyday life, as awesome as the shaman leader's powers to deal with the cosmos might have been, he was not treated in any formal way as someone of a different status. No one addressed the shaman leader as such, as '*ruwa*', for instance. Piaroa use no direct titles suggestive of hierarchy. There was no address except through kinship terms, or nicknames, used between adults. Moreover, although he might be considered as 'the *ruwa*', that is, the wisest of men, his wife was similarly considered as 'the *ruwahu*', the wisest of women. Her powers among women, for instance in the creation of large and beautiful gardens and her capabilities for giving birth to her children,[6] were considered of equal worth to her husband's in his travelling of the universe (Overing 2006b). What is more, on one level or another, all men were *ruwatu* and all women *ruwahutu*. Each adult considered themselves as '*ruwa*' or '*ruwahu*', for each was the master of their own skills, which were appropriate to their gender. Such gendered skills, or modes of power, are for many reasons, crucial to our discussion of power within the Amazonian context (e.g. see Thomas 1982; Overing and Passes 2000a, 2000b). For instance, sociopolitical equality between the sexes is not unusual in Amazonia (e.g. see Passes 2004 and forthcoming), and given proper reflection, we find that Piaroa emphasize time and again the importance of the political power of women. Such power was noted in many areas of practice, and not only in the matter of the chorus, which is spoken of below. For instance, if a family wished to move from one territory to another, the husband and wife were required *separately* to seek formal permission from head shaman of the new area. He would decide whether he would provide them protection, treating each as a separate case. Husband and wife were thereby treated by the *ruwa* as political equals.

Each adult was obliged to work on the mastery of his or her own power, so as not to cause harm to others of the community (Overing 2006b).The decision-making of each was a personal matter, to be respected: but all needed to work towards preventing the emergence of violence within their community life. Thus there was the emphasis upon laughter, joking, the play of words; and there was talk of their beautiful 'beads of knowledge', which allowed for beautiful behaviour, beautiful etiquette. The achievement of community was an individual matter – and the responsibility of all individuals. There were few mechanisms for 'the community' as a group to chastize a kinsperson. Actions remained a matter of personal desire. Yet, each person was highly attached to their own distinctive community's ways of doing things (see Overing 1993a). The reason for Piaroa reluctance to hierarchy is obvious. Through it's violence the delicate and convivial relations of community life could be drastically disturbed.

Because of the might and considerable knowledge of the shaman leader, he was always considered a possible threat to the highly valued tranquillity of community life. He could be dangerously prone to madness (Overing 1985a). His strong powers for fertile creation could become perverse, threatening, rather than generative of safety and well-being. Because of this risk, his behaviour was closely monitored, particularly by the women, for any evidence of self-aggrandizement, arrogance, aggression or paranoia. Successful leadership demanded the constant demonstration of a firm mastery of the passions. Thus, the behaviour of the *ruwa* entailed a conspicuous display of personal modesty and humility, to be seen in his demeanour and style of life (see Overing 1975). If given a gift, he distributed it to his people (cf. Lévi Strauss 1967, on the Nambikwara). In practice, he was expected to be the most social member of the community. His great mastery of the verbal arts lent considerable strength to his social skills: in everyday life he was the talented jokester of the community, and the competent host to visiting strangers. His own laughter, joking and wordplay were to oil the social wheels of all daily activities. The children enjoyed him. They hung on to him, tending to the mites on his legs as they listened to the fabulous stories he told them of the dangerous grotesque antics of creation time gods. Through such stories he taught them the importance of the arts of social decorum, and of the aesthetics of community life (see Overing 1989). He worked hard towards creating an emotionally comfortable life for the members of his community, and teaching the means to achieve it.[7] He continually displayed his own skills for living a socially convivial, and therefore a human sort of life: he ever worked though his personal powers for the health of the community. Such behaviour was expected of him. Nevertheless, all the while, the people were

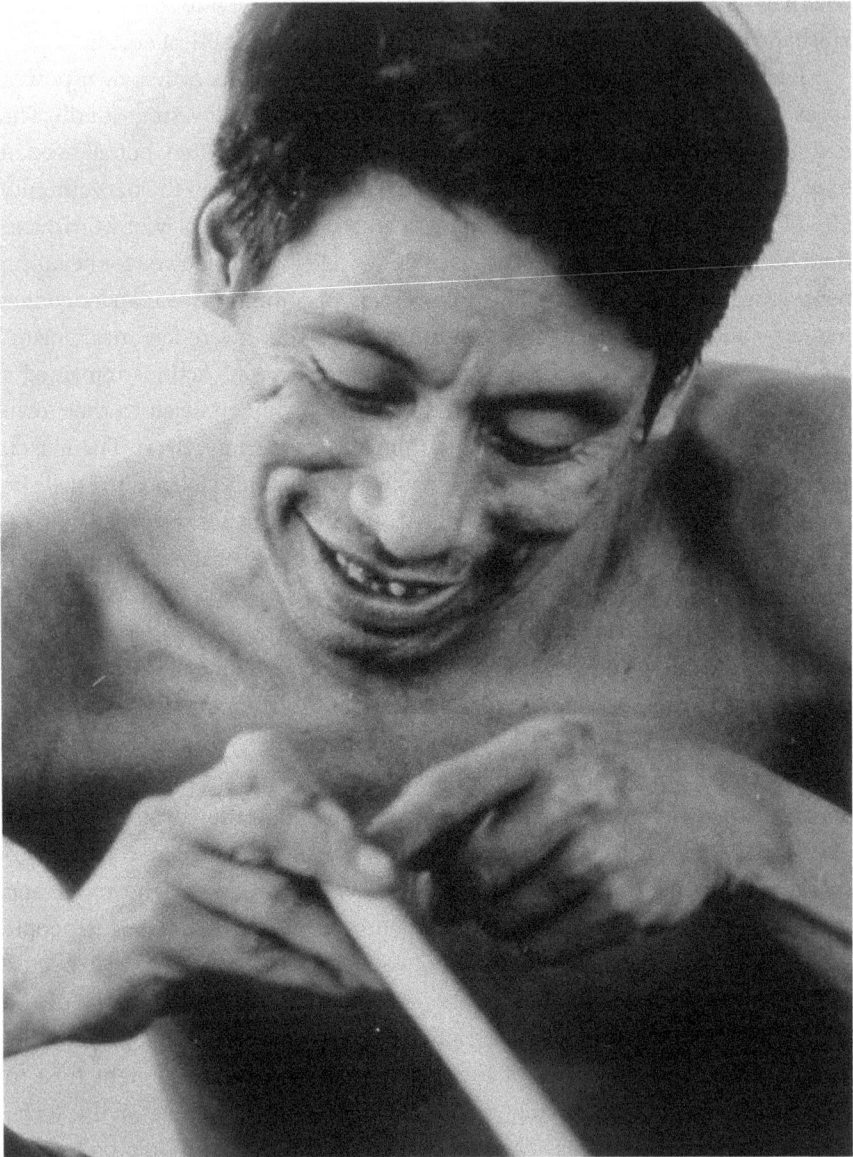

Figure 3   As the shaman whittles a sacred flute and has enraptured children sitting at his knee, he tells colourful stories of mythic time which stress the hilarious dangers of misbehaviour (see page 72).

watching for any sign of his misuse of his power – of a development on his part of hubris – and insanity.

An important political role of women was to monitor the relative mastery of power by the men of the community, but particularly of the most powerful. The expression of such female power was performed through the chorus of their voices. These were public, but occasional, events, taking place within the large patio area in front of the communal house. The work of such a chorus could be staged in a variety of ways:

> A group of women surround a grumpy shaman, to tease and thus shame him for an arrogant lapse of etiquette. They must be light hearted in this performance, for they want him to laugh, and not to become dangerously angry. There is the woman alone marching behind her brother, as he slowly walks across the patio. She is berating him for the danger of his lack of decorum in teaching the anthropologist (female!) some of the most powerfully dirty vocabulary of mythic chanting (see Overing 2000). There are two old women, sitting on the patio, facing each other, engaged in a formal wailing session, telling for all to hear their grudges against miscreant kinsmen who were not displaying sufficient appreciation of the enormous work and contributions of these two old women.

In each of these cases, the focus is upon the dangers to society of a wayward man's asocial actions, his lapse of attention to the delicacies of convivial living. The intent of each chorus was to remind its audience (most of the village) of the moral criteria upon which their convivial society was based. The chorus (always female) was addressing the audience to bear witness to her, or their, moral concerns (also see Passes 2004 and forthcoming, on the political work of the female voice among the Palikur of French Guinea). The audience became part of the performance. Each person stood still, listening intently. Everyone listened, but did not rebuke or speak. No matter what the mode, whether teasing, wailing, or scolding, each chorus was respectively accepted as a female political performance of consequence. This was a society where female skills, knowledge and strengths were publically acknowledged.

Women and shamans may work together. The job of the shaman was not to rebuke, but to teach people of the dangers of hubris, and ritually to cure them of their wayward or excessive behaviour (Overing 1975). It would have been much too dangerous to societal tranquillity for a man, and especially a powerful shaman, to publicly rebuke a person, and especially one who was also a shaman. Shamans do however listen to the female chorus, and in an extreme situation take action. There was the case of a powerful shaman who became crazy, and very angry, when all the people of his community migrated to the village of a younger shaman, perceived to be more capable. Arrogantly, the crazy shaman proceeded to retaliate by killing through sorcery several of the children of the migrating families. The chorus wailed, and all the shamans of the region reacted by holding a conference. Their solution was to act together to withdraw all the powers of the elderly shaman who went mad. He then became benign, and left to live by himself, with one young woman to take care of his needs.

How do you find society in all this?
Piaroa people were obviously creating a highly interesting social state of being. Indications of their understanding of the relation of power to society are loud and clear – and expressed *knowingly* by them on a daily basis. Power was attached to the individual. Such personal autonomy was necessary for the skilful creation of society, a human community of relationships, within which children could be safely raised to adulthood. Society was in the hands of each individual, including the chief! It entailed a daily task of relating to others – socially and politically. One came to understand that it was society that needed to be daily regenerated through social practices that would keep the negative aspects of power at bay. Each day, members of the community were presenting such accomplishment anew – self-consciously and through their beautiful and skilled practices of the culinary arts (their powers) (see Overing 2006b). This was a political fact, a dangerous fact – this business of creating kinspeople within the context of community. Their programme was to stress, indeed enact, the positive and generative, and not the negative side of power, that would entail violence and coercion (Overing 2000b). From our sociological point of view, the translation of the political and societal ways of such a people is not easy.

What is clear is that Piaroa people worked against the possibility of the institutionalization of power, such as the eruption of a stable hierarchy would create. It is precisely because of the State's juro-political paraphernalia, and attached bureaucratic ways, that I do not see Amazonian peoples being so much 'against the state' – such institutionalized violence was in large part beyond the pale, unfathomable to them.[8] What they did recognize as odious was the use of violence by individuals 'of the state', such as their fondness of commanding. It is the violent tyrant that Amazonian peoples want to prevent. The tyrant that destroys the very possibility of community. It certainly is the case that Piaroa people *did* understand the complexities of power: they each relied on the use of an array of forces of power for the daily process of successfully living within a society of relationships – the powers for gardening, hunting, fishing, cooking, giving birth – and for creating comfortable relations with each other. It was also the case that, for them, the shamanic 'chief' was expected to use daily, and nightly, the impressive powers with which he was endowed, in the service of members of the community, their protection, their comfort and their fertility. On the other hand, as Piaroa understood the matter, the violence of power nevertheless lurked at the heart of the social. This is the dilemma to be unravelled shortly. It was a cosmological matter, ever intruding itself within society (Overing 2004, 2006b). Power was a matter about which Amazonian peoples thought about in very interesting, and productive, ways. Their emphasis was upon the powerful, possibly poisonous, transformational powers of the person that were considered to be necessary for the achievement of a human sort of life.[9]

How do we achieve conversations on the violence of power: imageries of power

Again, it is clear that we tend to find that Amazonian egalitarianism is better understood through the lens of societal values and organization the modern West lacks. For instance, why is there little poetics attached to our political talk? Why is poetics – and also laughter – so important in Amazonia (see Overing 2000, 2006b, Lagrou 2006)? How do our imageries of power differ? Why in the West is domination viewed as such an important path to power? We do, nevertheless, find interesting overlaps in political concerns, and by exploring these we can begin a conversation. For instance, why do we find in both the assumption that violence resides at the heart of the social? Central to any moral system or political doctrine which values equality and personal autonomy (even if only for the few) is the vision of power as 'a problem'. The question of the source of such power, which enables the transformation of the resources of the earth for human use, must be answered. And then follows the question of who, if anyone, is morally, legally or cosmologically responsible for such powers? The violence of this power cannot help but enter into these discussions, for the transformation of the earth for use is a violent matter, as too can be the distribution of the transformed products. Power, as a force with coercive, violent and repressive aspects, is then seen as something that must be dealt with. The control and handling of this violence, or potential violence, is the central concern of both indigenous peoples of Amazonia and Western theories of personal freedom. The puzzle is how to handle competition over resources and still have a decent social life. As mentioned above, while these concerns may be similar, the solutions are often very different.

In conversing with Amerindian people about our common social and political concerns, I am not denying the value of our own sociological categories to the anthropological task. In order to unfold their concerns and solutions, we need to study the history of our own values of 'equality' and 'freedom' and the treatment of 'power' and 'constraint'. The overthrowing or neutering of monarchy, the emergence of capitalism and the nation state, the development of natural-law theory and the doctrine of 'the primacy of rights' are historical facts that have weighed heavily in the shaping of our own particular constructions of such notions as 'freedom', 'equality', 'power', 'society' and the 'individual'. Within such a context, how do we include the Amazonian emphasis upon poetics and affect, when we are talking about the sociological? Yet, on the subject of egalitarianism the same topics tend to arise time and again: those related to the idea that violence lies at the heart of the social.

Let's look very carefully at differences in envisioning power, and its positive and negative aspects; and also at our differences in understanding the role of the passions, and their relation to power. We find that modernist theory of the West tends, with regard to power, to emphasize the negative passions, while Amazonian peoples tend to dwell upon the interplay of the negative and positive sides of both power and the passions. This difference of emphasis leads as well to difference in their respective understandings of the relation of knowledge and power. We know that a major message of Foucault's is that knowledge and the political form together. For him, the play of passions is critical to his arguments for this relationship.

Foucault, Nietzsche and Piaroa on power and the negative passions

Foucault argues (see 2002)[10] that if we really want to understand knowledge, apprehend it at its root, we must look not at philosophy, but politicians. We must, he argues, study the manner in which people hate one another; how they fight, dominate and exert power relations over one another. Note that Foucault is relativizing political practices, and in so doing also relativizing the practices of knowledge. He argues, for instance, that the West, in devising complex techniques of judicial inquiry, laid the foundation for science – which led in turn to very distinct social and political controls.

Foucault picks up his notion of the relativity of knowledge from Nietzsche, who is taking pot-shots at philosophers. There is, for example, Nietzsche's declaration, time and again, that knowledge is a surface effect, a result of the passions (e.g. see Nietzsche 1974:296–97; 1989:First Discourse). In his theory of knowledge, it is not created through logic and the rational, but on the activity of instincts, in struggle against the chaos of the world (e.g. see Nietzsche 1974:168). Nietzsche argues that the relation between knowledge and known things is a relation of power and violence, a violation of things to be known. Thus, he stresses the point that the *negative instincts* – laughing (mocking), hating, lamenting – are at the heart of knowledge (see Nietzsche 1974[1882] aphorism 333). For him, the relation between knowledge and known things is arbitrary, ever establishing *particular* relations of power and violence. The will to power is a play of destructive desires, and it is these desires that produce knowledge practices (e.g. see Nietzsche 1967). We will find that the

Piaroa theory of the *origin* of the relationship between power and knowledge is quite similar. We begin to understand these conversations of Nietzsche and Foucault can be a rich starting point for engaging in discussions on power with Amazonian people.

Is this idea that destructive passions give rise to knowledge a unique insight into peculiar Western values? Or is it more generally true? Foucault is interested in knowledge as the basis of relations of force and political relations in the history of Western society. A central theme within this history is the development of judicial systems of inquiry, inquisition and examination. We need to look carefully at the Social Contract, and its controlling ways; and also at our rights-centred ethics, a judicial notion. A major question within such examinations and ethics turns out to be 'what can you get away with and not be punished?'. *An entirely negative phrasing.* Is such negativity general? [11]

In Amazonia, we find that the passions are treated differently than in most Western theory. Amazonian people emphasize the interplay of positive and negative passions, especially when dealing with the question of power (see Overing and Passes 2000a; Overing 2006b). For them, the Western judicial realm would be anathema. Piaroa people recognized the negative side of power, but strived for the positive: theirs was a virtue-centred ethics.[12] They ask what are the positive things (in society)? What can we do so as to avert violence? Don't taunt. Don't be greedy. Don't be arrogant, and especially don't make others angry. Rather, retain respect for the integrity and dignity of others. These are the matters they think carefully about, and not our considerations about which trespasses we must punish or how far we can go without being punished. We have here two different attitudes to freedom. In Amazonia the stress is upon the relational, not just the individual. Subjectivity includes the other.

Yet – also for Piaroa – there was the recognition of the violence of knowledge, and its relation to the violence of certain passions. They especially recognized, and pondered over, relations of violence to knowledge and power in mythic/cosmic time. Their stress was upon the violence of the teaming of power/knowledge in mythic times. This was what the myths, in shamanic exegesis, were mostly all about: the repercussions of gods acquiring too much mighty knowledge. Poisonous knowledge resulted in the expression of terrible passions: bad laughing, hating, lamenting, desire for revenge, murder. Because Piaroa were dependent on the poisonous knowledge created and used by their crazy gods of creation time, such relations of violence were ever a possibility within their own human society (see Overing 1985a, 2006b). Because mythic-time gods created and used knowledge through hate, greed, hubris, arrogance, mockery - negative passions – society in mythic time became impossible. Raising families, living in communities, became impossible.

Perhaps Amerindians understand Western power relations at a deeper level than Westerners can ever understand theirs.

The teaching of societal values through genres of grotesque realism and the sublime

Shamanic chanters of Piaroaland taught virtue-centred ethics in large part through grotesque realism. This was the genre they usually used in their nightly chanting, and also during the day when vignettes on mythical misbehaviour were narrated for the enjoyment of audiences of both adults and children. Such vignettes, usually hilarious and bawdy in the telling, had pedagogical as well as entertainment intent. For this reason, the narrations, unlike chanting, which used a 'creation time' vocabulary, were delivered in the more easily understood 'today time' language. Thus children, as well as adults, could better understand the ethical message. The shaman, with great wit, mocked the miscreant, crazy creator gods and their absurd, treacherous behaviour. In so doing he was underlining the dangers to society of the negative passions. The hubris of the gods inevitably led to ridiculous, asocial, violent outcomes. By the means of the genre of grotesque realism, the shaman played the same role as Foucault. Through it, he explored the ambiguities and violence of knowledge and power as used in mythic time, and their effect upon the task that humans have of creating society today (e.g. Overing 1990, 1995, 2004, 2006b). For Piaroa people, their ways of knowing were created through mythic-time hubris: all that taunting, plotting, murdering. The chanter/ narrators dwelt on this point more than any other. It was important for people to recognize this problem of hubris, to reflect upon and talk about the negative passions of the creator gods, Wahari and Kuemoi, the tyrants, doing their damage. There was the denial of sociality and a contempt of kinship. Such an attitude led to incest, betrayal and attempted fratricide. The tone of the chanting was usually slapstick, for such dreadful behaviour must be laughed at. To mock hubris was a duty of grotesque realism, as it unfolded the calamity of the negative passions of the gods.

As mentioned, the modern West stresses the negative passions in its judiciary procedures. It is also the case that 'civil society' itself is understood to be the realm of competition, a combative field of play. In such a view there lurks the idea of the competitive, combative, social other as a positive phenomenon. In Piaroaland, with regard to both social and political procedures, it was a matter of systematically teaching the use of positive passions rather than negative. They agreed that knowledge, which for them is embodied, is tied to both the passions and the senses, as well as to the intellect (Overing 1985a). Interestingly, the passions most valued, socially, were good laughter and empathy, those passions helpful for 'other-regarding'. Knowledge for them also pertained to aesthetics (Overing 1989). To attain the social, they understood that they must act through such positive passions to counteract the violence of the origins of their knowledge. They certainly understand that knowledge in itself is poisonous, dangerous (the gods made it so): the question was how to cleanse it, beautify it, as it flows through the blood of their bodies (Overing 2006b). They sought solutions for overcoming social violence. Their self-reflective knowledge practices (i.e. understanding the social implications of mythic violence) worked toward this end.

The shamanic genre of 'the sublime' also added a strong incentive for people to make good use of the positive passions (see Overing 2006b). Through this genre the chanter spoke to a human capacity for achieving beauty in action which the dances of the senses could provide. The genre of the sublime captured the beauty of seeing, hearing, feeling, smelling (good cooking, for instance). It noted the relation between social virtues, health and procreation (gods had no normal procreation). At this point we do not want to fall into trap of citing 'good' passions for the social and 'negative' for the political. For Piaroa people, the point is that regardless of whether we classify as 'social' or 'political', the question of violence must be addressed. There must, therefore, be solutions that work toward erasing the relation of distance and hatred of the social other. For instance, the practice of extending an ethics of other-regarding kinship throughout the community works toward peace, and not violence.[13] Certainly for Piaroa people the competitive and combative would not have been social (Overing 1992) – nor beautiful! Exchange relations within the community would be deadly, given their knowledge practices.[14] As an ironic point, we find that for Western theorists what Amazonian people regard as 'social' is asocial, and in turn, for Amazonian peoples Western ('civil') society is asocial – and not very pretty.

For Piaroa, it was through poetics that the ambiguities of the mythic tale could be properly expressed. Through the slapstick humour of grotesque realism, power that is pompously, egotistically, arrogantly displayed can be scoffed at. Through the genre of sublime, they could understand the seriousness of attaining beauty in their life. Piaroa people learned how to be social beings through poetics, not dogma or ideology. They learned though laughing. Of course there was day-to-day rhetoric supporting these messages. But the ambiguities, contradictions and dilemmas of life as unfolded through poetics are fundamental to the understanding of a Piaroa vision of the social, and who they are politically.

To understand Piaroa explanations of violence, we need to look at how they comprehended the relation of knowledge to power in their own social life. First of all, there was always a danger of violence in the use of their daily knowledge practices, in that they were, in origin, the work of their crazy

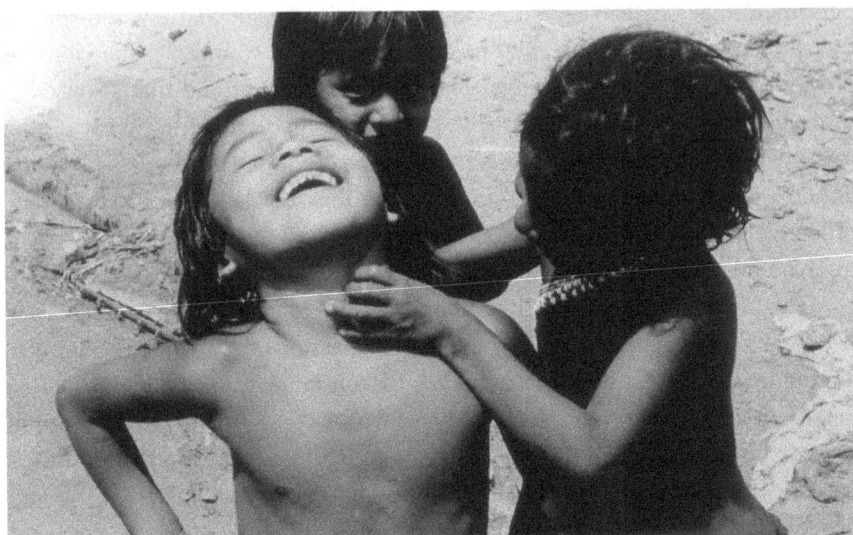

Figure 4   The cheerful children who were taught by the amiable, knowledgeable shaman.

creator gods. Secondly, because individuals had knowledge, they individually also had power. This having of power in Piaroa terms entails an interplay of consciousness, the sensory and the intellectual in their own conducting of knowledgeable practices (Overing 1985a, 2006a).[15] Power, and therefore knowledge, became a matter of how people inter-related – as dangerous to, or procreative of others – in their carrying out of knowledgeable practices. The idea of the tyrant, and his making, is critical to this story of power and its uses. A summary of Piaroa creation time is in order.

The lynching by the Piaroa of Wahari, their creator god – 1

Toward the end of creation time, Piaroa killed Wahari, their own creator god. The political question is why? At this point I shall provide a summary of important events within Piaroa cosmology.

The Shaman chanter relates Wahari's death as a tragic event, employing the genre of tragedy rather than grotesque realism. Wahari was the god of the forest, and both creator and benefactor of human beings. At the beginning of creation time, he was clearly a god of unity. He created human beings from fish, and taught them all the ethical values they would need to live a human sort of life, within a community. He created the 'sky of the domesticated' for them (Overing 2003), and put the moon and the sun in it to give them light. But over time he plummets, so to speak, into hell and ill-will, as he tries to acquire, and then to create on his own, wonderful culinary arts to give to his people, the Piaroa. He fails – terribly.

Over time, through their reciprocal violence, Wahari became twinned with Kuemoi, his crazy, violent arch-enemy and the original owner and creator of the culinary arts. Kuemoi, with the hallucinogenic knowledge to create such potent practices, was poisoned by their might from birth. He was owner of all the knowledge for hunting, and of all fruits and vegetables of the world. He owned fire for cooking and all knowledge of gardening. This was a god who was truly violent, because he had too much knowledge. Thus Kuemoi, from the start, was a crazy, malicious, plotting little murderer: the god of water and fire, and the tyrant who preyed on human beings of the forest. Wahari, trying to steal the culinary arts that were owned – and poisoned – by Kuemoi's knowledge traps,[16] became all of these things. While at first Wahari was a rather naughty trickster, in time his antics became extremely dangerous. Crazed by Kuemoi's poisonous power, he refused his kinspeople, becoming a promiscuous wanderer who committed incest, taunted his relatives and friends, attempted fratricide, and tried to kill his sister and even his son. On one thieving journey he killed his own grandmother. In the end, his own people killed him. *Piaroa killed the tyrant.*

This mythic tale of the emergence of collective violence is an Amazonian study of the violence of power – and its limits. As such it concludes with an egalitarian solution. To shed further light on this type of collective violence, I shall use as comparison Foucault's (see 2002) interpretation of Sophocles' *Oedipus Turannos*.[17] We find that, politically speaking, Amazonia, in many ways, may not be all that unusual.

Foucault's understanding of Sophocles' *Oedipus Turannos* – a story of a fall from power

Sophocles' Oedipus the Tyrant, according to Foucault, should be understood as a 'man of power', and not as Oedipus the incestuous or the committer of patricide. For him it is not a story of our desires and our unconscious, but is related to a history of political power.[18] The Thebans' first greeting to Oedipus was 'Oedipus the all-powerful!' The people in the end strip him of this power. Thus a major theme of the play is the nature of his political power. He was not the innocent, the ignorant one, lacking knowledge. Nor was he Freud's man of unconsciousness. The name Oedipus, or *Oida*, as Foucault reminds us, translates as 'to have seen', or '*to know*'. In the imagery of Sophocles, Oedipus Turannos *knew too much*. The play dwells on his *use* of power as he relates to the people of Thebes. He never defends himself as innocent. His chief concern is with remaining in power. The people appealed to him to save them from the plague. He did so – to preserve his own kingship.

According to Foucault, Sophocles' use of the word *'Turannos'* was not unusual, in that it was a common term for 'leader' used from the end of 6th to 5th century BC. We might understand the term to be closely akin to a mythic stereotype of a hero – or even a shaman. It was by no means a totally negative status. There was, however, the typical erratic history of a 'tyrant' – an outcast child, a lost soul, a vagabond, with years of wandering. Who then becomes the most powerful of men. Tyrants typically experienced both misery and glory. Although they reached the apex of power, they were always under threat of losing it (all this is relevant to the history of Oedipus). There was always an *ambiguity to tyrannical knowledge.* Many tyrants were nevertheless known as 'good' leaders, and as generous, They gave much to their cities, and were known for their justice – raising their cities by just economic distribution and just laws – like Solon of Athens.

The political role of the female chorus
Why did the people of Thebes strip Oedipus of his power? Foucault's reading of Sophocles is that they strip him of kingship so that he could no longer command. The people told him not to try to be master anymore. Thus this is a story of the process through which people took possession of the right to judge. Oedipus did not lose power because of his 'sins' – his incest and his killing of his father – but because of his arrogance. He displayed too much the negative qualities of the tyrant. Thus, the chorus reproached him: 'you think the city is your own, and not ours too'. The people were fighting for their egalitarian ways, where the people work with the leader, and have a say that is listened to. Oedipus had no respect for the laws, replacing them with his whims. It is not justice he was interested in, but in being obeyed. The chorus reproached him for these things.

At this point we can note that for the Thebes of ancient Greece, as for Piaroa of the Orinoco Basin, the chorus, often female, is very important for its warnings of emerging violence. We need to pay attention to this chorus, for it has power. It is not a 'collectivity' in our own sense of the term. Rather, the chorus in Amazonia, as in the plays of ancient Greece, is comprised of individual 'citizens' powerfully commenting on a situation (see also Passes 2004 and forthcoming). Each member of the chorus is taking responsibility for the outcome. As in Amazonian ethnography, we find in the story of Sophocles' Oedipus individual voices watching power and judging it. In both cases, women are crucial to the process. Through the work of the chorus, people become enabled to take action. As Foucault notes, the aim of the chorus is to give the alarm regarding the emergence of violent power working against the people. For Piaroa of Amazonia, and for peoples of ancient Greece, there was good reason for women to pay close attention and then assess the knowledge practices of their leaders.

The tyrants of ancient Greece rose to power because of the uniqueness of their knowledge, which was born of their (sometimes shady) unique experience in the world. Foucault notes that the tyrant's knowledge was a solitary knowledge, and for Oedipus this was taken to an extreme. Sophocles' Oedipus took power because he possessed knowledge superior in efficacy to that of others. He succeeded by means of his own thought, his own knowledge. Through it, he was able to solve the riddle of the sphinx. He was *sophor*, wise. But he always solved problems through *eureka*, his very own mode of knowledge. As hyper-tyrant, he got help from no one else.[19] Like the crazy Piaroa gods, he bragged about his accomplishments. He taunted the people, and also the prophet: 'I delivered Thebes all by myself!' A proclamation somewhat akin to Wahari's bragging – 'I am the master of all the world' – every time he went mad.

In fact, Foucault could have gone even further, to show that Oedipus was a thoroughly *asocial* leader; for as Foucault notes, he was the man of the solitary gaze. The monsters often met in Amazonian myth are understood to be beings of solitary knowledge, and beings who make their own solitary decisions. These are beings to be truly avoided. The whimsical violence of these monsters with excessive knowledge and power can be mighty (e.g. see Overing 1996).

What Foucault does understand, important for our discussion, is that it is because Oedipus was a man of autocratic gaze that he was naive about his power – he fell into traps. He didn't listen well; just like Wahari in his relationship with Kuemoi. Oedipus, a tyrannical and solitary power, aloof from the oracle of the gods, and aloof from what people said and wanted, craved to govern all by himself. He proved to be a true tyrant in our use of the word. However, such tyrants were also beginning to emerge in Sophocles' day, and it was they whom he was in fact attacking. These were tyrants ruling through both power (of might) and knowledge, representative of the tyranny of the ancient East, as in Assyria, where magico-religious power – the power of thought – became wed to the forces of might. Foucault notes that Sophocles, as Aristotle later, was fighting for the return of the egalitarian polity. The crime of Sophocles' Oedipus was the *social injury* that he inflicted upon the people of Thebes. His arrogant, autocratic ways of ruling became a disruptive force for the entire society. Thus the people of Thebes expelled Oedipus the tyrant from their boundaries. The female chorus played a major role in this tale of power lost.

The lynching by Piaroa of Wahari, their creator god – 2

Sophocles' story of Oedipus fits well the story of the tyrant Wahari and his
fall from power. The chanter narrator of Piaroa mythic cycles dwells upon
the events that led to his descent into tyranny. The signs of such violence
increased: from the arrogant gaze, to one that was crazy and then murderous.
He, like Oedipus, also became perceived by his own people as superfluous to
society, as his violence became too serious a danger for his own kinspeople.
Wahari, originally twinned with the gods of unity, refused that status to
become twinned with the archetypical god of violence – Kuemoi – the original
owner of all knowledge. Wahari finally murdered Kuemoi, with good cause.
The murder occurred when Kuemoi had a bad cold, which Wahari had sent
him as joke. Kuemoi retaliated by giving Wahari a dish of soup with Wahari's
own son, Lapa, roasted within it. Wahari, after gazing at his soup, and seeing
an arm of his son there, transformed into Eagle Hawk, and with his talons
grabbed Kuemoi by his dripping nose. He flew around the world with him,
then flung the monster onto the rocky cliffs below, smashing him to bits. This
was a story told as *comedy*. Wahari, as a true hero, slayed the 'real' monster.
But Wahari, who became twinned with Kuemoi through their mutual violence,
in time turned on his own people. He gave a great feast, inviting many of the
(human) inhabitants of the forest to it. When they became drunk, Wahari
transformed them into animals to be treated as game. And this is when the
lynching took place. His kinsmen silently, relentlessly, chased him down, and
killed him as if he were the animal of prey.

The telling of this story is through the poetics of tragedy. This is a sociality
in which the individual is always responsible for his or her own frailty or folly.
Thus, the group enters only in extreme cases. In this case it was reasoned
that for society's sake group action was necessary to kill the great tyrant, to
stop his genocide once and for all. A reasonable solution. Yet, murder is an
extreme solution, and murder by group decision even worse. It is understood
that violence breeds violence, difficult enough if by an individual, but chaos
if by a group of conspirators. Their murderous deed was certainly to stop the
epidemic of violence that Wahari had initiated, But once group action took
place, extreme violence spread throughout Piaroaland.

Unlike Girard's (1977) version of collective scapegoating, in which society
is supposed to become ever so calm and happy after such a lynching, the
communities of Piaroaland instead went mad with violence: mad from the
violence of Wahari, crazy from their own violence. Communities began
cannibalizing each other, and Piaroaland became a zone of war. It was
Wahari's female sibling, Cheheru, twinned in infancy with him, who ultimately
became responsible for saving society. She with whom he committed incest,
and he who later tried to kill both her and their son. It was also she whom he

Figure 5   A feather crown used by a ruwa in formal ritual to display the beauty of his powers.

taunted, and sold for six boxes of matches to the creator god of white people! It was Cheheru, who, no longer twinned with him, was able to repair society by taking all the poisonous knowledge created on earth during mythic history up to a new celestial land of gods. She locked up that knowledge in what became the 'crystal boxes of the gods'. In present-day time, human beings had to ask for this knowledge, which they received in small doses only, from the beatific, singing mountain gods of today's time, of whom Cheheru is the most revered. In mythic time, because of her anger with the antics of her brother (Wahari), she became a bit crazy as a promiscuous, wandering woman, the creator of monkey-urine perfume, and the mother of monkeys. Now, in today's time, she lives forever the chaste life of a chanting, sublime and beautiful goddess. She is generous, but careful, in her gifts of culinary arts to Piaroa people. She protects them, providing them with the generative powers to live a human sort of life – to hunt, cook, garden, create children. In Piaroaland, it then became the chorus – the voice and judgements of individual people – that detected and ejected a tyrant in the making, the one who took more knowledge from the gods than he or she could master. It became the important political role of women to watch attentively for expressions of arrogance and anger, or the egoistic use of knowledge. These were the signs of the emergence of the tyrant, he who is poisoned by too much poisonous knowledge – the one who had become superfluous to society.

In conclusion, Piaroan political theory stresses the poisonous effects of violence upon social stability and tranquillity. It also links violence with excessive knowledge, which in their understanding is inevitably allied to excessive power. Piaroa work toward solving this problem of violence through an egalitarian social system that is based upon virtue-centred ethics. In this case, we find a strong regard for personal autonomy being linked to the arts of paying regard to others. The arts of the mastery of knowledge practices and those of subjectively relating to others are intertwined – for both women and men. As with many other Amazonian societies, sociality in general morally privileges the positive emotions and practices (Overing 1989, 2006b; Overing and Passes 2000a, 2000b; Passes 2004, forthcoming). Society is daily created through affective arts of generosity, trust, friendship, cooperation and sharing (Overing 2003; Passes 2004, forthcoming). Within such a society, stinginess appals and anger is feared. Both are known to prompt violence in others (e.g. see Belaunde 2000). A moral gaff has both social and political consequences.

We can perhaps come to understand that this particular example of an Amazonian polity might well be one that is used more widely by a number of egalitarian sorts of people, and not only in Amazonia. However, we, ourselves, come from a highly controlling polity. Are we capable of understanding one that refuses such violence – intellectually, passionately? We must ask: what is the aim of a polity? What is the aim of a society? Amazonian people think greed is unworthy. This is a political point. Either as individuals or as a group of people, Piaroa could not own the resources of the earth. To do so would be considered a terrible impingement on other people, and other beings – and therefore inconceivably dangerous. To own such resources was considered a violence against others. Just imagine, Amazonia used to be classified in accordance to all those 'social' and 'political' qualities they didn't have – and which they abhor.

How *do* we talk about an Amazonian type of political and economic freedom? Just try to talk about the social and political implications of indigenous poetics, cosmology and aesthetics. How *do* we talk about an Amazonian woman's political and economic freedom, and their parity with men in the creation of society (see Heckler 2004; Overing 2003, 2006a; Passes 2004, forthcoming)? The details of the female chorus are central, whether set in ancient Thebes or Piaroaland, for they speak of the knowledge and skills attached to the women's political role in generating and repairing egalitarian types of society. Attempt to express any of these matters through the patronizing and paranoid gaze of Western social theory (Overing 2006a)? We are obviously in need of new visions of 'the sociological', a widening and extending of the anthropological endeavour beyond the restrictive, self-serving borders of modernist sociological theory. We need a more inspired perspectival gaze to allow us to consider seriously the relativity of knowledges, polities and socialities.

NOTES

1   See recent literature. For instance, Overing 2006b, and the books of McCallum 2001; Belaunde 2005; Lagrou 2007.
2   But see recent Amazonian ethnography (e.g. Overing and Passes 2000b) which speaks strongly to the *work* of achieving comfort.
3   Throughout Clastres' discussion he speaks of 'primitive' or 'archaic' societies. I replace this vocabulary with 'Amazonian societies' or 'peoples of Amazonia'. This does not distort his arguments for most of the ethnography he includes is from Amazonia.
4   I use the past tense because nowadays Piaroa communities (and also individuals) vary in their retention of the values I am relating here, based on my fieldwork of 1968 and 1977. It is also based on the extensive fieldwork of the 1990s carried out by Paul Oldham (1996), who worked with Piaroa in creating the first national indigenous organization in Venezuela. True to form, Piaroa people worked for 'direct democracy'. At that time the values I recognized were those of Piaroa. Nowadays, communities (and individuals) vary immensely in the degrees and ways of relating to the Venezuelan State.
5   On the 'shadows of language', see discussions by Edwin Ardener (in Chapman 1989:91, 94, 100 and 105).
6   A powerful *ruwahu* (wife of a powerful *ruwa*) tended to have more children than other women.
7   See Lévi Strauss (1967) on the Nambikwara leader's powers for unity, good will, his concern for the health of the community, and his generosity.

8   See David McKnight (2002) on the devastating effect of the state incorporating Australian Aborigines within its system.

9   For other Amazonian examples, see Guss (1989) on the Yukuana, Belaunde (2005) on the Airo Pai, and Lagrou (2007) on the Cashinahua,

10 Throughout the discussion of Foucault and Nietzsche, I am especially referring to the 2002 Penguin edition of selected essays by Michel Foucault on Power, specifically the selections on 'Truth and Juridical Forms'.

11 See Baier (1994) on the violence of such negativity, and on her arguments for transforming such ethics and system of judicial practices.

12 See Alastair MacIntyre (1982) on the use of virtue-centred ethics earlier in our own western history.

13 See Oliveira (2003) on the Mebengokré (Kayapó) who extend the ethics of kinship to include all community members. He argues well for this being a political, not just kinship, matter.

14 Thus actual male in-laws, for instance, must not be in an exchange relationship. They relate, instead, though a mutual flow of 'free gifts'.

15 Piaroa spoke of the importance of an individual's 'thoughts standing up' – that is cleansed and reflected upon – if her or his knowledge practices were to be properly positive. See Overing 1985a.

16 For instance he would leave 'wonderful' bags filled with the means for hunting, such as curare, hanging around the forest or delivered as a deadly 'gift'. Along with powers for hunting, such bags would also be filled with the poison of paranoia. When the victims went mad with this disease, Kumoi hoped they would die, so he could eat them.

17 Again I refer throughout this section to the chapter 'Truth and Juridical Form' within the Penguin edition of *Michel Foucault: Power – essential works of Foucault 1954–1984*.

18 Foucault is perhaps wrong about the topic of desires. There is certainly in Sophocles' Oedipus a strong lust for power.

19 Contrast the situation of a Piaroa *ruwa*. Each night that he chanted, all the men of the community placed their hammocks around him to provide him vocal support in his journeys travelling through mythscapes of the past. The men formed a nightly chorus, united in chanting at intervals refrains of the shaman's own repertoire. They were encouraging him in his dangerous work of protecting his people from cosmic mischief.

REFERENCES

Alès, Catherine, 2000, 'Anger as a marker of love: the ethic of conviviality among the Yanomami'. In *The Anthropology of Love and Anger: The Aesthetics of Conviviality in Native Amazonia*, eds J. Overing and A. Passes. London: Routledge.

Baier, Annette, 1994, *Moral Prejudices*. Harvard University Press: Cambridge, MA.

Belaunde, Louisa Elvira, 2000, 'The convivial self and the fear of anger amongst the Airo-Pai of Amazonian Peru'. In *The Anthropology of Love and Anger: The Aesthetics of Conviviality in Native Amazonia*, eds J. Overing and A. Passes. London: Routledge.

——— 2005, *El recuerdo de luna: genero, sangre y memoria entre los pueblos amazónicos*. Lima: Universidad Mayor de San Marcos.

Chapman, Malcolm (ed.), 1989, *Edwin Ardener: The Voice of Prophecy and other Essays*. Oxford: Blackwell.

Clastres, Pierre, 1977, *Society Against the State: The Leader as Servant and Humanity of Power among the Indians of Amazonia*. Oxford: Basil Blackwell.

Diamond, Stanley, 1987, *In Search of the Primitive: A Critique of Civilization*. New Brunswick, NJ: Transaction Books.

Foucault, Michel, 2002, 'Truth and juridical forms'. In *Michel Foucault – Power: Essential works of Foucault 1954–1984*, ed. James D. Faubion. London: Penguin Books.

Girard, René, 1977, *Violence and the Sacred*. Baltimore: The John Hopkins University Press.

Graeber, David, 2004, *Fragments of an Anarchist Anthropology*. Chicago: Prickly Paradigm Press.

Gow, Peter, 2000, 'Helpless – the affective preconditions of Piro social life'. In *The Anthropology of Love and Anger: The Aesthetics of Conviviality in Native South America*, eds J. Overing and A. Passes. London: Routledge.

Guss, David, 1989, *To Weave and Sing: Art Symbol, and Narrative in the South American Rain Forest*. Berkeley: University of California Press.

Heckler, Serena, 2004, 'Tedium and creativity: the valorization of manioc cultivation and Piaroa women', *JRAI* 10(2):241–61.

Lagrou, Els, 2006, 'Laughing at power and the power of laughing in Cashinahua narratives and performances', *Tipiti* 4(1 & 2), *Special Issue in Honor of Joanna Overing, In the World and About the World: Amerindian Modes of Knowledge*, guest eds Fernando Santos-Granero and George Mentore.

——— 2007, *A fluidez da forma: arte, alteridade e agência em uma sociedade amazônica (Kaxinawa, Acre)*. Rio de Janeiro: Topbooks.

Lévi-Strauss, Claude, 1967, 'The social and psychological aspects of chieftainship in a Primitive tribe: the Nambikwara of northwestern Mato Grosso'. In *Comparative Political Systems*, eds R. Cohen and J. Middleton. The Natural History Press.

Londoño Sulkin, Carlos, 2000, '"Though it comes as evil, I embrace it as good": social sensibilities and the transformation of malignant agency among the Muinane'. In *The Anthropology of Love and Anger: The Aesthetics of Conviviality in Native Amazonia*, eds J. Overing and A. Passes. London: Routledge.

MacIntyre, Alastair, 1982, *After Virtue: A Study in Moral Theory* (2nd Edition). London: Duckworth.

McCallum, Cecilia, 2001, *Gender and Sociality in Amazonia: How Real People are Made*. Oxford: Berg.

McKnight, David, 2002, *From Hunting to Drinking*. London: Routledge.

Oldham, Paul, 1996, 'The Impacts of Development and Indigenous Responses among the Piaroa of the Venezuelan Amazon' (Ph.D. thesis, University of St Andrews).

Nietzsche, Friedrich Wilhelm, 1967 *The Will to Power,* Translation by Walter Kaufmann and R. J. Hollingdale. New York: Randam House.

——— 1974 (1882) *The Gay Science*. Translation by Walter Kaufmann. New York: Vintage Books.

——— 1989 (1887) *On the Genealogy of Morals*. Translation by Walter Kaufmann and R. J. Oliveira, Adolfo, 2003, 'Of Life and Happiness: Morality, Aesthetics, and Social Life among the Southeastern Amazonian Mebengokre (Kayapo), as Seen from the Margins of Ritual' (Ph.D. thesis, University of St Andrews).

Overing, Joanna, 1975, *The Piaroa: A People of the Orinoco Basin: A Study in Kinship and Marriage*. Oxford: Clarendon Press.

——— 1985a, 'There is no end of evil: the guilty innocents and their fallible god'. In *The Anthropology of Evil*, ed. D. Parkin. Oxford: Blackwell.

——— 1985b, 'Introduction'. In *Reason and Morality* (ASA Monograph 24), ed. J. Overing. London: Tavistock Publications.

——— 1989, 'The aesthetics of production: the sense of community among the Cubeo and Piaroa', *Dialectical Anthropology* 14:149–75.

——— 1990, 'The shaman as a maker of worlds: Nelson Goodman in the Amazon', *Man* (NS) 25:601–19.

——— 1992, 'Wandering in the market and the forest: an Amazonian theory of production and exchange'. In *Contesting Markets: Analyses of Ideology, Discourse an Practice*, ed. R. Dilley.

——— 1993a, 'The anarchy and collectivism of the "primitive other": Marx and Sahlins in the Amazon'. In *Socialism: Ideals, Ideologies and Local Practice* (ASA Monographs 31), ed. C. Hann. London: Routledge.

——— 1993b, 'Death and the loss of civilised predation among the Piaroa of the Orinoco Basin', *L'Homme* XXVI–XXVIII (*La Remontée l'Amazone*):195–215.

——— 1995, 'O mito como historia: um problema de temp, realidade e outra questoes [Myth and History: the problem of time, reality and other matters]' *MANA, Estudos de Antropologia Social* 1(1):107–40.

——— 1996, 'Who is the mightiest of them all? Jaguar and conquistador in Piaroa images of alterity and identity'. In *Monsters, Tricksters and Sacred Cows* (New World Series), ed. J. Arnold. University Press of Virginia: Charlottesville, VA.

——— 2000, 'The efficacy of laughter: the ludic side of magic within Amazonian sociality'. In *The Anthropology of Love and Anger: The Aesthetics of Conviviality in Native Amazonia*, eds J. Overing and A. Passes. London: Routledge.

——— 2003, 'In praise of the everyday: trust and the art of social living in an Amazonian community', *Ethnos* 68(3):293–316.

——— 2004, 'The grotesque landscape of mythic 'before time'; the folly of sociality in 'today time': an egalitarian aesthetics of human existence'. In *Kultur, Raum, Landschaft*, eds E. Mader and E. Halbmayer. Frankfurt am Main: Brandes and Apsel/Südwind.

——— 2006a, 'The backlash to decolonizing intellectuality', *Anthropology and Humanism* 31(1):11–40.

——— 2006b, 'The stench of death and the aromas of life: poetics of ways of knowing and sensory process among Piaroa of the Orinoco Basin', *Tipiti* 4(1 & 2), *Special Issue in Honor of Joanna Overing, In the World and About the World: Amerindian Modes of Knowledge*, guest eds Fernando Santos-Granero and George Mentore.

Overing, Joanna and Alan Passes, 2000a, 'Introduction: the opening up of Amazonian anthropology'. In *The Anthropology of Love and Anger: The Aesthetics of Conviviality in Native South America*, eds J. Overing and A. Passes. London: Routledge.

——— 2000b, *The Anthropology of Love and Anger: The Aesthetics of Conviviality in Native South America*. London: Routledge.

Passes, Alan, 2004, 'The place of politics: powerful speech and women speakers in everyday Pa'ikwené (Palikur)', *JRAI* 10(1):1–18.

———forthcoming, 'Loud women: creating community from the domestic in Amazonia'. In *The Domestic Space Reader*, eds Chiara Briganti and Kathy Mezei. Toronto: University of Toronto Press.

Rapport, Nigel and Joanna Overing, 2000, *Social and Cultural Anthropology: The Key Concepts*. London: Routledge.

——— 2007, *Social and Cultural Anthropology: The Key Concepts* (2nd edition). London: Routledge.

Rivière, Peter, 1984, *Individual and Society in Guiana: A Comparative Study of Amerindian Social Organization.* Cambridge: Cambridge University Press.

Rubenstein, Steven, 2002, *Alejandro Tsakimp.* Lincoln, London: University of Nebraska.

Sahlins, Marshall, 1972, *Stone Age Economics.* Chicago: Aldine.

Thomas, David, 1982, *Order without Government: The Society of the Pemon Indians of Venezuela.* Urbana: University of Illinois Press.

Williams, Raymond, 1983, *Keywords.* London: Fontana.

CHAPTER 3

Tribalism and power in Iraq

Saddam Hussein's 'house'

⚜

HOSHAM DAWOD

This chapter examines the formation of Saddam Hussein's political power and, more widely, the Ba'athist state in Iraq from 1968 until the second Gulf War. The discussion then briefly explores the understandings of the occupying US forces of Saddam Hussein's political base, with specific reference to 'tribalism'. Through a series of re-engagements with anthropological sources, the aim is to develop some key themes, arising both from my own work and that of other Middle East researchers. These are: politics and different models of the organization and devolution of power; the tribe and the current retribalization of a part of Iraqi society (Iraq, however, being hardly unique in this phenomenon); and the overarching question of why people are today inclined, constrained or even encouraged to regroup themselves into large domestic units, such as tribes (real or fictive). What collective and individual interests link them and are reproduced through the tribal system? What is the meaning of the contemporary resurgence of tribalism when the dominant discourse, for several decades now, has been couched in the language of world processes and globalization?

For anthropologists, just as for other contemporary social scientists, societies are particular, their histories always singular – and yet here and there one can see the reproduction of comparable processes: tribes and their chiefdoms recur in different epochs and in different societies which have no contact with each other. One only has to look at the current socio-political map of Africa, Central Asia, Amazonia and Oceania.[1] To acknowledge this is not to abandon standards of anthropological debate: if grand evolutionary theories are dead, it is still true that social structures and ways of life and human thinking have evolved in the course of history and will continue to do so. The issue is how to make the best reconstruction of this evolution and this history.

Yet, at the same time, for twenty years or more there has existed a clear (negative) convergence between the grand paradigms: Marxism (at least in its Soviet and Third World versions), liberalism and modernism, to cite only three major ideological currents. In consistently underestimating the importance of all phenomena below the level of the state structure, these doctrines have left themselves unable to register the current tendency for kinship relations to become invested with political power (especially the higher levels of political power), the new forms of local solidarity, the ethno-cultural differences between peoples and so on. This current proliferation of tribal phenomena is simply relegated to the old banal headings of tradition/modernity as mapped by the linear scale of progress. Yet, there is much empirical evidence to show that the breaking down of the old social structures under the influence of industrialization, modernization and globalization, has produced some unforeseen consequences. Far from cooling off, the passions and diverse forms of tribal *assabiyya* (solidarity, *esprit de corps*), religious-denominational and ethnic, are undergoing an undeniable resurgence.

In considering theories of the origin and character of the tribe and the ethnic group, it is crucial to jettison the theme of their essentially archaic character, as in the conventional contrast with a 'modernizing rationality', in which all social change is reduced to the passage from the traditional to the modern, from simple to complex, 'particularism' to 'universalism'. From this perspective, tribal and ethnic phenomena belong to the 'particularist' or 'pre-modern' world; located on the side of the obsolete and hence ahistorical and suspect, to be designated 'obstacles to change' or the result of 'incomplete modernization'. Thus preconceived at the start, the ethnic group and the tribal structure are naturally of minor interest to the theorist. All that is offered by the new mode of dependency theorizing is an 'updated' version of the same old story: the role of contemporary capitalist globalization is merely to accentuate societies' tendency towards integration into a world system, a global economy dominated by the West, China and Japan. In relation to the tribe and the ethnic group, globalization gives a renewed stimulus to modernity and the modernist vision in peripheral societies, but now with the global trimmed to the measure of the local and vice versa. At the same time, we are witnessing how the political and cultural level is moving in precisely the opposite direction to economic integration, via a process of segmentation. New nation-states appear and multiply, each seeking to affirm their identity and legitimacy, ancient and modern. And it is precisely here that we observe, at the infra-state level, a revival of tribal and ethnic sentiments (real or reconstituted) that irreparably undermine modernity's image of its own origin. This fact obstinately demands attention, and was in fact already noted at the beginning of the 1980s by Louis Dumont, who insisted that even in the 'modern' or 'advanced' or 'developed' world, there existed a number of ideas/ values (in the holist sense that Dumont gives these terms) which one could take as most intensely modern and yet which are in fact the result of a history in the course of which modernity and non-modernity, or more precisely individualist ideas/values *and* their contraries, are imbricated with each other and intimately combined (Dumont 1985 and 1991, esp. 'Introduction').

Iraqi Studies: a brief survey

From the perspective of these opening propositions, what, then, is the current state of social science research on Iraqi society? The least one could say is that it presents a very strange and paradoxical situation: here is a society that is notoriously among the most 'mediatized' in the world (particularly since the first Gulf War of 1991), yet which remains enigmatic and largely misunderstood. Very little of the available work (of which certain examples will be given here) truly deserves the name social science.[2] This situation can be explained in terms of certain key failings.

The first failing I would see as a direct – and, putting it mildly, 'odd' – consequence of the Gulf Wars. The quantity of political literature produced about Iraq is huge, yet strikingly limited in its claims to knowledge. On the one hand, there is apologetics: the appeal to Iraq's romantic past, already a rich source of motifs of loyalty for the Iraqi political authorities, and which translates, in turn, into favours and privileges granted to researchers in the 'Orientalist' tradition, primarily European and North American archaeologists – by contrast to the blatant refusal of access to the same territory when it comes to anthropologists, sociologists and political scientists. On the other hand, there is the exaltation of the 'Civilizing Mission' of the New (read 'Western') World Order. This partly explains why social anthropology even today – even after refining and de(ethno)centring its theoretical and methodological apparatus – is treated as suspect and tainted with colonialism in the eyes of many African and Asian societies. Of course, the task of 'decentring' anthropology in relation to 'the West, its native home' remains always incomplete (see Godelier 1995). Even today, most Arab-Muslim societies perceive contemporary social anthropology (unjustly) as nothing more than a colonial science. Nonetheless, the paucity of anthropological research on the Middle East cannot be explained solely by such ideological-political accusations, nor their equivalent at the level of the petty administrative and police interference that ethnologists – as those not 'belonging' to the country – have to deal with. Other causes must be sought. The most significant are undoubtedly to be found in the cultural density of Iraqi society: a population that has been in a process of continual mixing since the Neolithic, a Muslim society for more than a thousand years, yet constantly mutating and, at the same time, historically continuous with other still more ancient inhabitants, a complex tangle of societies bearing the weight of history, rapid urbanization and other factors of change (Digard and Bernand 1986).

A second weakness lies in the area of social-science techniques: the problem of making comparisons when terms and categories are neither standard nor simple: 'tribe' and 'tribalism', 'house' (we use here, with caveats, the term 'house' [*maison*] in Lévi-Strauss's sense, to which we shall return),[3] 'domestic unit', 'kindred'; 'kinship' and so-called 'Arab marriage', 'power' and the like.

The third deficiency is the lack of any large-scale data on the distribution of the social phenomena being studied. Obviously, no map will be without its blank spots, but, even so, the sum of credible available information is very weak.[4]

The fourth problem is rather more difficult to pin down, it concerns the nature of the explanation that we aspire to. More specifically, how can we explain the reappearance of a social phenomenon? Are there devolutionary – like evolutionary – phenomena? If irreversible phenomena and processes exist, are there then also some aspects of reality that are reversible (see Godelier 1998)? This issue has been raised by Edmund Leach, Maurice Godelier, Jonathan Friedman and others, when faced with two forms of organization of power in the same society. They asked, therefore, whether one of these forms of power could be evolved from the other (Leach 1954; Godelier 1988; Friedman and Rowlands 1977; Friedman 1979).

Contemporary Iraqi society: some landmarks

The First World War brought vast and sudden change to Mesopotamia, as elsewhere in the Arab-Muslim world: after more than twelve centuries of Muslim domination, four of those centuries under Ottoman rule, the country found itself under the guardianship of a Western Christian state. On 6 November 1914, Anglo-Indian troops disembarked at Fao in the extreme south of Iraq and, a few days later, occupied Basra. The English, having occupied the provinces of Basra and Baghdad for most of the war, promised to deliver the population from the Turkish yoke, while the Turks saw it as a holy war (*jihad*) against the infidels. Most of the tribes adopted a 'wait and see' stance, although the holy Shi'ite cities (Nadjaf and Karbala) sought to rid themselves of the Turks. The defeat and subsequent dismantling of the Ottoman Empire had major consequences for the political evolution of the region. In effect, three years after the First World War, a modern Iraqi state had been founded under the regime of the 'peace settlement', and Great Britain was designated the Mandatory power in the new system of international guardianship established by the League of Nations. The victorious allies parcelled out amongst themselves the Arab provinces of the former Ottoman Empire (see Sluglett 1976).

Even though in the past certain regions of the country had been united under the same government, the entity that emerged in 1921 had not previously existed as an independent nation-state. Great Britain arranged for Emir Faisal (son of the Hashemite Chief Hussein of Mecca) to come to Baghdad and be proclaimed King of Iraq. In parallel, the British supervised the setting up of an Iraqi administration, a 'constitution' and a formal legislative apparatus which was, from that time onward, theoretically in the hands of the Sunni Arab notables trained at the Ottoman school. The Mandate – a form of indirect rule with Arab ministers and officials in place but closely supervised by British advisors whose 'advice' (read orders!) they were expected to 'follow' – came to an end in 1932, when Iraq gained admission to the League of Nations as an independent state. During this period, Great Britain had guaranteed the existing northern borders of Iraq, keeping a watchful eye on this area because of the concession for oil prospecting and exploitation conferred on the Iraq Petroleum Company, a conglomerate of British, Dutch, French and American oil interests. The British also created a social base for the monarchy by recognizing, for 'appropriate' tribal chiefs, full legal possession of the hitherto customary property of 'their' tribes. Great Britain also kept military bases in Iraq and generally continued to exercise a powerful political and economic influence. As for the economy, initiatives remained limited largely to the construction of various roads and railways. The field of agriculture saw the introduction of various botanical research projects and a more systematic basis of pedagogy, and some vast irrigation projects were initiated – but concretely, the only novelty was the appearance of motor pumps on certain river banks. Altogether, the period of the Mandate could hardly be characterized as leading to progress, whether in terms of civil peace or civil engineering, nor economic development, teaching or health.

In 1932, the year of independence, power was held by a handful of large Sunni houses, grouped in factions and divided by multiple intrigues. If it is true that Arab unity expanded in the 1920s, for the masses nationalism remained the expression of exclusion. The most influential men of politics – such as Yassin Pacha, Rachid 'Ali al Gaïlâni, Nouri Saïd – were preoccupied with consolidating the domination of the rising new social classes which they represented (landed proprietors, large merchants, 'growing' foreign investments, the emerging bourgeoisie) at a country-wide level (see Batatu 2004, esp. ch. 6). The next step was reinforcing the army, which began to be deployed in the 1930s, first against the Assyrians and then the Kurds, finally repressing the last great tribal uprisings in the Mid-Euphrates in the summers of 1935 and 1936. However, repressing the tribes in this epoch was no easy matter, even with a regular army. Notoriously, it was estimated that in 1933 the tribes possessed 100,000 rifles against the army's 15,000!

After 1936, the relation of forces was inverted in an irreversible way. The tribal sheikhs would henceforth attempt to win the favours of government rather than oppose it. This presupposed profound transformations, simultaneously regrouping tribal structures and communal proprietors, and devolving power within the tribes – in short, unsettling the entire ensemble of social relations. For the state authority was seeking expansion by coupling itself in a previously unheard-of alliance with the new rich urban social classes and urban tribal sheikhs. While various sources of urban capital were invested in the countryside (financing pumps, agricultural equipment and so on), the Government backed the authority of the sheikhs, launching with them the great river irrigation projects aimed at increasing the area of irrigated land. The tribal authorities, in turn, collaborated in raising tax levies. Many sheikhs, attracted by the new forms of consumption, installed themselves in the towns where they dispensed important funds, thus reinforcing their links with urban proprietors.

However, three new factors appeared. The take-off of communications (ports and railways), the exploitation of petroleum at Kirkuk and the undertaking of the great dam projects gave birth to a class of wage-employees – and eventually a trade union movement which manifested itself in the strikes of 1931. At this point, within the new Iraqi bourgeoisie, various individuals moved towards clearly reformist socio-political positions.[5]

The Second World War did not have any immediate repercussions. Certainly, nationalist groups had been aware of Hitlerite propaganda[6] for a number of years. In 1941, a group of Iraqi army officers led a short-lived resistance movement against Great Britain which resulted in a second British occupation until the end of the Second World War. The war provoked great difficulties of provisioning, and hence an increase in demand for agricultural products, which led the landed proprietors and the sheikhs to increase the areas under cultivation and the prevailing prices.

Between 1945 and 1958, the country was governed by a succession of 24 cabinets, composed for the most part of coalitions endlessly regrouping the same individuals. Many Iraqis in the countryside as well as numerous tribes (and this is a new development) thought that the most urgent need for the country was national independence, from which would follow socio-economic reforms, especially agricultural reform. The state was almost universally accepted as the 'natural' means of taking these reforms forward to a beneficial conclusion. This way of thinking – usually, but not always associated with socialism – was also very widespread in other parts of the Middle East and North Africa.

Wealth remained concentrated in the hands of a small number of houses (*bayt*, plural *beyoutat*), which, far more than kinship itself, organized the control of wealth of private commercial and industrial companies. Falling far behind these houses in status and fortune were the middling and small landowners, religious dignitaries and local notables, wholesale and retail merchants, manufacturers, small shopkeepers etc. The evident social contradictions manifest in the (mostly foreign-owned) large enterprises and the large landed estates meant that the poorer fractions of the population were extremely conscious of the flaws of the political system: they saw the solution in national independence, which became the supreme political goal (Batatu 2004:53–361 and 465–82; Fernea and Roger 1991).

The major socio-political and economic changes that took place very rapidly between 1920 and 1958 should not obscure the fact that Iraqi society was composed of elements that had never before been closely associated with an independent state (Batatu 2004:ch.6; Al-Wardi 1965: chs 3 and 6). As now, the population was divided into diverse but overlapping categories, corresponding to social and ethnic origin, religious denomination, occupation and regional and tribal affiliation. Apart from the Christian communities (3.6 per cent before the recent exodus), Sabean and Yazidi (1.4 per cent), about 95 per cent of Iraqis are Muslim. Almost one quarter of these Muslims are ethnic Kurds who are mostly Shafi'ite Sunnis, while the other Muslims are Arab. These Arab Muslims are, in turn, divided into Hanafite Sunnis and Ja'farite Shi'ites, the latter forming the largest homogeneous religious community in the country as a whole. Naturally, none of these communities or denominations constitutes a simple monolithic entity (Dawod 1994:34–56; see also van Bruinessen 1992; Bozarslan 1997). To the extent that it is possible to calculate (since only gross religious categorizations – Christian/Muslim – are registered in the Iraqi census) some 72 per cent of Iraqis are Arabs, 22 per cent are Kurds and the rest are Turkeman, Armenian and 'other'.[7] Almost all the Kurds (except the Yazidi) and Arabs (with the exception of a tiny (Christian) minority) are Muslim. To this extent, the heterogeneity of Iraqi society should not be overplayed, since some 70 per cent of the population is both Muslim and Arab, and recent manifestations of Sunni/Shi'ite sectarianism are more the product of political conflicts and competition for power than a reflection of any 'fundamental hostility' between the two denominations.[8]

The position of the Kurds (who are of Indo-European origin) and, more generally, their political aspirations, is determined essentially by ethnic considerations. The Kurds see themselves as sharply distinguished from their Arab and Turkish neighbours by their language, which links them to Iranian populations. Their socio-political traditions before the arrival of the state in the Middle East were shaped by Islamicization in the Shaf'ite form of Sunnism. In the Ottoman era, even though tribal structures and modes of belonging were predominant in Kurdish society, this population was already forming itself into a distinctively ethnic community among others subordinated to the power of the Ottoman Empire. Their consciousness as one ethnic group among others, founded above all on their linguistic particularism and their socio-cultural and secular way of life, took off after the fall of the Ottoman Empire when their territory was divided by new frontiers between Turkey, Iran, Iraq and Syria, and other Kurdish populations were cut off in the USSR (today in Russia and in various republics of Central Asia).

Between two-thirds and three-quarters of the Arab population is Shi'ite. Setting aside Baghdad, which has mixed Sunni and Shi'ite neighbourhoods alongside those that are exclusively Sunni or Shi'ite, it is generally true that Sunni (specifically Hanafite) Arabs live in the north of the country, in the area known as the Sunni Triangle in the north-west, in the High and Middle Tigris regions (Mosul, Tikrit, Samarra and Dur), and also in the High Euphrates ('Ana, Rawa, Haditha, Hit and Ramadi). The Shi'ite (specifically Ja'farite) Arabs live in the south of the country. Historically, Sunni Arabs were found mainly in the urban population and have always been politically dominant, as much under the monarchy as under the republic. This derives principally from the fact that the Ottoman empire was a Sunni institution and tended to employ only Sunnis in the administration. This Sunni pre-eminence continued under the republic to the extent that in 1958, and continuing under the system put in place by the Ba'ath Party, Sunnis occupied the high offices in the civil and military bureaucracy and held the real political power.

However, such monocausal political explanations are insufficient to understand the situation; there are sociological and historical reasons as well. For example, even when modern public teaching first appeared in Iraq at the end of the nineteenth century, few Shi'ites, to the extent that there were any at that time, went to the new state schools. Consequently, when the Iraqi state was created in 1921, there were few qualified Shi'ites able or willing to participate in the government, administration or army. This situation continued at the level of ministerial participation throughout the period of the monarchy (although there were some Shi'ite ministers) and at the level of key power positions under the republic. At the same time, however, Shi'ite tribal chiefs were among the richest land-holders, and Shi'ite businessmen among the richest merchants, in the period of the 1958 revolution, while the rapid progress of the education service did produce an increasing number of Shi'ite officials. Thus, by the mid 1950s, the dividing line between Sunnis and Shi'ites had begun to lose its importance. In addition, the wish for national independence in the 1930s, 1940s and 1950s had a unifying effect which would persist for some years despite the deep political divisions that appeared after the revolution. The 'secular' climate, in turn, and the optimism that prevailed in Iraq and the whole of the Middle East in the 1950s and the early 1960s sustained the hope that the importance attached to religious denominational divisions would gradually 'disappear'.

Today, at the beginning of the third millennium, the situation seems far removed from those times. Largely under the influence of Middle East 'experts', a highly simplistic image of Iraqi society has appeared (Farouk-Sluglett and Sluglett 1992): on the one side, the 'Sunni Arabs' were supporting the 'Sunni' regime of Saddam Hussein and, on the other, 'the Shi'ites', somehow 'not quite real Arabs' (a sort of Iranian fifth column) in strong opposition, with the Kurds located somewhere else entirely. It is undeniable that revival of Islamic sentiment, the Iranian revolution, the Iraq–Iran war and the cold war worked together to create a resurgence and reaffirmation of religious sensibilities.[9] In fact, one of the most decisive of all these factors (at least at the political level) was the persistence and renewal of a type of factional allegiance and spirit of solidarity (*asabiya*) among members of the same tribe, at the heart of the domestic group or coming from a common region and so on.[10] The question to ask, therefore, is whether the persistence of these types of attachment serve to consolidate the political 'revival' of Islamism or, on the contrary, weaken it? And, following from this, which of these denominational groups, Shi'ism or Sunnism, adapts itself best to tribal structures?[11] Islam, as a universal religion, has long faced this contradiction. Thus it seems that the reaffirmation of these forms of *asabiya* goes together with the promotion of forms of life and a system of values that are deeply anchored in an Arabic-Islamic consciousness, particularly in the countryside. But it is also true that Shi'ite institutions in Iraq (as instances of the supra-tribal, supra-ethnic national) adapt themselves to tribal realities with more difficulty.

Contemporary Iraqi society is divided along many lines: ethnic, religious, denominational, social (social class and also other socio-professional groupings) and between urban and rural. In fact, the disappearance of the nomadic world and the reduction of society to two poles are phenomena of very recent origin. For it is not so long since Iraqi society, like all Arab societies, was divided into three interdependent yet strongly antagonistic groups: nomads, agriculturalists and town-dwellers. Rapid and massive change has meant that, in a very short time (several decades), nomads, who in the nineteenth century still represented about 35 per cent of the total population, and then 4 per cent by 1957, now constitute less than 1 per cent. Despite this rapid decline, the Bedouin tribal model has profoundly influenced the rural population and also the newly settled populations of small- and medium-sized towns in the

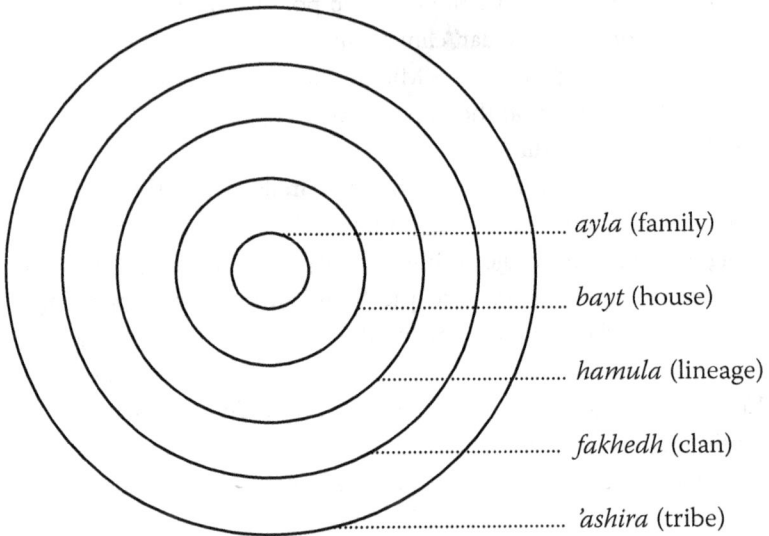

ayla (family)

bayt (house)

hamula (lineage)

fakhedh (clan)

'ashira (tribe)

Figure 1   Nested terms of association.

western and southern regions and the Mesopotamian plain, both its social
organization and its way of thinking. This character and tribal structure
distinguishes the rural Arab Iraqi world very strongly from other peasantries
of the Middle East: Egypt, Syria and even Kurdistan. Generally speaking, the
tribes of the West and the Mid-Euphrates, in direct contact with the desert,
have maintained (or re-created) some of their traditions far more than those
of the East, mixed as they have long been with settled populations (of course,
there are always exceptions: the grand tribal confederation of Beni Lam, for
example). It is fascinating to observe how the symbolism employed by Saddam
Hussein imitated, almost to the point of caricature, the Bedouin model of
western Iraq (dress, having a little herd of camel, keeping a link with the desert
and so on) to such an extent that he displayed total scorn for the peasants of
the east and the south of Iraq (the pejorative employed is 'M'adan'). A second
important effect of the decline of the nomadic world, here at the level of basic
social morphology, is the rapid transformation in social relations and former
structures, undertaken in order to undermine the opposition between town
and country.

More fundamentally, and arbitrarily limiting our analysis here to internal
factors (acknowledging that there are many exterior causes as well), factional
allegiance and the spirit of *asabiya*, types of allegiance now functioning
on a new base, have been reinforced at two historical moments and for

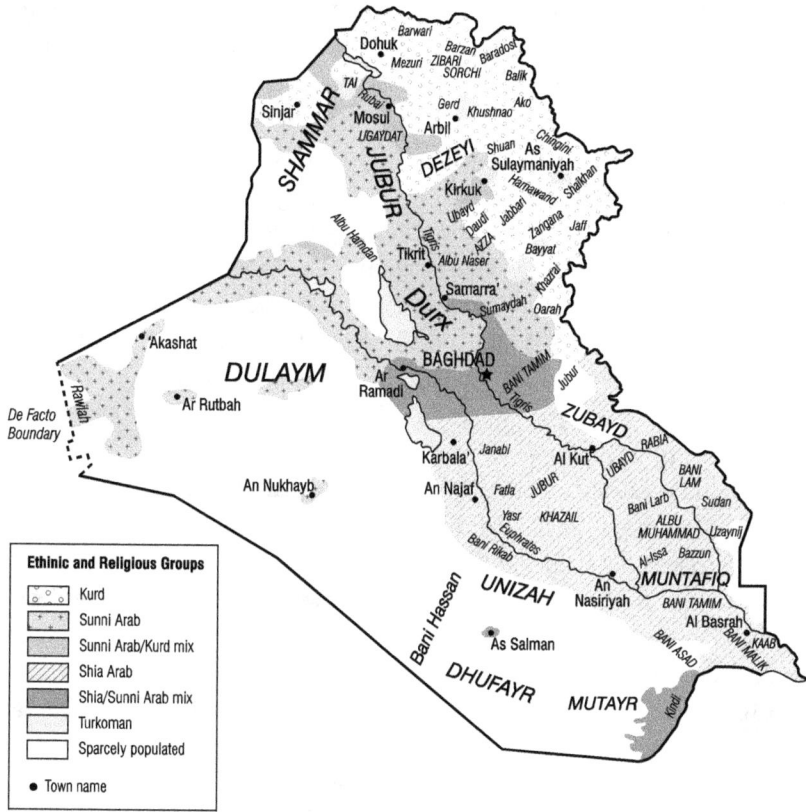

Figure 2   Ethnic and religious groups in Iraq.

two contradictory reasons: the first – and here disputing Bertrand Badie's thesis (1992:249–52, 1993) concerning the state and new phenomena in the international situation – is that in Iraq it was the universalist state in all its power (initially through the 1970s and 1980s) which was the prime mover in maintaining, subordinating and then propelling certain forms of tribal and clan structures. For it was the absence of individual power in the face of an arbitrary state, and the lack of any intermediary social bodies (without which there is simply the pure universalist Hobbesian state; alternatively the state functioning according to the Weberian model) that drove men and women to turn to infra-ethnic and infra-state levels, both to protect themselves or, conversely, to seek political and social promotion within this same state. The central Iraqi power itself consolidated this process with its frequent appeals to kinship relations and tribal elements as a way of managing politics. The second reason (and the second historical moment) was precisely the weakness of the Iraqi 'sovereign' state, specifically its incapacity (particularly since the 1990s) to assure the security of the population and territoriality of the country. Here, it was the state's inability to lead that induced individuals to return to their infra-state layers. Thus what Bertrand Badie calls 'empty social spaces' (*'espaces sociaux vides'*), that is, social spaces that escape the authority of the state (Badie 1995 and 1999: esp. ch. 4), are nothing more or less, in my opinion, than a devolved form of power in the national and new world context. In the Iraqi situation, recourse to such layers signifies a reinforced engagement with a tribe, a region or a particular house. In this, the central Iraqi power (through yesterday's strength or today's 'weakness') has contributed just as much to the reproduction and promotion of heterogeneity as to its disappearance.

What is an Iraqi tribe?

This is a double question: on the first hand, what is the nature of tribal organization in Iraq and, on the second, what are the conditions of their reactivation today? Let us begin by examining certain terms relating to tribal organization that are in current usage in the Arab regions of Iraq. It is always difficult to present a terminological analysis of Arab tribal nomenclature, which varies historically and geographically. Consider a few examples: *sha'b* – 'small tribe', meaning springing from a distant common origin, e.g. the Qahtan origin of the Arabs of Southern Arabia, Adnan for those of the North; *qabila* – a generic term designating a tribe or confederation of tribes; *'imara* – a sub-tribal structure, and a rarely used term which, in former times, metaphorically evoked parts of the body (*sadr*, chest and *'unuq*, neck) and subsequently came to mean 'flourishing'; *'ashira* – a sub-tribe or tribe, though for the Turks and the Kurds *qabila* means clan and *'ashira* means a big tribe or confederation of tribes; *batn* – clan, a term that according to the ancient Hebrew is derived from the word for stomach, though for other groups, Hebrew or Arab, it also means 'womb', which is why in Robertson Smith's (1966:38) evolutionist vision *batn* means a matrilineal clan preceding the era of patrilineality; *fakhith* – means patrilineal clan for the Arab tribes of the north-west of Iraq, while for the southern tribes of Iraq, as for the tribes of other Arab societies, it refers to a lineage;[12] *fasila* – a house (*bayt*) or extended family, but also, according to the metaphorical language of the body, the lower part of the leg; *firqa* (Varisco 1996) – lineage; *hamula* – lineage for the tribes of the north-west, but 'clan' for the tribes of the south;[13] *bayt* – house; *Mashaykh* (Sheikhdom) – chiefdom. In Iraq, only *'ashira, fakhith, hamula* and *bayt* remain in current use, along with various other terms of which some are specific to this region: *albu, fenda, âl* and *al-gurmeh*.

The terms *'ashira, fakhidh, albu, fenda, hamula* and *bayt* describe the fundamental relations constituting Iraqi social tribal organization, as much among the urban as the rural population. They each denote a particular order of relations allowing each individual to situate themselves in the social system. In this context, how should one think of continuity in relation to earlier tribal organization? How to situate this evolution in relation to the opposition/ complementarity between state power and tribal power? In which ways does contemporary tribal organization differ from earlier forms?

In local cultural usage, the term *'ashira* (tribe) signifies an ensemble of individuals and groups speaking the same language and dialect, split into multiple sub-groups: many *fakhidh*, many *hamula*, many *bayt* and in each *bayt* many *aïla* (families) of variable number and size, defining themselves by their common patrilineal descent, more often fictive than literally true. The appropriation of a territory claimed by the tribe as its own (whether through inheritance, conquest, by right of customary use or received from the central power) and which it is prepared to defend by force, constitutes another fundamental element of this reality. In fact, what is called an *'ashira* is a socio-political entity which exercises a large or limited sovereignty over a determined territory. In depicting the diversity of tribal structures, one notices how relations of kinship and consanguinity, real or fictive, are made primary in explaining rights, loyalties and obligations between persons and groups. Certain tribes collect sometimes thousands of people around a sheikh (one man) who regulates the tribe's internal relations and represents the tribe as a whole, and its interests, in relation to other groups and the central power.[14] The structural novelty that characterizes the contemporary Iraqi tribe is its dependence on the state to reproduce itself, and hence a relative loss in its larger political and territorial sovereignty. It is clear that contemporary tribal phenomena clearly cannot be understood in isolation from Iraqi central state power.

Apart from this reconfiguring of the political field of the tribe through its new dependence on the state, what are the other major differences between former and contemporary Iraqi tribal structures? In the period prior to British colonization, most of the tribes were in the process of regrouping themselves into grand tribal confederations (*'ashai'r*) under a *shaykh al-mashayikh* as supreme leader (a sort of chiefdom – *shaykhdom*). In theory, the sheikh of each tribe did not enjoy hereditary power: rather, through exercising his leadership capacity and his political ability to maintain the unity of his group as a whole, playing the role of arbiter within the tribe or the confederation, he would show his appropriateness, whether by the suppleness of his manoeuvres or in his ability to gain the consent of the tribal members to the use of force in order to maintain order within the tribe or gain prestige in the outside world. Hence the members of a tribe are associated with the sheikh's control of the territory and its resources. Nonetheless, transmission of the title of sheikh from father to son is not absolutely prohibited, provided that the new sheikh lives up to the expectations of status and can defend himself against possible rivals. If not, a man of the same house (*bayt*), or even another, is entitled to cut him off from his claim and take over the title. Thus, from early on, and contrary to the arguments of certain segmentarist authors (see particularly Middleton and Tait 1952; Gellner 1969; Hart 1981; Akbar and Hart 1984), the presumption of the title to power has long favoured the emergence of a particular house, that of the sheikh, and operated against other claimants – a reality that goes against the 'egalitarian' image which in principle may seem to reign within the tribal structure.

This 'non-egalitarianism' has been reinforced by the socio-economic transformations Iraq has undergone since the end of the nineteenth century. The classical *'ashira* (of the Bedouin type, or functioning according to a Bedouin ideology) has undergone profound alterations since the Ottoman reforms of the nineteenth century. The Ottoman Porte introduced the requirement to register land (*tapu*) by those who had worked it for a period of ten years. These use rights entailed exemption from state taxation, with the state retaining the right to repossess non-exploited land. This reform gave birth to a regime of peasant private property and profoundly modified the social and political relations at the heart of the tribe as well as its relations with the outside world. Under the British Mandate, the English repealed the Ottoman laws and introduced more radical measures, including many that politically favoured the power of the sheikhs. Sheikhs were no longer elected, but compelled recognition on the basis of their wealth and trans-local political alliances.

Consequently, the links of solidarity among tribe members weakened, without entirely disappearing, and a massive rural exodus to the cities threw tribal members back on the connections of their *hamula* and their house (*bayt*). This segmentation was encouraged and accelerated by the agrarian reforms of 1958 and 1970, conferring private property according to the principles of redistribution of land to peasants, offering them various technical aid and resources, thus making the peasantry more autonomous as a group. In this short period, in which the settled population sought to 'de-tribalize' the country, new forms of political cohesion appeared, totally or partly based on lineage solidarities. This tendency also marked the urban social fabric structured by houses. Part of local political power (particularly in the countryside) thus passed from the tribe and the sheikhdoms to the state. The development of the state brought in its wake the disappearance of tribal organizations to the extent that the tribe is a political entity requiring a certain autonomy of decision-making in order to continue to exist. At the local level, village communities survived or developed with certain forms (at the level of internal solidarity) more or less similar to classic tribal organization – but with the difference that the village communities exercised local control without imposing political power over a larger region or neighbouring communities of the same type.

Thus, generally speaking, the appearance and development of the post-colonial state saw the tribes continuing to exist, integrating themselves more or less easily within the state order which, often by violence, became pluri-ethnic and pluri-tribal state. In very recent Iraqi history, one can point to certain groups being arbitrarily transformed into 'tribes' in the successive censuses, as the state sought to control the population, or being encouraged (by pragmatism or fear) to put themselves under the protections of a long-established tribe.

Of course, there are other factors explaining this expanded use of tribal affiliation: in our fieldwork in the region of Bahdinan, we have established that Iraqi Kurdistan has suffered the consequences of the wars, deportation, repression, immigration and the loss in land value of vast tracts, as well as industrialization, globalization, etc. All these factors have invariably favoured the re-emergence of tribes and other types of particularism, ever-new tribes. However, it is interesting to observe how these factors have produced a double and contradictory effect. On the one hand, they have undermined the bases of influence of the old tribal groupings by liberating individuals from links with their groups of origin; on the other hand, they have brought about new social realities over which the old tribes had yet to extend their control. The distribution and attribution of these social and symbolic material 'surpluses' have become the 'broth' of culture that nourishes the new tribalism in its claim to participate directly in the political and economic mechanisms of the country. Hence the question: will these types of tribal identity – whether invented, dumped or reactivated – survive in a society whose social relations are completely disarticulated and deformed?

To pose the issue this way is not to subscribe to the idea that all tribal reality, or tribalism, is simply an invention of colonialism (yesterday) or the post-colonial state (today). Despite the modern current that has recharged tribal phenomena, this 'institution' is inscribed within a history of the *longue durée*, within a complex system of ethnic, religious, religious denominational, social and politico-military relations. Certain tribes living in Iraq today have an active history going back several centuries! Furthermore, tribes and local groups are not totally devoted to a permanent quest for political power: the relations between the majority of members of the large and important tribes are generally limited to the sphere of everyday social life. In retrospect, at the level of the sheikhs and the main houses, the links of filiation, descent and alliance have taken a quite different form. Undoubtedly, their mobilization and their proximity to the central power could confer various advantages on the rest of the tribe and increase the success of members' claims to benefit from the distribution of land, arms, economic means and honorific positions, or assure access (for them or their children) to certain politico-symbolic positions, for example, entry into the regime's elite paramilitary forces (Saddam's Special Presidential Guard and Republican Guard), or the military-industrial complex. Such practices in turn exert a reciprocal pressure of subordination on tribe members and a sense of having an asymmetrical debt towards the sheikhs and, via them, to the central power.[15]

Under these conditions, the relations between the various tribes close to the state power may develop relatively peacefully or, on the contrary, be accompanied by violent conflicts. In most cases, the struggles occur mainly between the old established groups and new groupings seeking a political role. In the absence of any strong competition, the new tribes have no chance of gaining tangible power. Even if successful, the position of any new tribe tends to be unstable and fragile in the long term. Nor was the force of the old grouping necessarily diminished by the loss of various high-level posts in the state. For example, most of the tribes in the Sunni Triangle in north-west Iraq who participated in or supported the central power in Iraq before the rise of the Ba'ath Party in 1968 are still very much present on the political military and national scene. This explains why the appearance of any new tribe close to the governing group can result in very serious social and political conflicts. But, equally, the reduction, just as much as the enlargement, of the number of tribes involved in decision-making can unsettle the politico-social equilibrium.

The structures of Saddam's political power

It is profoundly wrong to reduce Saddam Hussein's political power base solely to the tribal dimension, especially since the tribal group, house (*bayt*) and kindred (*ahl*) occupy a determinate place within the state. The political system combined three overlapping levels: the religious denominational cum political; the tribal cum regionalist (on which we focus here); and the politico-institutional order (not subject to analysis in the present essay). However, in reality these levels do not present themselves neatly separated. For example, the politico-institutional power was articulated around eight centres of decision-making:

1. the Revolutionary Command Council (RCC), which was officially the most important Iraqi political institution;
2. the Special Presidential Guard (around 14,000) in charge of Saddam Hussein's security and placed under the command of the President's own direct kindred (his younger son Qusai);

3. the Republican Guard, a hand-picked military unit of about 35 men usually commanded by members of the Albu Nasir tribe (Saddam Hussein's tribe) or by someone from the town of Tikrit;

4. the militias, which were composed of two organizations, the more important being Saddam Hussein's Fedayin or Commandos, about 60,000 men; the other, the Popular Army 'Al-Jaysh al Sha'bi', also about 60,000 men, a sort of party militia;[16]

5. the intelligence and security services;

6. the regional command of the Ba'ath Party;

7. the army; and

8. the government.

Of course, all these centres are not of equal importance. For example, belonging to the RCC and being under the direction of the Ba'ath Party would not totally guarantee having the ear of Saddam Hussein. But to be direct kindred or from the same house or tribe and in the Special Presidential Guard would assure a very important position in the hierarchy of the regime.

Saddam's personal mythology

Saddam Hussein reinforced his position of power by identifying himself, publicly, with many figures drawn from Mesopotamian, Islamic and modern Arab/Third World history. For example, he sometimes presented himself as descended from the neo-Babylonian king, Nebuchadnezzar; and in other circumstances as a direct descendant of the Bani Hashim house (*bayt*), which is the house of the Prophet Muhammed and his cousin and son-in-law, Ali, even going so far as to rebaptize his natal village (Al-'Ouje near the town of Tikrit) as Um Al-Qura (the name used by Arabs in the time of the Prophet for the town of Mecca). He had the words Allah Akbar (God is Great) inscribed on the Iraqi flag. Saddam Hussein also gave himself the name Al Mansur Bi-Allah (honorific title of the Caliph conquering Andalusian Omawide – Mohammad Ibn Abi 'Amir, called 'the victorious' or, more precisely, 'the one to whom Allah gave victory'). On top of this, and following the Muslim theological texts which recognize the 101 names of God (Allah), the official Iraqi media displayed 100 names attributed to Saddam Hussein! Hundreds of books, colloquia, articles, films etc. by Iraqi, Arab and European authors were devoted to legitimizing this enterprise. Here I mention only one example (Al-Rijebi al-Hussayni 1980), very little known either to the public or specialists, which for political reasons and reasons specific to Saddam Hussein's own family, was very quickly banned and withdrawn from Iraqi libraries.

Saddam's house

Let us now examine the articulations that operate between powers (central and local political power, military, religious) and the contemporary tribal structure, focusing on the case of Albu Nasir, the tribe of Saddam Hussein and most of those who occupied the key positions in the Iraqi state between 1968 and 2003.

I

Above all else, the effectiveness of any group that aspires to a political role is determined by its size and political importance. This explains why tribes as large as Dulaymi, Juburi, Albaydi and Shammar maintained important positions and their closeness to state power despite the change of regimes. Tribes at the heart of the state might have as many as hundreds of active members. Saddam Hussein's tribe (Albu Nasir) was initially at a major handicap, knowing that its tribe, its own house (even its nuclear family), was not of a size sufficient to 'furnish' a cadre of active members. Which is why the tribal orbit grew to include distant relations (kin), friends from the same region, favourites and old companions on the road to political power.[17] Very quickly, the numerical 'weakness' of Saddam's tribe was transformed into a force of quasi-monopolization of key posts by the descendants of the Albu Nasir – to such an extent that, over the years, Saddam Hussein succeeded in building a complex power structure in which the tribe, the house and kindred were his first circle of protection. Even early on, it was due to his distant cousin Ahmed Hassan al-Bakr, the first President of the Ba'athist republic after the 1968 *coup d'etat* (by origin from the same tribe but a different house, Albu Mosallat is the house of Saddam's mother, and Albu Khattab is the house of his four half-brothers), that Saddam Hussein became the second most important person in the regime. It was thus in his cousin's shadow that Saddam Hussein put together the power that allowed him to succeed him in 1979.

Saddam Hussein's father being dead, it was with the help of his mother's house (in particular his maternal uncle, Khairallah Tulfah) that he found the capacity to advance himself. In 1963, he married his matrilateral cross-cousin (Sajida Khairallah Tulfah). She gave him five children, two sons and three daughters. Naturally, cross-cousins and half-brothers very soon occupied important posts. His brother-in-law and matrilateral cross-cousin, Adnan Khairallah Tulfah, passed rapidly from the rank of colonel to a post of Minister of Defence and would become one of the few military members of the RCC, the supreme organ of power in Iraq. Three of his half-brothers, from the second marriage of his mother with one of his cousins, Ibrahim Hassan of the lineage of Albu Khattab, occupied positions of responsibility from 1974 onwards, notably in the field of security. This overburdening weight of maternal cross-cousins and half-brothers was counterbalanced from the second half of the 1980s with a massive influx of parallel patrilateral cousins (notably of the lineage Albu Ghafour and the house of al-Majid). The most celebrated of these was Ali Hassan al-Majid, a member of the regional command of the Ba'ath Party, who was for a time Minister of Defence, and responsible for the military and security aspects of part of the north of the country (the Kurdish region) and later for the province of Salah al-Din (Tikrit and the region of Saddam Hussein). It did not take long for the two branches, maternal and paternal, to begin contesting the division of power. For, as distant as the tribal and family links may be, and despite the image given by this 'collective' participation, definitive decisions are taken in a supremely authoritarian and brutal character, contrasting with the familiar 'collectivism' of the Middle East. Saddam Hussein thus did not hesitate in the mid 1980s to temporarily cut off his three half-brothers when they protested against the marriage of his two daughters to his parallel patrilateral cousins, the famous Hussein Kamel al-Majid and his brother Saddam Kamel al-Majid, who were assassinated by men from their own tribe.

The second circle of power was formed around the Tikritis, already numerous in the army under the British on the eve of the First World War. They were very well represented in the security services. At its height, the phenomena was such that Saddam Hussein, from the end of the 1970s, issued a decree prohibiting the use of the name of the region after a person's surname (*laqab*). From 1973 he stopped calling himself Saddam al-Tikriti and used Hussein, his father's name.

The third circle of Saddam Hussein's power involved the tribes of the Sunni triangle: the Dulaymis, the Juburis, the 'Ubeydis and the 'Azzawis. All the same, he kept long-standing faithfuls, from whom he had nothing to fear, close to himself, and in particular at the heart of the RCC and in regional command of the Ba'ath Party.

II

The effectiveness of the tribe depends equally on its own internal relations. The most acute problem on any tribe's agenda is the relation between its constitutive kindred base, patrilateral cousins (close and distant), the members of the same house, and the members 'recruited' though marriage. The latter (those not of Albu Nasir origin) are given the inferior status of 'outsiders' by contrast to the 'principal' and pure relations. Yet this probably does not have as much effect on the degree of political sympathy as the preferences of non-blood relations often being more conditioned by material and political interests. Which is why close relations (kin) are often given positions as personal servants of the chief and his guard, allowing them to exercise an informal supplementary influence over the leader.

Any modification of the rank, status and function of members of the tribe linked to the genealogical kernel and its generational renewal can represent a serious threat to those in the first generation. At some point, if conflicts at the heart of the group are not settled then it cannot sustain further blows. This became very clear at the end of the 1970s, with the political and then physical liquidation of the former President (distant cousin and descendant of the house of Albu Bakr) and his entourage by the house of Saddam (from the lineage of Albu Ghafur). The second renewal (again violent) was in the 1990s, when the subtle equilibrium which had been established between the three major groups was broken: the first group was the parallel patrilateral cousins who had become sons-in-law (descendants of Albu Ghafur); the second was the half-brothers who were linked to the lineage of Albu Khattab (by blood/ filiation and marriage); the last was the direct kindred (*Ahl*) of Saddam, and who in fact functioned as the core active group (his two sons and in particular his oldest son Udai. After the 30 years of strategic alliances and marriages, conflicts and physical elimination, the conclusion to be drawn was that it was not the members of the Albu Nasir tribe, with all its lineages and houses, who united members around the central power. Rather, it was the kindred (*Ahl*) who stood at the forefront, even when the tribal ethic (surviving or revived) held it together internally. But the weakening of the tribe and the house to the benefit of kindred, in turn, reduced its cohesive force and the absolute hegemony of persons belonging to the kernel of kindred, and hence bears finally on the competence of the group. For kindred can neither substitute for political, juridical and social structures nor for kinship and tribal organization.

III

Another important factor for the political success of a tribe is the personality of its chief. In the old, large tribes, the faults of the chief could be partly compensated by the competence of his close entourage; in the new tribes which have a major political role, it is simply not possible to confer the leading role on a weak personality (except in certain African countries or in the Arab-Persian Gulf, for example, where the weak personality of the chief is consolidated by support of 'foreign bayonets'). Access to such a position by an outsider is thus always fleeting.[18]

The moment of succession of a new chief is linked to all sorts of 'ill-omened' consequences, whether the tribe is old or new. If, for the old groups, the form of transmission of power was relatively elaborate; the majority of the new ones disintegrate with the loss of their leaders. This is what happened, for example, with the clans of Idi Amin or Bokassa. Of noted contrast is the record of 'longevity' of the clans of West Africa (M. Keita, Sekou Touré), whose origins go back to the Middle Ages, or of the Sharifite line of Hassan II in Morocco and the descendants of the dynasty of Ibn Saud in Arabia, whose active political role is attested since the eighteenth century.

But equally, within the tribe, the vulnerability of both old and new factions at the moment of chiefly succession also comes from the fact that, willingly or not, the chief may have to crush their families for the sake of the 'wider picture'. The departure of the chief creates a particular void which cannot be filled except at the price of sharp confrontations and 'settling of accounts'. The cohesion of factions within a tribe is sorely tested when important political successes are at issue. At the time of the succession of a chief of a faction to the supreme post in the state, the style and the character of his relations with his near entourage changes considerably. Typical pretexts for violating tribal or factional unity at this stage include discord between 'kindred', or contempt for certain rules and basic tribal traditions etc.

IV

A further feature necessary for the political prosperity of the tribe is a feminine element in the chief's entourage. Even in societies where the cultural tradition ascribes mothers and wives a very secondary role, the positions of spouses or even mothers of the chief are always important. It is true that the role played by women in this type of masculine-dominated tribal society remains very polyvalent and deeply misunderstood. On the one hand, local tradition ordinarily grants mothers and wives, even if of chiefs, secondary roles. Nonetheless, at the higher levels of political power this role becomes very important. We know that Sajida Khairallah Tulfah, the wife of Saddam Hussein (his cross cousin) and Sabha Tulfah (his mother) have helped the political career of their husband/son considerably. The wife or the mother of the chief exercises an undoubted influence over the daily mood and are in touch with the secrets of the most confidential political business. Sustaining rigorous respect for certain traditions, and hence the affirmation of internal unity, also depends very much upon the savoir-faire and mode of communication of these pre-eminent ladies. They supply the appropriate tone to relations between women and seek to manage family conflicts. It is precisely these kind of moves that Saddam Hussein employed, at first without success, in the episode of the flight of Hussein Kamal, his cousin and son-in-law to Jordan, before eventually achieving an internal settlement with a group of secessionists in 1996.

On the other hand, and still following the logic of the tribe, we can find among the group associated with Saddam Hussein much recourse to alliance strategies of a close marriage (so-called 'Arab marriage'). This may also be explained by the negative role very often imputed to women from the point of view of group development. For, if the matrimonial links of the chief become excessively numerous and wide ranging, feminine favouritism may obscure the internal rules of the game within the tribe and thus reduce its capacity to act as a unified group. This fear of group dislocation is well illustrated by the events of the second marriage of Saddam Hussein, in 1989, with Samira Shabandar, the ex-wife of the Director General of Iraqi Airways (and an outsider to the Albu Nasir tribe). This second marriage unsettled the position of the entire Albu Musallat and Albu Khattab lineages inside the state, and, especially, the house of Tulfah, and precipitated the physical elimination of the Minister of Defence, Adan Khairallah Tulfah (matrilateral cross-cousin and brother-in-law of Saddam Hussein).

In other cultures and societies, strategies of matrimonial alliance have played an important role in political success, notably for Ferdinand Marcos and B. Aquino in the Philippines, Ali Bhutto in Pakistan and others across the world, thanks to the kinship links of their wives or mothers. This is because strategies of this type create conditions particularly favourable to rapid expansion of the role of these groups. Polygamy especially makes it possible to form, in a very brief time, the genealogical kernel of a tribe and associated substructures of birth, and guarantees an introduction to a different level of the social hierarchy. In one generation, the group can be in a position to constitute a ramified system of links as much at the heart of the social elite as with their client groups of inferior social strata. Having taken this initial step, the new political clans quickly become almost indistinguishable from classic tribes, whose positions are so difficult to breach from the outside.

V

The stability and the unity of many tribes are reinforced by various types of cult, the public glorification of the chief being one of the most widespread forms ideological influence over the members of the concrete group and the social environment. Such cults serve to isolate and, ideally, to distinguish the tribal community spiritually and politically from the rest of the population, thereby affirming the *asabiyya* – solidarity based on the links of kinship as the supreme value in life. Although often aided by other specific religious practices (for example, confraternities) to secure a monopoly of influence over the members of the group, the aspiration of the tribal hierarchy may be realized by other routes. Thus in the Bahdinan region (Iraqi Kurdistan), where religious traditions are solidly attached to the Naqshbandi Sufi order, this is in turn largely legitimated and ensconced within the absolute political authority of the Barazani chiefdom and the centralization of decision-making on all questions large and small that confront the members. The exercise of these spiritual-political legitimations creates another ideological effect, affirming among the members of the group not only the differences that distinguish them from others, but also their superiority. For example, the belief held by various Shi'ite houses and groups, of having a direct genealogical link with the honoured ancestors (the prophet, Ali and so on) articulates the political group's objectively combative mood.

VI

The viability of tribes or clans involved in the political game grows tangibly with the enlargement of their activity outside the initial sphere of their principal occupation. This involves guided migration by members of the group, but equally the activation of links with adjacent kin and or compatriots of a different division. The new ecological niche creates possibilities highly favourable to quantitative evolution of tribal/clan structures. The groups that leave the peripheral ethnic regions for the capital undergo particularly noticeable transformations. Positions of responsibility, foreign travel or access to the centralized system of distribution of material goods by one member of the tribe offer openings for social betterment (although unequal) for all of the substructures. A further consequence of migration is the appearance of a network of ramified groups, arising from the permutations of the leader; this, if physically extended to other regions, will 'acquire' in each new area a clientele with which the leader's followers will maintain contact. This is why the relations of forces of the governing elite concentrated in capital cities is determined not only through formal nomenclature but also by tribal links maintained in the periphery.

VII

Lastly, in order to understand more fully aspects of tribalism in Iraq it is necessary to go back some fifty years or more to a time when Iraq was evolving in three different ways. Initially there was a contradictory trend: on the one hand, a process of modernization had been launched by the state and the authoritarian Ba'ath party; while, on the other, the top levels of political organization were drawing on the resources of tribalism in order to hold on to power. In addition, prior to the Iran–Iraq war (1980–9) there was a retribalization of polities and society imposed from above (i.e. by the authorities). People were recruited to certain state institutions and the elite army corps essentially on the basis of their tribal and regional origins, to the extent that some military, police and intelligence bodies came to almost perfectly reflect tribal structures in their set-up. Hence, the 1980s and 90s saw the beginnings of 'the tribalization of the state', particularly in its coercive functions. This led in the 1990s to tribal leaders declaring their allegiance to Saddam Hussein. Tribalism came to form the fourth pillar of the Ba'ath regime, alongside a form of politicized Islam, Arabism and the country's glorious Mesopotamian heritage.

None of these characteristics of the political groups (tribe, large house or regional group) are speculative abstractions. They are directly related to the viability of tribal groupings, and their constructive and destructive aspects will periodically erupt in the course of ongoing political evolution.

Tribalism after the Second Gulf War: the early occupation (April 2003 – July 2004)

The Americans' initial political plan once they had 'landed' may be summed up as democratization, liberalization and modernization: in short, the exact opposite of the received idea of tribalism, which was conceived as a vestige of the past rather than as a plan for the future. Nonetheless, certain voices within the US civilian and military administration insisted on the 'useful contribution' that the tribes could make in stabilizing the situation on the ground, particularly in the area of security.

After a few months of wavering, and during which the Americans did not take the tribal factor into account, the tribes returned to the scene, no longer regarded as an outmoded tool of governance but as sociopolitical structures of considerable strategic utility on the ground. In November 2003, when real difficulties were first encountered, US military personnel posted in Iraq produced a document setting out a potential role for tribalism in reconstruction policy, albeit with some exaggeration:

> At least three quarters of the population of Iraq belong to one of the one
> hundred and fifty of the nation's tribes. Many large tribes contain a mix
> of religions and ethnicities ranging from Sunni to Shia, Kurd to Arab to
> Persian. Tribal confederacies can date thousands of years, or can be the
> creation of political expediency in the past decade. If properly engaged by
> CPA and CJTF-7, Iraqi tribes can become a key factor in the promotion of a
> safe and secure environment in Iraq.
>
> (Alexander, Kyle and McCallister 2003:1)

Although this document greatly overstates the extent of tribal affiliation among Iraqis, these US servicemen were clearly conscious of the role tribes could play, since they perceived them as politically oriented structures:

> An individual's stated attachment to a particular genealogical heritage is,
> at the tribal level, partly a political act ... In claiming a particular ancestry,

people necessarily align themselves with a given political charter and
strategy, which cannot be glossed simply as kinship.

(ibid.:8)

Towards the end of 2003 the US army started working to influence tribal
positions without the local Iraqi players, such as Islamicist (Sunni and Shi'a)
and ethnic (Kurdish) parties, realizing the significance of this step. Because
of their ability to mobilize or cause trouble on the ground, tribal chiefs were
courted for different and even contradictory reasons: the Coalition (US and
British) forces wanted to ensure security, while certain Iraqi politicians and
groups wanted them to provide support on the ground, to counterbalance
other competing political parties, or merely to act as vote-catching machines.

In 2004, several Iraqi politicians were already appealing to tribal legitimacy
in order to attain positions of power in the national hierarchy. The first Iraqi
interim government appointed 1 June 2004 included several members of
important tribes: in addition to President Ghazi al-Yawar (nephew of the
sheikh of the powerful Shammar tribal confederation), there was Adnan
al-Janabi (Secretary of State without portfolio, from the Janabi tribe; his
father had held an important position under Saddam Hussein), Malik Dohan
al-Hasan (Justice Minister, Jebur tribal confederation), Leila Abdul-Latif
(Employment Minister, al-Tamim tribal confederation) and Luay Hatem
(Transport Minister, his father was the leader of the Ors-Erris tribe). All these
people also had impressive CVs (with doctorates, directorships in foreign
companies, fluency in foreign languages, long lists of important contacts etc.),
which illustrates just how much sheikhs have changed: no longer measured by
their bravery, guns and raiding success, they have become a symbolic asset,
blending tradition and modernity.

Tribalism after the transfer of sovereignty (June 2004)

By the end of June 2004, sovereignty had been partially transferred to the
Iraqis. At the same time, an interim government of national union had been
formed. In July, a national conference of 1,000 people felt to be representative
of Iraqi society was set up, including a moderate proportion of tribal
representatives (70 members, as against 140 representatives of the political
parties, 170 academics etc.). In parallel with this formal political development,
the insurrection had already regained most of the Sunni Arab region, and
there had been considerable activism from certain Shi'ite militias, particularly
those supporting Muqtada al-Sadr.

As a response to the spread of this political and military crisis, the US
army made considerable efforts in the second half of 2004 to hold successful
negotiations with the main tribal groups in the Sunni triangle, so as to regain

control of the towns north and east of Baghdad without having to intervene militarily. That was at the height of the *jihadi* insurgency in Fallujah, between April and November 2004. The following year, 2005, turned out to be a pivotal year in the modern history of Iraq: for the first time in centuries, a Shi'a-dominated government was formed in Baghdad and a constitution acknowledging this new status quo was approved by referendum. At the same time, the Sunni Arab population, still reeling from the shock of 2003, found itself marginalized and sank into an insurrection that was becoming increasingly *jihadi* in nature. Given the ineffectiveness of the Iraqi government forces and the collapse of the coalition forces, the Americans turned *en masse* to the main tribal groups in the Sunni triangle before taking control of this region.

The arrival of General David Petraeus as Commander-in-Chief of US forces in Iraq in 2006 accentuated this situation still further. Having studied history at Princeton, he did not hesitate in appointing dozens of anthropologists to advise him, including the former Australian army colonel David Kilcullen and the anthropologist Montgomery McFate. For the first time since Vietnam, the Pentagon established a programme, with a budget of some US$ 40 million a year, to place anthropologists within combat units on the ground (the 'Human Terrain System').

The US decision to strengthen the tribes

After many setbacks, the Americans finally realized that empowering the tribes as political actors and partners at a national level made little sense, given their interests and allegiances at local levels, unless they were used as government intermediaries in the fields of territorial and social control. They could secure critical zones by distributing resources, arm quasi-militias, gather intelligence by infiltrating networks and liaise directly with local authorities etc. Indeed, through the tribal revival movement (*Sahwa*, 'Awakening'), the Pentagon made use of tribes as local power networks in its counter-insurgency strategy, distributing aid designed to win hearts and minds. This tribal policy meant supplying them with funds, support and weaponry, in the form of tactical air support, communications and even Abrams M1 tanks, as in the case of the measures taken to protect Sheikh Sattar Abu Risha (Klein 2007). One of the results of this policy, however, was a rather lax attitude towards crime (particularly the substantial illegal trade in oil) and iniquitous practices such as vendettas and honour-based justice (Graff 2007). This destabilized the central authorities at a time when the Iraqi security forces were not fully operational and before the overhaul of the legal system was complete.

While some 'experts' were quick to promote the 'stabilizing' role of tribes,[19] the actors on the ground soon found they had to deal with constraints and contradictions resulting from the tribes' strategies for holding on to local power. The tribes are highly pragmatic and focus on their own economic and political interests, to the extent that they are often accused of double dealing. They sabotaged infrastructure facilities and sites formerly under their protection, on the excuse that they had been unfairly deprived of these facilities. Similarly, many tribal members were implicated in the insurrection and in taking part in militias or terrorist activities. To counter such activities, the US army established a number of channels of influence and action in certain areas, in parallel with other initiatives to engage with people in authority: businessmen, retired military officers, Muslim clerics, neighbourhood or village headmen (*mukhtars*) and elected officials.

As was the case in Fallujah, it is often not contact with the tribal sheikh that works best, but instead the relationships that can be built with the imams in the mosques or with the *mukhtars*.[20] In this respect, the net outcome of the tribal Awakening (*Sahwa*) movement in non-security fields (such as on the social front, or in reconstruction) remains equivocal. The factors that led the tribes in al-Anbar province to side with the US army were their rejection of al-Qaeda's ideology and practices, as well as the insurrection's adverse effects on commercial activities, both legal and illegal. General Petraeus rightly remarked that the tribes in al-Anbar 'all have a truck company, they all have a construction company and they all have an import-export business', and that meant that al-Qaeda 'was bad for business' (Eisenstadt 2007). In other words, although the tribal alliance was necessary, it was not in itself decisive in reducing the fighting or satisfactorily securing administrative, military and economic sites in the country. Consequently, the tribes' engagement with security remained limited overall:

> Nevertheless, the coalition's engagement efforts have yielded a number
> of modest but important benefits. Because the sheikhs are generally well
> connected and plugged into various tribal and non-tribal networks (essential
> if they are to look after the interests of their tribe), they have generally
> proven useful as sources of information and advice and as vectors of
> influence among their tribesmen...
>
> On the down side, tribal engagement has not brought about a total halt
> in attacks in tribal areas of influence. It is not clear whether this is due to the
> sheikhs' inability to influence younger fighters – who are heavily represented
> in the ranks of the insurgents, or certain sections or subsections of their
> tribe.
>
> Furthermore, efforts to employ tribes to protect strategic infrastructure
> such as oil pipelines and electrical power lines have failed. And until
> recently, sheikhs have rarely delivered on promises to provide tribal levies

for anti-AQI militias such as the 'Desert Protectors' in Husaybah and the Albu Nimr police force in al-Furat or to provide large numbers of conscripts for the Iraqi Security Forces. This is particularly telling, given the high rates of unemployment in Iraq today. (ibid.)

The limitations of the tribal *Sahwa* were mitigated in US strategy by the recruitment of civilian militias, the 'Concerned Local Citizens' (CLC). These included many former insurgents, jobless young men, demobilized soldiers from the former army and even ex-criminals, roughly 103,000 men in total, who were paid US$10 a day by the US commander up until January 2009. The *Sahwa* councils and the CLC were concentrated geographically in the area around Baghdad and in al-Anbar province and were composed largely (80 per cent) of Sunni Arabs. This sector of the population was confined in gated communities created by the Coalition using barriers, encircling walls (made of sandbags or concrete blocks) and a biometric census. This solution – walling off towns and neighbourhoods – seems to have brought about a lull in the fighting, but can hardly be considered a step towards reconciliation. Instead, it creates divided communities, reinforcing barriers in people's minds: the Sunnis fearing that they will be the victims of violence and economic isolation once the US troops return to their bases, and the Shi'as imagining Sunni neighbourhoods and towns to be hotbeds of Salafi terrorists. Yet the tribal councils and the CLC were presented by the Coalition as a means to promote local security, to protect critical installations and to establish a system for contacting and gathering information from local people.

Concluding remarks: the future of tribalism in Iraq

In the eyes of the political and military authorities in Iraq, tribes are either useful local players or, conversely, factors that destabilize the social order.

Tribes today certainly need the support of the state, or even of other, more global, forces. It is local factors, however, that govern the reproduction of their legitimacy and power. That is precisely the point that Islamic *jihadi* organizations such as al-Qaeda have not grasped. It is worth recalling the example of al-Anbar province, where the strategy devised by US general David Petraeus had some success. He understood that a *jihadi emir* will always try to seize power in the name of an abstract, global, hard-line, radical form of Islam, and will see the local people as just a fraction of the *umma* that he has to lead along God's path. A tribal sheikh, in contrast, draws his legitimacy from his local power base and his relations with the state and beyond. That is precisely what became apparent after 2004. A major conflict of interests and legitimacy between the Sunni Arabs of western Iraq and the Islamic *jihadis* and radicals was therefore inevitable (for further examination of this question, see Dawod 2004).

The US army's partial success in the Iraqi tribal context is not without its contradictions, however. It makes use of the tribes solely for security purposes, but once mobilized they cease being passive and become actors in their own right on the political stage, where they seek to make gains both locally and nationally. They then try to dominate other tribes and demand that their own customs and habits should prevail over those of the state.

Finally, while Iraqi society is not tribal in its entirety, it does includes tribes that, however, no longer enjoy the autonomy they used to have. They seek the support of the state and/or US forces so as to remain or become political actors, often to the advantage of certain sheikhs who aspire to local or even national political office. To achieve this end, tribes often clash with political parties or religious or ethnic representatives over their respective interests. This is seen to be happening in Iraq still today.

Acknowledgements

I am much indebted to Maurice Godelier, Jonathan Friedman, Lucette Valensi, Edouard Conte, Chris Ballard and Naâma Trabelsi for their comments and assistance.

NOTES

1   For some, this is to be explained as a consequence of the logic of society. This was already the position, a century ago, of Taylor and James Frazer and the first generation of the English school of anthropology. Frazer said (and it was also the opinion of Taylor) that one should privilege the study of the same phenomena appearing in societies without contact with each other. For him, this showed at work the deep social and anthropological processes that *societies have in common*, setting aside their differences. Now, precisely, accenting difference has been the chief specialty of the French school of anthropology – Marcel Mauss and his *'total social fact'*, which is in reality nothing but a *specific* complex of a given society. Mauss also launched a rather excessive attack on Frazer and through him the whole of English anthropology: 'Intellectualism considers only resemblances … To give a scientific picture, it is necessary to consider the differences and for that one needs a sociological method' (Mauss, *Année Sociologique* 1:161). For a 'holistic' presentation of this episode, see Dumont 1979, esp. pp. 324–50.

2   It has been repeatedly shown that, when it comes to Iraq, some Western researchers are often reduced to relying on reports with hidden purposes or ends dictated by the politico-military and financed by the intelligence services of certain regional or world powers.

3   Claude Lévi-Strauss makes a connection between Boas's analysis of the Kwakiutl
     house and European noble houses. By underlining the similarity between these
     institutions, he defined the house as 'a moral person holding an estate made up of
     material and immaterial wealth which perpetuates itself through the transmission
     of its name down a real or imaginary line, considered legitimate as long as this
     continuing can express itself in the language of kinship or of affinity, and most
     often, of both' (Lévi-Stauss 1983: 174). See also Lévi-Strauss 1984 :189–241, 1986;
     Lévi-Strauss and Pierre Lamaison 1987. The later writings by Lévi-Strauss on the
     house have provoked a large number of colloquia, seminars, articles and other
     types of anthropological literature around the world (see, for example, Macdonald
     and members of ECASE 1987; Carsten and Hugh-Jones 1995).

4   Among the factual studies of tribes in Iraq that I would consider valuable, at least
     in part (some are a little dated), are Al-Hassan 1937; Salim 1955; Al-Wardi 1972;
     Al-Tahir 1972; and, following the instructions of the Iraqi authorities, in particular,
     the Minister of the Interior and the *Office of Tribal Affairs*, a 'well oriented'
     encyclopaedia has been published, al-'Amiri 1992–5.

5   In invoking the case of the new Iraqi bourgeoisie, one must be aware of how the
     'native' utilization of sociological terms and categories, such as 'social class' relates
     to Iraqi social realities. According to what Maurice Godelier would call the classic
     definition of class, the starting point is in relation to the process of production,
     i.e. ownership of land and other means of production. Thus we become workers
     or masters etc. But this notion of class is very specific and does not correspond
     to that existing in the former Ottoman provinces that made up the Iraqi state in
     1921. Why? Because during this epoch of modern Iraqi history, as within many
     societies across the world, it was only through birth that once could receive rights
     to ownership of a means of production that could be communal (for example,
     for all the members of a lineage, house or tribe). Of course, certain lineages or
     houses had undoubted advantages over others in the division of common goods
     (a point to which we shall return). Thus, belonging to a social class (according to
     the Weberian or Marxian definition) is not restricted by economic definitions. It is
     only when individuals are free in their person that they rediscover their economic
     mode of class belonging, as such and such a class which, Marx says: exists in itself
     after having become conscious of itself as such. See Godelier 2001.

6   In 1940, the Grand Mufti of Jerusalem, Haj Amin al-Husseini sought refuge in
     Baghdad, from whence he issued violent anti-Jewish denunciations. Together with
     the apparent English weakness, and encouraged by the Germans, this agitation led
     to the military coup led by General Amin Zaki Sulaiman and Rashid Ali al-Gailani.
     On 1 and 2 June 1941, the Jews of Baghdad (in a highly anti-Zionist epoch) were the
     object of violent attacks (the *Farhoud*).

7   Until recently, Iraq had an ancient and very important Jewish community.
     Enjoying, like Christians, a community status under the authority of an exilarch.

During the Abbasside period and up until the Hashemite monarchy, Jews had an important administrative role in the country and also as artisans, in commerce and banking. Speaking Arabic or Kurdish – according to the ethnic regions – seemingly well-integrated with the rest of the population, Iraqi Jews were not touched at first by the Zionist movement. Around 1935, however, they suffered various attacks by Muslims and anti-Semitism grew in Iraq after 1940. The governments of Nouri Saïd and his successors in effect saw an easy way to defuse various social tensions arising from their political programmes through government propaganda accusing Jews, whether of Zionism or communism. These governments played a key part in encouraging the hostility of part of the population against them, a movement that was in turn exacerbated by the Arab defeat in 1948. Even though a number of Jews were involved side by side with Muslims in the founding of the Anti-Zionist League, which was dissolved in 1947 on the pretext of communism, Iraqi Jews were forced to emigrate by government measures taken against them. In 1947, there were about 120,000 Jews, making up 2.6 per cent of the total population but 7 per cent of the urban population of Iraq: it has been estimated that around 80,000 of this number left Iraq in the years that followed. Other waves of emigration took place in 1956, 1967 and 1968–9; this last wave followed attacks, repressions and public assassinations by the public political power directed by the Ba'ath Party (at the time, by Ahmed Hassan Al-Bakr – Saddam Hussein). At the beginning of the 1990s, a new and perhaps final wave (of several thousands) of Kurdish Jews (or those claiming to be) emigrated to Israel via Turkey. Today, it is impossible to know if there are still Jews in Iraq and the exact state of their community (whether in the Arab or Kurdish parts of the country). For an idea of this tragic episode, see Shiblaq 1987.

8 For an approach to the changing nature of relations between Sunnis and Shi'ites, compare the two articles by Sluglett and Farouk-Sluglett 1978 and 1993. On Shi'ism more generally, one could usefully consult Nakash 1994a and b.

9 Equally, it could be that large fractions of the Sunni population who, under other circumstances, would not have supported Saddam Hussein, were led to do so by the fear of a fundamentalist Shi'ite regime. At the same time, outside the holy cities of Karbala and Najaf, many 'secular' Shi'ites probably shared these fears and supported the regime for similar reasons.

10 For a very interesting account of how a society constructs its political universe (taking the case of Morocco), thinks its relation to power and follows a mechanism of allegiance, see Tozy 1999. The work of the Moroccan anthropologist, d'Abdella Hammoudi (1997) also remains very useful (even though the data on the Arab societies of Mashrek is out of date).

11 See various seminars given by the great Ayatollah Mohammad Sadiq al-Sadr (several years before his assassination in 1999 by the Iraqi powers that be). These

seminars were collected and printed in a pamphlet which was rapidly banned in Iraq and then secretly distributed: *Al-Fiqh al-'ashari* (Tribal Jurisprudence).

12 The term *fakhidh* is in general usage by Iraqis to designate patrilineal kinship groups arising from the application of a principle of unilinear descent in which the kinship links extend over four to five generations. A *fakhidh* is thus a set of men and women who consider themselves related as kin (*awlad 'am*) through patrilineal descent from a common ancestor. But, in reality, there is an equivocation around this term: the use of the word *fakhidh* has long been very polyvalent, depending on the region. Other words exist to designate such structures: *bdida* (plural: *bdayid*) or *fnda* (plural: *fned*). Linguistically speaking, the term *fakhidh* signifies 'thigh', as indicated above, while *fnda* is the meaty part, the flesh without the bone. Each *fakhidh* has its chief and often its own name and a specific territorial seat, generally corresponding to a single village or even a part of a village.

13 The word *hamula* means 'carry away' in Arabic. The root *hml* evokes the mutual aid that men of the same *hamula* are supposed to bring to each other. This word, which does not belong to Iraqi Arab society, is used as much in the countryside as among town-dwellers without reflecting the same social structure. Thus, the *hamula* is a group articulated in an agnatic idiom and composed of a variable number of patrilineal units invoking a common ancestor, real or fictive, which the genealogy can trace back – the patrilateral line – for five or six generations. It is virilocal (patrilocal), that is, on marrying, the wife goes to live in the house of the father of her conjoint husband, or in a neighbourhood of the *hamula*, or in the home (*dar*) of their husband. The size of the *hamula* is very variable. There are small *hamula* that number dozens or hundreds of individuals and large *hamula* that can go up to many thousands. The number and the dimension which make up a *hamula* is an important factor determining its power. This factor combines with its political force (access to local and national power), and material wealth. If a large *hamula* is poor and has not succeeded in weaving relations with other larger *hamula* in the local, regional and national ladder, it cannot secure its power and social prestige either in the village or in the urban milieus, nor, consequently, in the area of central political power.

14 In the case of Iraq, the relations that link tribes to the central power pass principally through three channels: the *Bureau of Tribal Affairs*, directed personally by Saddam Hussein and his younger son, Qusai ; the Minister of the Interior through various politico-security representatives; and the Ba'ath Party, through various security services, the paramilitary militia and the Army.

15 Following and elaborating on this logic of the creation of asymmetric debt, *hiba*, Saddam Hussein presented himself for a number of years as Shaykh al-Mashayikh, i.e. the sheikh of all sheikhs, a title used in the great sheikhdoms of the past. This new title suggested to various rich tribes and houses, to build, in the suburbs

of Baghdad and in other towns, various *maudhif* 'guest-houses' in the name of Shaykh al-Mashayikh, i.e. Saddam Hussein.

16 The Commandos were set up by Uday, the elder son of the President, in 1994. They were in charge of (among other things) the security of all those with powerful positions. In the wake of an attempted assassination in 1996, with serious injuries inflicted on Uday, this militia moved to the command of Hussein's younger son, Qusay: he was named responsible for the inter-army Umm al-ma'arik ('mother of all battles') and as Joint Supreme Chief of the armies (jointly with his father). The Popular Army was entrusted to an old comrade of Saddam, Taha Yassine al-Jazrawi (originally from Mosul), who was part of the core group around Saddam Hussein.

17 In 1968 the Ba'ath Party had very few active members and did not have a credible political base among the population from which to draw officers prepared to manage the affairs of state. That is why, after the *coup d'etat* of 1968, the majority of powerful men came from the same tribe (Albu Nasir), the same town (Tikrit), the same region (the Sunni Triangle in the north-west), the same religious denomination (Sunni Islam) and the same ethnic background (Arab). See Farouk-Sluglett and Sluglett 1987.

18 The most delicate question for a tribe or a clan with a role politically situated at the head of the state is to assure the passing of power within the group, and thus to establish a succession without interior disturbances. The cases of Syria, Jordan, Morocco etc. show that one can direct affairs in such a way as to establish a seeming 'tradition' giving direct/immediate kindred (filial) primacy over full-blood brothers, cross-cousins and their descendants. This is not necessarily easily done: in Syria, Rifat al-Assad's refusal to allow power to pass from his late brother (Hafiz al-Assad) to the latter's son (Bashar); in Jordan, the dismissal of Crown Prince Hassan in favour of the sons of Abdullah II.

19 These were the same experts who recommended promoting the tribalization of political relations throughout the Middle East, such as the Israeli Amatzia Baram:

> Provided it maintains a solid cadre of specialists in tribal affairs, the central government in Baghdad has a good chance of being able to use the tribal system to increase social stability in rural areas and keep the country in one piece. By contrast, an attempt to ignore the tribes or dismantle the tribal system would be destabilizing and could even increase the chances of armed conflict.
>
> (Baram 2003)

20 See Eisenstad 2007; and also the account of Operation Alljah in Fallujah by Lt Col. William F. Mullen, commander of the 2nd Battalion, 6th Marine Regiment: 'As for the awakening, that is more of a tribal thing. Tribes have little influence inside Fallujah because of how mixed up the population is.' (Smith 2007a; see also Smith 2007b).

The idea that the Sahwa experience might work in the tribal area of Pakistan is questionable. The *New York Times* published a 'secret' Dept. of Defence report suggesting that US special forces would be sent to organize the tribes in Waziristan in the fight against the Taliban and al-Qaeda (US$350 million over several years to consolidate a tribal border force of 85,000 men). The tribes in this area have long been involved in recurrent alliances and misalliances with the Pakistani armed forces and with Taliban and al-Qaeda combatants, and unlike the Iraqis in al-Anbar, they tend to accept Salafi fundamentalism. See Roggio 2007 and Schmidt, Mazzetti and Gall 2007.

References

Akbar, S. and D. Hart (eds), 1984, *Islam in Tribal Societies. From the Atlas to the Indus*. London: Routledge & Kegan Paul.

Al-'Azzawi, Abbas, 1937, *'Asha'ir al-'Iraq* [The Tribes of Iraq, 3 volumes]. Baghdad.

Al-'Amiri, Thamer 'Abd al-Hassan, 1992–5, *Mawso'at al-'asha'ir al-'iraqiyya* [Encyclopaedia of Iraqi Tribes, 9 volumes]. Baghdad.

Alexander, Christopher (Sergeant), Kyle, Charles M. (Captain) and (Major) William S. McCallister, 2003, 'The Iraqi insurgent movement' (http://www.comw.org/warreport/fulltext/03alexander.pdf, accessed 8 July 2011).

Al-Hassan, Amin, 1929, *Al-hala al-ijtimaiyya li'al-'asha'ir al-'iraqiyya* [The social situation of Iraqi tribes]. Baghdad.

Al-Rijebi al-Hussayni, al-Sayid Ahmad, 1980, *Al-Noujoum al-zawahir fi Shajarat al-sayid al-amir Nasir*. Baghdad: Dar al-Houriya li-tiba'a.

Al-Tahir, 'Abd Al-Jalil, 1972, *Al-'Asha'ir al-'iraqiyya* [The Tribes of Iraq]. Baghdad.

Al-Wardi, Ali, 1965, *Dirasa fi Tabi'at al-mujtama' al-'iraqi* [A Study of the Nature of Iraqi Society]. Baghdad.

——— 1972, *Lamahat ijtimaiyya min tarikh al-Iraq al-hadith* [Social Aspects of the Modern Histories of Iraq, 6 volumes]. Baghdad.

Badie, Bertrand, 1992, *L'Etat Importé, l'Occidentalisation de l'Ordre Politique*. Paris: Fayard.

——— 1993, 'Ruptures et innovations dans l'approche sociologique des relations internationales', *Revue des Mondes Musulmans et de la Méditerranée (RMMM)* 68–9(2–3):65–74.

——— 1995, *La fin des territoires, essai sur le désordre international et sur l'utilité sociale du respect*. Paris: Fayard.

——— 1999, *Un monde sans souveraineté, les Etats entre ruse et responsabilité*. Paris: Fayard.

Baram, Amatzia, 2003, 'The Iraqi tribes and the post-Saddam system', *Iraq Memo* 18 (July 8), (http://www.brookings.edu/views/op-ed/fellows/baram20030708.htm, accessed 9 July 2011).

Batatu, Hanna, 2004, *The Old Social Classes and The Revolutionary Movement In Iraq* (3rd edn). London: Saqi Books.

Bozarslan, Hamit, 1997, *La Question Kurde*. Paris: Presse de Science Po.

Carsten, Janet and Hugh-Jones, Stephen, 1995, *About the House: Lévi-Strauss and Beyond*. Cambridge: Cambridge University Press.

Dawod, Hosham, 1994, 'Ethnicité et Etats au Moyen-Orient: le cas Kurde', *Peuples Méditéranéen* 68–9(July–December):39–56.

Dawod, Hosham (ed.), 2004, *Tribus et pouvoirs en terre d'Islam*. Paris: Armand Colin.

Digard, Jean-Pierre and Bernand, Carmen, 1986, 'De Tehran à Tehuantepec: L'ethnologie au crible des aires culturelles', *Homme* 26(1–2) :63–80.

Dumont, Louis, 1979, *Homo Hierarchicus, le système des castes et ses implications*, Paris: Gallimard, Col Tell (expanded edition).

——— Louis, 1985, 'Identité collective et idéologie universaliste: leur interaction de fait', *Critique* 435:506–18.

——— 1991, *Essais sur l'individualisme: une perspective anthropologique sur l'idéologie moderne*, Paris: Éditions du Seuil.

Eisenstadt, Michael, 2007, 'Tribal engagement lessons learned', *Military Review* (September–October).

Farouk-Sluglett, Marion and Peter Sluglett, 1987, 'From gang to elite: the Iraqi Ba'th party's consolidation of power 1968–1975', *Peuples Méditerranéens* 40 (July–Sept):89–114.

——— 1992, 'L'Irak et le Nouvel Ordre Mondiale', *La Pensée* 285:7–28.

Fernea, Robert A. and Louis W. Roger (eds), 1991, *The Iraqi Revolution of 1958: The Old Social Classes Revisited*. I.B. Tauris: London & New York.

Friedman, Jonathan and M.J. Rowlands (eds), 1977, *The Evolution of Social Systems*. Liverpool: Duckworth.

Friedman, Jonathan, 1979, *System, Structure and Contradiction in the Evolution of Asiatic Social Formations* (Social Studies in Oceania and Southeast Asia, vol. 2). Copenhagen: National Museum of Copenhagen.

Gellner, E., 1969, *The Saints of the Atlas*. Chicago: Chicago University Press.

Godelier, Maurice, 1995, 'Is social anthropology indissolubly linked to the West, its birthplace?', *International Social Science Journal* 143:141–59.

——— 1998, 'Afterword: transformations and lines of evolution'. In *Transformations of Kinship*, eds, Maurice Godelier, Thomas R. Thrautman and Franklin E. Tjon Sie Fat, pp. 386–413. Washington and London: Smithsonian Institution Press.

——— 2001, 'Formes et fonctions du pouvoir politique. A propos des concepts de tribu, ethnie et l'etat', *La Pensée* 325:9–21.

Graff, Peter, 2007, 'Harsh justice where U.S. relies on Iraq tribes', *Washington Post* (4 September).

Hammoudi, d'Abdella, 1997, *Master and Disciple: The Cultural Foundations of Moroccan Authoritarianism.* Chicago and London: University of Chicago Press.

Hart, D., 1981, '*Dadda Atta and his Forty Grandsons: the Socio-Political Organisation of the Ait Atta of Southern Morocco.* Middle East & North African Studies Press: Cambridge.

Klein, Joe, 2007, 'Operation Last Chance', *Time* 170(2).

Leach, Edmund, 1954, *Political System of Highland Burma.* Aldine.

Lévi-Stauss, Claude, 1983, *The Way of the Masks* (trans. S. Modelski). London: Jonathan Cape.

——— 1984, *Paroles données*, Paris: Plon.

——— 1986, 'Histoire et ethnologie', *Les annales E.S.C.*: 12–17.

Lamaisan, Pierre, 1987, 'La Notion de Maison: Entretien avec Claude Levi-Strauss', *Terrain* 9:34–9.

Macdonald, Charles and members of ECASE (ed.) , 1987, *De la hutte au palais: sociétés à maison' en Asie du Sud-Est Insulaire.* Paris: Editions du CNRS.

Mauss, *Année Sociologique* 1:161

Middleton, J. and D. Tait, 1952, *Tribes without Ruler.* London: Routledge & Kegan Paul.

Nakash, Yitzhak, 1994a, *The Shiis of Iraq.* Princeton, New Jersey: Princeton University Press.

Nakash, Yitzhak, 1994b, 'The conversion of Iraq's tribes to Shi'ism', *International Journal of Middle East Studies* 26(3):443–63.

Roggio, Bill, 2007, 'The Pakistan problem and the wrong solution', *Weekly Standard* (21 November 2007) (weblog – http://www.weeklystandard.com/Content/Public/Articles/000/000/014/383wutvv.asp, accessed 9 July 2011).

Salim, Shakir Moustafa, 1955, Ech-Chibayish: An anthropological study of a Marsh village in Iraq. Ph.D. thesis, University of London.

Schmitt, Eric, Mazzetti, Mark and Carlotta Gall, 2007 'U.S. hopes to use Pakistani tribes against al-Qaeda', *New York Times* (19 November 2007).

Shiblaq, Abbas, 1987, *The Lure of Zion.* London: Al-Saqi Books.

Sluglett, Peter, 1976, *Britain in Iraq, 1914–1932.* London: Ithaca Press.

Sluglett, Peter and Marion Farouk-Sluglett, 1978, 'Some reflections on the Sunni/Shi'i question in Iraq', *Bulletin of the British Society for Middle Eastern Studies* 5(2):79–87.

——— 1993, 'Sunnis and Shi'is revisited: sectarianism and ethnicity in authoritarian Iraq'. In *Iraq: Power and Society*, ed. Derek Hopwood, pp. 75–90. Oxford: Ithaca.

Smith, Herschel, 2007a, 'Operation Alljah and the Marines of 2nd Battalion, 6th Regiment', *The Captain's Journal* (22 August 2007) (weblog – http://www.captainsjournal.com/2007/08/22/operation-alljah-and-the-marines-of-2nd-battalion-6th-regiment, accessed 9 July 2011).

——— 2007b, 'The special forces plan for Pakistan: mistaking the Anbar narrative', *The Captain's Journal* (26 November 2007) (weblog – http://www.captainsjournal.com/2007/11/26/the-special-forces-plan-for-pakistan-mistaking-the-anbar-narrative, accessed 9 July 2011).

Smith, Robertson W., 1966 [1903], *Kinship and Marriage in Early Arabia.* Boston: Beacon Books.

Tozy, Mohamad, 1999, *Monarchie et Islam, Politique au Maroc.* Paris: Presses de Sciences PO.

van Bruinessen, Martin, 1992, *Agha, Shaikh and State: The Social and Political Structures of Kurdistan.* London: Zed Press.

Varisco, Daniel Marin, 1996, 'Metaphors and sacred history: the genealogy of Muhammad and the Arab tribe', *Anthropological Quarterly* 68(3):139–56.

CHAPTER 4

An altered state?

Continuity, change and cosmology in Rwandan notions of the state

CHRISTOPHER C. TAYLOR

Introduction

In a 2001 article, M.R. Trouillot questions whether the present anthropological use of the term 'state' is appropriate or consistent. In expressing this sentiment he echoes one of the reservations expressed earlier by Radcliffe-Brown (1970), who pointed out that in most cases what analysts mean by the term 'state' could be more accurately described by the term 'government'. C. Nagengast (2002) has also warned that anthropology has taken the state as a given and has neglected genuine analysis of it. Yet another attack on the meaningfulness of the term 'state' comes from transnational and globalization theorists, who emphasize the role of social entities that are not easily bounded by states: infra- and supra-national institutions such as religious groups, NGOs and multi-national corporations, and global flows of capital, consumer goods and ideas (Appadurai 1996). Trouillot sees a path towards something of a clearing by building upon Philip Abrams's statement that the avenue toward understanding the state is that of power (1988:76):

> The state ... is not an object akin to the human ear. Nor is it even an object
> akin to human marriage. It is a third-order object, an ideological project.
> It is first and foremost an exercise in legitimation ... The state in sum is a
> bid to elicit support for or tolerance of the insupportable and intolerable by
> presenting them as something other than themselves, namely, legitimate,
> disinterested domination.

Trouillot follows Abrams's lead in seeing power as the central issue in understanding the state and advises us to study the state as a set of processes rather than as an entity. Both these aims can be accomplished by observing the state's effects at border sites, where encounters between individuals and states are most visible. Although I do not differ with Trouillot in his insistence that the state be studied as a set of processes rather than as a fixed entity or apparatus, I question whether an analysis which places power at its centre exhausts all that may be important about the state. I also question whether a pronounced emphasis on power, following the influences of Gramsci and Foucault, does not end up reproducing Western ontological assumptions. Are all processes of the state determined by power? Are all conceptualizations of power the same cross-culturally? In specific localities, are there no other forces or factors that condition power's expression? Is it always correct, following Gramsci, Foucault and Abrams, and reminiscent of Hobbes, that the state be theorized as an ideological entity productive of hegemonic and disciplinary practices that are independent of cultural influences?

In posing these questions I take inspiration from Sahlins (2000), who warns us that by persistently situating power at the centre of analysis we may be doing violence to more complex cultural content. We may be collapsing this content into a Western and culture-bound vision that is largely instrumental in nature, yet presumed to be universal. When all that is social becomes power, we assume that the intentionality driving every action, belief or practice is necessarily purposive, and that the purpose is either to maximize power or to resist it. In place of *Homo economicus* we posit a structurally homologous *Homo politicus* and a kind of tautological functionalism returns, as if through the back door.

Uncritically transferring what I believe are Western notions of being and personhood to non-Western examples of the state runs the risk of dissolving local diversity into a single explanatory matrix subtended by assumptions of maximizing individuals and repressive collectivities. In this chapter, using the example of the pre-colonial Rwandan state headed by a sacred king, I will attempt to show power's encompassment by cosmology. I do not believe that the Western dichotomy which opposes the individual as a desiring machine to the state conceived as power, coercion or discipline adequately captures the specific ontological dimensions of the pre-modern Rwandan state,[1] though it may have more relevance for the modern state after decades of colonialism, missionization, and involvement in the capitalist world economy. This does not mean that considerations of power will be absent from the discussion. It is rather that I view these as dependent upon religious, cosmological and ontological conditions that were specific to early Rwanda. Then I will compare these pre-modern aspects to those which characterized the modern Rwandan state headed by President Juvenal Habyarimana during the pre-genocidal times of 1990–4. Following Trouillot, the Rwandan state must be observed as a process with specific effects, although in this case – an extraordinary time characterized by the ascendancy of 'wild sovereignty' and the reduction of many lives to 'bare life' (Agamben, 1998) – these were more visible within the borders of Rwanda than outside of them. Pre-colonial cosmological notions of the state and of leadership, including those suggestive of 'wild sovereignty', were manifest in popular media during the period leading up to the Rwandan genocide of 1994.

Wild sovereignty and bare life

Following Agamben (1998), whose analysis of Roman sovereignty bears some resemblance to Luc de Heusch's discussion of central African kingship in *The Drunken King or the Origin of the State* (1982), the sovereign is an outsider, and as such, possessed of wild potencies. He is the outsider brought into the social fold who then uses his preternatural force to impose order. And yet, as an outsider, he is free to act independently of the laws and constraints that he imposes on others. However, many of the others against whom he asserts his control are also outsiders in the sense that they do not willingly submit to the sovereign order. As Kapferer puts it, the sovereign is 'that externality which asserts itself unconstrainedly against another externality' (Kapferer 2005:7). 'This externality, like the sovereign, is defined as an asocial, amoral being – in Agamben's analysis, "bare life" and beyond the protection of the sovereign order, open to being killed with legal and moral impunity' (ibid.). Like the Roman sovereign, the African sacred kings that de Heusch discusses never completely shed their association with the wild and never permanently divest themselves of the risk of being reduced to 'bare life' and summarily killed. Neither do those to whom these kings are simultaneously opposed and equivalent, those defined as external whether outside or within the state's borders. Modernity does not radically change things for Agamben, who sees evidence of continued 'wildness of sovereignty' and the capacity to reduce persons to 'bare life' in many times and places. As Kapferer says, 'the examples are legion: the situation of Jews up to and including the Holocaust, of Romanies even today, of Palestinians in the West Bank and Gaza, of Tutsi and various other African populations, the prisoners of Guantanamo Bay, and those in refugee camps in Australia, Europe, and elsewhere.' (ibid.).

De Heusch's analysis of the myths that surround sacred kingship in the Congolese savanna demonstrates that the Roman *Homo sacer* was hardly alone in the pre-modern world, for it reveals two contradictory symbolic orders underlying sovereignty, *bufumu* and *bulopwe* (de Heusch 1982:32). *Bufumu*, associated with the unbridled forces of nature, with incest and human sacrifice, is very much like Agamben's notion of 'wild sovereignty'. *Bulopwe*, associated with fecundity, exogamy and refinement, constitutes the 'rule of law' or the domesticated aspect of sovereignty. Rwandan sacred kingship, despite some differences with the Congolese varieties, incorporates similar opposing principles in the person of its mythical ancestor, Kigwa, said to have fallen from the sky and to have practiced incest with his sister, and a later mythical king, Gihanga, decorous and exogamous, who 'introduces a refined and truly royal cultural order' (de Heusch 1982:74). Also divided were the ritual and political functions of Rwandan kings in any single dynastic cycle of four kings. The first and fourth kings were said to be peaceful and were forbidden to engage in wars of conquest. They were confined within the two sacred halves of the Rwandan kingdom defined by the Nyabarongo River. The second and third kings were warlike, enjoined to transgress the sacred boundaries, and to conquer new territory. Two of the four kings within each dynastic cycle thus had the responsibility of conquest, while the other two had the responsibility of consolidation and renewal. Once again, this opposition corresponds roughly to *bufumu* and *bulopwe*, the mutually constitutive aspects of sovereignty in its wild and domesticated forms.

Earlier symbolic forms, Rwandan sacred kingship and its symbolism

In order to understand cosmological aspects of the pre-colonial Rwandan state, it is necessary to understand the religious concepts in which notions of the state were embedded. Let us begin with the Rwandan concept of *imaana*. Before Christian evangelization (early twentieth century), *imaana* referred to the notion of a supreme being, both as a specific though unfathomable personality and as a more generalized 'diffuse, fecundating fluid' of celestial origin whose activity upon livestock, land, and people brought fertility and abundance (d'Hertefelt and Coupez, 1964)[2]. Elaborate state rituals called *inzira* or 'paths', which often took months to complete, aimed at channelling the fertility effects of *imaana* to the entirety of the Rwandan polity. The Rwandan king (*umwami*) and his coterie of ritual specialists (*abiru*) were charged with the responsibility of enacting these rituals, and their credibility and tenure were dependent upon tangible success. All Rwanda's kings, as well as most of their closest retainers, belonged to the pastoralist Tutsi group, who were much fewer in number than Hutu cultivators. Rwanda's first historical king was a pastoralist from the neighbouring kingdom of Ndorwa named Ruganzu Ndori. He established his realm in the latter half of the seventeenth century CE (Vansina 2001). Rwanda's last 'traditional' king was Yuhi Musinga, who usurped the throne in 1896 and then was himself deposed in 1931, when the Belgian tutelary authority and the Rwandan Catholic Church placed his mission-educated son, Charles Rudahigwa, on the throne.

In earlier work I discuss the ritual functions of the Rwandan sacred king, the centrality of fluid symbols (rain, milk, blood, breast milk and semen), and the symbolic opposition between orderly states of flow and disorderly ones (Taylor 1992). In essence, this opposition approximates the *bufumu/bulopwe* opposition discussed by de Heusch. For example, disorderly states of flow include drought, inundation, lack of menses despite being of childbearing age, lack of breast development despite being of childbearing age and incest (semen and blood flowing in a closed circuit), while orderly states of flow include rainfall in the proper measure, lactating cattle, fertile land and fertile people.

The king's legitimacy in pre-colonial Rwanda arose from his capacity to promote fertility by controlling the flows of substances along hierarchically defined trajectories. But he could only control these by selectively interdicting them (the enactment of 'wild sovereignty'), even though this carried the risk of total obstruction: drought, infertility and death. The exercise of 'domesticated sovereignty', in other words, required a measure of 'wild sovereignty', but this latter had the potential to gain the upper hand. In a similar way to that of the Merina of Madagascar that M. Bloch discusses, the blessing of life force can only be appropriated from nature through the controlled violence of ritual, but that violence always runs the risk of becoming excessive (Bloch 1986). In the best of times, the Rwandan king as an embodiment of *imaana* exerted just the right amount of pressure on the celestial udder. This is why in some instances, although ordinarily called *umwami*, he was referred to by the term *umukama*, which means 'the milker'. The king could enrich his subjects with his gifts of cattle and fertility, or he could impoverish them, either by withholding these gifts or by being an unworthy repository of *imaana*. In this latter instance, with the aspect of wild sovereignty eclipsing that of domesticated sovereignty, and the normally hidden side to kingship – its externality, its rootedness in 'bare life' – becoming visible once again, the king himself might be eliminated.

The killing of kings did not occur often. More frequently their connection to celestial beneficence and domesticated sovereignty that was publically extolled. In dynastic poetry, for example, the king was idealized as the creator Imaana's earthly representative, responsible for channelling fertility to the rest of humanity. In effect, the king's body could be compared to a conduit through which celestial beneficence passed. But this passage was neither immediate nor direct. The royal body retarded the descent of *imaana*, the flow of fertility. By temporarily serving as the obstructing agent, the king's role in catalyzing the process became tangible and visible. In one legend that I heard in 1987, for example, fertility power passed through the king's alimentary canal according to this delayed rhythm:

Ruganzu Ndori was living in exile in the kingdom of Ndorwa, a neighbouring kingdom to the north of Rwanda. There he had taken refuge with his FZ (*nyirasenge*) who was married to a man from the region. In the meantime, because the Rwandan throne was occupied by an illegitimate usurper, Rwanda was experiencing numerous calamities. The crops were dying, the cows were not giving milk, and the women were becoming sterile. Ruganzu's paternal aunt encouraged him to return to Rwanda to retake the throne and save his people from catastrophe. Ruganzu agreed. But before setting forth on his voyage to Rwanda, she gave him the seeds (*imbuto*) of several cultivated plants (sorghum, gourd and others) to restart Rwandan cultures. While en route to Rwanda, Ruganzu Ndori came under attack. Fearing that the *imbuto* would be captured, he swallowed the seeds with a long draught of milk. Once he regained the Rwandan throne, he defecated the milk and seed mixture upon the ground and the land became productive once again. Since that time all Rwandan kings are said to be born clutching the seeds of the original *imbuto* in their hand.

The king's body was a synecdoche of the cosmological system and a metaphor of it in human form; he was a part of the whole, but he was also the part that resembled the whole. Since he was the conduit between sky and earth, his body had to be kept open and this was imprinted upon his physiological processes (Taylor 1988).[3] In essence, by attuning the king's body to the collective symbolic order and then metaphorically extending this to the cosmos as a whole, it was hoped that the inherent randomness of weather, pestilence and human social life might be kept in abeyance, if not stymied once and for all. Early Rwandans were more than likely aware of the illusory nature of such a desire, despite the assertions of the king's ritualists to the contrary. Yet they might entertain this illusion – just as in the United States we tend to believe that the President is responsible for the economy – as long as a certain degree of prosperity prevailed within the kingdom and there was some semblance of predictability to human social life. This was, of course, tempered by the realization that states of predictability and order were relative and ephemeral, and that the default state of the universe was entropic. Everyone was aware, for example, that keeping calamity at bay came at a price, and this demanded sacrificial victims, in some instances the king himself. In circumstances of natural disaster (e.g. drought, epidemic, epizootic, flooding or crop failure) or of humanly caused disasters (e.g. military defeat, invasion by a neighbouring kingdom), the king might be seen as an inadequate conduit of *imaana*, and thus the ultimate human obstructer. Later, his death would be depicted in dynastic legends as an *umutabazi* sacrifice, i.e. as if the king had heroically given his life for the survival of Rwanda (d'Hertefelt and Coupez, 1964).

The function of *umutabazi* (pl. *abatabazi*) sacrifice was initiated by a mythical king named Ruganzu Bwimba, who chose to sacrifice himself in order to save Rwanda from conquest by the neighbouring kingdom of Gisaka (Coupez and Kamanzi 1962:87–104). While Vansina (1967) has interpreted accounts in Rwandan court history of king sacrifice as attempts to conceal Rwandan military defeats, de Heusch (1982) maintains, following Frazer, that the sacrificial function was more than a mere artifice to conceal national humiliation. It was a quality implicit in kingship itself. Whatever the historical and political realities of *abatabazi* (liberators) were, these were encompassed within symbolic representations of the king as an embodiment of *imaana*. Sacrificial bulls used in courtly divination were also embodiments of *imaana* and these substituted for the king in ordinary courtly sacrifices. But there were moments of danger so extreme that neither the blood of royal cattle, nor the blood of ordinary mortals could keep open the conduit of beneficence between sky and earth. Such times were moments when the survival of the kingdom was in question. In these instances, diviners would determine who, among those of royal blood should sacrifice himself for the good of Rwanda. Often, though not always, the lot fell upon the king himself, for obviously his was the most potent royal blood. Spilling this blood on enemy territory was thought to poison the territory for its inhabitants, rendering it easy prey to Rwandan conquest.

The vitiating effect of royal blood spilled in sacrifice resembled that of two accursed beings: *impenebere* (women of childbearing age who had not developed breasts, i.e. deficient in milk) and *impa* (women of childbearing age who had never menstruated, i.e. deficient in blood). Such women, as embodiments of *ishyano* (impurity), were thought to be sources of aridity and infertility to the entire kingdom. Often Rwandan armies sacrificed them on enemy land in order to spoil the land and render it susceptible to capture. In certain instances, therefore, the king could be considered the final repository of *ishyano*, the ultimate 'blocked being', or in Agamben's terms the ultimate repository of 'bare life' and 'wild sovereignty'.

The person of *umwami* Ruganzu Bwimba, the first king said to have died as an *umutabazi*, reveals something about the flow of royal blood. According to legend, Kigwa, who was said to be the founder of Rwandan royalty, practised incest with his sister. This hyper-endogamy kept the blood of royalty flowing in a 'closed circuit' and precluded all possibility for any of the king's subjects to share in the privileges of royalty ('wild sovereignty' at its extreme). Later, another legendary king, Gihanga, renounced incest and instituted the practice of hyper-exogamy by marrying women who were neither of royal blood, nor even from the Rwandan kingdom. Descendants of Gihanga continued a moderated version of exogamy by taking wives from Rwanda's three putative autochthonous clans (*abasangwabutaka* – 'those who were found upon the earth'): Zigaaba, Singa and Gesera. Because of these exogamous kings, the blood of royal consanguinity began to flow in a more open manner. Celestial-origin kings married women of terrestrial origin and engendered children who were mixed, ultimately producing a form of sovereignty whose externality and wildness were tempered by connection to the earth.

Ruganzu Bwimba ended the practice of exogamy when his mother's brother, Nkorokombe, a Singa, induced illness in himself in order to avoid having to sacrifice himself for Rwanda. (A sacrificial victim must be healthy and whole.) Under threat from the neighbouring kingdom of Gisaka, Rwanda's court diviners determined that a human sacrifice of high rank was necessary to save Rwanda from defeat. The *umutabazi* was to be Nkorokombe. Instead of accepting this responsibility graciously, Nkorokombe took the flowers of an irritating plant called *ibitugunguru* and inserted them in his anus. When Ruganzu Bwimba's messenger came to fetch Nkorokombe and bring him to the place of sacrifice, the latter displayed his swollen anus at the entry to his hut. Observing that the hoped for *umutabazi* was suffering from rectal prolapsus, the messenger departed and went to inform the king of the disappointing news (Coupez and Kamanzi 1962:97).

In effect, by stopping off his anus Nkororkombe had made himself into a 'blocked being' – someone capable of ingesting but not egesting. Metaphorically speaking, Nkorokombe had transformed himself into a 'closed conduit' – someone capable of receiving, but not giving up or passing on that which he has received. (Freudian psychosexual stages obviously come to mind here, and the personality characteristic known as 'anal retentiveness'.) No longer could a cycle of exchange be constituted in which such a being was a participant, and by implication, no longer were 'autochthones' suitable alliance partners with 'celestials'. To save Rwanda, the *umwami* himself, Ruganzu Bwimba, offered to take Nkorokombe's place. Shortly before his sacrificial death, however, Ruganzu Bwimba decreed that never again should potential Rwandan kings take wives from groups that were not of celestial origin, i.e. from clans other than those termed *ibibanda*.

Royal blood after Ruganzu Bwimba was shared in a manner that represented something of a compromise between the two extremes of hyper-endogamy and hyper-exogamy. Confined within the closed circle of 'celestial' clans, it was nonetheless a blood already partly diluted by several generations of intermarriage with autochthones. Ruganzu Bwimba, in correcting the individual action of a 'blocked being', indirectly reaffirmed the principle of the king's prerogative to enact 'blockage' himself, i.e. 'closed-circuit' exchange or 'wild sovereignty', by restricting the potential wives of kings (in effect, an externality acting against an externality).

Although the legend places ultimate blame for this on the cowardice of his autochthonous MB, Nkorokombe, we see that in effect the king exercises his domination by controlling 'flows' and that he can only do this by occasionally assuming the mantle of 'wild sovereignty'. But the legend also shows that this can cost him his life. This example demonstrates that the exercise of power in the pre-modern Rwandan state was dependent upon specific defining parameters presaged in myth and performed in ritual. Power in the pre-modern state did not emanate simply from the display or exercise of force, it was symbolically conditioned in its expression, and actions were only deemed to be powerful or not, as a result of local, pre-existing and shared models of interpretation.

King Habyarimana – *umutabazi*?

Rwandan journalists applied representations of sacred kingship to President Juvenal Habyarimana during the pre-genocidal years of 1990–4. Some transfer of sacred kingship notions to Habyarimana was quite conscious; in other instances I do not believe that journalists were fully aware of the deeper layers of Rwandan cosmology that they managed to touch in their images. Politically, this period witnessed the invasion of Rwanda in October 1990 by soldiers of the Rwandan Patriotic Front (RPF), a group composed largely of Tutsi exiles who had been living in Uganda but with some disgruntled Hutu weary of Habyarimana and his party, the Mouvement Revolutionnaire pour le Developpement et la Democratie (MRND),[4] which had been in power for close to twenty years. After this invasion, and for the next year or so, the tides of fortune veered back and forth between the RPF and Rwandan Government Forces (RGF), but by 1992–3 the advantage definitely lay with the RPF. Only extensive military support from the French, who mistrusted the Anglophone RPF, kept the teetering Habyarimana and his government from collapse. The events of this time also stirred up the most significant cleavages in Rwandan society, between Hutu and Tutsi on one hand and between northerners and southerners on the other. Finally, in August of 1993 at Arusha, Tanzania, a peace agreement was signed between the Rwandan Government and the RPF with the participation of Rwanda's democratic opposition parties.[5] According to the agreement, President Habyarimana was soon to be reduced from an autocrat to a figurehead, and the RPF were to play a significant role in the new government. Before the end of the year, a broad-based transitional government was to take over and to organize presidential elections.

Unfortunately, because of the intransigence of Hutu extremists who loathed the thought of RPF participation in the government, and the President's own reluctance to cede power, these accords were not implemented by the end of 1993, nor by early 1994, nor even by March 1994. Finally, regional leaders summoned Habyarimana back to Arusha in April 1994, and warned him that if he continued to delay implementing the accords he risked bringing the whole region down in flames. Returning to Kigali on 6 April 1994, the President's plane was shot down by a shoulder-fired missile as it approached Kigali airport; everyone aboard was killed. This was the straw that broke the camel's back. The push to genocide could no longer be contained. At around 3 a.m. on 7 April 1994, we[6] heard the sound of hell breaking loose, when Rwandan Government Forces (RGF) attacked the RPF garrison in Kigali and the genocide began in earnest.[7] The following morning, Rwandan radio advised everyone to stay at home, as Kigali's neighbourhoods turned into killing fields. For the next seventy hours, we remained ensconced in our house and, at times when the explosions seemed frighteningly near, sheltered in the innermost corridor with mattresses on either side. Occasionally, when there was a lull in the fighting, I ventured onto our front porch to have a look. From there I could see just above the courtyard wall and into the street, where every now and then a loaded car or pick-up truck raced by. At other times I could make out the bobbing heads of looters carrying booty on their heads, as people in the neighbourhood were killed and their houses pillaged. It was genocide for some, opportunity for others.

Then on the afternoon of Saturday 9 April, a USAID employee banged loudly on the outdoor gate and yelled, 'Chris, get your stuff. You've got five minutes. We're being evacuated.' By land convoy we travelled first to Bujumbura, and then a few days later took a plane to Nairobi. Once settled there, I began to visit Rwandan refugees housed at the Shauri-Moyo YMCA. From them I learned about a diviner named Magayane, who two years earlier had predicted the genocide, the president's death, and a number of other occurrences. These predictions had been printed in one of Rwanda's numerous cheap political magazines. One of Magayane's predictions, that Habyarimana would be the last of Rwanda's Hutu kings, particularly intrigued me. Although during the time of the monarchy all Rwanda's kings had been Tutsi, here Rwanda's foremost Hutu, Juvenal Habyarimana, was being spoken about as if he too were a king. At the time I wondered how significant this identification was between former kings and Habyarimana.

The pre-sentiment that Habyarimana would not live beyond March 1994 was stated more than once in the popular political literature of the time, and not just by the diviner, Magayane. Here, in *Kangura*, one of the more infamous and widely read Hutu extremists' organs (Chretien 1995), Habyarimana's death is predicted four months in advance. He is also depicted as doing the bidding of RPF leader, Paul Kagame. I was first shown this cartoon by a Hutu friend in

Figure 1   *Tutsi ingratitude: Habyarimana will die in March 1994. (Kangura, December 1993, no. 53, p. 3)*
Kagame: 'On to Kigali'.
Habyarimana: 'I've done everything I could to make you Tutsi happy.'
Kagame: 'Who asked you?'

January 1994. His comment at the time was that there was more than a bit of truth to the idea that Habyarimana had become Kagame's beast of burden. For many extremist foes of the Arusha Accords, Habyarimana by early 1994 was no longer to be trusted as the champion of Hutu ethno-nationalism. Indeed, Habyarimana by that time was a leader alone. Deserted by increasing numbers of extremists, he had long since been abandoned by Hutu moderates, although obviously the two camps differed on why they deemed him a bad ruler. When I asked a Rwandan friend late in 1993 why it was that Habyarimana never appeared in public anymore, I was told that if he did, he would be subject to verbal and possibly physical assault by the population.

No one has ever claimed responsibility for killing the president, but the two most credible hypotheses place the responsibility either on Hutu extremist members among Habyarimana's own followers or on members of the rebel group at the time, the Rwandan Patriotic Front (RPF). Felip

Reyntjens, for example, once an adherent to the Hutu extremist thesis, has more recently given credence to the RPF thesis (Reyntjens 1999); this has also been supported by articles that have recently appeared in the French newspaper, *Le Monde*. Although I lean more in the direction of the Hutu extremist explanation, there is certainly merit to the RPF thesis as well. The death of President Habyarimana could have served the political interests of the extremists, just as it could have served the interests of the RPF. Many of the extremists, for example, were convinced that Habyarimana had become soft on the Tutsi, and that he needed to be replaced by someone more unequivocally genocidal. As for the RPF, they saw the president as an obstructionist who was delaying full implementation of the Arusha Accords and thus preventing their participation in a coalition government. Looking at the event in hindsight, and in terms of its psycho-social and symbolic efficacy, one would have to say that Habyarimana's death did more to rally moderate Hutu (those unwilling to engage in full-scale massacres against Tutsi civilians) to the extremist cause, than it did to rally Tutsi and moderate Hutu to the RPF cause. If the RPF or certain officers within the RPF were responsible for killing Habyarimana, they grossly underestimated the effect that this was to have on the Rwandan Presidential Guard, the Rwandan Army, the Interahamwe militias,[8] and even many among the Hutu population in general.

In the two years preceding Habyarimana's death, the path was being prepared in Rwanda's print media for something of a king sacrifice. At first we see hints of this in the opposition press and its portrayal of the president as a tyrannical or incompetent ruler that the country would do well to be rid of. Later, even Hutu extremists deserted him (as indicated in the cartoon above). Rwandan journalists attacked the president in ways that constituted a radical departure from the timidity that had prevailed during the 1980s. This was due in part to the democratization, supported by France and other Western powers, that occurred during the 1990s and to which Habyarimana and the MRND were forced to acquiesce. The press became free and open, but the sudden easing of restraints did not coincide with a corresponding rise in concern for journalistic standards. Innuendo, calumny, veiled and not so veiled calls for assassination characterized the printed and spoken media of the time (see Chretien 1996). More often than not, followers of the President, who occupied many of the key positions in the national media including control of the infamous 'hate radio' station, Radio Television Libre de Mille Collines (RTLM), used the weapons of fabrication and exaggeration against the President's perceived critics and rivals. The President's critics, however, were not above the occasional smear campaign, the use of obscenity and the liberal use of disinformation (ibid.).

Comparing Habyarimana in the popular political literature to a traditional sacred king was not without irony, for the President was Hutu (all former kings had been Tutsi) and much of the avowed ideology of his party, the Mouvement Revolutionnaire National pour le Developement et la Democratie (MRND), was anti-monarchist and, superficially at least, egalitarian. In addition to the predictions of Magayane, there were many examples of President Habyarimana and other leading political figures in the political literature (between 1990 and 1994) that show the influence of the kingship institution.

In hindsight it is not difficult to perceive some equivalence between the Rwandan presidency and the country's former monarchy. When I began my first period of fieldwork in Rwanda in 1983, I quickly became aware of the cult of personality surrounding President Habyarimana and the autocratic nature of his reign. At the time Habyarimana was running for re-election and MRND party faithful were very busy campaigning. There was little chance of his losing the election, though, as he was running unopposed and the MRND was the country's only authorized political party. Shortly after he overthrew the country's first Hutu president, Gregoire Kayibanda, in 1973, Juvenal Habyarimana assumed the presidency on a supposedly emergency basis. Later, he established the Mouvement Revolutionnaire National pour le Developpement (MRND), a party whose most enthusiastic support derived from his natal region of north-western Rwanda. In the 1983 elections Habyarimana asked for, and was reported to have won, an incredible 99 per cent of the vote. For many years afterwards, it seemed as if he would hold power forever.

Rwanda was a closely controlled military dictatorship at the time, with very few people daring to raise a dissenting voice. Rarely did one hear a critical word being muttered against Habyarimana and the army's tight control of the Rwandan state. Those who did oppose the president, in word or deed, usually found themselves in prison or dead under mysterious circumstances. In the capital of Kigali, the presence of army and gendarmerie was pervasive. Commitment to the government was obligatory. Every Saturday morning people everywhere in Rwanda, especially employees of the state, but many others as well, would meet to participate in *umuganda*, community service. They would come with their shovels and hoes and fill in the ruts of dirt roads deeply gouged by the rain; they would repair municipal buildings; they would plant trees. There was very little complaining. Even most Rwandan Tutsi during the 1980s supported Habyarimana, recalling the violence of 1973 when Habyarimana and the army stepped in, stopped the violence against Tutsi, and then took power from then President Kayibanda and his central and southern Hutu supporters. Of course, along with the paternalism of the Habyarimana regime came the army's close surveillance of the population and the threat of force.

At the time, adulation of Habyarimana was *de rigeur* for Rwandans; it was a key element in the enactment of their *civitas*. Virtually everyone had a portrait of the President hanging on a wall at home, and many wore the MRND party button on their shirt or blouse. On Wednesday afternoons groups met to practice chants and skits in celebration of the Rwandan state, its overthrow of the Tutsi monarchy, its rejection of the *ubuhake* cattle contract signifying Hutu servitude to Tutsi, and, most of all, to honour the country's president, Juvenal Habyarimana. Termed *animation*, it didn't seem to bother anyone that these Wednesday afternoon get-togethers took people away from their jobs and did nothing to augment the country's gross domestic product. Even songs on the radio seemed to equate Rwanda, its beauty and relative prosperity with the person of its president.

Of course much of this adulation was self-interested. The state, with Habyarimana at its head, was the country's primary source of patronage. Showing support for it and its leader could never hurt your career. Even in contexts where there was nothing obvious to be gained, however, many people expressed their admiration of the country's president. Some people made comments about the appropriateness of Habyarimana's name, from the verb *kubyara* (to engender) and *imaana*, which together could be translated as: 'It is God who gives life'. Nothing could have been more appropriate in a Catholic, anti-abortion and basically pro-natalist culture, yet very few names could have at the same time resonated so well with the more 'traditional' themes of fertility, prosperity and good luck, manifestations of the 'diffuse fecundating fluid'. Yet it seemed at the time to hold true. During most of the 1980s Rwanda was doing well economically (in comparison to neighbouring states), and many Rwandans attributed this to the good stewardship of its president. The orchestrated affection for Habyarimana was part theatre, certainly, but there were many who were sincere.

Closely associating the country's fertility and prosperity with the person of the president was not the only way in which we see the lingering influence of the representations of sacred kingship. We also see this influence in references to the country's rivers, the body and violence. Sometimes the assimilation of Habyarimana to a Rwandan sacred king was explicit. At other times it was more implicit, bordering on the unwitting. In many cases the association was intended to be flattering, in other instances it was intended to be critical. Let us look at some examples.

Ngo Kiliziya yakuye kirazira.

Muri mirongo inani HABYARIMANA· baramubwiye ntiyumva kandi
ibintu byari bigifite igaruriro, bimaze kuba agasitswe ati: Ndi IKINANI...

Figure 2   Headline beneath the cartoon: 'In 1980 when things could have been
           arranged, we told Habyarimana, but he wouldn't listen. When things
           flew out of control, all he could say was: I am Ikinani [the invincible]'.

           Habyarimana (upper left): 'We are well dressed [i.e. in military
           uniforms]. We are descending to the Nyabarongo to conduct the
           campaign. Try to spare a few so that they will tell the story of
           Ikinani's victory. But once we have crossed [i.e. the Nyabarongo],
           my children, what I haven't told you, figure out for yourself.'

           RPF (upper right): 'What are they thinking in Rwanda!? Is it true that he
           wants the votes of cadavers!?'

1 Rivers

In one popular political journal, *Umurangi*, closely associated with the party
known as the Mouvement Democrate Republicain (MDR) and opposed to
the MRND, Habyarimana is pictured in proximity to the Mukungwa and as
about to attack southern Rwanda with his army and militia (*Umurangi* 13, 27
November 1992). *Umurangi*'s indirect allusion to the boundaries of the sacred

kingdom and to Habyarimana is not intended to flatter. In this cartoon we see the three major democratic opposition parties, the Mouvement Democrate Republicain (MDR), the Parti Social Democrate (PSD) and the Parti Liberal (PL) poised close to the Nyabarongo and preparing to fend off Habyarimana's descent into what was once the most sacred territory of the Rwandan kingdom. To the north-east we see the RPF, delighted that southern Hutu (MDR, PSD and PL) and northern Hutu (MRND and CDR) are divided among themselves. At another level, the cartoon seems to be saying that Habyarimana is an illegitimate pretender to the throne, a northerner, an outsider and one responsible for terroristic killings in the south and centre.

2 The amoral body and its reduction to 'bare life'

Many of the explicit references to the former kingship institution are ideologically motivated, and this accounts for the differences seen among the various Rwandan political factions in their depiction of Habyarimana and others. Other linkages cannot be explained solely as ideological, for they appeal to a deeper, more ontological level (see note 1). Indeed, the various Rwandan factions were contesting who would control the power of the state, but the contest was being waged through the mediation of a common body of symbols. For example, imagery of the body as conduit is where ideological motivation gives way to a realm of thought having to do with a specifically Rwandan way of imagining the body as a being in time and space, a being that acts as the focal point of physiological and social processes redolent with cosmological import – a being through which *imaana* should pass in its descent from sky to earth. Although the following cartoon manifests the symbolic pattern of 'body as conduit', it adds to the instantiation of the pattern, its negation. Here Hutu opponents of Habyarimana portray his body as a 'flowing' conduit, but one which turns all flows back upon itself.

The headline reads: 'In the MRND they continue to excrete on the plate from which they eat and into the water from which they drink'. At the left an MRND youth holds up a severed leg and says: 'Let's kill them, let's get rid of them, let's eat them'. Habyarimana replies: 'Yes, let's descend on them all right'. To his right, one CDR man and another who is MRND exclaim sarcastically: 'In the Rwanda of peace, there sure is a lot of delicious food'. Beneath the cartoon are the words: 'The politics of the cattle thieves causes problems'.

Much is condensed in this illustration. At an ideological level, Habyarimana and his MRND and CDR followers are being compared to cattle thieves. It is also quite obvious that the President, according to his detractors, is a man who eats shit. But there are other elements that are not directly ideological or even logical in an ordinary sense. What serves as Habyarimana's latrine in the picture is Rwanda and its hapless population. The spoon that we

Figure 3   Top: 'In the MRND they continue to excrete upon the plate from which
they eat and into the water that they drink.'
Bottom: 'The politics of the cattle thieves causes problems.'

see him moving from beneath his anus and about to place in his mouth is
labelled 'taxes'. The Rwandan people's taxes are swallowed by Habyarimana,
excreted by Habyarimana, only to be swallowed by him again. Only if you are
a follower of his are you likely to get anything to eat, as with these CDR and
MRND party members who manage to grab the occasional severed limb, the
occasional errant turd. Habyarimana reverses the flow of beneficence. Instead
of it descending downward from the sky, passing through his body, and then
to the earth and people, it moves from down to up, from people to ruler. Once
there, most of it is continually recycled in a sterile 'closed-circuit flow' within
his body. What little passes through him gets gobbled up by his lackeys.

At an ontological level a more profound message is being communicated:
Habyarimana is an inadequate conduit of *imaana* and thus not a worthy king.
He is an inversion of Ruganzu Ndori. A king like Ruganzu Ndori would never
have selfishly allowed his bowels to retain the mystical powers of the original
imbuto. Ruganzu Ndori's body was a moral conduit, one through which *imaana*

could pass from sky to earth, a body capable of performing 'open-circuit flow', a potentially good alliance partner, a giver and not simply a receiver of gifts, an adequate embodiment of Imaana on earth. King Habyarimana is the antithesis of Ruganzu Ndori and the embodiment of *ishyano* (ritual impurity). He has re-assumed the 'wild' aspect of sovereignty and, in doing so, reduced himself to 'bare life'. These cartoons seem to be saying, at a level beneath, yet more powerful than, the ideological, 'Habyarimana must be sacrificed'.

Conclusion

In this chapter I have tried to show that, despite the changes brought in the wake of colonialism, Christian evangelization and post-colonial independence, there were lines of continuity in the cosmological conceptualization of the Rwandan state between the pre-modern period when the state was led by a sacred king and the modern period when the state was headed by a military dictator, President Juvenal Habyarimana. This continuity shows the persistence of local notions of 'wild sovereignty' and can be discerned in representations of the President that appeared in popular political literature during the pre-genocidal years between 1990 and 1994.

In contrast to views of the state advanced by Trouillot, Abrams, Gramsci and Foucault, which see the state primarily as an apparatus of power, I have attempted to problematize power and to shift analysis to those subjacent aspects of meaning upon which power itself was constructed, both in pre- and post-colonial Rwanda. I have proceeded in this way because I see something of a flaw in analyses which privilege power. When power becomes the sole or dominant analytic concern, perceived here, there and everywhere, it is also seen nowhere. Power is as much a metaphor as a lived reality, and as such can only be dependent upon other metaphors, and these require symbolic interpretation. We cannot fully understand the state, even the state as a wielder of power, without understanding the religious, cosmological and ontological determinants in which power is embedded, deployed and interpreted.

Sovereignty in pre-colonial Rwanda depended upon the balanced interplay of two metaphorical potencies I have labelled 'wild sovereignty' (following Agamben) and 'domesticated sovereignty'. These correspond closely to the qualities of *bufumu* and *bulopwe* encountered in nearby regions of central Africa and discussed by de Heusch. As long as these two potencies were perceived to act in tandem and for the benefit of the social group, the sovereign's origin in the realm of the wild could be overlooked. It was only when the wild and domesticated aspects of sovereignty became separate and visible that the king exposed himself to the risk of being reduced to 'bare life' and that his life and others were in danger. Wild and domesticated sovereignty were in turn dependent upon another set of metaphors encapsulated in the central cosmological notion of the pre-modern Rwandan state – *imaana*, the 'diffuse, fecundating fluid' – whose ordered descent to the earth was the central preoccupation of the rituals of Rwandan sacred kingship. Understanding *imaana* requires understanding the nature of symbolism having to do with liquids and their movement. According to this symbology, perturbations in fluid flows were negatively valued such as blockages or overly abundant fluid flows. The sacred king's responsibility was to catalyze and direct these flows, but he could only do this by enacting aspects of 'wild sovereignty'. Acting as the human focal point of the polity as cosmological process, the king made flows of beneficence tangible and visible, but only by temporarily obstructing them. Yet the king forever risked being perceived as overly obstructing and overly wild and thus responsible for the cessation of beneficial flows in times of crisis. This is when he was susceptible to being judged as an inadequate conduit for *imaana* and reduced to 'bare life'. Usually his death then was a foregone conclusion. However, collective remembering of such events in dynastic histories usually followed the model of *umutabazi* sacrifice, masking tragedy and making it appear as if the sovereign had died a selfless and heroic death.

We see a similar pattern in the person of President Habyarimana and in the intimations that he was to become, like some of Rwanda's past sacred kings, an *umutabazi*. In the print media before the genocide, we find images of Habyrimana where his exercise of sovereignty is compared to, and thus defined by, the constraints of sacred kingship. Most dramatically, we sense the move towards the veiled accusation that Habyarimana had become a 'wild sovereign', an inversion of Ruganzu Ndori, for Habyarimana is portrayed as a sovereign who reverses flows, who retains beneficence within himself, and who arrests that which should pass through him. He becomes a bad king, one who seeks profit for himself and his immediate followers and who impedes the descent of *imaana*. He turns the world upside down as he channels beneficence from bottom to top and as excrement becomes aliment. It is in this way that he changed from a Gihanga into a Kigwa during his final days, an obstructer, a 'wild sovereign'. It was because of this that he could be reduced to 'bare life'. Like the proverbial genie, however, once 'wild sovereignty' detached itself from 'domesticated sovereignty', it was impossible to put the contagion of 'bare life' back into its bottle. By his death, Habyarimana became the catalyst for further death, as he became the rallying cry behind which Hutu extremists mobilized their genocide against all Tutsi, who were blamed for his assassination.

NOTES

1   By ontology I mean a culturally specific way of constructing being and personhood in a given nation-state. As Kapferer states: 'The reasoning or logic of the respective nationalist ideologies has ontological dimensions; that is, these ideologies contain logical elements relevant to the way human beings within their historical worlds are existentially constituted.' (Kapferer 1988:19).

2   I will use Imaana when I am speaking of *imaana* as a specific deity.

3   In some instances this was quite literally the case. Every morning the king imbibed a dose of liquid called *isubyo* which was intended to counteract any poison he might have ingested or drank the previous day. *Isubyo* possessed powerful laxative qualities.

4   The Mouvement Revolutionnaire pour le Developpement or MRND changed its name in 1991 to Mouvement Revolutionnaire pour le Developpement et la Democratie after multi-party democracy was authorized in Rwanda. It retained the acronym MRND.

5   The democratization wave pushed by Western powers during the late 1980s and 1990s also touched Rwanda. Feeling that it would have to open its political system in order to continue receiving aid from Western donors, Rwanda allowed other political parties besides the MRND to come into existence, although most power continued to rest with the president. Many different political parties quickly saw the light of day, but the principal ones besides the MRND were: the Mouvement Democrate Republicain (MDR), the Parti Liberal (PL), and the Parti Social Democrate (PSD). In an effort to scramble the situation the MRND also created other parties that were in effect clones of itself, such as the Parti Ecologiste. The CDR party, Coalition pour la Defense de la Republique, was an MRND splinter party that was more openly anti-Tutsi and anti-RPF than the MRND. Later in the 1990s, President Habyarimana and other Hutu extremists managed to split off anti-RPF factions from the MDR and the PL parties that became known as 'Hutu Powa' (Hutu power) factions. Many later supporters of the genocide were recruited from the 'Hutu Powa' groups.

6   At the time that these events transpired, I was living in Kigali, Rwanda, with my fiancée, Esperance. I was employed as a behavioural research specialist by Family Health International and USAID.

7   As part of the Arusha Accords, the RPF was allowed to station one battalion of its troops in Kigali in order to protect its political representatives. Although the first violent incidents that followed the President's assassination were against prominent Hutu opponents of the genocide and some individual Tutsi, the RPF garrison was attacked early on 7 April 1994. It then asked and received permission from the United Nations Mission to Rwanda to leave the confines of its garrison in order to defend itself.

8   Interahamwe means 'those who attack together'. Most Rwandan political parties
    had youth wings and for the MRND party (the party in power at the time of the
    genocide), theirs was the Interahamwe. Recruited largely from among un- or under-
    employed young males who had drifted into Rwandan cities, the Interahamwe
    received political and arms training from MRND party officials, Rwandan
    Government soldiers, and possibly also from French military advisors. Practically
    every urban neighbourhood, and in the rural areas every hillside, possessed at least
    one Interahamwe member. They aided the pre-genocidal apparatus in keeping
    regularly updated lists of all Rwandan opposition party members and all Tutsis.
    Before the outbreak of wholesale massacres, the Interahamwe intimidated people
    on their lists with actual or threatened violence and extorted 'protection' money
    from some of them. Even before the genocide Interahamwe were occasionally
    given authorization to set up roadblocks and to rob, beat and sometimes kill the
    people they had trapped, or to steal or damage their vehicles. On two occasions I
    narrowly avoided being trapped in such a roadblock and on one of these occasions
    bricks hit my vehicle just beneath the windshield. On another occasion at a small
    barrier, consisting merely of a motor bike straddling a Kigali back street, a Tutsi
    friend of mine and I were caught and hassled for twenty minutes or so by a group
    of Interahamwe and in the presence of two Rwandan police officers. After lengthy
    negotiations with the police officers, who were probably nonplussed by the
    presence of a foreigner, the Interahamwe released my friend although not before
    they had cut him slightly near the eye. During the genocide Interahamwe weapons
    of choice were the machete, the nail-studded wooden club and the grenade.

REFERENCES

Abrams, Philip, 1988, 'Notes on the difficulty of studying the state', *Journal of
    Historical Sociology* 1(1):58–89.

Agamben, Giorgio, 1998, *Homo Sacer: Sovereign Power and Bare Life*, trans. Daniel
    Heller-Roazen. Stanford: Stanford University Press.

Appadurai, Arjun, 1996, *Modernity at Large: Cultural Dimensions of Globalization*.
    Minneapolis: University of Minnesota Press.

Bloch, Maurice, 1986, *From Blessing to Violence*. Cambridge: Cambridge University
    Press.

Chretien, Jean-Pierre (ed.), 1995, *Rwanda: Les Médias du Genocide*. Paris: Karthala.

Coupez, André and Kamanzi, Théoneste, 1962, *Recits Historiques Rwanda*. Tervuren:
    Musee Royal de l'Afrique Centrale, Annales, Serie in 8, Sciences Humaines
    no. 43.

Foucault, Michel, 1977, *Discipline and Punish: The Birth of the Prison*. New York:
    Vintage Books.

Gramsci, Antonio, 1992, *Prison Notebooks*, trans. Joseph A. Buttigieg and Antonio Callari. NewYork: Columbia University Press.

d'Hertefelt, Marcel and André Coupez, 1964, *La Royaute Sacree de l'Ancien Rwanda*. Tervuren: Musee Royal de l'Afrique Centrale, Annales, Serie in 8, Sciences Humaines no. 52.

Heusch, Luc de, 1982, *The Drunken King or, the Origin of the State*. Bloomington: Indiana University Press.

Hobbes, Thomas, 1998, *Leviathan*. Oxford: Oxford University Press.

Kapferer, Bruce, 1988, *Legends of People, Myths of State*. Washington DC: Smithsonian Institution Press.

——— 2005, 'New formations of power, the oligarchic-corporate state, and anthropological ideological discourse', *Anthropological Theory* 5(3):285–99.

Nagengast, Carole, 2002, 'Innoculations of evil: symbolic violence and ordinary people: an anthropological perspective on genocide'. In *Annihilating Difference*, ed. Alex Hinton. Berkeley: University of California Press.

Radcliffe-Brown, A.R., 1970 [1940], 'Preface'. In *African Political Systems*, ed. M. Fortes and E.E. Evans-Pritchard. London: Oxford University Press.

Reyntjens, Felip, 1999, *La Guerre des Grands Lacs: Alliances Mouvantes et Conflits Extraterritoriaux en Afrique Centrale*. Paris: Harmattan.

Sahlins, Marshall, 2000, 'The sadness of sweetness; or, the native anthropology of Western cosmology'. In *Culture in Practice*. New York: Zone Books.

Taylor, Christopher, 1992, *Milk, Honey and Money*. Washington DC: Smithsonian Institution Press.

——— 1999. *Sacrifice as Terror*. Oxford: Berg Publishers.

Trouillot, M.-R., 2001, 'The anthropology of the state in the age of globalization', *Current Anthropology* 42(1):1–24.

Vansina, Jan, 1967, 'L'évolution du royaume Rwandais des origine à 1900', *Cahiers Internationaux de Sociologie* XLIII:143–58.

——— 2000, *L'Histoire du Royaume Nyiginya*. Paris: Karthala.

Cartoons from:

Kangura. Rwandan popular political magazine.

La Medaille-Nyiramacibiri. Rwandan popular political magazine.

Umurangi. Rwandan popular political magazine.

Zirikana. Rwandan popular political magazine.

CHAPTER 5

Post-war realities in Sri Lanka

From the crime of war to the crime

of peace in Sri Lanka?

❧❧❧❧❧

BRUCE KAPFERER AND

ROSHAN DE SILVA WIJEYERATNE

Introduction

Sri Lanka's civil war, which had lasted over thirty years, came to an end on 19 May 2009 with the extermination of the leadership of the Liberation Tigers of Tamil Eelam (LTTE), including the founder, Velupillai Prabhakaran, by the Sri Lanka Army. The event was marked by the slaughter of thousands of Tamil civilians who were trapped in a confined area by the Sri Lanka military advance. The LTTE prevented the escape of these civilians, but the 2011 UN report on war crimes in Sri Lanka makes it clear that the carnage that the Tamil civilian population suffered was mainly the result of government fire that was not only directed at combat zones, but also at agreed safe havens as well as hospitals and UN posts.[1] The whole concluding episode of the war is one of a number of significant crimes of war against the civilian population for which the Sri Lanka government bears much if not the full blame[2] .

The last months of the civil war drew their violent intensity, a rage of the state, not from the mere fact of the violence which is war (of the 'war is hell' kind), but, we consider, from the passions of ethnic nationalism (Sinhalese and Tamil) that had built through the preceding decades (in peace as much as in war). Thus the final events of the war could be interpreted as part of a larger policy of a Final Solution to what could be described as the long-standing Tamil National Question which has assumed particular significance within the building of Sinhalese nationalism.[3]

Although the international focus, especially through the United Nations, has been on the atrocities of the Sri Lankan armed forces as the war reached its grizzly end, this has tended to deflect attention away from ongoing processes in Sri Lanka connected with the transformation of the state and the role of nationalist discourse in this. There is much evidence demonstrating the continuation of the suffering of the Tamil population in the east and especially in the war-ravaged north, which from many accounts sustains many of the features of a concentration camp. There, almost two years after the end of hostilities, the military is in virtual total control, civil liberties are drastically curtailed, civilian 'disappearances' continue, and land, in the control of the Tamil population for centuries, is being appropriated.[4] While a welcome peace has settled over much of the Sinhalese population in the west, central and southern regions of the island, and the dreadful anxieties of the last twenty years or so of war have been lifted, this is far from the case for Tamils. However, we stress that this is relatively so, for Sinhalese critics of the government – especially journalists – continue to be harassed, and freedom of expression, as well as other civilian liberties, continues to be constrained in a context of heightened state control and nationalist triumphalism.

Even prior to the end of the intensification of the Sinhalese-Tamil conflict after the anti-Tamil pogrom of 1983, Sinhalese and Tamil nationalisms had effected a thoroughgoing ethnic polarization, as well as dimensions of ethnic cleansing, that were nowhere as apparent forty years ago, when Kapferer first started visiting Sri Lanka. Even though Tamil communities in the south of the island were small, they were nonetheless present and their religious temples active. Kapferer well recalls attending Hindu festivals in the Galle area in the early 1970s that involved the enthusiastic participation of members of Sinhalese Buddhist communities. These have long since been discontinued. Most of the Tamils who once lived in the south have fled. For some communities along the western seaboard, north and south of Colombo, the distinctions between ethnic Sinhalese and Tamils had often been fuzzy, to say the least. Many people who considered themselves to be ethnically Sinhalese spoke Tamil domestically and carried Tamil names. This highlighted the often close interpolation of Sinhalese and Tamil populations, and the risks of assuming clear cut cultural and social distinctions. So much of the ordinary ritual world of the Sinhalese, even today in the south, bears a strong trace of Tamil influences. But nationalist rhetoric and war have destroyed much of this sense, and has realized the firm exclusive boundaries of a nationalist imaginary.

Our stress here is on the apparent continuities in the nationalism of the Sri Lankan state with that which obtained before and during the war and into the post-war situation. It is this which is implicated in what we call a 'policy of the Final Solution' that has, as a major effect, pressured Tamils to leave the island. The 'ethnic cleansing' that was a feature of the attacks on a helpless civilian population at the conclusion of the war is a dimension of continuing policies.

Such a direction was always a potential of government approaches to the Tamil Question as these developed in the decades preceding the war, though they were then generally held in check (and largely only evident in relation to Tamil tea-estate workers imported into Sri Lanka by the British). In the sense that is developed by Gilles Deleuze and Felix Guattari (1974), what was *virtual* (or immanent) is now actual. This has been achieved through transformations in the state order, mediated in the course of the war in the context of larger geopolitical shifts connected with processes of globalization. Thus the period of the war was one in which global neo-liberal forces gathered momentum, and saw a shift away from the order of the nation state to that of the corporate state (Kapferer 2010, 2012). Part of this involved a radical restructuring of elite and oligarchic control (essentially a change within the dynamics of class relations) and an associated intensification of nationalist discourse. That is, what seems to be continuity in nationalist rhetoric is so only by means of a radical shift in the socio-political order of the state. In other words, nationalist ideology has been turned in the interest of a new class hegemonic function that has resulted in the maintenance of restraint over civil liberties.

As already mentioned, we consider that a major effect of this has been the actualization of a policy that has all the features of a Final Solution in relation to the Tamils. This has been exacerbated by the global shift in political economic power from the erstwhile imperializing West to the newly imperializing East. It was, of course, this shift that has enabled the Rajapakse government – the spearhead of new post-colonial elites – to be relatively immune to international criticism of its excesses. We stress that what we discuss as the continuation and in certain senses an intensification of Sinhalese nationalist discourse into the post-war context and a realization of its implications, is a consequence of dynamics of state transformation in the larger setting of a shift in global political and economic power and influence.

Sinhalese nationalism – the power of myths

Nationalism generally thrives on its own mythology, to which it assigns particular significance. Kapferer wrote of this in the wake of the 1983 anti-Tamil riots and with a consciousness of certain parallels between the rise of Nazism and its exterminating populist violence and what was happening in post-colonial Sri Lanka. Thus a quotation from Ernst Cassirer's *The Myth of the State* (1946), written on the eve of the Second World War, begins the analysis of Sinhalese nationalist myths in *Legends of People, Myths of State* (1988, Chapter 2, see also new edition and appendices 2011). Cassirer asserted that matters concerning the historical empirical truth or falsity of nationalist myths are of little matter. Ominously, he declared that their 'truth', as in Nazi mythologies, was not in the myths themselves (a *virtual* in the

Deleuzian sense, i.e. a domain of potential that is real but not actual), but in their particular realization through practical implementation, or in the actualization of their logic and potential in their political application. This was the argument that was developed in *Legends of People, Myths of State*, showing how those in power in Sri Lanka brought ancient stories of kings and princes into operation to legitimate the very contemporary and entirely modern claims to hegemony and the exclusive national territorial right of ethnically defined political leaders and their followers. Here, it was also argued that the myths in themselves had certain possibilities of interpretation. Undoubtedly they had ambiguities, but there were logical potentials in them to be realized if they became activated in the contemporary situation of ethnic nationalism. This was all the more so, if dimensions of their logical schemes entered within political consciousness, where, in contemporary circumstances, they could assume both original and dreadful possibility. That is, and following Cassirer, the myths could achieve all the potency of the most destructive weaponry, as well as giving the violence of war particular focus and intensity.

The point was not that a mytho-logical consciousness that had such possibility was already present in the everyday consciousness of citizens. Rather, the argument was that it could be created through the particular narrative structures of contemporary nationalism, and *made to achieve a truth of sorts*. Thus no matter how cynical the use of ancient stories in modern nationalist rhetoric might have been, there is always the danger that leaders and followers can actually come to believe the stories that they tell. This is a widespread phenomenon, and certainly not limited to Sri Lanka. However, populations in Sri Lanka were particularly vulnerable to such beliefs, because the stories and particular interpretations of them were present in popular everyday ritual. These were not relevant to modern politics, having import largely for personal existential difficulties often to do with healing. But nationalist politics, by engaging such stories, bridged ritual realities into contemporary political matters. The politicization of mythology out of its ritual register had the potential of creating impassioned commitment, and of effectively creating a political consciousness of dangerous proportions. There is much evidence to show that political leaders among the Sinhalese were doing more than putting the stories to cynical use. Some began to embody their possibility.

This was so with President Premadasa (murdered by the LTTE), who came to conceive of himself as virtually the last in line of Tamil-fighting Sinhalese kings (Bastin 2012). He was committed to the idea of Dutugemunu, and wrote a popular novel about him and his restoration of Sinhalese hegemony.[5] A hoarding near the official residence of Sri Lanka's currently triumphal president associated him explicitly with Dutugemunu. The point was that modern political leaders, however erroneously, became internal to their own stories, as did many of their followers. They became potentially committed and imprisoned in a consciousness and logic of their own insistence. That is, they brought into central place a mythological reality. This was given entirely contemporary significance unrelated to any reality hitherto, save some ritual realities that were quite independent of modern politics. Through nationalism, lived realities were, as Ricouer (1978) has noticed for some recent European history, re-mythologized. With this re-mythologization, a past (one which in all probability never existed in the terms of its mythic imaginary) became integral to the understanding of present experience, and a force in the working through of ongoing political realities.

Reterritorialization and mythological violence

One dimension of this process is a conception of land and territory as the exclusive and relatively unchanging ethnic Sinhalese birthright, legitimated in a history that myth reflects. An aspect of this conception is that ethnic Sinhalese have a right to settle in areas which were 'once theirs'. We will not go into the many criticisms of this view, which are well known and have been discussed by scholars from all sections of Sri Lanka. A dangerous 'truth' is, however, being created. In a visit Kapferer made to the Eastern Province three years ago, after the disastrous – for the LTTE - division in the ranks of the LTTE leadership, and when the LTTE was being driven from the region, various mythical and ritual sites were in a process of being redefined or creatively invented. Thus sites of important Sinhalese mythical personages (e.g. the mother of King Dutugemunu) were being discovered by Buddhist monks (interpreting references in the *Mahavamsa*, the national storybook). Mythological legitimation was being used to redraw or reterritorialize land from Tamil to Sinhalese inhabitation, and was further mediated by military and security pragmatics in the context of the extra-legal methods adopted by Tamil nationalists.

Our suggestion is that the programme of Tamil resettlement in the 'liberated' Eastern Province of the island is one of ethnic reterritorialization in which Sinhalese nationalist mythology is a motivating force as much as, and perhaps more than, the needs of security. Tamils have long feared such a process, since well before there was any indication of the civil war that was to come. In the late 1940s and early 50s the Gal Oya irrigation and resettlement scheme in the Eastern Province was seen by Tamils as driven in Sinhalese nationalist mythology. The Gal Oya was envisioned as a colonization scheme to settle Sinhala farmers from other areas of the island in a region hitherto dominated by Tamils. Part of the imaginary behind the scheme was to realize the past in the present, for it was conceived as a region of the great irrigation civilizations ruled by ancient and medieval Sinhalese kings. A nationalist vision was to realize the Sinhalese hegemony that it believed had been disrupted by the Colan invasions from south India that had driven ethnic Sinhalese out. The effect of the civil war, and the mythology engaged to it, is to render the imagination of a past a contemporary reality.

The Tamil resettlement programme, or their 'temporary' relocation, may disguise more sinister objectives that the International Community's humanitarian interests may both be oblivious to and unwittingly assisting (Klein 2008). It is conceivable that what has already been happening in the east has a bearing on the restrictions on international humanitarian intervention by Colombo, both during the end game of the war in the north and now in relation to the parlous situation of the huge number of Tamil civilian victims, and the potential for dispossession of Tamil owned land in the current ordering and security processes of the state. The Sri Lanka Government might not be able to hide objectives of an ethnic cleansing nature, if it did not thoroughly control the way outside humanitarian intervention is orchestrated.

An unsettling ominous sign regarding the future, and of the reterritorialization taking place, was the visit of the Sri Lanka president's wife to Jaffna, at the northern tip of the island, on Friday morning, 5 June 2009, soon after the end of hostilities. She accompanied a statue of Sanghamiththa, the first woman Buddhist missionary to Sri Lanka, and the daughter of Emperor Asoka. The statue was to be enshrined in a newly built Buddhist temple in Maathakal in the High Security Zone.

The propaganda of peace and a blueprint for the future?

On 18 January 2009, Dr Susantha Goonatilake published 'After the victory: full-scale development in the north but no racist appeasement', an article in the English language *Sunday Times* printed in Colombo. Goonatilake is an outspoken apologist for Sri Lanka government policy, and a champion of Sinhalese rightist groups. He has made it his mission to attack what he would regard to be liberal and leftist academics and intellectuals in Sri Lanka.

Writing of significant government victories, the capture of Kilinochchi and Elephant Pass, that were preliminaries to the demise of the LTTE, Goonatilake writes:

> It was a victory reminiscent of Dutu Gemunu who over 2,100 years ago as
> a child in the deep South described the helplessness of being pushed into
> the country's extreme corner by a Tamil invader. Gemunu broke loose. But
> keeping with Buddhist ethos he paid homage to his dead adversary Elara.
> Prabhakaran is no just adversary. He must be eliminated.
>
> (*Sunday Times*, 18 January 2009).[6]

Goonatilake goes on to excoriate far more moderate Sinhalese opinion and to find parallels linking contemporary heroes and villains within the Sinhalese community with both ancient and more recent pre-colonial Sinhalese kings. Rajasinghe, a king who was a scourge of both Portuguese and Dutch colonial power, is equated with Gotabhaya Rajapakse, the president's brother and immediately responsible for the government military campaign as head of the Ministry of Defence. He effectively makes the suggestion that the international community and its intervention have a colonial ring to them. Goonatilake makes much of the Tiger emblem of the LTTE and the events of the Colan invasion of the eleventh century *'that laid us waste'* (*Sunday Times*, 18 January 2009, emphasis added).

Goonatilake undoubtedly engages in metaphoric hyperbole, but there is more than a hint of belief in the kinds of historical continuity that he expounds, and which he certainly expects among sections of his readership. Goonatilake epitomizes in his own Newspeak the dangers of the mythologizing of which we have written. The article also indicates the contemporary forces that drive the mythologization. The strong resentments in Sri Lanka against the colonial past are undoubtedly vital in Goonatilake's mythologizing, and are part of a populist legitimation of the government's antagonism to foreign intervention (read Western European involvement, especially that of Britain, where significant and influential members of the Sri Lankan Tamil community reside). The anti-colonial rhetoric obscures aspects of a radical internal colonialism that is now taking place.

Alarming in Goonatilake's rhetoric is the extraordinary doublethink whereby he implies that the 'appeasers' are racists – i.e. they are for the fragmentation of national territory along ethnic lines. (The reference is to various solutions that were discussed involving as a minimum some form of power-sharing and relative autonomy to Tamil dominated north-east; solutions that were dismissed by both the LTTE and the Sri Lanka government). Goonatilake follows with his 'non-racist' idea of a settlement. It is set in a language of egalitarianism and liberalism that makes a completely and scurrilous mockery of such ideals. It masks an intent that is the extreme inverse. We cite his Final Solution of the Tamil problem:

> Sri Lankans should have the freedom to settle anywhere in the country as indeed tens of thousands of Tamils have recently done in Colombo. The mono-ethnic nature of the North should be dismantled. All Sinhalese and Muslims expelled by the LTTE should be resettled with compensation. People from all communities should be settled in the empty lands of the North and commercial enterprises employing all communities started. Like Indian 'Defence Colonies' defence settlements should be established all over

the North. Retired husband and wife ex-employees of the armed forces
should be settled in such strategic settlements. Like mainland China, and
earlier in Korea, Armed Forces owned industries should be established in
these areas for both defence and civilian production. Our forces should be
further strengthened to deter any future attempts.

(*Sunday Times*, 18 January 2009)

Goonatilake finishes his piece with a rhetorical flourish, 'For the areas
won: rapid development, absolute and full equality and dignity. But no
appeasement of racism.' What bad faith! He in fact recommends the
thoroughgoing militarization of the North and the incarceration of its
population. Goonatilake sets out a plan for the further dispossession of Tamils.
Implicit in his position is an attitude that casts an entire population under the
shadow of enduring suspicion: a population made continually subordinate
to a controlling Sinhalese gaze and routinely committed to a secondary and
policed status in the nation as a whole. The falsity of his position is betrayed
by his comments on Colombo as a zone that exemplifies the future. Here,
the site of the terrible fury of the 1983 anti-Tamil riots, Tamils have in recent
years been increasingly regulated and made subject to the 'midnight knock.'
Since June 2006, Tamils living in Colombo and in the hill country have been
required to be registered at police stations. Both private and public businesses
have been required to register details of Tamil employees. It remains to be
seen if these restrictions will be lifted. Tamils in Colombo and elsewhere have
for a long time now been made to feel very vulnerable, especially in Sinhalese
dominated areas. Members of the Tamil elite have been subject to kidnapping,
murder and extortion. This has been occurring in a general climate in
which liberal-minded Sinhalese concern for genuine reconciliation has been
largely silenced, except for the critical voice of a few remarkably courageous
journalists who have been subject to threats, brutal beating and murder by
what seem to be government-supported thugs. Goonatilake often writes the
intellectual equivalent of this violent repression.

What is most alarming, is that the spectre of Goonatilake's vision could
actually be taking shape. Despite restrictions on entry into the militarized
north, there are unnerving reports of ethnic cleansing and extra-judicial
killings.[7] The internment camps have largely been disbanded, although there
are reports of some being maintained.[8] Lack of medical attention, food, and
ordinary facilities continues. In the north the presence of the military and
its control is thoroughly evident. While this may be necessary for security, it
could also be grasped as a long first stage in a process of ethnic cleansing and
territorial clearing. This may be all the more a possibility given a Sinhalese
nationalist mythological sensibility that tends to see Sri Lanka as a whole as

the primordial property of Buddhist Sinhalese, and positions Tamils as later violent and destructive intruders.

At a time when national reconciliation is most needed, there are suggestions that Sri Lanka government policy may be caught in the coils of the nationalist serpent and which may continue to realize its awful truth. The humanitarian situation of Tamils in the north and east continues to be shocking. The immediate concern is to ensure relief. But the situation is likely to endure – even should the government eventually acquiesce to some international assistance – if the structural and ideological forces integral to Sri Lanka government policy are not addressed. Should there be a failure to do so, then the humanitarian concern risks becoming instrumental in the very reproduction of the abjection it may wish to overcome. This is especially so if the condition for assistance, as imposed by the Sri Lanka government, is silence regarding the human rights abuses it appears to be condoning.

Much of the discussion to date in the aftermath of the war has focused on the matter of war crimes. However important this is – and little headway has been made – many of the conditions that gave rise to these remain and may become entrenched in the kind of peace that is being forged. That is, the crimes of war may be giving way to crimes of peace in which a whole population is made victim.

What we are witnessing appears to be the apotheosis of a strategy first envisioned by N.Q. Dias – Susantha Goonatilake is merely the latest advocate of such an approach. The relegation of the Tamils to second-class status has been well documented – while the International Community and Sinhalese liberals have spoken out against this strategy, it has been to little avail. The agenda appears to have been driven by the Rajapakse clan – Gotabhaya Rajapakse and Basil Rajapakse in particular; the latter, as head of the all-purpose Ministry of Economic Development, has occluded the participation of Tamil civil society groups in the redevelopment of the north-east.

Thus all signs point to the continued physical, administrative and legal encompassment of the Tamils.[9] Since the end of the civil war, and simultaneous with the increasing economic role of the military, the 'controlling agents of the corporatized Sri Lankan state are redrawing the internal ethnic and social delineations of the state in line with popular sentiment, but no less in the oligarchic interests of those who are in command of state machineries' (Kapferer 2010:143). As a further example of the encroachment of former military officers into the life of the north-east, in December 2011 the former Navy Chief of Staff, Mohan Wijewickrama, was reappointed as the governor of the Eastern Province. The current Government Agent for Trincomalee District in the Eastern Province is also a retired army officer. The consequence of placing retired Sinhalese military officers in charge of the distribution of state resources in Tamil/Muslim dominated areas, is to undermine the authority and capacity of Tamil public servants in the north-east (ICG 2011a:15).[10] This contributes to the general Tamil resignation to second-class status (ICG 2011a:16–17). Sri Lanka's present and future is clear – 'the emergence of Bonapartism centred on the capture of centralised state power' (Kadirgamar 2010:24).

Major General Mahinda Hathurusingha, the army commander of Jaffna, was at least open about the strategy of the state. Jon Lee Anderson, in an extended piece of journalism for *The New Yorker*, observed that both Hathurusingha and other senior military figures in Jaffna conceded that in order to gather intelligence the armed forces had 'infiltrated the Tamil population and installed electronic surveillance systems' (2011:49). We can assume that this new panopticism directed against the Tamils is here to stay – its multiple forms are military encirclement, Sinhalese 'colonization' of traditionally Tamil/Muslim owned/occupied land and militarized forms of development. Other more fluid (but potentially static) forms of panopticism are also evident. On the Colombo–Jaffna road, Anderson notes that 'cafés and picnic grounds had sprung up by the side of the road, with signs identifying them as "People's Rests" and "Army Welfare Canteens." They were occupied by soldiers and busloads of Sinhalese tourists' (ibid.:49). He continues that his Tamil aide and translator Siva 'remarked, "They are increasing, not reducing their presence. This is permanent." Entire military cantonments, made out of special materials supplied by the Chinese, were being erected all over the north. We passed many more Army camps along the road.' (ibid.:49).[11]

In a strategy that echoes with that of the Khmer Rouge in Cambodia, the violence of the state has also extended to eviscerating the memory of the Tamil struggle in the north-east.[12] Anderson notes that the army has

> ...methodically erased all traces of the Tigers in the north. Kilinochchi's cemetery had been totally eradicated. Pointing to mounds of broken gravestones and piles of rubble, Siva explained, 'The Army has come along and just bulldozed them.' In the center of Kilinochchi, the Army had erected a victory monument: a giant concrete cube with a bullet hole cracking its fascia and a lotus flower rising from the top. Soldiers stood at attention before a marble plinth, whose inscription extolled the Rajapaksas' leadership during "a humanitarian operation which paved the way to eradicate terrorism entirely from our motherland, restoring her territorial integrity and the noble peace.
>
> (ibid.:49–50)

We would add that this is indicative of the firmer establishment of the state as a dictatorial order, rather than a more democratic one committed to reconciliation: effectively extending the *state of exception* introduced in the circumstances of civil war into the post-war situation. This leaves Tamils, particularly in the liberated areas of the north and east of the island, effectively maintained in a situation approaching that of 'bare life' Agamben (1998) describes in *Homo Sacer*. Tamils, as is their potential conceived through the mythologies of Sinhalese nationalism, are that externality within the political order of the Sri Lankan state that sustains the political order of the *state of exception* that has become exemplary of post-war civil society in Sri Lanka.[13] This is, of course, in continuing dynamic formation, and we suggest is conditioned by the global context of what may be called the corporate-state assemblage, in which a shift in the imperial structuring of global political-economic relations is occurring, with China at the forefront of this restructuring.[14]

Conclusion

The end of the civil war presaged a future that has now been borne out. Moreover, this is apparent in a reformation of the state, occasioned in the *state of exception* of the civil war in which nationalism, as a technology of the state, is integral to the transmogrification and reconfiguration of the state and its apparatuses to support the formation of a dictatorial socio-legal order. That is, the *state of exception* conditioned in a civil war persists into the peace with the conquered Tamil population as perceived from a position within Sinhalese nationalist rhetoric. Apparatuses that were thinly disguised as pragmatic necessities of the war (the need to ensure the security of the state, for example) now seem to be (re-)occurring as the realization of some of the worst fears of the Tamil population. Such fears were instrumental in encouraging Tamil diaspora support for another ill-fated example of the many "cruel little wars" as Joxe calls them that have been and are being pursued in post-colonial realities across the globe.[15] Sinhalese/Tamil fears were promoted in a Tamil nationalism of self assertion in reaction and resistance to a Sinhalese nationalism that as the war endured grew in its passions further fanning the flames of fear on both sides. The immediate aftermath of the defeat of the LTTE has assumed the proportions of a Sinhalese nationalist triumphalism well in excess of mere pragmatic necessity.

NOTES

1   Report of the Secretary-General's Panel of Experts on Accountability in Sri Lanaka (2011), pp. 55–65.

2   http://srilanka.channel4.com/index.shtml

3   We are drawing an analogy here with the Nazi Final Solution to the European Jewish Question. We are not suggesting similarities in the form of extermination directed at the Tamils, for the Jewish Holocaust was a highly organized and bureaucratized process (Bauman 1989), but we are suggesting similarities with reference to the content of certain traditions in Sinhalese Buddhist nationalism which focus on the evisceration of memory, seeking to annihilate (and also physically marginalize) the physical presence of Tamils in a significant part of the north-east of the island.

4   http://colombotelegraph.com/2012/01/28/the-king-is-naked-and-fonsekas-lion-cubs/

5   Dutugemunu was a 2nd century BCE ruler from the south who defeated the Tamil ruler of Anuradhapura, Prince Elara. The story has been subjected to Sinhala nationalist revaluation (Kapferer 2012, 86; Kemper 1991, 59–65).

6   http://www.tamilnet.com/art.html?catid=13&artid=28217

7   International Crisis Group (ICG), *Reconciliation in Sri Lanka: Harder than Ever*, Report No 209, 18 July 2011a.

8   About 5,000 alleged former LTTE combatants remain in what the state refers to as 'rehabilitation centres'. This last group truly inhabit an exceptional space devoid of legal representation. (International Commission of Jurists Briefing Note, September 2010 – http://www.icj.org/dwn/database/BeyondLawfulConstraints-SLreport-Sept2010.pdf; while the figures may well be dated, even by the time of publication, the analysis remains relevant).

9   Anderson (2011:49); see also Tisaranee Gunasekara, http://www.thesundayleader. lk/2011/10/30/oppressed-north-lawless-south.

10   The militarization of the north-east is also having a devastating impact on the lives of Tamil women who are now heading households – there is evidence that Tamil women are been subjected to sexual assault, prostitution and sex slavery under the eyes of the Sinhalese military (ICG 2011b:1–49).

11   For an up-to-date account of militarization of civil life in the north-east see Tisaranee Gunasekara – http://www.thesundayleader.lk/2012/01/29/militarization-dynasty-and-democracy.

12   '[A]lmost all LTTE memorials and graveyards in Jaffna and Vanni constructed for their dead have been destroyed' (http://groundviews.org/2010/05/25/the-importance-of-not-forgetting/). The evisceration of memory has extended to the Sinhalizing of Tamil town names in the Eastern Province (De Votta 2007:48).

13 Here we note a similarity between Agamben's argument in *Homo Sacer* with the use by Kapferer (1988 [2011]) of Dumont's (1980) concept of hierarchy as applied to Sinhala nationalism where Tamils are an effectively subordinated externality in a Sinhala-dominated socio-political order and paradoxically integral to that order.

14 Following Rajapakse's visit to Beijing in 2007, the Chinese further increased military aid to Colombo. China had previously viewed the LTTE's challenge to state power as a purely internal matter for Sri Lanka, but this was no longer the case (http://www.timesonline.co.uk/tol/news/world/asia/article6207487.ece). It has become clear that other diplomatic options were open so far as guaranteeing Sri Lanka's territorial integrity was concerned. China would step in and offer Colombo a blank cheque for military assistance. They would extract a high price, but it was one that Sinhala nationalists were prepared to pay (http://www. thesundayleader.lk/2010/02/07/hambantota-in-the-great-game-of-the-indian-ocean; http://in.reuters.com/article/2009/07/01/idINIndia-40731520090701). There has emerged a common synergy between the increasingly authoritarian regime that Rajapakse is heading and the regime in Beijing (www.tamilnet.com/ art.html?catid=13&artid=31237). China's efforts after war's end has extended to providing technical assistance to Colombo to block access to Tamil diaspora web sites which provided alternative news sources on events in the island (Kapferer 2010:138–9).

15 Joxe (2002).

REFERENCES

Anderson, Jon Lee, 2011, 'Death of the Tiger', *The New Yorker*, 17 January 2011.

Agamben, Giorgio, 1998, *Homo Sacer: Sovereign Power and Bare Life.* Translated by Daniel Heller-Roazen. Stanford: Stanford University Press.

Bastin, Rohan, 2012. 'Empty Spaces and the Multiple Modernities of Nationalism' in Bruce Kapferer, *Legends of People, Myths of State*: Violence, Intolerance and Popular Culture in Sri Lanka and Australia. Berghahn Books: New York.

Cassirer, Ernst. 1946, *The Myth of the State.* New Haven: Yale University Press.

De Votta, Neil, 2007, *Sinhalese Buddhist Nationalist Ideology: Implications for Politics and Conflict Resolution in Sri Lanka*, Policy Studies 40. Washington: East-West Center.

International Commission of Jurists, 2010. *Beyond Lawful Constraints:Sri Lanka's Mass Detention of LTTE Suspects.* Geneva, Switzerland.

International Crisis Group, 2011a, *Reconciliation in Sri Lanka: Harder Than Ever,* 18 July 2011.

——— 2011b, *Sri Lanka: Women's Insecurity in the North and East,* 20 December 2011.

Joxe, Alain, 2002, *Empire of Disorder.* Los Angeles: Semiotext(e).

Kadirgamar, Ahilan, 2010, 'State Power, State Patronage and Elections in Sri Lanka'in *Economic and Political Weekly* xlv(2):21–4).

Kapferer, Bruce, 2012 (1988), *Legends of People, Myths of State: Violence, Intolerance and Popular Culture in Sri Lanka and Australia.* Berghahn Books: New York.

Klein, Naomi, 2008, *The Shock Doctrine: The Rise of Disaster Capitalism.* London: Penguin.

Ricouer, Paul, 1978, *The Rule of Metaphor* (trans. R. Czerny with K. McClaughlin and J. Costello). London: Routledge & Kegan Paul.

CHAPTER 6

The Hindu epics, theatre and the Indonesian state

Violence and cosmic regeneration
– a Balinese perspective

ANGELA HOBART

The chapter examines how far the Hindu epics the *Ramayana* and *Mahabharata* have influenced rulers in Southeast Asia in the formation and maintenance of the state. I shall focus on Indonesia, and more specifically on Bali. My aim is to shed light on the complexities of power in the Indonesian state, and, more generally, on the dynamics of nationalism in relation to the anguish and suffering of human beings.

There are more than 300 languages spoken in Indonesia, with as many different cultures. With a population of about 220 million, Indonesia is the fifth most populous country in the world. Ninety percent of the people are Muslim, at least nominally, but the state is not. Bali, a small island in the Indonesian Archipelago, is predominantly Hindu.

Political processes and nationalism inevitably depend on imagery – on myth, ritual, theatre, ceremony and architecture. In Southeast Asia it is, above all, the Hindu epics that have provided the people with role models, and with a means to aestheticize politics. To see what this can mean, we need but think of Thailand, where the Rama story (*Ramakien*) became so revered that the first king of the Chakri dynasty (1782–1809) took the official title of Rama I, and named the capital after Rama's mythical kingdom of Ayodya. Interestingly ASEAN, the Association of South East Asian Nations, is now promoting cultural projects based on the epics. In the words of the late Balinese scholar Bagus (2000):

[While the *Mahabharata* and *Ramayana*] depict war, rage, conceit, arrogance, and hate, in the end the great message of the two epics is is peace and human welfare.

Hence the epics could contribute to cooperation and mutual respect between nations.

It is no accident that the national airline in Indonesia is named after the heavenly bird Garuda, god Wisnu's mount in the *Mahabharata*. Garuda is also a prominent emblem in the coat of arms of the Republic of Indonesia. Although soap operas, pop songs, Chinese, Indian and Western films have become popular these days, the epics are televized and illustrated in books. Yet it is primarily through dance and drama that the epics become accessible to the whole population. This applies above all to the shadow theatre, *wayang*.[1] In Peacock's (1968:4) words the shadow theatre 'is regarded by Javanese as the most important vehicle of 'Javanese religion, that complex of mystical beliefs which most Javanese treasure more than Islam'. The earliest reference to what might be this theatre genre is datable to AD 907. Despite its Hindu associations, the shadow theatre is one of the few feudal institutions that Communists and hard-line Muslims alike have venerated. It is also relevant to note that the shadow puppet theatre in Bali, Lombok, Java, as well as in peninsular Malaysia, is one of the key cultural icons of Indonesia, recognized by UNESCO in 2003 as a Masterpiece of the Oral and Intangible Heritage of Humanity.

The known history of Indonesia extends from the era of kingship and empire building, to colonialism and post-colonial state formations. Recently intense ethnic and religious strife have racked such remote provinces of the country as Aceh in northern Sumatra, Ambon in the Moluccas, Timor, and Irian Jaya/West Papua. Historical data indicates that warfare and strife go back to Indonesia's earliest recorded times. The realities of Indonesians were and continue to be mythologized; they cannot be comprehended satisfactorily through the secular orientation of most Western contemporary philosophers and social scientists. As Dufrenne reminds us: 'the real loses its flatness only through the unreal, which puts the real into perspective and situates us in the midst of things' (1973:357). Intrinsic to this statement is the fact that imagery is never free-floating, but is grounded in the complexities of everyday actions and relations. It is only by exploring how the varied social and ideological threads interweave that we can gain an understanding of the power of the epics, and their associated imagery, in destroying or healing social tensions and divisions.

This chapter is divided into three parts, preceded by general comments on Indonesia, with specific reference to south Bali, a fertile rice-growing region where more than half of Bali's (over) two million people live, and my research area. The island is of special interest as its unique heritage, blending Hindu, Buddhist and Tantric elements with indigenous traditions of ancestor worship, animism and sorcery, has been used, simultaneously, to promote tourism and Indonesian nationhood (Picard 2000:102). Initially I will say something briefly about notions of the early Indonesian nation-state and introduce the epics. Secondly, mention is made of sorcery and healing practices in Bali as they emphasize the potency of the mythic imagery. In the third part the focus is on the Balinese shadow theatre. The discussion will oblige us in the fourth part to confront issues about the significance of narrative and imagination, and the potentially regenerative effects of performances for participants more widely in Indonesian society.

Java and Bali
Early notions of the nation-state and the epics
The known history of Indonesia extends from the era of kingship and empire building, to colonialism and post-colonial state formations. Indic influences arrived in the region from the fourth century onwards and remained prominent in Java up to the fifteenth century. The most remarkable archaeological remains are in the plains of central Java, where the colossal temple complexes Borobudur and Prambanan (also called Lara Djonggrang) were built around the tenth century AD. The former is Buddhist and the latter Hindu. In their grandeur and aesthetic complexity they dwarf anything comparable in India. The first detailed reliefs illustrating the *Ramayana* epic are at Prambanan. Fontein (1990:40) suggests that the high drama of the narrative reliefs reflect the oral tradition of storytelling in Java, with specific references to the shadow theatre.

Heine-Geldern's (1943:15–30) study of the religious basis of the palace-cities is the first developed model of the Indonesian state. He argued that the structure of the great temple complexes in Southeast Asia, whether Angkor Vat in Cambodia or Borobudur and Prambanan in Central Java, were modelled on Buddhist and Hindu cosmological ideas: the monuments replicate the universe on earth, in an attempt to perpetuate the harmony between the heaven and earth without which the kingdoms could not thrive. At the centre of the human world (Jambudvipa) rises the cosmic mountain, Mount Meru, where the highest gods dwell – gods whose power the king of the realm partakes in. Heine-Gelden's study of the early state was succeeded by Weberian ideas of the patrimonial state (Wisseman, 1985:3). The influence of these two scholars shaped later studies of state formation in Southeast Asia. Indian cosmological ideas also have a bearing on the shadow theatre.

Influential studies of early Indonesia politics emphasize the interrelations of art, religion, literature and politics in the Central Javanese period – a trend that has prevailed up to the present, especially in Bali and Java. Concomitantly Anderson (1979:43) argued that Javanese rulers achieved power through acquiring spiritual and moral knowledge, and by adhering to aesthetic modes of behaviour. Although power was fluid and unstable, the ruler was supreme in his world-state. The sign of his power was his 'mystic light of royalty', *teja* (Schrieke 1957:83). The masses were considered stupid and unenlightened. Accordingly, the state and capital city, Negara – etymologically there is no difference between them – was typified by its centre, and not the perimeter.

Later scholars (Fontein 1990:102–3; Wisseman 1985:3), however, point out that inscriptions and literary sources indicate that the bureaucratic administration was not as centralized as Heine-Geldern suggested. The importance of regional trade is ignored as is the complex relationship that must have existed between the elite and populace. These cosmological notions served to legitimize the courtly power centres.

Wolters' approach to the early city-states in Java is noteworthy in this context. Historical records, he suggests, reveal a 'patchwork of often overlapping mandalas, or 'circles of kings' (1982:16) – what Tambiah (1985:252) coined a 'galactic polity'. A mandala depended on a network of loyalties that could be mobilized to provide armies for leaders, who are best viewed as 'big-men' or 'men of prowess' (Wolters 1982:25). During life they participated in the authority of gods, which allowed them to act as mediators between the celestial and human realms. This is dramatically borne out by the fierce eleventh-century image of Garuda carrying the god Wisnu at Belahan (Figure 1). It is a posthumous 'portrait' of the great Javanese King Erlangga, of Balinese descent. In Wolters's (1982:61) opinion, Wisnu, the reincarnating god, provided a divine metaphor for exalting the king over the centuries.

A wealth of narrative reliefs based on the epic tradition is depicted on monuments erected during the Majapahit era in east Java. Bali became part of the Hindu-Javanese cultural world during this period (Wolters 1982:26). The mighty Majapahit Empire, or mandala centre, claimed suzerainty over most of the archipelago and beyond. The empire lasted for three hundred years. It disintegrated at the end of the fifteenth century with the gradual rise of Islam. The style of the narrative reliefs radically changed during the thirteenth and fifteenth centuries. In their positioning the flat figures recall those in ancient Egyptian paintings. They are in so-called *wayang* (puppet) style and resemble figures in the Balinese shadow play. Javanese puppets became highly stylized after the Majapahit era, probably because of the Islamic proscription of image-making (Holt 1967:135).[2] For the first time, royalty on some of the carved panels are accompanied by their dwarfed attendants[3] who are indispensable

Figure 1   Erlangga posthumous image as Wisnu carried by Garuda, from Candi Belahan, East Java, eleventh century. Now in the Museum of Moyokerto. Courtesy of Universitas Udayana, Department Pendikan Nasional.

to the shadow theatre. Although the cult of the kings declined in the fifteenth century, the epics have continued to inspire dance, drama and literature up to the present.

Generally it is said that the high castes (*triwangsa*) in Bali are descendants of aristocrats who came over when the Javanese kingdoms fell to the onslaught of the Islamized coastal sultanates. The people themselves distinguish between the insiders (*jero*) and the outsiders (*jaba*). The insiders are of noble birth, in contrast to the commoners who make up over ninety per cent of the population.

Bali was the last island to be incorporated into the larger framework of the colonial state in the early twentieth century. The Dutch affected power relations throughout the archipelago at the regional and national level by radically altering village organization, irrigation and patterns of landownership. The old kingdoms were replaced by colonial rule from the beginning of the nineteenth century to 1942 (when Indonesia was occupied by the Japanese), entailing an externally imposed bureaucracy that rendered the indigenous courts militarily and politically powerless. With regard to Bali, the Dutch sought to foster the idea that the island represented a 'living museum' of Java's Hindu heritage, the aim being to encourage tourism. Irrespective of Bali's history of warring kingdoms, slavery, mass suicides and feuds into the early years of the Republic, Indonesian presidents, Westerners and Balinese, alike, sought to perpetuate the image of Bali as a 'paradise island', where the royalty were patrons of the arts. President Sukarno, who led Indonesia to independence and nationhood in the 1940s, had a special relationship with Bali because his mother was Balinese. As the original (*asli*) culture of Indonesia, the island mirrored the kind of nation-state Sukarno wanted to recreate (Vickers 1989:180).

These images, as well as early studies by such scholars as Heine-Geldern (1943), undoubtedly influenced Clifford Geertz in his renowned work on the Balinese 'theatre state' in the nineteenth century – a system of government he claims was once widespread in Southeast Asia. According to his model, the king and his courts are placed in the 'exemplary centre' of the state and capital city. In Geertz's (1980:11) words:

> The kings and princes were the impresarios, the priests the directors, and the peasants the supporting caste, stage crew, and audience.

The statement emphasizes the expressive nature of the state, which was geared towards spectacle and 'the public dramatization of the ruling obsessions of the nobility: social inequality and status pride' (ibid.:13). Although Geertz's vision is evocative, it is static and timeless. The image of the theatre state is moreover belied by actual theatrical performances, particularly the shadow play in Bali to which I now wish to turn. In passing, it is, however, crucial to realize that this theatre genre is equally popular in Java, but there it was assimilated into Islam[4] and between the eighteen and twentieth century was developed into a highly sophisticated form of drama under the patronage of the sultans.

The epic tradition

Initially it is important to introduce briefly the epics in order to gain an understanding of their power and associated imagery in the shadow theatre and mundane life. Founding myths and legends stimulate the imagination and ignite the passions of nationalists almost everywhere. Said (1993) argued that English and French literature have provided a crucial setting in which the 'other' is imagined and created. Although many myths have been perpetuated and disseminated in Indonesia, the Hindu epics, the *Mahabharata* and *Ramayana*, are the key myths of national identity. Their impact has remained vital over the centuries, largely because they are articulated ever anew through visual and dramatic arts in the public domain.

The *Mahabharata* originally derived from India. The Indonesian *Mahabharata* comprises nine out of the eighteen volumes (*parwa*), present in the Indian tradition. The earliest volumes were composed around the tenth century in Java in Old Javanese prose. The central theme of the epic concerns the tragic conflict between the five Pandawa brothers, who were begotten by gods, and their first cousins, the one hundred Korawas, ogres incarnate. This culminates in the Great War, the *Baratayuda*, in which the Korawas, and their ogre followers, are defeated. The heroes of most stories are the Pandawa princes – gentle Yudistira, powerful Bima, comely Arjuna, and the twins, Nakula and Sahadewa. Their mentor is the brilliant and crafty Kresna, an incarnation of the preserver god, Wisnu.

The *Ramayana* is a long poem, which resembles the *Mahabharata* in language. It had been transmitted from India to Java by the eight century. The poem recounts the abduction of beautiful Sita by the demon-king Rawana. Rama, with the help of the monkey god Hanuman and his army of monkeys, rescues his wife from the demon's clutches. Rama, like Kresna, is an incarnation of Wisnu.

Myths drawn from the *Mahabharata* are particularly beloved in Bali and Java because they entail moral dilemmas, political intrigue, romantic overtures and family strife. The *Ramayana* has special appeal to statesmen. Nationalist pursuits may be crystallized in metaphors of conflict and violence derived from the epic. Rama epitomizes the righteous and benevolent ruler (*raja adil*).[3] President Sukarno commissioned performances of the *Ramayana*, for surprised visitors, to illustrate his authority and capacity to subdue wild 'unreason' in the nation-state.

Mention should here be made of the servant-clowns who do not appear in the Hindu epics, but have a crucial role in dramatic performances, making them accessible to the humblest of villagers. The servant-clown Semar in Java, or Tualen, his equivalent in Bali, is descended from the highest gods in folk myths.[4]

Bali
Magically images in healing and sorcery
Before turning to the shadow theatre, it is pertinent to say a few words on healing and sorcery rites in Bali, as they indicate the significant potential that this genre of theatre can have in certain medical and socio-political circumstances. Scholars, such as Obeysekere (1981) and Kapferer (1988:29–32), have long noted connections between forms of political authority, power and the traditional healing system, with specific reference to Sri Lanka. For the Balinese, myths, cosmic symbols and heroic images of political rhetoric familiar from the shadow theatre are enshrined in their medical practices. This is illustrated by so-called magical 'tools' (*pakakas;* Hobart 2003:62–73) made by sorcerers for clients. Sorcerers or scholarly healers are generally male and high caste. They are the most revered ritual practitioners on the island for their learning derived largely derived from the palm leaf manuscripts and their accredited power, *sakti*, which allows them to manipulate the forces of the dark. The tools are often in the form of charms or amulets and may contain drawings with images that closely resemble epic characters from shadow theatre. Practitioners explain that a drawing, once folded up and placed in a 'tool', transmits cosmic energy directly to supplicants in accordance with its orientation. Two examples of such magical drawings that folk healers may give clients during rituals are included. They include the Pandawa prince Yudistira (Figure 2) and the ogre Gundul (Figure 3). The drawing of Yudistira is given to village headmen or government officials to augment their authority and benevolence, enabling trust to be incited in others. The ogre is destructive in intent.

The mantas, incantations, that sorcerers or healers breathe into these 'tools' during the rites give an inkling of their performative immediacy, and the life-giving or murderous energies that practitioners and clients seek to engage in order to affect the consciousness of a person adversely or creatively.

Figure 2   Magical drawing of Yudistira who imparts authority and benevolence. Obtained from a healer/sorcerer. (Original in palm-leaf manuscript.)

Mantra to evoke the qualities of Sang Yudistira (called Darmawangsa in Bali)

Ong, Sang Hyang Darmawangsa (Yudistira)
reside in the centre of the world.
Manifest the 'essence' (*suksema*) of Dharmawangsa.
May white light from your forehead illuminate the world.
May gods and humans give homage.
May malign motivations of others be transformed
into reverence and compassion.
Ong, so be it.

The man to whom the sorcerer gave the 'tool' with the black magic (*pangiwa*) drawing of the ferocious ogre Gundul wanted to destroy the consciousness of his younger brother in order to take over all the family rice land after their father's death (ibid. 2003:86). The younger brother died not long afterwards. By rights, the land ought to have been shared between the brothers whereby it is important to emphasize that inheritances are among the most acrimonious issues in Bali.

Mantra to evoke the ogre Gundul

Ong, may I embody destructive power.
I am the powerful ogre/witch Gundul.
(Gundul) will pluck out the spirit of I Salem (the victim)
and remove his vital force.
May he cough up blood.
May he die.
Ang Ah (Sky Earth).

Healing and sorcery practices manifest cosmological principles and images that power can assume in theatre, as well as in everyday life in Indonesia (cf. Kapferer 1997:263–87). Ogres, for instance, in plays based on the *Mahabharata* support the Korawas, themselves incarnate ogres. To villagers ogres and demons are associated with the passions and furies that literally 'blind' (*buta*, denoting also demon) consciousness and fragment reality. The two examples of magical tools illustrate that the magico-medical system is a symbolically mediated mode of apprehending and acting on the world that can only be understood within a web of interpersonal processes that have moral connotation. Kleinman and Kleinman (1997:115) already drew attention to the importance of moral imagination cross culturally in relation to notions of suffering and responsibility. Thus the medical practices, I would contend, give impetus to both the destructive and the reconstituting potency of the embodiments of the figures – the kings, princes, princesses and ogres who dance in the shadow theatre to whom I now want to turn.

Shadow theatre in the early twenty-first century
The shadow theatre, *wayang kulit* (or *wayang purwa*)[1] has remained a rural dramatic art (Hobart 1987). It has never been tied to the elite, as in Java. *Wayang* may be derived from *yang* or *hyang*, deified ancestors, or may mean shadow (from *bayang)*. Some scholars argued that the shadow play developed out of ancestor rites (cf. Holt 1967:132). Ancestor worship is intrinsic to Balinese life. Ancestors can either be of benefit to descendants or bring

Figure 3　Magical drawing of ogre who brings destruction. Obtained from a sorcerer/healer. (Original in palm-leaf manuscript.)

affliction, if not revered. Traditionally, a person who did not know his clan ancestry was likened to one who 'gropes in the dark' (*wenten peteng, ten panggih napi*); suffering will follow. This has a bearing on our subsequent discussion.

Initially it is relevant to comment on the importance of sight in Balinese culture. Pinney (2004:8) has stressed the impact of visuality in India which endows religious–nationalist images with great efficacy in the public sphere. Images are not just representations; they can do something. Sight in Hindu-Bali has similar connotations: it is considered the primary sense in cognizing the mundane world. Westerners tend to focus on discourse as the prime means for comprehending the other. Balinese and Javanese, on the other hand, are intensely observant of the demeanour and actions of others which are

Figure 4   Stage of shadow theatre with puppeteer and musicians. Photographed by
            P. Horner.

generally considered more reliable than words that are delusive and cannot be
trusted. Unsurprisingly sight connotes ideas relating to insight, knowledge and
philosophy.[5] Such notions help account for the significance of the shadow play
in the society, and theatre genres like masked plays or contemporary drama
that follow its conventions.

The main occasion for a shadow play performance is in association with a
temple ceremony or sacrificial ritual, *panca yadnya*, when it is chosen because
of its moral and religious overtones. Spectators pay no fee for attending a
show; the village community sponsors it. The audience primarily comprise
men and young boys. Women often say they are not interested in the political
content of the stories, and do not like the long, drawn-out battle scenes.
Tourists rarely sit through performances as the stories are obscure.

The puppeteer, *dalang*, is the producer and sole narrator of a mythic
story. The gods are said to inspire him, if skilled, so that his narrative delights,
instructs and stimulates the audience. The following human or non-human
agents in the society are considered teachers: the ancestors, the rulers, village
headmen, school and college teachers, the parents, specifically the father,
and the puppeteer. Unsurprisingly, the Institute of Indonesian Narrators,
established in 1958 in Java, stipulated that puppeteers, who recount the

Figure 5   Shadows on screen (from left to right): Tualen, Yudistira, Kunti, Merdah and Bima. Photographed by G. de Caterina.

epic myths and founding legends of the nation, should play a part in the development of the Indonesian state (Moerdow 1982:53). The myths were viewed as integral to national sovereignty.

The puppeteer manipulates the puppets (the actors), projecting their shadows onto a cotton screen, to the accompaniment of the sweet and acid sounds from metal-keyed instruments (Figure 4). Most of spectators sit huddled together in front of the screen watch the dancing silhouettes. Some scholarly Balinese refer to them as *maya*, illusion (in Sanskrit) – a term that alludes to the illusionary and paradoxical nature of the phenomenological world (Figure 5).[6]

A performance at night takes place in an elevated booth. In Hindu-Balinese philosophy the stage is considered a microcosmic replica of the cosmos. Special attention should be given to the main scenic item in a performance, the Kakayonan, the Tree of Life or Cosmic Mountain (Figure 6) which creates the sacred setting of a play. It is the first and last silhouette to appear on the stage and marks important episodes in the story. Its form brings to mind the symbolism of ancient Javanese monuments. The Kakayonan is the main mediating figure between the seen and unseen realms, continually reaffirming that a progressive embodiment of macrocosmic processes is being unfolded during a show.

There are four main groups of characters derived from the epic stories: the celestial beings, the nobility, the Satriyas, the servant-clowns, and the ogres. During the show, the more righteous groups, the Pandawas and gods, in the *Mahabharata*, always enter from the right of the puppeteer, and the

Figure 5   Kakayonan, World Axis, and an ogre. Photographed by A. Hobart.

less righteous, the Korawas and ogres, from the left. Yet the ethical cleavage
between them is not absolute, for many characters are highly ambiguous.

The emphasis given to sight has a bearing on the puppets. Mention was
made to the fact that, they have a lingering affinity with figures on east Javanese
temples of the fifteenth century. As new puppets are made by copying old ones
puppet forms are relatively standard throughout the island. Hence spectators
immediately recognize main heroes as the shadows flit across the screen. The
eyes are the most important feature. Most of the characters in a collection of
about 150 puppets are nobility. Refined nobles have elongated, narrow eyes.
Ogres and coarse nobles, like the Korawas, have bulbous fiery eyes, implying
a hot-headed and uncontrolled disposition. Characters in performances
are further revealed by their voices and dance which are in tune with their
iconography. So refined heroes, like Yudistira or Arjuna, dance gracefully and
speaks with sweet eloquence. Coarse looking characters, on the other hand,
tend to move in a bold, abrasive manner.

The four servants stand out from the nobility by their idiosyncratic body
forms, and individualistic voices, gait and gestures in line with their multi-
faceted roles as clowns, court gestures, commentators, mediators and village
sages.

In view of the emphasis placed on the visual, it can be suggested that this
component encourages the aestheticization of politics through the medium
of theatre.

The performance and narrative

A number of prominent scholars have drawn attention to the socio-political significance of the shadow theatre in Java (see, among others, Anderson 1972 and McVey 1986). This aspect is also evident in Bali. In line with a society where sensitive issues are communicated in veiled terms (Hobart 2003), references to the Indonesian state and its leaders are merely alluded to in plays. Yet learned spectators immediately understand what is implied. This emerges in the few short extracts from performances that I witnessed and recorded in 2001 and 2002. The meaning of the dialogues was commented on by villagers in my fieldwork area. Inevitably, my own voice is interwoven with theirs. These short dialogues give a flavour of the Balinese shadow theatre, of one kind of dramatic practice in a loosely textured, multi-dimensional socio-political fabric that is ever-changing. The generative process and underlying structure of a play in relation to state building are discussed in the next section.

The first *wayang* performance, from which I have selected two example dialogues, was given during a collective cremation (*ngaben*) in the village Tegallalang in south Bali in 2001. The story was drawn from the *Mahabharata*, and was chosen to fit the occasion. The puppeteer improvised considerably, as is usual. The play begins with the Pandawa princes expressing their anguish to Kresna that many kin and innocent people had been killed in the Great War, the *Baratayuda*. Kresna consoles them, and advises them to carry out the burial rites (*pitra yadnya*) for the deceased spirits, in order to purify them. War breaks out between the princes and the ogres, who are vanquished.

The dialogues included are paraphrased, as they are highly idiomatic and repetitive. As is standard in *wayang* plays, the epic characters say little, and use archaic Javanese. The servant-clowns bring the stories to life by elaborating and translating their masters' speech into colloquial Balinese. The following dialogue takes place after the Great War. The servants, Tualen and Merdah, translate and comment on Kresna's and Yudistira's words.

Yudistira	I feel great sorrow for many have died in the Great War.
Tualen	I will translate what Sang Yudistira said. Forgive me [to the mythic princes and the audience] for any mistakes I make. We have won the war, but Sang Yudistira is overcome with sorrow, especially for his mother (Kunti) who lost her son, Karna, in battle. Other kin and many subjects died.
Kresna	Don't dwell on the past, brother. You defeated those who lack virtue (*adarma*).
Merdah	And who were the protagonists of the Pandawa – the hundred Korawa! They were consumed by greed and self-interest (*angkara*). It is proper that they die (*pantas kematiang*).

Tualen	It is difficult to destroy all the 'roots of evil' (*akah ane jele*) in a country. Even after ailing trees are cut down their sick roots will contaminates everything. The land must now be purified.
Merdah	Let us carry out the rites for the dead, so that the deceased spiritis do not become unruly demons (*buta cuwil*) who bring strife (*ngai kali*) to the community.

It was evident to learned spectators that Tualen was referring to the corruption in Suharto's era. Commoners and high castes alike pointed out that 'dross' (*lulu*) in a nation can only be regenerated by killing those responsible for it (see 'Cosmic regeneration', below).

After some banter, the two servants focus their attention on the complexities of power and status in the kingdom. They set out the present-day cosmological conception of the Indonesian state at the village level.

Merdah	[to his father] There are nine important administrative positions in the government. This tallies with the nine-fold division of the cosmos, the *nawa sanga* (the eight directional gods and the unifying god of the centre). The ruler is number one. He is followed by the generals of the army (TNI) and the police (POLRI) – both belong to the Indonesian National Armed Forces (ABRI).
Tualen	That accounts for three positions. What are fourth and fifth?
Merdah	The People's Consultative Council (MPR) and The House of Representatives (DPR). Below them are the governors of the Provinces of Indonesia (*bupati*), the heads of the districts (*camat*), the heads of the sub-districts and village headmen (*klian* and *lurah desa*).
Tualen	And then?
Merdah	The Supreme Court (Mahkamah Agung).
Tualen	You have missed out number nine?
Merdah	The people! The ruler and subjects must unite in order to ensure ensure prosperity and order in the country [returning to the epic], the kingdom of Rawana is in chaos.

Puppeteers, as mentioned, are informal teachers. This particular puppeteer shows remarkable knowledge of the present-day structure of the government.[7] The cosmological order, the *nawa sanga*, emphasizes the values of harmony and equality, and to a lesser degree hierarchy. It is not clear from the dialogue whether it is the ruler or the ordinary people who are at the 'centre' of the cosmic order.

When I spoke to the spectators after the play, they expressed empathy with the servant-clowns. Mere mention of the state makes villagers feel powerless. This was conveyed through a proverb: 'While the elephants fight with one another, the mouse deer [*kancil*] between them is squashed and dies.' The metaphor graphically illustrates the detrimental effect of a regime where officials play 'money-politics', and often clash with one another, ignoring their subjects' (i.e. 'the mouse deer's') needs. There are many instances of this, for example, the anti-Chinese riots of Jakarta in 1998, or the intimidation and notorious murdering of proponents of Timorese Independence in 1999.

The next extracts are drawn from a story based on the *Ramayana*. The play was performed during the anniversary celebration of the temple Duur Bingin in the district Gianyar in early 2002. The story ends when the hero-prince, Rama, is united with his devoted wife, Sita. In one of the final episodes the monkey-god Hanuman and the monkey armies enter Rawana's kingdom, Alengka. Rama kills Kumbakarno, Rawana's powerful brother. During the fray, the monkeys savagely hack off his limbs and tear pieces of flesh from his body. Although Kumbakarna's sympathies are with Rama, he is a sacrificial offering of the conflict, for he remains loyal to his home of origin. The dialogue is between Rawana's servants, Delem and Sangut, who comment on his tragic death.

Delem	Rama has shot an arrow into Kumbakarno's mouth.
Sangut	*Aduh,* Kumbakarno does not resemble an ogre. He is noble and powerful (*sakti*). [Rama shoots another arrow at Kumbakarno so that he ceases to suffer – *sangsara* – and his head falls off.]
Rama	[to Kumbakarno] May you be released and become a deified ancestor.
Sangut	Once Rama is in charge of Alengka. He will divide the land between the monkeys.
Delem	How should the land be divided?
Sangut	In the same way as Kumbakrno's body is apportioned. Rama will give each monkey his due, so that the flesh is shared fairly.

This dialogue alludes to a sensitive subject: land ownership. The Suharto family, Indonesian companies based in Jakarta and foreign investors have all bought thousands of acres of potential agricultural land in Bali and Lombok. While this usually involves the use of middlemen (*calo*), it is inescapable to Balinese that the 'thieving family' (*keluarga pemalingan*) of Suharto and their friends own many hotels and golf clubs on the island, particularly the luxury complex of Nusa Dua on the Bukit peninsula. Villagers speak with special scorn of Suharto's notorious son, Hutomo 'Tommy' Mandala Putra and his siblings Tut and Bambang, who are linked to numerous business concerns, from supermarkets to fuel supplies. Villagers have either been enticed by 'sweet talk' (*kalemesin*) or by intimidation from gangs of thugs (*sekan penjahat*) to sell their land. Police could not be trusted because they were often implicated in these dealings. Recently peasants have been able to retrieve some of the land so bought (see Liem, 2002:214).

In line with modernization and mass education, radios and televisions are found in most homes, and young Balinese read newspapers avidly. Spectators these days speak reasonably freely about political issues; also women voices are heard. Yet during President Suharto's rule villagers used to fear government reprisals if they openly criticized the state apparatus. They could be jailed, or forcefully taken away from their homes at night.

In the next example Rama's two servants Tualen and Merdah discuss the sad events which led to the capture of Sita and the brutal death of Kumbakarno.

Tualen	I am sad [at witnessing the previous events]. My sorrow cannot be cured by medicine.
Merdah	Your stomach is hot (*basing kebus*), your lips chapped (*bibih kepit*), your blood pressure high (*darah tinggi*). Go to a doctor and let him examine your eyes. If they are yellow, you have jaundice (*penyakit kuning*); if red, you are stressed.
Tualen	Don't make fun of me!
Merdah	If your eyes are blue you are like a foreigner who is rich. The doctor will examine you carefully.

This dialogue highlights the attitudes of most villagers towards tourists. They 'throw away their money' (*ngentungang jinah*), seemingly buying anything they desire. On the one hand, this incites anger at the government for failing to improve the standard of living of the commoners; but, on the other hand, 'thank heavens' (*keswecan antuk Sang Hyang Widi*) for tourists, as they are crucial to the livelihoods of many people.

Tourism accounts for eighty per cent of Bali's economy. The island has, therefore, been severely affected by the bomb attacks in Kuta Beach in 2002 that killed over two hundred people. Some English newspapers described the Bali as 'Paradise Lost' immediately after the event. As tourism is Indonesia's second largest source of revenue, after oil and gas, economic malaise in the whole country has increased as a result of the bombing (*Indonesia Newsletter*, January 16, 2003).

More recently, after the bomb blasts I witnessed technically innovative shadow theatre and drama performances that responded to the disaster (Sedana, 2003:73–86). New large puppets were made in the form of violent demons, *buta-kala,* who in plays possessed villagers to become terrorists; intense suffering followed in their wake. At the time I investigated the works of NGOs, with specific reference to the International Medical Cooperation

Figure 7   Servants in contemporary drama. Photographed by A. Hobart.

that was largely funded by the Australian Red Cross. The organization, realizing the popularity of theatre in the community to entertain and heal put on contemporary drama shows (Figure 7) throughout the island, drawing attention to the medical services they offered victims of the bombs. Yet the stories narrated were simplistic and had little appeal in rural areas. Nevertheless performances sought to illustrate how the wild is tamed by restoring the balance between the demonic and divine through human mediation. Demons are intrinsic to the Balinese cosmos. As emerges in sorcery practices they are associated with the passions and desires that can destroy life-worlds. They must be continually purified and transmuted through rituals.

Interrelated with the above is the important concept of *tri hita karana* which refers to the harmony that must prevail between the gods, the society and the environment for stability to prevail. Performances explicitly referred to this concept after the bomb blasts in order to help empower villagers to create order out disorder in the community.

Each performance is, of course, unique and transient, whilst making references both to earlier and current performances. Yet these short examples of dialogues from performances give an inkling of how socio-political issues are embedded in the narration.

A few general comments on the shadow theatre and the structure and logic underlying the performance are here relevant. A show continues for about three hours. There are three principal phases that flow into one another. The cause of the conflict is set out in the first phase. A theme of contention that always reappears is who the rightful heirs to the throne are.

Many scenes in the second phase take place outside the palace, in the forest, and are enacted by the servant-clowns. While elucidating the moral values upheld by their masters, the servants delight and entertain the spectators. They dance playfully or vulgarly, laughing, burping and farting. They either subvert or sustain order with their jokes, puns and oblique allusions to socio-political issues.

Negotiation breaks down in the third phase when the camps involving mainly nobility confront one another in battle that is often fierce and prolonged. The righteous dominion of the ruler re-emerges in this phase. Interaction between two conflicting groups accords to the fundamental principal of complementary opposites (*ruwa-bineda*) in Bali and Java: the demonic coexists with the celestial, the rough (*kasar*) with the refined (*alus*). It is not possible to have one with out the other; balance between them must be sought ever anew.

In the next section we will explore how the structure and regenerative dynamic of shadow theatre performances contributes to legitimizing different political claims and perceptions in everyday life.

Interweaving myth and reality: cosmic regeneration through theatre

How does the above discussion on the shadow theatre interpret into political and social reality? Villagers in south Bali describe government officials in Jakarata as 'big fathers' (*bapak besar*) who 'dance' (*mesolah*) while playing power politics; their subjects (*para panjak*) merely watch. Fittingly the setting of political discourse in both theatre and life is the family, and as Nadine Gordimer (2000:5) pointed out, morals and politics have a family connection, politics' ancestry being morality. An immediate link is made in these statements to the shadow theatre, which conjures up political and cosmic processes to Balinese. Victor Turner (1990:16–17) already drew attention to the continual interaction of social drama and stage drama, aesthetics drawing power from the social and vice versa. The shadow theatre is a unique vehicle in this context. Although it cannot be shown that the epics have causative power in the society,[8] the logic and aesthetic principles underlying the shadow play enable people on occasion to penetrate beneath the confused surface of daily life, allowing them to pull meaning from the tangle of events, perceptions and experiences, giving them direction and impetus. This comes to the fore in relation to three issues that are central in political discourse: legitimate descent, conflict and violence, and the interaction between rulers and subjects. A few words will be said by each of these.

It is crucial to realize that the shadow theatre expresses a view of historical reality in which history and myth merge. Sacred time and space were there in the beginning, underlie the present and help determine the future. In line with this, Brandon (1970:16–18) wrote that the cycles of shadow plays can be viewed as linked series, dramatizing the legitimate descent of Javanese kingship from the gods and ancestors, via the epic characters, to generations of Javanese kings and rulers of the twentieth century. The apical ancestor is Wisnu, the Preserver God, represented by Kresna or Rama in the epics. This is laid out in the included diagram (Figure 8, adapted from Brandon's [1970:17] condensed version of Javanese dynastic genealogy).

With secularization and modernization, this view may be less pronounced in Java these days. Yet it has still resonances in Bali where intellectuals and villagers continue to use epic heroes as character templates (see Holt 1996:145) by which to evaluate statesmen, while at same time endowing them with almost magical potency. Ruth McVey (1986:22) argued that situations and places might also be seen in terms of events dramatized in plays.[9] It is intriguing to explore briefly in what ways the people perceive that recent rulers are analogous to figures in the shadow theatre, whereby account is taken of their appearance, behaviour and character traits.[10] Rulers, too, may publicly compare themselves to *wayang* heroes they desire to emulate. This is

Wajang form	Dramatic cycle	Wajang hero	Historic period
	Rama	Rama	
		(seven generations)	
		Abijasa	
Wajang Kulit (or wajang purwa)	PANDAWA	Pandu	Ancient mythology (the ancestors)
		Ardjuna and brothers (knesa)	
		Abimanju	
		Parikesit	
		(two generations)	
wajang madya	Djajabaja	Djajabaja	Legendary Javanese kings
		(eleven generations)	
wajang gedog	Pandji	Pandji	Kedri Singosari (c.1000–1293)
		(eleven generations)	
wajang klitik	Damarwulan	Darmarwulan (Brawidaja)	Madjapahit (c.1293–1520)
		(fifteen generations)	
wajang Djawa	Diponegro	Diponegoro	Java War (1825–30)

THE DUTCH COLONIAL PERIOD (c. mid 19th century to 1945)

Wajang hero	Historic period
Karna, Birna	Sukarno (1949–67)
Hanuman, Duryodana, Desamuka/Butasiya	Suharto (1968–98)
Karna	Habibie (1998–2000)
Dastarastra	Abdurrahman Wahid (2000–1)
Yudistira, Drupadi, Srikandi	Megawati Sukarnoputri (2001–4)
???	Susila Bambang Yudhoyono (2004–present)

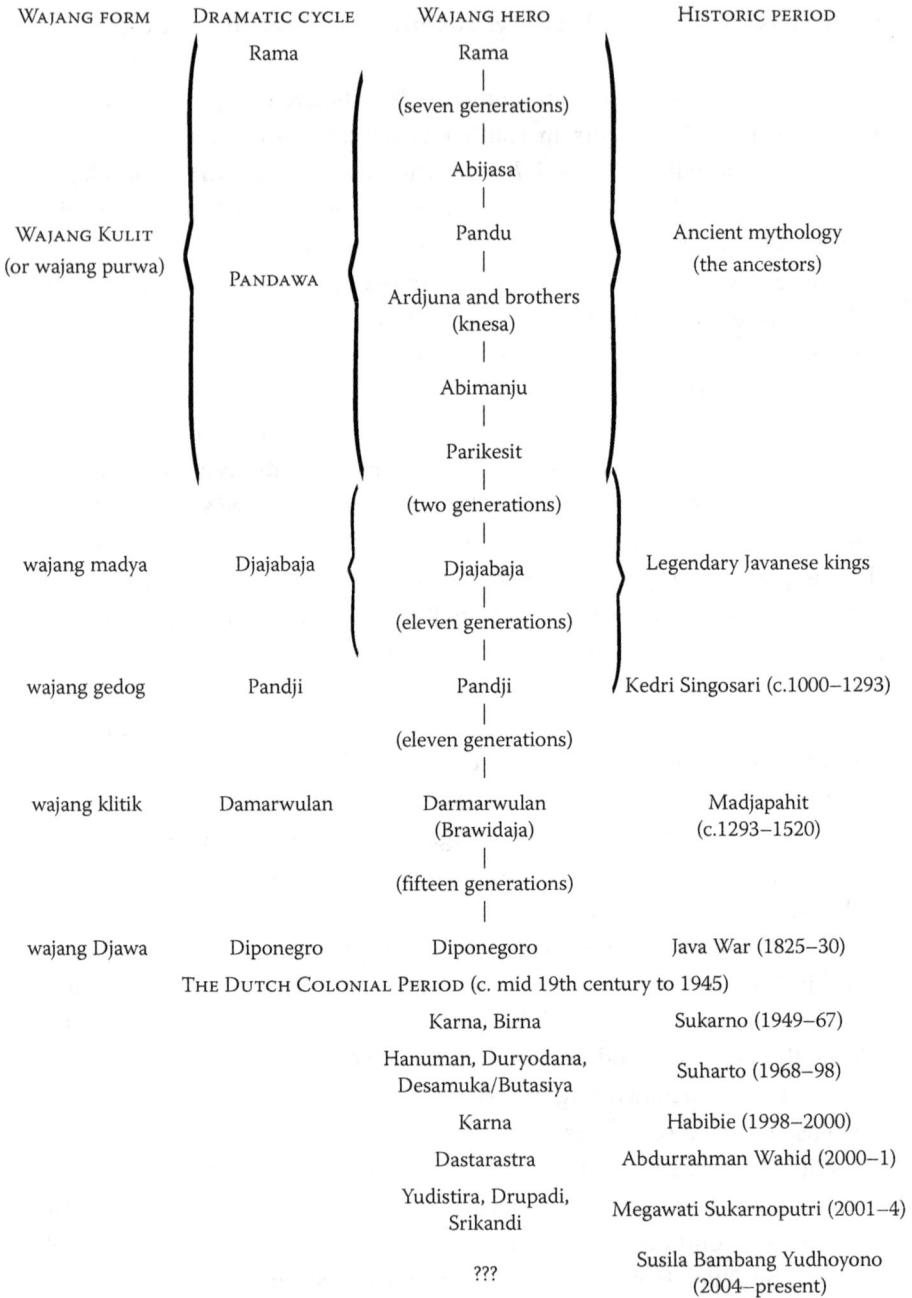

Figure 8   Javanese dynastic genealogy and epic characters, with added information given by Balinese villagers. CAPITALS indicate most important wajang form, dramatic cycle and wajang hero. Lines connecting heros indicate direct descent; intervening generations are also directly descended. Adapted from Brandon 1970:17.

a performative act, the purpose of which is to entice the imagination of their subjects towards perceiving them in the same light. This comes to the fore in relation to three recent presidents – Sukarno, Suharto and Megawati. The diagram, moreover, highlights how tenuous people's perceptions are: they may change over time. Villagers indeed stress that only after death does it emerge which epic hero a politician most closely resembles.

President Sukarno established the new Republic of Indonesia in 1950, four years after the end of the devastating struggle with the Dutch. His father was Javanese, and his mother was a Balinese Brahmana. As Sukarno was a sickly child, his parents named him Karno, after the epic hero Karna, illegitimate son of the Sun God, in order to transfer his potency to their son (Hering 2001:9). In his youth Sukarno gave himself the pen name Bima (Peacock 1968:4), the name of the mighty Pandawa Prince. Bima is also known for his fidelity to his ancestors.[11] Members of Sukarno's party, the Indonesian National Party (PNI), as well as the public, referred to him as either Bima or Karna. In mythic stories both Karna and Bima ruthlessly overcome all obstacles. The names are fitting, as Sukarno brought unity to a ravaged country. While a flamboyant, controversial leader, he retained respect with the masses that perceived him as supporting the Indonesian urban poor.

Like a strong father-figure and charismatic teacher, Sukarno declared Indonesia a guided democracy in 1958, and he defined the ethical principals, the *pancasila*, of the Republic – Belief in one God, Humanism, Nationalism, Sovereignty of the People, and Social Justice. These state-sanctified principles were later accepted as a key element in the national ideology. They were identified with the five Pandawa princes, and a special shadow theatre was created to convey their struggles against the ogres (Moerdowo 1982:25). In passing, it is interesting that the terms politics, or justice, only entered the Indonesian language during Sukarno's time. Justice, *keadilan*, is Arabic in origin. *Dedayan*, meaning cunning, shrewd and deceitful in Balinese, is the closest term to politics.

Balinese and Javanese (Anderson 1972:13) still today compare Sukarno to an adept puppeteer, *dalang*, because of his amazing oratory delivered in the 'mixed language of Indonesia's identity' (fundamentally Indonesian, but with borrowings from other foreign languages), and his skill in manipulating politicians of conflicting loyalties behind the scenes. During his leadership of the 'theatre state', in Vicker's (1989:178) deliberately chosen words, Sukarno sought to present the appearance of 'unity in diversity' (Bhinneka Tunggal Ika) the national motto, to Indonesians and outsiders alike.

Suharto envisaged himself as Sukarno's legitimate successor. Hence he called himself Hanuman, the name of the monkey-god, and Bima's mythic, half brother. Bima and Hanuman are semi-demonic figures, both embodying dangerous, paradoxical Tantric potencies. Suharto came from a farmer's family, and rose through the ranks of the military to presidency in 1965. His background is reflected in the name Supersemar, which was given to him in the letter of ascent to the presidency of 11 March 1966 (Magnis-Susena, 1999:221). The appellation Supersemar alluded to the enigmatic servant-clown Semar (called Tualen in Bali). Suharto preserved Bali's special place in Indonesian culture, and encouraged mass tourism as a source of national revenue. Initially, he seemed to bring prosperity to Indonesia. Yet his New Order revolved around himself. Corruption, collusion and nepotism (KKN) seeped through all sectors of the society. The Indonesian scholar Magnis-Suseno (ibid.:222) wrote that his lacklustre radiance, his family's greed and his insensitivity to the well-being of the people placed him on a par with the Korawa who did not listen to their faithful servants (Togog and Suraito in Javanese shadow theatre). Unsurprisingly, after Suharto's dramatic and bloody fall in 1998, Balinese liken him to the ignoble Korawa king, Duryodana, who is defeated in the Great War, or to his wrathful emanation Dasamuka ('the ten-headed' demon-god).

The succeeding two presidents Habibie[12] and Abdurahman Wahid[12] only governed the nation-state briefly. Irrespective of the fact that they are Muslim, Balinese have no hesitation in comparing them to *Mahabharata* characters, albeit to members of the Korawa camp. Although both tried to encourage civilian supremacy, they are perceived as supporters of the Suharto clan. Megawati Sukarnoputri became president with strong backing from the military and police, but her government is weak and impotent. The analogies that villagers make between her and epic characters illustrated a wistful wish to endow her magically with power and the necessary capacities to revitalize social and political realities, implicit to which is democracy at the grassroots level. At the beginning of her presidency many Balinese compared her to Yudistira, who is known for his sense of duty and compassion.[13] Yudistira is an effeminate *wayang* prince, whose hair is styled in a female bun. He is mild, modest and says little. This description tallies with Megawati's description in German newspapers as '*eine Hausfrau*' who enjoys shopping in Singapore and is taciturn at public meetings, letting her ministers justify her stance. Megawati has, of course, to tread warily in a strife-ridden country that is predominantly Muslim, particularly as orthodox Islam does not approve of women leaders.

Susila Bambang Yudhoyono was installed as President in 2004. He stands out as a moderate Muslim who is the most Western-friendly leader in Indonesian history. Yudhoyono's outlook is relatively secular. He composes love ballads and likes popular music. Balinese say it is too early to know what *wayang* figure he is comparable with. The *Frankfurter Allgemeine Zeitung*

(9 September 2004) likened him to an enigmatic character in the shadow theatre. A few Balinese suggest he has traits of Prince Bima as he is large in stature and his manner imposing. He has also brought in reforms and there is greater freedom of speech. Yet a number of villagers question how attuned he is to the concept of *tri hita karana,* referring to 'harmony between the gods, humans and the environment', as during his time in office the country has been beset by the 2004 Tsunami and other natural disasters.

As mentioned, contradiction and violence are intrinsic to dramatic performances. Tambiah painted a similar picture of the Balinese kingdoms of the nineteenth century. He ably refuted Geertz's argument that Balinese kings of the nineteenth century were 'still points' of exemplary centres, and as such immobilized and passive (1985:316–37). Traditional political dynasties were unstable and shallow, being characterized by conflict, intrigue and violence. The recurrent wars of succession related to control of resources and manpower. Rulers had to legitimize ever anew their claims to power through concerted, often contrived, links to the core descent line, or 'title line' (ibid.:334). Personal prowess and the capacity to ensure the people's welfare demonstrated their connection with the unseen world and their right to rule.[14] Schulte Nordholt (1996:334–6) pointed out that recurrent conflicts – albeit covert – continued to beset the kingdoms during colonial times. The kingdoms were never centralized polities. The *negara* is best described as a heroic polity in which the ruler was the pivot of significant events (cf. Schulte Nordholt 1985:32–54). Within this greater cosmic reality, warfare can be viewed as periodic revitalization in which the administrative apparatus is recharged with moral potency. Taussig's (1987:374) evocative imagery comes to mind:

> The space of death is notoriously conflict-ridden and contradictory,
> a privileged domain of metamorphosis, the space par excellence for
> uncertainty and terror to stun permanently, yet also revive and empower
> with new life.

Does this image resonate in the politics of the nation-state in contemporary times? Two examples are suggestive in this context. Corruption, tensions over land tenure, and the factionalism that arose during the colonial period all intensified during the Sukarno era and culminated in the bloody coup in Jakarta in 1965 that led to the massacre of the Communists (PKI) at the hands of the Nationalist Party of Indonesia and other anti-Communists. Thousands of people were slaughtered in Java and Bali. The killings provided a pretext to settle old grudges. For instance, numerous Chinese were executed, in part because of envy at their business success (Vickers, 1989:172). During the genocide both the Communists and Nationalists identified themselves with

*Figure 9   Masks of Osama bin Laden and President George Bush among demons
at Hong Kong Toy show. In* Jakarta Post, *23 October 2001. Courtesy of
Reuters.*

the Pandawas and their opponents with the Korawas. The Communist Party
even utilized Arjuna, the third Pandawa brother, by identifying his magical
arrow, Pasopati, with the hammer and sickle insignia. Some Balinese viewed
the killings as 'a sort of mystical cleansing of all the island's problems and ills'
(ibid.:173).

The next example brings us to the twenty-first century. After September
11 and the United States attack on Afghanistan, President Bush and Osama bin
Ladin were both put on a par with the Korawas. This is vividly demonstrated
in the photograph of a booth with masks in the market of Hong Kong that
was published in *The Jakarta Post* in 2001 (Figure 9). The two men are not
simply portrayed as mindless masks or puppets among demons and monsters.
Mention has been made of the importance of sight in Bali. Bush is squinting
and bin Ladin has one blind eye. To the Balinese defective eyesight implies
limited vision, a person consumed by narrow egoistical interest. Despite the
respect given to Westerners for their modernity (see Colmbijn and Lindblad
2002:18) anti-American sentiments were aroused by the invasion of Iraq
without international support; it was considered an 'act of terror' (Moestafa
2003). The epics are renowned throughout Southeast Asia and in this instance
they provide a powerful means for the people to understand and judge world
politics.[15]

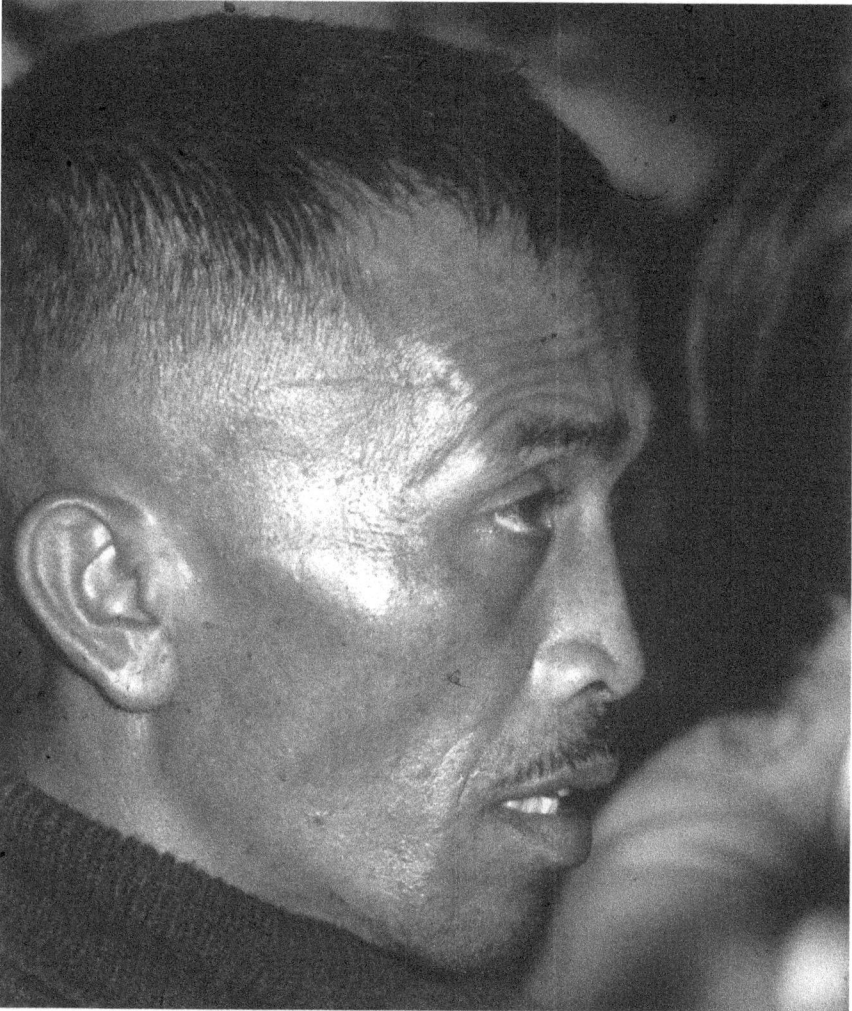

Figure 10   Villager. Photographed by A. Hobart.

Recent scholars have agued that the use of violence is legitimate in Indonesia – 'sometimes it may even be considered a good thing' (Colombijn and Lindblad 2002:15). The country is still beset by economic, political, ethnic, religious and educational problems. It is one of the poorest countries in the world. Anderson (2001:18) has drawn attention to the general absence of law and the corrupt judicial sector of the government. Hence there are few legitimate means for conflict resolution. In these circumstances, discord leading to violence is likely and recurrent. It is plausible in this context to suggest that the dynamics revealed in theatre, and echoed in healing and sorcery practices, may be resonated in actual situations of dissension and strife.

In both life and theatre, it is the commoners, the subjects, who represent the wit, the playfulness, the common sense, the rhetorical irony and wisdom inherent in the society (Figure 10). In so doing, they celebrate the dynamism and versatility inherent in village culture and as Bakhtin (1981:403–6) put it: laughter purifies dogmatism, pedantry, naiveté and sentimentality. In drama the servants are called *pandasar,* 'the basic ones', i.e. the basis of the society. Yet their power in relation to their masters is fluid and paradoxical. This applies to everyday existence. The authority of the ordinary people is in part illusory – at least at the national level. Despite the democratic processes initiated by Bambang Susila since he came to power, villagers interviewed in Bali despair of corruption abating. They describe civil servants as 'a type of lizard with big ears that do not hear' (*sekadi kuping alu*), as the suffering and pain of the subjects is not heeded sufficiently. It is, above all, theatre that continually draws attention to the commoners, the people at the grass roots level, for it is they who ultimately imbue society with strength and vitality.

Conclusion

It is evident that the epics provide Indonesia with the key nationalist myths and legends. This applies to much of Southeast Asia, allowing them to act as unifying force in the region. The potency of their imagery (and its dynamics) has to be seen in conjunction with the sacred shadow theatre. It is through theatre that myth has essentially become history, and history myth. This certainly still applies to Bali. As such, the epics, particularly when dramatized, furnish the indigenous people with a wide range of possibilities whereby they can legitimize different political claims and perceptions of realities. The diversity of images and interpretations that are thrown up during a show relate to the fact that the voices of the mythic characters, ancestral spirits and poet-priests interlock with the silent voices and hum of the audience. The mosaic of voices are interwoven and intertwined in a thousand ways ever anew during each performance. There is a continuous interchange between self and other, leader and subject, prey and parasite, performer and beholder; one is the mirror image of the other. A poem by Breytenbach[16] eloquently captures this duality.

O my snow-white shadow Death
O my own secret police
I will be yours forever
and you are
mine mine mine

(Coetzee 1966:227)

This theme has universal resonance. The Kakayonan, or World Axis, the main mediating figure between the seen and unseen realms in the shadow theatre, echoes it. In high Balinese, Kakayonan is derived from *mapikayun,* meaning the capacity 'to think' or 'to reflect'. The implication is that once alert, we can gain deeper understanding of the ambiguities and conflicts that are present in the depths of our consciousness, as well as in the world.

The figure, as it oscillates back and forth – between creation and destruction, laughter and tears, fragmentation and integration – during a performance, hints at our common humanity and the continual renewal that is possible when humans are centred within the cosmic processes, and imbue relevant situations and social relationships with healing force.

Acknowledgements

I would like acknowledge here I Ketut Suta Temaja who for many years has been an invaluable research assistant. His eldest son I Wayan Suardana, competently and patiently, helped me tape-record and transcribe theatre performances. I also want to express my gratitude to the Brahmana priest and healer, Padanda Gede Putu Ggenjung, the puppeteers I Wayan Wija and I Dewa Rai Mesi for the deep knowledge they shared with me about their healing and performative art and its socio-political significance in the society.

ABBREVIATIONS AND ACRONYMS

ABRI	*Angkatan Bersenjata Republic Indonesia* – Indonesian Armed Forces
DPR	*Dewan Perwakilan Rakyat* – House of Representatives
KKN	*Korupsi, Kolusi, dan Nepotisme* – Corruption, Collusion and Nepotism
MPR	*Majelis Permusyawaratan Rakyat* – People's Consultative Council
PNI	*Partai Nasional Indonesia* – Indonesian National Party
POLRI	*Polisi Republic Indonesia* – police.
PKI	*Partai Komunis Indonesia* – Communist Party
TNI	*Tentara Nasional Indonesia* – Indonesian National Army

NOTES

1   *Wayang* is the generic name for a variety of genres of theatre, the best known of which is the shadow play, *wayang kulit* (*kulit* means skin or leather). The shadow theatre is also referred to as *wayang purwa* (*purwa* implyies primeval, original; the term is associated with *parwa* or *parwan* in Bali, indicating the volumes comprising the *Mahabharata*.

2   Muslim Javanese even credited the Islamic sage Sunan Kalijaga with creating the shadow theatre; the five Pandawa brothers were said to represent the five principles of Islam.

3   Javanese rulers traditionally valued having clowns and dwarves in the palace. They were deemed to embody power that augmented that of kings.

4   To be just, benevolent and fair (*adil*) is one of the eight qualities of an ideal statesman as laid out in the epics; they are referred to as Hasta-Brata (Moerdowa 1982:68). Balinese point out that no human is capable of being just to all. Only water can be deemed 'fair', for it flows to the fields of both high and low castes without discriminating between them.

5   In high Balinese the eye, *panyurianan*, is derived from *surya*, sun. The Sun God, Batara Surya, brings clarity and light to darkness (Hobart 2003).

6   The indigenous concept of reality is complex. It bears resemblance to India (cf. O'Flaherty, 1984). The shadow theatre hints at the ambiguous nature of reality implicit to which is the interplay between the seen and unseen, the mundane and the spirit realm.

7   The government structure elucidated in the dialogue is essentially accurate, though simplified. For instance, the puppeteer does not mention the two quasi independent bodies the Supreme Advisory Council or the Supreme Audit Board which support the executive role of the government.

8   Locals, however, may point out that in certain circumstances a performance can directly affect political situations. For example, in 1957 a performance was given of the Great War in which Prince Karna was killed. That same night students threw grenades at President Sukarno, his namesake (see text) in Jakarta (Mulder 994:41). He in fact preferred to identify himself with Bima.

9   Interestingly, part of the far-flung island of Subawa, in eastern Indonesia, was given the name Bima, after the Pandawa prince. This probably testifies to the historical links that Subawa had with the kingdom of Majapahit (personal communication from Professor Michael Hitchcock, 2003).

10   Some *wayang* characters may be somewhat differently perceived in Java than in Bali. For instance, Javanese respect Karna's loyalty to Duryadana. Thereby Karna showed his gratitude to the king for honouring him despite his apparent lowly origins (Anderson 1965:15). Although Karna is intelligent and capable, Balinese, criticize him for supporting the Korawas (see Diagram 1, Habibie).

11   Bima is the hero in the *Mahabharata* who descended into the underworld to rescue his parents and bring them to heaven. To Balinese and Javanese Sukarno was acutely aware of his predecessors who enabled him to legitimize his claim to power. In Bali the deified ancestors continue to assist descendents if proper homage is given to them (see text).

12   Dastarastra (Diagram 1, Wahid), the father of the Korawas, was blind. Wahid, too, is blind in one eye and had a stroke. To Balinese his vision is blurred. Through

political manoeuvres he became president, rather than Megawati, who received most votes. During Indonesia's occupation of East Timor, Timorese fled to Bali and told of atrocities committed by the army. Many Balinese (probably erroneously) held Wahid responsible for these (Liem, 2002:215).

13 Some Balinese compare Megawati to the *wayang* heroine Srikandi, who is bisexual, as the president has a male role. Interestingly, Sukarno gave the name Srikandi to the first woman guerrilla of Indonesia in the 1962 liberation campaign (Anderson 1965:26).

14 Traditionally royal legitimacy was linked to the possessions of heirlooms, such as *krises* (daggers) and palm-leaf manuscripts, that were imbued with power from the unseen. In contemporary times, President Sukarno and Suharto are said to have consulted healers and worn magical charms to protect them.

15 This also applies to the past. For example, during the conflict between rulers of Surakarta in the eighteenth century, the Javanese often identified the Dutch with the wise servant Semar because of their shrewd manipulations in assisting the sultans. In the early nineteenth century, Javanese perceived both the British and Dutch as ogres or witless servants in *wayang* (Carey 1993:75). For a detailed account of how *wayang* became an important area of negotiation between the Javanese and the Dutch, see Shears'(1996) work on colonial discourse and Javanese tales.

16 These lines are taken from one of Breyten Breytenbach's poems written while imprisoned from 1975–82 for opposing the apartheid regime of South Africa. Many of his prison writings are dominated by the figure of a man looking into a mirror who realizes that 'you' and 'I' need not stand for fixed positions.

BIBLIOGRAPHY

Anderson, B., 1965, *Mythology and the Tolerance of the Javanese.* Ithaca: Cornell University, Modern Indonesian Project.

——— 1972, 'The idea of power in Javanese culture'. In *Culture and Politics in Indonesia,* ed. C. Holt. Ithaca: Cornell University Press.

——— 2001, 'Introduction', In *Violence and the State in Suharto's Indonesia*, ed. B. Anderson. Ithaca: Cornell University, South-east Asia Program.

Bagus, I. Gusti Ngurah, 2000, 'Welcome Address', *The Second Conference-Seminar on Ramayana and Mahabharata*, Denpasar, Udayana University.

Bakhtin, M., 1998 [1981], *The Dialogic Imagination.* Austin: University of Texas Press.

Boon, J., 1977, *The Anthropological Romance of Bali 1597–1972.* Cambridge: Cambridge University Press.

Brandon, J., 1970, *On Thrones of Gold.* Cambridge, MA: Havard University Press.

Carey, P., 1993, 'Dance drama (*wayang wong*) and politics at the court of Sultan Hamengkbuwana III (1812–14) of Yogyakarta'. In *Performance in Java and Bali*, ed. B. Arps. London: School of Oriental and African Studies.

Coetzee, J., 1996, *Giving Offence: Essays on Censorship*. Chicago: University of Chicago Press.

Colombijn, F. and Lindblad, J., 2002, 'Introduction'. In *Roots of Violence in Indonesia*, eds. F. Colombijn and J. Lindblad. Leiden: Royal Institute of Linguistics and Anthropology.

Dufrenne, M., 1973, *The Phenomenology of Aesthetic Experience*. Evanston: Northwestern University Press.

Fontein, J., 1990, *The Sculpture of Indonesia*. Washington, DC: National Gallery of Art.

Geertz, C., 1980, *Negara: the Theatre State in Nineteenth-Century Bali*. Princeton: Princeton University Press.

Gordimer, N., 2000, *Living in Hope and History*. London: Bloomsbury.

Heine-Geldern, R., 1943, 'Conceptions of state and kingship in Southeast Asia', *Far Eastern Quarterly* 2:15–30.

Hering, B., 2001, *Soekarno: Architect of a Nation 1901–1970*. Amsterdam: Royal Tropical Institute.

Hobart, A., 1987, *Dancing Shadows of Bali*. London: Kegan Paul International.

——— 2003, *Healing Performances of Bali: Between Darkness and Light*. Oxford: Berghahn Books.

Holt, C., 1967, *Art in Indonesia: Continuities and Change*. Ithaca: Cornell University Press.

Indonesia Newsletter of the Embassy of the Republic of Indonesia in London, Volume 22, 16 January 2003.

Kapferer, B., 1988, *Legends of People Myths of State: Violence, Intolerance, and Political Culture in Sri Lanka and Australia*. Washington, DC: Smithsonian Institute Press.

——— 1997, *The Feast of the Sorcerer: Practices of Consciousness and Power*. Chicago: University of Chicago Press.

Kleinman, A. and J. Kleinman, 1997, 'Moral transformation of health and suffering in China'. In *Morality and Health*, eds. A. Brant and P. Rodin. London, New York: Routledge.

Liem, S.L., 2002, 'It's the military, stupid!'. In *Roots of Violence in Indonesia*, eds. F. Colmbijn and J. Lindblad. Leiden: Royal Institute of Linguistics and Anthropology.

Magnis-Suseno, F., 1999, 'Langsir Keprabon: new order leadership, Javanese culture, and the prospects for democracy in Indonesia'. In *Post-Soeharto Indonesia: Renewal or Chaos*, ed. G. Forrester. Singapore: Institute of Southeast Asian Studies.

McBeth, J., 1999, 'Political update'. In *Post-Soeharto Indonesia: Renewal or Chaos*, ed. G. Forrester. Singapore: Institute of Southeast Asian Studies.

McVey, R., 1986, 'The *wayang* controversy in Indonesian Communism'. In *Context, Meaning, and Power in South-east Asia*, ed. M. Hobart. Ithaca: Cornell University Press.

Moestafa, B., 2003, *The Jakarta Post*, Jakarta, 1 January 2003.

Moerdowo, R., 1982, *Wayang: its Significance in Indonesia Society*. Jakarta: Balai Pustaka.

Mulder, N., 1994, *Inside Indonesia Society*. Bangkok: Duang Kamol.

Obeyesekere, G, 1981, *Medusa's Hair*. Chicago: University of Chicago Press.

O'Flaherty, W.D., 1984, *Dreams, Illusions and Other Realities*. Chicago: University of Chicago Press.

Peacock, J., 1968, *Rites of Modernisation*. Chicago: University of Chicago Press.

Picard, M., 2000, '*Agama, adat, budaya:* the dialogic construction of *"kebalian"*', *Dialog: Journal Internasional Kajian Budaya*. Denpasar: Udayana University.

Pinney, C., 2004, *Photos of the Gods: The Printed Image and the Political Struggle in India*. Oxford: Oxford University Press.

Said, E., 1993, *Culture and Imperialism*. London: Chatto and Windus.

Schrieke, B., 1957, *Ruler and Realm in Early Java*. The Hague: Van Hoeve.

Schulte Nordholt, H., 1996, *The Spell of Power: a History of Balinese Politics, 1650–1940*. Leiden: Royal Institute of Linguistics and Anthropology.

——— 2002, 'A genealogy of violence'. In *Roots of Violence in Indonesia*, eds. F. Colmbijn and J. Lindblad. Leiden: Royal Institute of Linguistics and Anthropology.

Sears, L., 1996, *Shadows of Empire: Colonial Discourse and Javanese Tales*. Durham, NC and London: Duke University Press.

Tambiah, S., 1985, *Culture, Thought, and Social Action*. Cambridge, MA: Harvard University Press.

Taussig, M., 1987, *Shamanism, Colonialism and the Wild Man: A Study in Terror and Healing*. Chicago: University of Chicago Press.

Turner, V., 1997 [1990], 'Are there universal of performance in myth, ritual, and drama?'. In *By Means of Performance: Intercultural Studies of Theatre and Ritual*, eds. R. Schechner and W. Appel. Cambridge: University of Cambridge.

Vickers, A., 1989, *Bali: a Paradise Created*. Berkeley: Periplus Editions.

Wisseman, J., 1985, *Theatre States and Oriental Despotisms: Early Southeast Asia in the Eyes of the West*. The University of Hull: Centre for Southeast Asian Studies, Occasional Papers No. 10.

Wolters, O, 1982, *History, Culture, and Region in Southeast Asian Perspectives*. Singapore: Institute of Southeast Asian Studies.

CHAPTER 7

The death of divine kingship in Nepal

Nepal's move from autocratic monarchy

to a fragile republican state

BAL GOPAL SHRESTHA

In the reign of the king curfew turns every house a jail
Yes, the stupid kings have been imposing curfew for ages
However, people never stopped pulling down pillars of the palaces
This time again, the people are rising from every direction
They are marching forward violating the curfews
Chopping off hands, legs and neck of the monarch
The people are already in the path of a people's republic of Nepal.
– Bikram Subba[1]
(An acclaimed poem during the 2006 people's movement in Nepal)

Introduction

Nepal's interim parliament declared the country a 'federal democratic republic' on 28 December 2007. In May 2008, the first meeting of the elected Constituent Assembly (CA) formally removed the king from power. In the perception of most Nepalese, this was a historic moment. The chairman of the Communist Party of Nepal (Maoist), Prachanda, asserted that 'there was no chance of the revival of the monarchy'. Yet the transition from the autocracy of the king, via Maoist insurrection, to democratic rule has emerged as problematic and complex. This chapter discusses the dynamics of resistance and control in the Nepalese state by examining the role of the monarchy, the socio-political processes underlying state power and the people's struggle for democracy.

When the 2006 people's movement was launched, it targeted the authoritarian king. People from all walks of life, including the Janajatis ('indigenous nationalities'), the Madhesi (the people of Tarai[2]), the Dalit (low and untouchable castes) and women, participated in the movement aimed at defeating the king, with the aspiration of turning Nepal into an all-encompassing, accommodating and democratic state in which all citizens enjoy equal rights. These groups had remained oppressed and neglected for almost two-and-a-half centuries under the rule of the Shahs, while the high-caste Hindu Hill Bahun (Brahmin) and Chetris within the Khas ethnic group controlled the power structure. After 2006, however, state power simply shifted from the king to these very same Hill Hindu Bahun and Chetri high-caste elites, led by Girijaprasad Koirala, who became Prime Minister for the fifth time. His interest in Bahun supremacy did little to change the fate of the oppressed and disadvantaged section of the society. The Bahun and Chetri elites sidelined the neglected groups when the interim constitution was promulgated on 15 January 2007. Even the 'revolutionary Maoists', who had fought a guerrilla war against the 'feudal centralized state', supported the elite, disregarding their earlier promises to 'empower' the oppressed segments of the society. The Maoists joined the Seven Party Alliance (SPA)[3] to bring down the king, as they no longer thought that a 'final victory' could be achieved in the war against the 'oppressive state'. This resulted in them sharing state power with their one-time 'class enemies'. Unsurprisingly, the Janajatis and the Madhesi remained discontented, and violence erupted in the Tarai, coinciding with the promulgation of the interim constitution. The government showed little inclination to address the issue, fearing that to do so would help the Maoists politically. So the Tarai problem escalated, and continues to detrimentally affect the economy and security of the country.

Kingship has always been repressive in Nepal. The history of democracy in Nepal can be perceived as a constant power struggle between the state and the people. The Nepalese population have expressed their wish for democracy through repeated, massive people's movements, but time and again they were deceived (see Thapa 2006).

As an institution based on the traditional concept of divine power, the kings of Nepal did not feel it necessary to abide by democratic norms. In this context, this chapter examines the difficulties of establishing a democratic government in Nepal, and provides explanations for the Maoist's war. Issues related to the April 2006 people's movement illustrate the fears and hopes that accompanied the transition of the country from autocratic monarchical state to a fragile democracy, and from a fragile democracy to a fragile federal democratic republic.

The successor to the Shah dynasty

Scholars such as Marie Licomte-Tilouine (2004) presumed that the Maoists leadership under the hill Bahun elites might succeed the king. In analysing the fierce warrior strategy of the Maoists during the fight against the feudal kingship, she presumed that the Bahun leadership of the Maoists would be the most likely successor to the Shah kings. However, no full victory transpired, as they joined the SPA to defeat the king, and became part of a government accepting Girijaprasad Koirala, a 'bourgeois' chieftain, as an all-powerful premier and the head of state in the 'New Nepal'.[4] The Maoists had aimed for a victory that allowed them to become the new, and sole, rulers of the country, saviours of all the oppressed and disadvantaged groups; but that did not happen. Therefore, they repeatedly demanded that Nepal be made a republic, instantly, and that Koirala become the first president. The latter initially refused, wanting to wait until after the CA elections. The Maoist party then presented its leader, Prachanda, as the only viable candidate for the 'first president of Nepal' during the 2008 the CA election. But although the Maoist Party emerged as the largest party in the CA election, it failed to obtain a working majority of seats, and was prevented from implementing any of its programmes. The dream of making the Maoist Chairman Prachand the first president of republic Nepal was not to be realized.

In fact, Girijaprasad Koirala very reluctantly accepted the 'republic' the Maoists' pressured for, supporting the monarchy until the last minute. Some, like the Nepali Congress Party leader Gopalman Shrestha, even opined that King Gyanendra be made the first president of Nepal, so as to smoothen the transition towards a republican set-up.[5]

Scholars such as Keshavman Sakya (2007) believe that the 'anti-king' war was in reality largely between the two high Hindu castes, the 'Bahuns' and 'Chetris', with the Bahuns enjoying victory after the defeat of the Chetri king. He thinks, since the leadership of the SPA, including the Maoists, is in the hands of Hill Bahuns, they are now the true rulers of the country. They were able to grab state power and discard the king when the Janajatis and the Madhesi put their weight on their side. The balance of power might change any time if these groups change their positions. During the interim period (2006–8), the Bahun-Chetri elites again tried their best to retain their supremacy over other ethnicities. Therefore, the Janajatis and the Madhesi are on the warpath with the ruling Bahun-Chetri elites because the latter failed to fulfil their aspirations. The oppressed Janajatis, too, are determined to have their share of state power. However, nothing is crystal clear about the future of the king, federal structure, republic or the successor to the Shah dynasty, because it appears that the king and the ruling Bahuns will not easily relinquish the power they have enjoyed for hundreds of years.

Figure 1   *A cartoon showing how the Nepalese Brahmins are determined to keep control over the resources, depriving Janajati (indigenous nationalities), Madhesi (people of the plain) and Dalit (lower caste) in the name of nationalism. Drawn by Rabin Sayami 2008.*

Some senior Maoist leaders talk about a 'democratic coup' against them. They also fear 'Pakistani-style political assassinations' in Nepal. Similarly, leaders of other parties accuse the Maoists of hatching a 'nationalist coup' as they began seeking support from the former royalists, in their bid to strengthen 'nationalist forces'[6] in the 'republic of Nepal'. If a 'coup' or 'assassination' of any leader does take place, the whole political process will be at a stake.

State and power in Nepal

At present, the words 'country', 'nation' and 'state' are frequently used interchangeably. However, in a deeper sense, they carry distinct meanings. When we speak about a state, we are talking about the domination of a political unit over a certain geographical area. Nepal was divided into several tiny monarchical and tribal states before the development of centralized feudal power. Historians such as Dhanavajra Vajracharya (1999:11) suppose the boundaries of ancient Nepal to be as large as those of the present day. Inscriptional evidence tells us that rulers in ancient Nepal, such as Manadev and Amsuvarman, proclaimed themselves to be great feudal masters (*mahasamanta*), and were proud of their supremacy and influence over the lands and people they ruled. In a later period, Nepal disintegrated into several small states and principalities. These came under the domination of one single administrative unit after the 1769 Gurkha expansion. As elsewhere, the 'dominance of the victors of history' is apparent in Nepal. Max Weber's definition of 'monopoly on the legitimate use of physical force within a given territory' is evident in Nepal. The various Janajatis that lost their lands to the Gurkha Empire, and remained oppressed by Khas (Brahmin-Chetri) chauvinism under the pretext of Nepali nationalism, are now actively asserting their distinct national identities by restructuring the state into a federal set up.

From the dawn of Nepal's history till today, kings and feudal chiefs controlled the lands and monopolized taxes. They punished and rewarded people as they wished. The kings in Nepal behaved no differently than Louis XVI of France, who proclaimed 'I am the state'. The king's word was the law. For centuries, state power in Nepal revolved around the kings and the royal palace, and it continued to do so until recent events. The Nepalese kings controlled the sovereignty of the state until the political changes of 1990 forced King Birendra to relinquish it, thereby empowering the Nepalese people themselves as the sovereign power. Janajatis in Nepal are, furthermore, no longer ready to accept centralized state power; rather they desire a decentralized federal state.[7] These developments in Nepal fit the arguments of modern-day scholars such as Michel Foucault, who believe that the notion of a sovereign, centralized state is outdated (Foucault 2000:123). King Gyanendra reclaimed sovereignty when he became king in 2001, and behaved as the centre of power, but the Nepalese people discarded him, and the April 2006 people's movement compelled him to cease his attempt to regain power.

Kingship, the state and the political background

Ancient Hindu scriptures put the king at the summit of the mechanism of the state. As a ruler, the king was an agent of the gods, a god in himself, or at least supposedly possessing some divine powers. Divinity gave the highest position in the state to the king (Bühler 1969:216; Kane 1977:1639). As a king, his duty was to maintain and protect law and order, and no man was supposed to disobey him (Heesterman 1986:1). It was his divinity that authorized him to reward and punish his subjects and led him to be considered the supreme or sovereign power of the state.

The belief in the king as god is a pre-historic tradition in Nepal, and the kings have abided by it till modern times. The Licchavi kings (464–878 AD) claimed that they were descendants of the God Sun. Their successors, the Thakuris (879–1200 AD) and the Mallas (1200–1769 AD), made similar claims. The Malla kings also identified themselves with the terrifying god Bhairava, a form of Lord Shiva. The Goddess Taleju was their tutelary goddess.[8]

The Malla kings began the tradition of worshipping the Living Goddess Kumari, believing her to be a manifestation of the Goddess Taleju in human form. Inhabitants say that the Goddess must put *tika*, a mark of blessing, on the forehead of the reigning king on the last day of the Festival of Indra in Kathmandu, in order to re-endorse his rule for the coming year. If she refused, he might lose his kingdom. According to one story this indeed happened to Jayaprakash, the last Malla king of Kathmandu. Prithivinarayan Shah, the warrior king of the Gurkhas, launched a surprise attack on Kathmandu, and conquered it on the day that the people were celebrating the Festival of Indra. Prithivinarayan Shah then arranged for himself to receive *tika* from the Goddess Kumari, legitimizing his conquest. His descendants continued this tradition. In 2007, King Gyanendra went to receive *tika*, but only after the Prime Minister, as head of state, had received his. King Gyanendra feared an evil spell might affect him if Kumari did not bless him with *tika*. After the CA election in 2008, when the rule of Nepal passed to a President, the former king was banned from attending any religious and cultural programmes in the capacity of head of state.

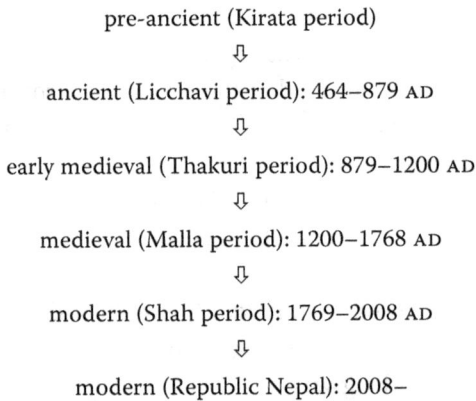

pre-ancient (Kirata period)
⇩
ancient (Licchavi period): 464–879 AD
⇩
early medieval (Thakuri period): 879–1200 AD
⇩
medieval (Malla period): 1200–1768 AD
⇩
modern (Shah period): 1769–2008 AD
⇩
modern (Republic Nepal): 2008–

Table 1   A timeline for Nepal.

The Gurkha rulers enforced rules based on Hindu religious scriptures that encouraged caste-based hierarchies, discrimination and, of course, the Gurkha kings' supreme position as a reincarnation of the Hindu God Visnu. The geographical boundaries of Nepal were reduced to their present size when in 1816 they were obliged to sign a treaty with the British Empire. Though Nepal never came directly under British colonial rule, from that point on, its rulers had to obey the British.

Internal power struggles between members of the Shah dynasty (Shah 1990; Stiller 1975) gave rise to the dictator Jangabahadur Rana (Stiller 1981). He established the notorious Rana oligarchy in Nepal, ensuring the post of the Prime Minister to his brothers, their sons and their cousin (1847 to 1951). As a result of a massive uprising, the Rana oligarchy came to an end on 19 February 1951, and Nepal achieved democracy. However, after the 1951

Figure 2   King Birendra and his family, who were massacred in 2001. Official website of Nepal's royal palace (defunct).

change, as a new democratic country, Nepal had to experience politically unstable period between 1951 and 1959. The conflicts among political parties helped strengthening power of the king. In this way, instead of consolidating democracy the political change only reinforced the Shah Kings. In 1955, with the death of King Tribhuvan, his eldest son, Mahendra, became the new king. On 12 February 1957, he promulgated a constitution, and the first parliamentary election was held in 1959. The Nepali Congress Party (NC) won this election and formed a government. On 15 December 1960, however, Mahendra staged a *coup d'état*, dismissed the elected government, banned political parties, and imprisoned all prominent political leaders[9] Mahendra's dictatorship introduced the Panchayat system, which lasted thirty years. This was an attempt to homogenize the country by enforcing the adoption of one religion (Hindu), one language (Khas) as Nepali, one culture and a one-nation policy, under the pretext of 'Nepali nationalism'. It systematically suppressed ethnic languages and cultures. In 1971, on the death of King Mahendra, his eldest son Birendra inherited the Panchayat system.

In 1979 a spontaneous students' protest forced King Birendra to proclaim a referendum, seeking the people's opinion as to whether to retain the Panchayat system with reforms, or to reintroduce the multiparty democracy in Nepal. The results of the 1980 referendum were Panchayat with reforms, so the political parties once again had to suffer prohibition. In fact, political parties in Nepal did not consider it as a fair referendum. However, they continued their struggles to restore multiparty system. Finally, on 8 April 1990, a People's Movement (*janandolan*), succeeded at obliging the king to lift the ban.

Prithvinarayan Shah (1768–1775) ruler of Gurkha from 1743

Pratap Singh Shah (1775–1777)

Ranabahadur Shah (1777–1799)

Girvanyudhabikram Shah (1799–1816)

Rajendrabikram Shah (1816–1847)

Surendrabikram Shah (1847–1881)

Prithvibikram Shah (1881–1911)

Tribhuvan Shah (1911–1955)

Mahendra Shah (1956–1972)

Birendra Shah (1972–2001)

Dipendra Shah (2001 king for three days)

Gyanendra Shah (2001–2008)

Table 2   A chronological list of Nepal's Shah kings.

King Birendra reluctantly transferred sovereign power to the people with the promulgation of the 1990 constitution.[10] The constitution failed, however, to address the problems of the neglected communities and ethnic nationalities (the Madhesi), the non-Hindu populations and the Dalit, socially disadvantaged low caste and women.[11] It also maintained Nepal as a Hindu kingdom and reasserted a single Khas language as Nepali, the official language of Nepal, just as the Panchayat system had.

In April 1991 the first general election returned the NC as the largest political party, enabling it to form a single-party government under the leadership of Girijaprasad Koirala. However, the ruling party could not fulfill the hopes and expectations of the people regarding social, political and economic changes. Corruption, nepotism and upper-caste dominance contributed little to the upholding of democratic norms. Inflation and rampant corruption angered and frustrated the populace. At the same time, inter- and intra-party conflicts increased day after day (Hacchethu 2006). On 10 June 1994, as the ruling party failed to pass a motion of vote of thanks for

Figure 3   Gyanendra standing in full attire and crown. Official website of Nepal's royal palace (defunct).

the king's speech, Koirala tendered his resignation, dissolved the parliament and announced a mid-term election in November.

The 1994 mid-term election proved disastrous, resulting in a hung parliament. The largest party, the CPN United Marxist and Leninist (UML), had to seek support from opposition parties to form its government, which lasted for only nine months. Nepal experienced a series of government changes, with no coalition surviving for more than a few months. In the general election of 1999, the NC was once again returned as the largest party, but its intra-party disputes did not cease. It seemed multi-party democracy was on course for failure.

The death of divine kingship

With the introduction of the 1990 constitution, the powers of the king were considerably reduced. However, neither he, nor other royal members, took the change easily. In general, King Birendra behaved as a constitutional monarch and acted as a stabilizing factor; but one faction in the palace led by his brother, Gyanendra, and the queen mother, Ratnarajya, always opposed the loss of royal power, and they played an active role in weakening political parties so as to regain the lost power of the palace.[12]

The modern history of Nepal refers to the palace as the seat of conspiracies (Dangol 2005). High posts in the army were reserved for the relatives of the kings and queens. In the 1 June 2001 royal-palace massacre, King Birendra and all the members of his family, his two sisters and youngest brother were killed. The Royal Investigation Commission blamed the crown prince Dipendra of committing regicide. He was made the king for two days while he was in a coma, before being declared dead. The Nepalese people, however, did not believe the report, instead accusing Gyanendra, the only surviving brother of King Birendra, who succeeded to the throne, of being the murderer. Gyanendra's multiple businesses were notorious before he became the king. Many link him to underworld trades, such as drug trafficking and the smuggling of Nepal's ancient treasures to other countries (Greenwald 2001:131–3). In addition, his only son, Paras, whom he made the crown prince, is a known criminal with a record of killings and brawls at nightclubs. Therefore, the Nepalese people do not see King Gyanendra and his son Paras as the successors to the Nepalese throne.[13]

The slaying of the king in a family feud, in a country where he was supposed to be an incarnation of Lord Visnu, was astonishing, but the 2001 incident made it clear that divinity did not protect him from his own son or brother, let alone his foes. This naturally shattered traditional faith in the power of the divine king. Even for the most religiously minded people, it was the end of the divinity of the king.

A widespread myth about the Shah dynasty is that the god Gorakhnath had bestowed King Prithivinarayan Shah and his descendents with the rights to rule Nepal for ten generations – ending with King Birendra's death. As both of his sons were also killed in the palace massacre, no natural line of succession remains. Therefore, the Nepalese people consider, the kingship has lost its authority. Although Gyanendra had succeeded Birendra, religious people did not accept him as a true king.

Political turmoil

Soon after the palace massacre, the game of toppling Koirala began within his own party. This time his own protege, Sherbahadur Deuba, was on the warpath, and indeed succeeded in bringing him down. On 22 May 2002, Premier Deuba dissolved the elected parliament, having failed to gain support from his own party members to extend the state of emergency for the third time. On 4 October 2002, however, King Gyanendra abruptly sacked Deuba and took over executive power, overstepping the constitution.[14]

Figure 4   Women marching with a banner saying 'Let's abolish the monarchy and establish a republic'. Photographed by Basanta Maharjan, 2006.

Against the king's authoritarian move, the five major political parties, though remaining loyal to constitutional monarchy, intensified their agitations. Amidst increasing anti-king agitations, Gyanendra reluctantly reinstated Deuba as the Premier on 5 July 2004. However, on 1 February 2005, King Gyanendra suddenly staged a *coup d'état*, further damaging the already unpopular monarchy in Nepal.

The situation compelled constitutional parties to join hands with the Maoist rebels. On 22 November 2005, a twelve-point agreement was signed between the Seven Party Alliance (SPA) and the CPN (Maoists) to end the king's arbitrary rule. While the twelve-point agreement was explicitly against the 'regressive kingship' (*nirankush rajtantra*), it was only implicitly for a 'republican' Nepal. The Maoists, however, reiterated that they were firm in their goal to turn Nepal into a republic. All parties, except for the royalist ones such as the National Democratic Party (Nepal), dropped their commitments to 'constitutional monarchy' from their party constitutions by 2006. During the April 2006 Movement, the Nepalese people's single demand was that Nepal declare itself a republic by ending the monarchy immediately.

The SPA, with active support from the Maoists, launched their decisive agitations from 6 April 2006. They drew massive support from people of diverse walks of life. The Movement spread from the Kathmandu Valley to major cities and the villages throughout the kingdom. At its peak, late on the night of 23 April, the king accepted the people's sovereignty in a televized speech, reinstated the parliament he dissolved four years previously and agreed to accept the SPA's roadmap, while still hoping to retain a certain form of kingship. By the time of his announcement, however, the people no longer wanted to retain kingship in Nepal. Throughout the country, statues of the present and past Shah Kings were smashed and hoardings with the quotations of the kings were torn apart or burnt down. It was clearly the end of the 240-year-old Shah dynasty's power in Nepal.

On 18 May 2006, the reinstated parliament revoked all the king's powers and declared Nepal a secular state. It also declared the nationalization of all the properties he had obtained by virtue of being king, such as palaces, forests and national parks, historically important heritage sites etc. Furthermore, the interim constitution came into effect on 15 January 2007 that completely deprived King Gyanendra of any executive rights.

1769	the Gurkha conquest of Nepal and the rise of the Shah dynasty
1846	the Kot Massacre and the rise of the Rana Oligarchy
1951	Nepal received democracy by ending the Rana rule
1959	the first general election was held in Nepal
1960	King Mahendra banned political parties and introduced the autocratic Panchayat system
1979	students' movement against the Panchayat system
1990	the reintroduction of the multi-party democracy with a constitutional monarchy
1996	the Communist Party of Nepal (Maoist) launched the 'people's war'
2001	the June 1 palace massacre, which killed King Birendra and his entire family
2002	
22 May	Prime Minister Sherbahadur Deuba dissolved the elected parliament
4 Oct.	deposing the Deuba government, King Gyanendra assumed executive power
2005	
1 Feb.	King Gyanendra staged a *coup d'état* and imposed a state of emergency
2006	
24 April	Gyanendra relinquished power in the wake of a massive people's movement

2007

January   the outbreak of the Tarai Madhesi unrest in the southern belt of
            Nepal
15 Jan.   Interim Constitution issued and the Maoists enter the parliament
1 April   the Maoist joined the interim government
28 Dec.   the interim parliament endorsed the country to be a 'federal
            democratic republic' but to be rectified by the elected Constituent
            Assembly (CA)

2008

10 April   elections to the Constituent Assembly (CA) to draft a new
            constitution
28 May   the newly elected CA formally declares Nepal a federal democratic
            republic
11 June   Gyanendra moved out from the Narayanhiti royal palace
21 July   the CA complete the election of the first president and
            vice-president
15 Aug.   members of the CA overwhelmingly elect the Maoist leader
            Prachanda as the first prime minister of the Republic of Nepal

2009

May   the Maoist led government falls on the issue of the sacking the of
            army chief, and Madhavkumar Nepal of UML becomes the new
            prime minister with the support of NC, Madhesi and other fringe
            parties

2010

28 May   the CA term extended for another year, as its agreed two-year term
            expires, and Madhavkumar Nepal resigns as prime minister.

2011

Feb.   Jhalanath Khanal becomes the third prime minister of the Republic
            Nepal
28 May   amidst considerable uncertainty, the term of the CA is extended for
            3 months

Table 3   A chronology of events.

The Maoists' people's war

The root cause of the Maoist movement in Nepal is the extreme inequalities
in income and political power within the country. Already in 1992, scholars
such as R. Andrew Nickson had predicted a Peruvian type of Maoist uprising
in Nepal. In February 1996, the CPN Maoists launched the people's war when
the then government ignored their 40-point demands.

The Maoists' 40-point demands were on three themes: nationalism, democratic rights and everyday life.[15] The first nine nationalist demands included the removal of all unequal treaties with India, and the end of the monopoly of foreign capital in Nepal's industry, trade and economic sector etc. The next seventeen demands related to democratic rights included the right to draft a new constitution by the people's elected representatives; curtailing of all the special rights and privileges of the King and his family; the bringing of the army, police and administration under the people's control; declaring Nepal a secular state; giving equal property rights to daughters and sons; the end of all kinds of exploitation and prejudice based on caste; autonomy for ethnic nationalities; the end of the status of Dalits as untouchables; the equal status of all languages; the arrangement of education in the children's mother tongue up to high-school level; and the guarantee of free speech and a free press. The remaining demands were related to people's everyday lives, such as tillers' rights over land, guarantees of work and welfare allowances to jobless people, free and scientific medical services and education to all, etc. Unfortunately, the government chose to suppress the Maoists instead of fulfilling any of their demands or finding a negotiated settlement. The ignoring of the demands merely helped spread support for the Maoists across the country.

The history of the communist movement in Nepal began with the establishment of the Communist Party of Nepal (CPN) in 1949. They actively contributed to Nepal's 1951 democratic movement only to be left in a limbo for years. They participated in the 1959 general election and were able to send just four members to the 108-member parliament. After the 1960 royal *coup d'état*, the party again had to function in hiding or from exile. Soon after the 1960 royal coup, sharp ideological differences surfaced within the party. While functioning underground during the 30 years of Panchayat regime, the CPN split into many factions. At the time of the 1990 people's movement, about a dozen different communist groups were in existence.[16]

In the aftermath of the 1990 changes, the CPN underwent both polarization and unifications. The 1991 election result showed that the main opposition UML and the United Peoples Front (UPF), a legal front for the CPN Unity Centre, as the two strongest communist parties (winning 69 and 9 seats, respectively, in the 205-seat parliament). Conflict between the ruling NC and the UPF increased as the latter's demands on behalf of underprivileged sections of society were ignored. In addition, the UPF experienced suppression in their constituencies. For them, their supposition that the parliament was not the right place to solve the people's problems was proving correct. They therefore boycotted the second general election in 1994, and initiated a new party: the CPN Maoist.

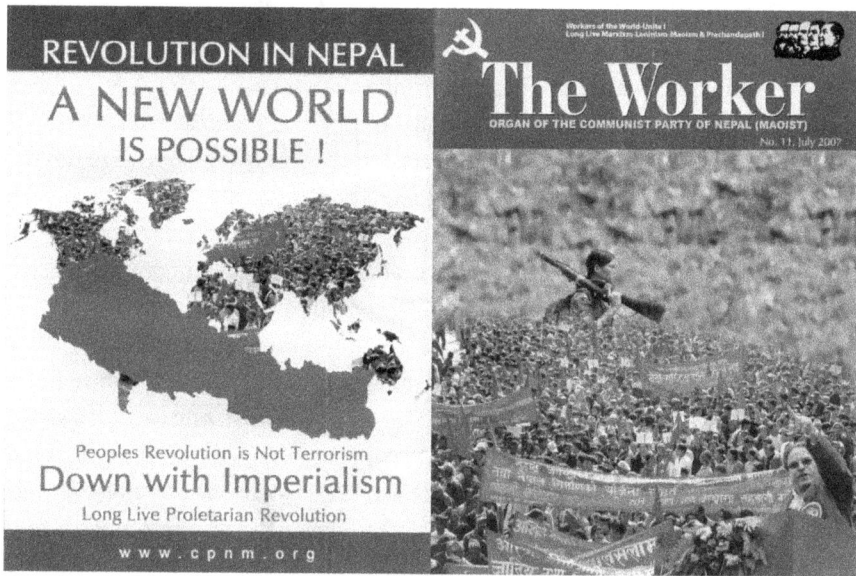

Figure 5   A cover of a Maoist Party magazine 'The Worker' (July 2007).

In 1996 they launched the people's war. Against general predictions, the Maoists insurgency sustained its guerrilla war for ten long years, and succeeded in influencing the entire country by 2006. The Maoists, although not very popular among the affluent populations, boast support at the grassroots. From November 2005 they began to collaborate with other parliamentarian parties to fight against Gyanendra's authoritarian rule. When the war ended in May 2006, more than 14,000 Nepalese had lost their lives, and more than 500,000 people had been displaced from their homes. The country experienced a deep economic crisis, and women and children in rural areas, especially, suffered a great deal because of the war.

The Maoists are tarnished by their extortions and atrocities, but they are admired for many social reforms and changes. For instance, in a country where women have been socially dominated for centuries, the Maoists recruited thousands of women in their people's army (PA), which even encouraged the government to recruit women in the royal army. The Maoists are also credited for awakening the rural poor, Janajatis, women and oppressed low castes against social injustice and discrimination. Political analysts such as Professor Lokraj Baral consider that Prachanadapath (Prachanda's doctrine), though principally based on Marxist, Leninist and Maoist values, is moulded according to the needs of the Nepalese context. He notes that the Maoists are flexible enough to accept a multi-party system and a pluralistic society, which has made it possible for them to cooperate with other bourgeois parties (Baral 2007).

The ultimate goal of the Maoists, however, was to establish a 'people's republic'. Some analysts claim that their 'joining the political mainstream is only a tactical move designed to weaken the state from within and seize power.' (Mehta 2007). The Maoist top leaders hoped for a 'final victory' during the CA election so that they could restructure the state according to their principles, but this did not happen. The coercive activities of its Young Communist League have had damaging consequences, despite its many commendable works.

After the Maoists signed a peace agreement with the government in November 2006, they agreed to confine their 31,000-strong people's army (PA) in cantonments and to lock their arms in containers under the control of the United Nations Mission in Nepal (UNMIN). However, the UNMIN has verified only 19,000 of 31,000 as PA, as some have left the cantonments and other were under-aged. The debate regarding the integration and rehabilitation of the PA is still going on over. The fear is there that if the Maoists and other parties fail to agree on this issue, then the peace process may break down.

International influences

Nepal, a country situated between two giant neighbours, China and India, is subject to multiple foreign influence, particularly from India, and more recently from America. The geopolitical realities, combined with historical, cultural, and economic links between the two countries, increased the importance of India for Nepal's politics. It was apparent already in the early 1950s, when Nepalese people began agitations against the Rana rule. While it is notable that it was with the help of India that Nepal achieved democracy in 1951, Nepal has also had to sign iniquitous treaties with India, such as the 1950 peace treaty that was signed secretly by the last Rana prime minister, Mohan Shamsher. During the 1951 uprising, to the call of the NC, the Nepalese people actively participated in the struggles to end the Rana rule, but it was the Indian prime minister, Jawaharlal Nehru, in Delhi, who decided the outcome of the uprising. Jawaharlal Nehru in Delhi arranged a secret agreement sign between the King and the last Rana Prime Minister, Mohan Sumsher, which forced the Nepali Congress Party to abandon their struggle against the Rana regime. Not only the people of Nepal, but also the leaders of the Nepali Congress Party who led the struggle, were unaware of the treaty. India's role in Nepal has not diminished in more recent times.

During the 1990 changes, India's role was vital (Parajulee 2000:177–219). In 1989 and 1990 there was a serious trade and transit dispute between Nepal and India, which contributed to economic hardship in Nepal and created a fertile ground for a movement aimed at regime change and democracy. India and its people provided moral support to the democratic movement, though the Indian government remained neutral (Hoftun *et al.* 1999:267–8). Similarly, the United States played an active role in encouraging the Nepalese elite to solve the problems through dialogue and negotiation. The European Union, Amnesty International and Asia Watch also contributed to the public opinion in favour of a democratic transition.

However, since 9/11 the world has changed. From that time, the 'war on terror' became more important than promoting democratic consolidation. For example, military, economic and political aid from the United States now strengthened the authoritarian regime in Nepal. Eventually, it encouraged Gyanendra to stage the 2005 *coup d'état*. In the early stages of the king's direct rule, America continued its support for him, with the hope for success in the king's attempt to wipe out the 'Maoist terrorists'. But mounting public dissatisfaction over the king's authoritarian rule pressured the SPA to cooperate with the Maoists, and thereafter the international community, India, America and the European Union all began to support the agitating parties. The SPA and the Maoists signed a 12-point agreement in New Delhi, and although they refute Indian government's involvement, it was widely reported that the Indian authorities facilitated the compact. Similarly, it was reported that the then American ambassador to Nepal, along with other envoys, supported the agreement.

Both India and America also tried until the last minute for a negotiated settlement to save the king. A student leader told the BBC that an American authority had even threatened to revoke their visas (they were planning their journey to America), if they did not stop their anti-king agitations. When the people's movement was at its peak in April 2006, Karan Singh, a special envoy of the Indian government, arrived in Nepal in a bid to rescue the king. Immediately after he left Nepal, King Gyanendra announced some concessions to the SPA that were instantly welcomed by India, the United Kingdom, the United States and the European Union. However, the agitating parties disregarded it and continued their protests. As the people prepared for a final showdown against the king on 24 April 2006, he announced his retreat late in the night of 23 April. Radhakrishna Mainali, then a royal minister, disclosed to the BBC that the king had done so, as the then Indian envoy in Nepal had assured him a form of monarchy would be retained. Indian leader Karan Singh was in Nepal as a self-deputed mediator between the King and agitating parties but the agitating parties were not in mood to listen him.

Since the success of the 2006 movement, Nepal has had yet more foreign influence come to bear on it, with India and America at the forefront (Mage 2007). This factor delayed the peace process, as both countries disapproved of the 'communist Maoists'. Even on his departure from Nepal at the conclusion of his tenure, the American envoy, James F. Moriarty, was not ready to shake hands with the Maoist leader Prachanda, because the Maoists had still not given up violence (Moriarty 2007).

The Prime Minister's door was open to high-level foreign visitors and diplomats more than it was to his own party colleagues and coalition partners. In an interview with the BBC, the then foreign minister Mrs Shahana Pradhan criticized Premier Koirala for his mindset. Foreign powers in Nepal are also blamed for escalating violence in the Tarai. In this regard, there is much talk about India's role, with Premier, Koirala even saying that the violence in Tarai could be ended within minutes if India wished it. During these troubled days, India is also seen to be encroaching on Nepalese lands at several disputed zones on the border. The Indian authorities are, however, quick to refute their involvement in any kind of disorder in Nepal.

China, on the other hand, has maintained a non-interference policy towards Nepal. It has always supported mainstream politics in Nepal, and that meant the king until he was made irrelevant in Nepalese politics. While the Maoists were fighting the Nepalese government, China never supported them. However, China has reaffirmed that they would not tolerate outside intervention in Nepal's internal affairs (Junmei 2007).

Interim constitution, indigenous nationalities (Janajatis) and the Tarai

Nepal received its interim constitution, and interim parliament that included the Maoist rebels, on 15 January 2007. However, the constitution failed miserably to address the longstanding demands of Janajatis and Madhesi populations. After the April 2006 revolution, there were lots of discussions on the restructuring of the state, but the Bahun and Chetri leadership of the major parties managed to secure a safe haven for themselves by denying any clear commitments to oppressed nationalities, Madhesi or low-caste people (Shrestha 2007a).

The Maoists advocated a federal state, autonomy and self-determination rights for the Janajatis in Nepal. Emphasizing autonomy, federalism and the right to self-determination, Maoist supremo Prachanda said 'People took part in the historic movement to put an end to the centralized feudal state and create a state in which everyone can have their say.'[17] In the aftermath of the April 2006 Revolution, the leaders of all the other parties, including the UML, and certain leaders of both the fractions of the NCP, began campaigning for a restructuring of the state into a federation, so as to grant rights of autonomy to Janajatis. However, the interim constitution they promulgated omitted any mention of these promises. Not surprisingly, various organizations

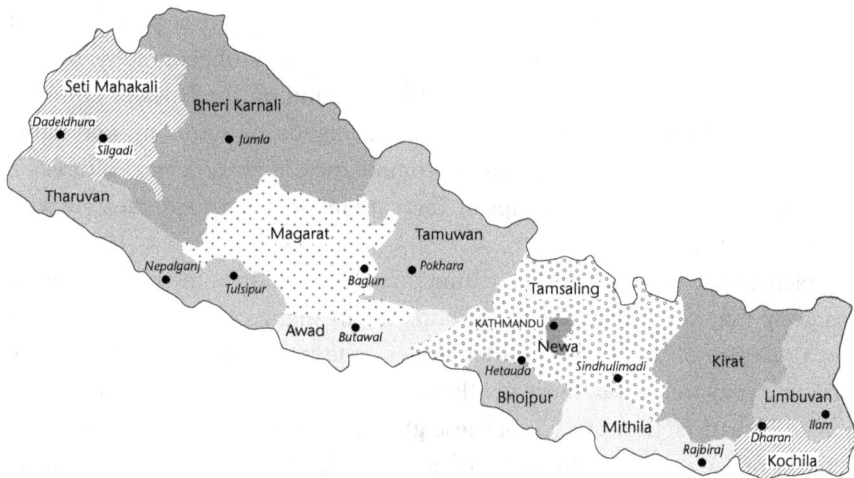

Figure 6   Map of New Nepal. Standard map modified by Bal Gopal Shrestha.

of the Janajatis under the umbrella of the Nepal Federation of Indigenous Nationalities (NEFIN),[18] as well as the Madhesi parties, protested vigorously against the constitution. It sparked unprecedented violence in the Tarai, which continued unabated, killing several dozen and displacing thousands of people of mountain origin (Pahadi) from the Tarai.

The open border between Nepal and India has helped to inflate violence and criminal activities in Tarai. There are at least a dozen militant groups spreading violence in the area. Many influential leaders from the Tarai recently abandoned their mother parties, and formed the Terai-Madhes Loktantrik Party under the leadership of a former NC leader Mahanta Thakur. These Tarai-based parties, which include the United Madhesi Forum, Madhesi Janadhikar Forum (MJF), Madhesi Liberation Forum, the fractions of the Sadbhavana Party and Janatantrik Terai Mukti Morcha are all determined to foment a decisive Terai agitation if the government does not fulfil their demands. At the same time, other Tarai groups led by Jaykrishana Goit and Jwala Singh advocate an independent Tarai.

The three main demands of the Madhesi and Janajatis are the immediate declaration of a republic, an electoral system based on all-out proportional representation, and a federal state with the right to self-determination. In the end the interim constitution adopted an electoral system combining first past the post and proportional representation in an attempt to satisfy all parties.

Nepal has been declared a 'federal democratic republic', but the government remains totally unclear about the federal structure of the state. The parliamentary parties and the Janajatis have conflicting views about its make up. Most Bahun Chetri elites, in all the major political parties, are of the view that the country should be divided along lines of geography; others, especially various Janajati groups, insist on division on the basis of ethnicity and language (Tamang 2006). The Janajatis' demands for autonomy and rights of self-determination are intended to promote their languages and cultures on an equal basis, and certain groups in Tarai are insisting on a federal state with rights to secede.

Nepal hosts more than sixty distinct nationalities. In some places a single ethnicity may form the majority group, but in many places the population has a mixture of ethnicities and languages. The implementation of a federal structure may well ignite more conflicts, if necessary homework is not carried out to the satisfaction of each of these groups. The Maoists have proposed a division of the country into nine to fourteen federal states based on ethnicity and geography, but this scheme is far from satisfactory to everyone. The other political parties have as yet presented no clear view on the matter, while the Madhesis are demanding that the whole Tarai be declared one single province for them, despite the fact that the Tarai is not inhabited by a single homogeneous group. If the government fails to address the Madhesis' and Janajatis' demands of autonomy with the right to self-determination, the separatist voices in Tarai will soon grow even stronger.

The delicate transition: some remarks and conclusion
It should be clear from the discussion here that transitional politics in Nepal is at a volatile stage. The 2006 popular movement forced the king to renounce state power, but the royalists still want to revive the monarchy. Many perceive that the former king is looking for an opportunity to strike back, albeit he would need the help of the Nepal Army. However, he has neither international nor national support.[19] As almost entire population of Nepal is against the monarchy, no miracle return of the king to power is foreseen.

Now the king has been defeated, the 'victors' are claiming shares in state power. The Maoists, the SPA, the Janajatis, the Madhesi, oppressed low-caste Dalits and women all claim that they have defeated the king, so each of them believe themselves to deserve a share in state power. However, as the leadership of all the major parties are in the hands of the high-caste Hill Bahun and Chetri, it is they that are now in charge of the state (Giri 2007). They act as if they are the ones in the position to dispense 'mercy' upon other groups: the Janajatis, the Madhesi, low-caste Dalits and women. However, these neglected segments of Nepal are no longer ready to depend on anyone's 'mercy', but rather seek an equal share for themselves in state power. Hence, they opt for autonomy, self-government and self-determination rights. They are determined to live in dignity as equal citizens of the state, with the same pride and power as any other citizen. To pacify them, the present interim constitution has turned Nepal into a 'federal republican state', but what the proposed federal structure might be remains completely unclear. At the same time, the ruling elites of the major political parties, particularly the NC and the UML, are against any federal structure, as they fear the loss of the power they enjoyed for so long under the monarchy. They think a federal structure will be divisive and fragment the country.

People believed the elected CA would cure many of the evils in Nepal. However, uncertainty is looming because of the clash of interests among stakeholders. In addition, interference of international power brokers, particularly India's open meddling, badly impedes political process in Nepal. Even if the CA successfully completes its drafting of a new constitution, its acceptability to the various parties is unpredictable. If the aspirations of all stakeholders are not properly addressed, we cannot predict against the disgruntled ones burning the new constitution on the day it is issued. Therefore, any forecasts of how smooth or fragile the transition of Nepal from a dictatorial monarchy to a federal republican state will be are premature, until such a time as the CA succeeds in promulgating a new constitution that satisfies the population of Nepal as a whole.

Epilogue: the aftermath of the CA election

The long-awaited election of the Constituent Assembly (CA) was completed in April 2008. Nepal now has an elected Constituent Assembly with 601 members. Winning 227 CA seats, the ex-rebel Maoists have become the single largest party, but they failed to win the majority that enable them to form a single-party government. The two old parliamentarian parties, the NC and the UML, won only 115s and 107 seats, respectively. As the two major parties of the post-1990 change in Nepal, this was an unpredicted and humiliating defeat for them both. The three new Tarai-based Madhesi parties, which were engaged in violent agitations to create a single province in the Tarai, won 82 seats in total, enabling them to bargain for power and rights. Other fringe parties and independent candidates won the remaining seats.

As announced in November 2007, the first sitting of the newly elected CA on 28 May 2008 declared Nepal a federal democratic republic. Subsequently, on 11 June, the ex-king Gyanendra Shah gracefully exited his palace. In a press conference hours before his departure, the ex-king publicly accepted the result of the CA, defended his actions as the king, and refuted the allegations he and his family members were involved in the 1 June 2001 palace massacre. He also denied having any properties in foreign lands in either his name or that of any member of his family. The ex-king now lives in Nepal as an ordinary citizen, but soon after leaving the palace his son Paras left Nepal to live in exile in

Singapore. Now and then he comes back to Nepal, and while he has expressed his desire to participate in politics, he has not changed in his rowdy behaviour.

On the 21 July the CA elected the president and vice-president of the newly declared republic. Since the post of president is a ceremonial one, the Maoists had been pleading for an independent candidate – from a minority community, a Madhesi community, a woman, or someone from a low caste. However, their appeal failed to convince other parties, in particular the NC and the UML, with the former wanting its octogenarian leader Girijaprasad Koirala to be the first president, while the latter wanted its ex-general secretary, Madhavkumar Nepal. At last, the three big parties proposed three different names, though, ironically, all were from the Madhesi community. A last-minute alliance among the NC, the UML and the Madhesi Janadhikar Forum (MJF) succeeded in defeating the Maoist candidate. Eventually the NC candidate, Rambaran Yadav, emerged victorious. It was a significant breaking with the traditional dominance of Hill Brahmins and Chetris that such a prestigious post went to a Madhesi for the first time.

Towards the end of August, almost five months after the election, the Maoists, as the largest party in the CA, succeeded in forming a new government with the UML, the MJF and a few other fringe parties; the NC, the second largest party, chose to stay in opposition. This, despite the Maoists claim that their first priority was to form a national-consensus government that brought all 25 parties, big and small, together. Amidst allegations and counter allegations, the NC filed Sherbahadur Deuba as its candidate for the post of prime minister, only to be defeated by the Maoist supremo Prachanda, who could garner support from the UML, the MJF and most of the small parties.

The interim constitution emphasizes consensus among the parties in the formation and running of the government in the process of making the new constitution. In June 2008, however, the NC, UML and MJF forced the Maoists to agree in amending the interim constitution in favour of a majoritarian system of forming a government. This has the basis for rival parties to engage in the same old game of toppling government after government as pushed the country into a state of turmoil in the mid 1990s.

As was predicted, the first elected government of the Republic of Nepal did not last long. It fell within the short span of nine months. The Maoist Prime Minister Prachand's resignation came as the President reinstalled the army chief whom Prachand had sacked. Prachand accused the President of an unconstitutional coup against the supremacy of the people. With the support of the NC and Madhesi parties, Madhavkumar Nepal, twice defeated in CA elections, succeeded to the post of Prime Minister. When the CA failed to allow discussion of the motion the Maoists presented against the president's move, the country became witness to prolonged street protests by the Maoists.

It is notable that the CA was elected only for a term of two years, and that its single major task is to make a new constitution. However, little progress towards the drafting of the new constitution was in fact made in the allowed two years. The Interim Constitution allows for the extension of the CA by six more months, but on 28 May 2010, at the last moment before its expiration, all the parties agreed to prolong the CA's life another year. Prime Minister Madhavkumar Nepal tendered his resignation at the same time, because the parties had agreed to form a national-consensus government. A lack of consensus between the squabbling parties then meant it took them nine months before they could elect the next Prime Minister. This was a significant setback to the possibility of agreeing a new constitution within the already extended period allowed.

Finally, in February 2011, Jhalanath Khanal, the chairman of the UML, was elected Prime Minister after seventeen tedious rounds of elections, but this time with the support of the Maoists. As the parties' skirmishes continued, the drafting of the new constitution remained unfinished, and the extended period of a year given to the CA expired on 28 May 2011. Amidst great uncertainty, the term of the CA was extended by another three months on the 29 May 2011. During this period, the parties agreed to complete the integration and rehabilitation of the Maoist army. If this was successful, drafting of the new constitution could be extended again by three months. Yet the situation remains extremely uncertain. Although the contending parties have promised to provide a national-consensus government this has yet to take shape.

Undoubtedly, the conflict between the parties will continue. The CA has already lost its credibility. If it fails to write a new constitution after all the extended time given, the country might face an unprecedented crisis. The Nepalese are anxious that the wrangling among the major political parties may instigate chaos. It would be unfortunate if this newly created federal democratic republic failed in its historic task, and the Nepalese are holding their breath, optimistically waiting for a miracle to happen.

Acknowledgments

This chapter was written within a broader project, 'Do some forms of democracy consolidate more easily than others?', which was financed by the NWO Social Sciences Research Council, the Netherlands. I am indebted to Dr Renske Doorenspleet, now at the University of Warwick, UK, for her support before and during this project, and the comments she made to this paper. I thank Professors Rudy Andeweg, Ruud Koole and Peter Mair, and other colleagues at the Department of Political Science, University of Leiden, for their support, where I was associated as researcher and assistant professor (2006–7). I am most grateful to Dr Angela Hobart of the Centro Incontri Umani, Ascona, Switzerland for her patience and the valuable comments she provided to an earlier draft of this paper. I also want to express my gratitude to Professors Bruce Kapferer of the University of Bergen, Norway, Tej Ratna Kandahar and Kamal P. Malla of Tribhuvan University, Kathmandu, Shailendra Sharma of the University of San Francisco and Christopher C. Taylor for their valuable comments to earlier drafts of this paper. Keshar Lall in Kathmandu, Swoyambhudhar Tuladhar in Geneva, Switzerland, and Kalsang Norbu Gurung made helpful comments to the final draft which I wish to acknowledge. Finally, I want to thank my wife Srilaxmi Shrestha in Leiden.

Appendix

The People and the King
*By Bikram Subba**
In the reign of the king
People's mouths are forcefully shut
It is not permitted to move around freely
It is forbidden to express grief or happiness at any open place
The king's law is in discomfort when people speak out their minds
But people's minds burst out as the songs of volcanoes
It seems the helpless crown has been caught in the blaze
That coming out from the funeral pyres the people set with the tyres
In the reign of the king
The roads are blocked, stating them a 'forbidden area'
As if the shameless king is taking a naked bath there
But the feet know only to walk
They enjoy walking through the restricted paths
Therefore people feel enchanted walking
Marching right through the forbidden areas
Happiness propels as if marching over the chest of the king
People have moved forward to establish a new Nepal excluding the king
In the reign of the king
Curfews are clamped already before the dawn
Whole morning, whole day and whole night
In the valley and beyond
In the streets and in the passages
In the reign of the king curfew turns every house into a jail
Yes, the stupid kings have been imposing curfew for ages
However, people never stopped pulling down pillars of the palaces
This time again, the people are rising from every direction
They are marching forward and violating the curfew
Chopping off hands, legs and neck of the monarch
The people are already in the path of a people's republic of Nepal.

*A free translation from the original Khas-Nepali language. This was an acclaimed poem during the 2006 people's movement in Nepal. Subba is Nepal's renowned progressive poet. He has several books to his credit.

NOTES

1   See Appendix at the end of this chapter for the full poem (Subba 2006).
2   The Tarai is the land stretching from east to west in the southern belt of Nepal, bordering India. Most of its inhabitants are Madhesi, people of the plains, whose religious traditions, language, caste system, food, dress, social customs and manners are similar to the people of Indo-Gangetic plains in the south. According to the 2001 population census, the Tarai occupies 23 per cent of total area of Nepal and contains 48.5 per cent of its population. This population includes many non-Madhesis: indigenous ethnic groups and recent migrants from the hills. Because of infrastructure, agriculture, industrial development and access to India across the open border, the Tarai area is crucial to the Nepalese economy.
3   The Seven-Party Alliance consisting of the Nepali Congress Party, the Nepali Congress Party (Democratic), the Communist Party of Nepal United Marxist and Leninist (UML), the Jana Morch Nepal (Communist Party of Nepal, Unity Centre Masal's legal front), the Nepal Sadbhavana Party (Good Will Party), the United Left Front and Nepal Workers and Peasants Party
4   The Maoists popularized the slogan of 'New Nepal', but at present it is the other parties talking about it. See (Kiran 2007) for the Maoists' concept of 'New Nepal'.
5   See a news report (Press Trust of India, September 14, 2006).
6   A section of Nepalese people that includes the supporters of the former King, Panchayat system, and certain fractions of Nepalese communists including the Maoists are levelled as radical 'nationalists' because of their strong anti-Indian sentiments.
7   A lot of discussion is going on regarding the restructuring of the state to empower ethnic nationalities (see, for instance, Tamang 2006).
8   The Goddess Taleju is a form of Sakti, the female power. There are also stories about a subdued erotic character to the relationship between the king and the Goddess Taleju (Hoek 1991:151).
9   He accused the NC of fostering corruption, encouraging anti-national elements and failing to maintain law and order (Joshi and Rose 2004:384).
10 See (HMG 1992:1). However, the constitution is criticized for its rigidity as its preamble forbids amending the 'Parliamentary System of Government and Constitutional Monarchy and Multi-Party Democracy', see Shrestha (1991:13).
11 See (Hachhethu 1994; Lawoti 2005).
12 See (Thapa 2006) for more on relations between kings and parties in Nepal.
13 In Nepal succession of kingship is in the line of father to son. Therefore, taking over of the throne by a younger brother of the slain King Birendra was unacceptable for Nepalese people. In addition, Nepalese people saw Gyanendra as the murderer of his brother and his entire family, though there is no evidence to prove it.

14 The King justified his actions with Article 127 of the 1990 Constitution, though the Constitution did not actually permit him to take such an action (HMG 1992:30).

15 Numerous publications discuss the Nepalese Maoists' uprising (e.g. Baral 2006; Karki and Seddon 2003; Thapa 2003; Hutt 2004; Shrestha 2004; Onesto 2005; Pathak 2005).

16 See S. Shrestha 2007 for a history of the communist movement in Nepal.

17 See *The Himalayan Times* online, 3 December 2006.

18 See (Gellner *et al.* 1997; Shrestha 2007b) for more on ethnic nationalism in Nepal.

19 A survey conducted from 28 March to 27 April 2007 showed that 59 per cent of respondents among 4,089 people spread over 40 districts of Nepal rejected the idea of retaining the king in Nepal (Pandey 2007).

REFERENCES

Baral, Lokraj, 2007, 'Prachanda on Prachanda doctrine', *The Kathmandu Post* (9 May).

——— (ed.), 2006, *Nepal: Facets of Maoist Insurgency*. New Delhi: Adriot Publishers.

Bühler, George, 1969, *The Laws of Manu*. New York: Dover Publications. First published in 1886.

Dangol, Sanubhai, 2005, 'Palace is like a package of conspiracies' In Khas-Nepali, *Janaastha* (November 23).

Foucault, Michel, 2000 (1976), *Truth and Power. In Power* (ed. J.D. Fearon). New York: The New Press.

Gellner, David N., Joanna Pfaff-Czarnecka and John Whelpton (ed.), 1997. *Nationalism and Ethnicity in a Hindu Kingdom: The Politics of Culture in Contemporary Nepal*. Amsterdam: Harwood.

Greenwald, Jeff, 2001 (1991), *Shopping for Buddhas*. London: Lonely Planet Publications.

Giri, Krishna, 2007, 'Brahmin and Chetri tyrants in Nepal', *eKantipur* (July 9).

Hachhethu, Krishna, 1994, 'Transition to democracy in Nepal: negotiation behind constitution making, 1990', *Contributions to Nepalese Studies* 21(1):91–126.

——— 2006, *Political Parties of Nepal*. Patan: Social Science Baha.

HMG, Ministry of Law Justice and Parliamentary Affairs, 1992. *The Constitution of Nepal 2047 (1990)*. English Translation. Kathmandu: Law Books Management Board.

Heesterman, J.C. 1986, 'The king's order.' *Contributions to Indian Sociology* 20(1):1–13.

Hoek, Bert van den, 1990, 'Does divinity protect the king? Ritual and politics in Nepal', *Contributions to Nepalese Studies* 17(2):147–55.

Hoftun, Martin, William Raeper and John Whelpton, 1999, *People, Politics and Ideology: Democracy and Social Change in Nepal*. Kathmandu: Mandala Book Point.

Hutt, Michael (ed.), 2004, *Himalayan People's War: Nepal's Maoist Rebellion*. London: Hurst & Company.

Joshi, Bhuwanlal and Leo E. Rose, 2004 (1966), *Democratic Innovations in Nepal: A Case Study of Political Acculturation*. Kathmandu: Mandala Book Publications.

Junmei, Ciwang, 2007, 'An interview with Professor Ciwang Junmei', *Nepali Times* 27(16): December 28.

Kane, Pandurang Vama, 1977 (1962), *History of Dharmasastra: Ancient and Mediaeval Religious and Civil Law in India*. Vol. 5 Part II. Poona: Bhandarkar Oriental Research Institute.

Karki, Arjun and David Seddon (eds), 2003, *People's War In Nepal: Left Perspectives*. Delhi: Adroit Publishers.

Lecomte-Tilouine, Marie, 2004, 'Regicide and Maoist revolutionary warfare in Nepal: modern incarnations of a warrior kingdom', *Anthropology Today* 20(1):13–19.

Lawoti, Mahendra, 2005, *Towards a Democratic Nepal: Inclusive Political Institutions for a Multicultural Society*. New Delhi, London, and Thousand Oaks: Sage Publications.

Mage, John, 2007, 'The Nepali revolution and international relations', *Monthly Review* (May).

Mehta, Ashok K., 2007, 'Uncertainty in Nepal', *Spotlight* (August 12).

Moriarty, James F., 2007, 'Obstacles to Nepal's peace process', *The Kathmandu Post* (June 12).

Nickson, R. Andrew, 1992, 'Democratisation and the growth of communism in Nepal: a Peruvian scenario in the making?', *Journal of Commonwealth and Comparative Politics* 30(3):358–86.

Onesto, Li, 2005, *Dispatches from the People's War in Nepal*. London: Pluto Press.

Pandey, Krishna, 2007, 'The state of Nepali democracy', *Nepali Times* 352 (8–14 June).

Parajulee R.P., 2000, *The Democratic Transition in Nepal*. New York: Rowman and Littlefield Publishers, Inc.

Pathak, Bishnu, 2005, *Politics of People's War and Human Rights in Nepal*. Kathmandu: BIMIPA Publications.

Shaha, Rishikesh, 1990, *Modern Nepal: A Political History 1769–1955* (2 vols). Delhi: Manohar.

Sakya, Keshavman, 2007, 'Conflicts between Bahun and Chetri started' (In Khas-Nepali). *MySansar.com* (30 December).

Shrestha, Bal Gopal, 1991, 'The question of sovereignty in the constitution of Nepal 1990' (in Newar), *Malah* 12(19):13–16.

——— 2007a, 'The interim constitution; the Madhesi turmoil.' *eKantipur* (1 February).

——— 2007b, 'Ethnic nationalism in Nepal and the Newars'. In *Contentious Politics and Democratization in Nepal*, ed. Mahendra Lawoti, pp. 199–225. Los Angeles, London, New Delhi, Singapur: Sage Publications.

Shrestha, Chudabahadur, 2004, *Nepal Coping with Maoist Insurgency: Conflict Analysis and Resolution*. Kathmandu: Chetana Lokshum.

Shrestha, Sambhuram, 2007, *Memories of My Political Life* (in Khas-Nepali). Kathmandu: Gwahali Guthi.

Stiller, Ludwid F.S.J., 1975, *The Rise of the House of Gorkha. A Study in the Unification of Nepal 1768-1816*. Patna: The Patna Jesuit Society.

——— (ed.), 1981, *Letters from Kathmandu: The Kot Massacre*. Kathmandu: Centre for Nepal and Asian Studies (CNAS).

Subba, Bikram (ed.), 2006, *Ganatantrako Kheti: Andolan Kabita [Cultivating Republic: Poems from the Movement]* , Part 1 (in Khas-Nepali). NepaliKabita.Com.

Tamang, Sitaram (ed.), 2006, *Restructuring of State in Nepal's Context* (in Khas-Nepali). Kathmandu: Samana Praksan, Nepal.

Thapa, Deepak (ed.), 2003, *Understanding the Maoist Movement of Nepal*. Kathmandu: Martin Chautari, Centre for Social Research and Development.

Thapa, Surya 2006, *Struggle between Monarchy and Political Parties in Nepal* (in Khas-Nepali). Kathmandu: Nawayug Publications P. Ltd.

Vaidya, Kiran 2007, 'Literature, Art and Culture in New Nepal'. *The Worker*, Number 11.

Vajracharya, Dhanavajra 1999. *Dhanavajra Vajracharyako Aitihasik Lekhasaṃgraha* [A Collection of Dhanavajra Vajraacharya's Historical Writings]. (In Khas-Nepali). Volume 1. Edited by Bhadraratna Vajrācārya. Lalitpur: Lotus Research Centre.

Weber, Max, 1994, *The Profession and Vocation of Politics. In Political Writings*. Cambridge: Cambridge University Press.

Newspapers

Nepali Times, The Kathmandu Post, Kantipur, Naya Patrika (Khas-Nepali language), *Sandhya Times* (Newar language).

Websites

www.nepalnews.com, www.kantipuronline.com, www.weeklynepal.com, www.thehimalayantimes.com; BBC Radio, FM radio stations in Nepali and Newar languages accessible at www.mazzako.com.

CHAPTER 8

Expectations of the state

An exile returns to his country

~~~~~~~~~~~~~~~~~~~~~

LAURIE KAIN HART

Petros is sitting in his garden in a small village at the north-western boundary of Greece. A few kilometers to the north-west and the north-east, across the broad lake that lies at the foot of the garden, the high ridges of Albania and of the (Former Yugoslav) Republic of Macedonia are visible. Petros was born a Greek citizen in 1943, in a nearby village that was destroyed in the Greek Civil War (1946–9). He was evacuated across this frontier to Eastern Europe in the final stage of the conflict in 1948.[1] His mother tongue, like that of the majority of regional farmers in this part of Greece, was Macedonian,[2] and he speaks Greek, Hungarian and some Russian as well. He returned to Greece in the 1980s after thirty-five years in Hungary as a political refugee, and settled in the northern Greek city of Thessaloniki. Eventually, he bought and reconstructed a small ruined house near his former paternal village.

In 1991, Petros was injured at his welding job, damaging his shoulder and arm. A few months later, while walking his grandson to school, he was injured again in a hit-and-run car accident. Disabled by his injuries, he applied for state assistance. Because he had worked for most of his life in Hungary, he was not registered for national disability insurance, nor did he understand the complex rules of Greek bureaucracy. For a year and a half he went from office to office to sort out the papers that would establish his qualifications, but the papers were never complete.

A sanguine and gentle man, he was finally overwhelmed by the uphill battle he had been waging on multiple fronts to gain recognition as a full citizen by the Greek state. He recounted the story some years later, still mystified by the emotional violence of the experience. In the end it was the way the bureaucrats spoke to him, he said, that made him crack:

I remember, I went only once a month [to the 'IKA', the workers' benefits office], so that I wouldn't annoy them. I would just ask for an update and then I would leave. They always greeted me with smiles; the girl at the desk knew me. Finally I had gotten the last slip of paper. 'If you have received that form', she said, 'we should get it soon too, so come back in two weeks and we'll tell you when you'll get your payment.' So I go back after two weeks, as the girl told me to, and I ask if it has arrived and she behaves like she has never seen me before. I said, 'Something is not making sense here.' She looked for the papers, but she didn't find them.

And it was the way she talked to me – the way she talked to me at that point – from all of the stress,[3] I just lost it. In other words my nerves had broken. And I began to howl. I remember and I am ashamed. I howled like a donkey , 'ou, ou, ou.' I exploded. I didn't know what to do. I went crazy. Because I couldn't find the door to get out of there. They brought the police, they did this and that, I don't know what went on, I wasn't aware. Until someone grabbed hold of me, held me down, and gave me a little water, and I came around. I didn't know where I was. From that point on I didn't really understand what was going on. They told me afterwards, 'You have to go to the "TEVE"[4] [the insurance for independent businesses], not the "IKA".' I couldn't go to the 'TEVE' because I couldn't go into an office again. I couldn't bear to see a civil servant.

The breakdown was profound. Petros said,

I couldn't get it together, I couldn't go out … I couldn't see people …
I wasn't that kind of person in Hungary. I went out, I had friends, happiness and pain. But I don't want to complain, I don't want to have a bad attitude towards my fatherland (*patrída*);[5] I want … but my fatherland doesn't love me.

1

Greece was liberated from more than three years of Nazi occupation in October 1944. In December fighting broke out in Athens between, on the one hand, the forces of the British and the British-supported Greek government (until 1944 in exile in Egypt), and, on the other, the Communist-led resistance forces of the National Liberation Front (EAM-ELAS, Ethnikón Apeleftherotikón Métopon–Ethnikós Laïkós Apeleftherotikós Stratós).[6] In February 1945 a settlement (the Varkiza Agreement), by which ELAS agreed to disarm, was reached between the rebels and the government installed by the Allies. There followed a period of 'white terror' reprisals against the Left and the reconstitution of the disbanded ELAS forces as the 'Democratic Army of Greece' (DSE, or *Dimokratikós Stratós Elládas*) in 1946. Armed conflict continued until 1949, when government forces backed by the US defeated the guerillas in the mountains of north-west Greece (see Close 1993; Iatrides and Wrigley 1995).

The Greek Civil War has been less well known internationally than one might expect, compared, most notably, to the Spanish Civil War that took place a decade earlier (1936–9).[7] Given the gravity and violence of the conflict, as well as its paradigmatic character as a theatre of post-war anti-communism and the impetus for the Truman doctrine of increasingly active global anti-communist intervention by the US, the international invisibility of the Greek Civil War is surprising. Post Second World War Greece was a crucial testing ground for US-supported experiments in economic development as well as militarized political repression.[8]

The belatedness of scholarship on the war (despite initiatives from US-based Greek scholars in the late 1970s; see Iatrides 1981, 1995)[9] is the result of cold war politics within Greece and beyond. Until well after the end of the military dictatorship of the Colonels in 1974, the anti-communist right controlled the representation of national history.[10] With the return of democracy and the shift of power to the left-of-centre Panhellenic Socialist Movement (PASOK) in 1981, the left asserted its own version of political hegemony. In a joint move 'for the sake of national unity' in 1989, a coalition New Democracy (conservative)/PASOK government destroyed the entire archive of police files kept since the 1930s on Greek citizens, thus precluding any future systematic examination of the punitive role of the state and para-state in the post-war period (Close 1995, 2004). Both sides were anxious to bury the past. A Communist Party (KKE) official suggested that burning the files would spare children the 'shame' of learning that that their partisan parents had signed the infamous 'repentance declarations'. (These were the oaths of loyalty repudiating communism that partisans and suspected fellow-travellers were forced to sign for release from incarceration or for post-war employment: Vervenioti, 2009a). The elimination of documents predictably worsened the 'epistemic murk' (Taussig 1984, 1987) surrounding the question of the repentance declarations and the war in general.

The collapse of the Soviet Union in 1989 brought about significant changes in the Greek political climate. By the mid 1990s, research on local memory and the micro-history of the war at the ground level (as well as its long-term consequences) began to appear more widely in the public media. The fall of the Berlin Wall and the dismantling of the so-called Eastern bloc of regional socialist states reduced the strategic valence of some highly charged issues, at least in official circles.[11] Nevertheless, as recently as 2006 an academic symposium on the Civil War was forced to change its intended meeting site because of local civic opposition.[12] All this is to say that those whose fates, from infancy to old age, were dictated by the conflict and its wake continue to bear the weight of this charged history in every dimension of their social and psychic lives. For the generation of the 1940s and their descendents, recent interest in their personal accounts and truths is an irreparably belated development.

Most former child refugees who have returned to their natal territory have had working-class lives characterized by limited resources. Some have retired on small pensions, some continue to work intermittently at odd jobs or fishing or agriculture. Despite these modest appearances, their lives have been unusual, blighted by multiple eras of personally devastating political turmoil. They have had to contend with a constantly resurrected fifth-column stigma. They have forged perspectives on the world that are often cosmopolitan and humanitarian; most of them speak several languages and have close relatives scattered across the globe. This cosmopolitanism is hard won: it is the result of being repeatedly swept off their feet by history.

2

The international border zone of the conjoined Great and Small Prespa Lakes in north-west Greek Macedonia was, and is, one of the areas most affected by the dislocations of the Greek Civil War. In the Greek sector, Prespa forms a kind of national cul-de-sac of about thirteen small villages, with no official border crossings.[13] Its protected topography, its position on the borders of the then newly socialist states of Eastern Europe, and its ethnically diverse population allowed it during the war to became the epicentre for the communist-led Democratic Army in its struggle with Greek Government forces. The devastation caused by the fighting in the 1940s was extreme: the Prespa region lost most of its inhabitants and entire hamlets were eradicated.

Slavic-speaking agro-pastoralists have constituted the main population group in this corner of north-west Macedonia since about the eighth century CE. Strategically labelled 'Bulgarian' by Greek nationalists[14] since the inception of nationalist movements in the Balkans, the local population was pejoratively associated in Greek majority discourse with what Greeks see as the major twentieth-century challenges to Greek sovereignty. These challenges include the 1903–8 Macedonian Struggle, a heroically celebrated struggle by Greek-affiliated forces against Bulgarian IMRO[15] guerrillas in Ottoman occupied Macedonia[16] for the control of the northern territories; the Axis invasion and the occupation of Thrace by fascist Bulgarian troops during the Second World War; and post Second World War Bulgarian and Yugoslav socialism and irredentism. In the mid 1990s, border tensions with the new ex-Yugoslav

Macedonian state (recognized by the UN in 1993) revived this Greek nationalist spectre of the internal enemy. Most recently depicted as 'Skopjan'[17] nationalists, the local Slavic-speaking population has been the subject of consistent ethnonational suspicion and political persecution in Greece from the 1940s up to the present.[18]

This case study examines how one political refugee[19] evacuated as a small child understands his moment in history, in the aftermath of his return to Greece in the early 1980s from a long post-war exile in the Eastern bloc. It focuses on his relationship to his place of birth and to his country of exile, and, specifically, on how his understandings of 'nation' (*éthnos*), 'country' (*patrída*), and 'state' (*krátos*) – or several permutations of states, from socialist to neo-liberal – have played out as he reclaimed his citizenship and resettled in his native country after four decades abroad. More importantly, an analysis of his experience, informed by that of others in this volatile border zone where I have been engaged in fieldwork since the early 1990s (Hart 1999, 2004, 2006, 2009) prompts the broader question: how do ethnonationalist ideologies colonize people whose own political experience would seem to demystify the very idea of national identity? By what biographical, social and psychological processes does what Renata Salecl (1994:15) calls the 'fantasy structure' of national hegemony[20] take hold? In the case of these former exiles, how has the state managed to place itself not just in a position of power but squarely at the centre of individual self-worth and as the condition of the possibility to thrive?

Close analysis of the impact of political categories on particular lives allows us to see how institutional power shapes individual subjectivity (see also Voglis 2002).[21] Because nationalist hegemony is realized through kinship and transgenerational transference as much as through public political experience, the close texture of life history is critical to understanding the state.

The social reality in which these former refugees live is conditioned above all by the 'long' cold war. Cold war political structures and dispositions retain a strong grip at Balkan borders both in local interactions and international diplomacy. These border dynamics have lately been re-energized by new strategic and material interests (Khalidi 2004). Reconfigured (but perpetuated) by Europe's strategies against terrorism, the control of undocumented labour migration and increases in income inequality, post-socialist borders have retained and modernized their powers of discrimination and selection. Long-enduring stakes in national identifications and asymmetries generated at the border do not disappear overnight: decades after the end of socialism, even more now than in the 'cold' past, a Russian 'feels himself', wrote the poet Yerofeyev, 'to be a cockroach in Europe' (Mignolo and Tlostanova 2006:211).

The international borders in north-western Greek Macedonia were established in the early twentieth century through the bloody conflicts of the

Balkan Wars and through Great Power commissions and treaties before and after the First World War. Both before and after those wars and treaties there were politically induced mass movements of population, as well as official 'exchanges' of populations calculated to render the borders ethnically legible (Hart 1999; Koliopoulos 1999:28–9; Ladas 1932; Pentzopoulos 1962). This attempt to solve the problem of border diversity through ethnic cleansing (the exporting and importing of people as well as internal deportation[22]) was supplemented with propaganda (Karakasidou 2000), the transformation of personal and place names (Cowan 2000:xiii–xvi), and the creation of restricted zones of passage (Rombou-Levidi 2008). This quasi-obsessional attention to the national question at the border did nothing to alleviate local poverty, which in turn exacerbated individual and communal tensions over rights to the few local resources (fundamentally, land, water, and civil-service employment). Relatively little research attention has been devoted to the pertinence of such local conditions at state borders to the maintenance and reproduction of nationalist antagonisms. As Riki von Boeschoten has noted, the general neglect of the periphery in twentieth-century Greek domestic policy (but see Carabott 1997) did not create regional solidarity: 'the politicization of the border … [simply] increased the feelings of estrangement from the state in each group separately' (Van Boeschoten 1999:92). The patterns of enduring social stratification associated with the border-straddling Slav-Macedonian population have been amply documented (e.g. Brown 2003; Danforth 2003; Karakasidou 1993, 1997; Van Boeschoten 2000, 1999:101–3, 1998). The local population at the border has felt the brunt on the one hand of too little, and on the other of too much, attention from the state, and is left with the conviction that it is both abandoned and persecuted.

3

In late winter 1948, scores of children from Prespa, led by young local women, walked across the border between Greece and Yugoslavia towards various destinations in Eastern Europe and the Soviet Union. They joined a massive exodus of some 25,000–28,000 children from rural Greek villages suffering starvation and aerial bombardment.[23] The children, who ranged in age from toddlers to adolescents,[24] were transported to the Soviet bloc countries and housed in camps, schools and daycare centres. As starvation and bombardment intensified during the last years of the war, children were both expatriated and internally displaced as part of war strategy on both sides of the Greek conflict.[25] Some travelled with one or both of their parents; others left parents at home or were orphans. Finally, in August of 1949, after five years of intense civil war, the Greek Nationalist forces defeated the communist-led rebels at Mt. Grammos. Villages in the Prespa area were destroyed or abandoned; some disappeared permanently.[26]

The struggle over the disposition of these children and adolescents drew immediate international and domestic publicity.[27] Minors had been displaced to schools, group homes and re-education camps within Greece (Papanicolaou 1994:151; see Vervenioti 2009b) as well as expatriated: in July 1947 Queen Frederika had opened the first of a half-dozen 'Childtowns' (*Paidopóleis*) for the housing and (re-)education of Northern Greek children.[28] In 1948 the government collected at least 10,000 children from Macedonia and Thrace to be 'transferred to the interior of Greece to prevent their forcible removal by guerrillas' (United Nations 1948:31). Parents reacted: the peasants of one village 'took their children away from Florina after learning that the Government intended to evacuate them to the south'(ibid.:31). In March 1948 the rebel Democratic Army publicly broadcast its policy of 'removing children "at the request of their families for their own safety"' (ibid.:156).

In response to protests lodged by the Greek government, the 1948 *Report of the UN Special Committee on the Balkans* explored allegations concerning the removal of Greek children from northern Greece to Eastern bloc countries. Removals were chiefly from two areas, the 'Slav-speaking area of Western Macedonia' and Thrace. The Greek Liaison Service charged that the removals constituted a crime of genocide (the intent to 'destroy the Greek race by alienating Greek children', United Nations 1948:29).

Radio broadcasts from the receiving countries claimed to the contrary that the transfers were a humanitarian effort. The children were welcomed with public celebrations by the socialist states. The Red Cross verified that the children were well cared for in their initial reports from the refugee hostels to which they obtained access (Premier Rapport 1949). While some witnesses reported the forcible removal of children from their families, in other cases witnesses reported that the exodus of children was supported by their parents, or the village priests and teachers, in the interests of their safety, and that some families had indeed also successfully refused to send children abroad (United Nations 1948:30–1). The reasons given by those interviewed at the time who did agree to send their children away were evenly divided between 'sympathy with the guerrillas', 'poverty and lack of schooling' and 'to escape the dangers of war' (ibid.:31). Given the politically charged and polarized context, these comments are not transparent; nonetheless former child evacuees and parents in the 2000s continue to emphasize the extreme conditions under which the moment of exodus occurred, the absence of alternatives and the attraction of promises of shelter and social welfare.

International and Greek efforts to repatriate the children taken from Greece to Eastern bloc countries began soon after the first convoys had left, but were thwarted by political stalemates between the Greek government and the various host countries, as well as by charges of false petitions and reverse child abduction (most children had at least one parent abroad as well). [29] Because of Tito's estrangement from Stalin and the KKE and his rapprochement with the West, Yugoslavia was the first to enter into an agreement with the International Red Cross and to engage in the identification and return of children requested by their parents or relatives. Other countries refused to recognize as legitimate the claims for children put forward by the Greek government (see Brown 2003) and/or had political reasons for retaining their charges and their families, just as Greece had political motives for reclaiming minors for 're-education'.

4

Their expatriation in socialist Eastern Europe at the opening of the cold war meant that Greek child refugees fell under the suspicion of communist and internationalist infection. The prevailing view in Greece was that 'Slav-Macedonian children were indeed being de-Hellenized and turned into fanatical Makedontsi' (Koliopoulos 1999:266), and this interpretation is still actively promoted in nationalist circles.[30] In reality, the blend of communist ideology, Greek national and cultural ideology, and autonomist or ethnic Macedonian consciousness promoted abroad was far more varied and subtle than this. Despite being accused not only of political but also of ethno-national disloyalty, many of these children grew up infused with an ardent Greek patriotism that they continue to profess in the 2000s. The communist party in the 1950s promoted its own official Hellenism in school curricula and public proclamations, as a means to refute Greek government propaganda; and this political Hellenism intensified by the more organic, and certainly emotionally complex and powerful, nostalgia that the exiled parents of the children sustained for their former villages and hamlets. The children were in this sense pushed by world events and the political imaginary toward a state that would inevitably reject them. They have gone on to play out, as adults, a scenario of return in stark contrast to the celebratory character of their arrivals as children in the Eastern bloc socialist states.

Their eventual struggle for inclusion in the *patrída* was more or less doomed from the start. The labelling of the transport of children popularly, officially and in the press as a '*paidomázema*' (against the preferred leftist term, '*paidofílagma*' or child protection) was an early and lasting victory for the political right (Vervenioti 2005). '*Paidomázema*' referred back to the *devshirme*, the infamous Ottoman levy of Christian children for induction into imperial military and court service and religious conversion. It construes the expatriation as an attempt towards the wholesale national, ethnic and religious

IRON CURTAIN HOLDS
GREEK CHILDREN CAPTIVE

GREECE MOURNS FOR HER 28,000 CHILDREN
ABDUCTED BY THE COMMUNISTS

Figure 1   Cover of Iron Curtain Holds Greek Children Captive: A Survey of the Case of the Kidnapped Greek Children. Published in Washington by the Royal Greek Embassy, Information Service, 1950.

conversion of a generation of Greek children. It construes the refugees as traitors to Greece and to Orthodoxy.

In 1994, a member of the Cultural Association of Greeks of Hungary gave me the newsletter that that she and others had produced to celebrate the 45th anniversary of the April 1948 arrival of the children in Budapest. In it, the former refugees rejected the terminology of 'abduction' and *devshirme* and remembered how it felt to be the object of taunts:

> They called it 'the abduction of children' (*arpagí paidión*) and 'the child levy' (*pidomázema* [sic]). There was a song that ran: 'They brought them to the Slavs, to make them slaves...' (*ta pígane stous Slávous yia na kánoun sklávous*)
>
> (Oungarias 1993:1)

The story the newsletter told about the evacuation was quite different and described children rescued from starvation and war on humanitarian grounds, and educated abroad as loyal Hellenes.[31] It explained that those who had first-hand experience of the bombs, lice and hunger knew the truth: 'Everyone thought it would be a short separation. Their relatives thought, "At least these will be saved"...'

5

The trope of the state as parent is common across very different political ideologies. In Greece in the late 1940s the drama of the removal of the children heightened the parental rhetorics and parental modus operandi of the state and party as these institutions inserted themselves increasingly firmly into the family's disrupted chains of caretaking and reciprocity.[32] On both sides, the domestic and international propaganda war of the late 1940s and 1950s was waged in the intense, romantic and corporeal language of motherhood: pamphlets[33] and radio broadcasts conjured helpless infants buried alive or sadistically cut from the arms of mothers (Omada 1948; Gouvernement 1949).[34] The Royal pamphlets are unambiguous and violent: they described the 'bandits' (DSE/communist rebels) as they advanced into war-torn villages, ripping children from their mothers' embraces and dashing them to the ground. The grieving mothers are presented in a cascade of metaphors and diminutives: *manoúla, miteroúla, i psychoúla* ...; their daughters are as 'beautiful as fresh water', the sons, 'golden boys of whom fate was jealous' (Omada 1948).

The sorrow of war did indeed overwhelm Greece in the 1940s; and the pain of parents was at least as searing, if not as saccharine, as these narratives suggest.[35] The drama of the maternal bond was effectively mobilized by the right in the propaganda battle over Greece's future in the late 1940s, and the *'paidomazema* narrative' has triumphed in social memory. Those mothers who willingly sent or accompanied their children abroad with the insurgency for safety – and there were many, given the constant bombardment of the villages – were silenced in the post-war record.

If maternal pathos was exploited, paternal authority, competence and commitment was destabilized in cold war ethno-politics. The frameworks of local society were dismantled by the devastation of villages by war. Able-bodied fathers had been conscripted either by the state or by the guerrillas; children could not, and sometimes did not want to, recognize their fathers when they returned to their villages from the mountains; and, more often, fathers did not recognize their children when presented to them in the collective repatriations from abroad or from the Queen's Childtowns (see Hart in preparation.) This contest over the ownership of children established an anxiety about both parental and state guardianship. It is not surprising, consequently, that this question takes centre stage in the affective lives of many former exiles. National sentiment depends not only on the horizontal fellowship of Anderson's 'imagined community' (1983), but also on an axiom of guardianship: the subject who 'loves' the state will in return receive its care.

The personalization[36] of one's sense of the state that is so manifest in crisis is not only metaphorical or psychological. The social and material rights and claims of the refugees have been at the mercy of party and state mandates mediated by local officials. Divided from their traditional peasant capital – both their landed properties and their kin networks at 'home' and scattered abroad – former exiles have been forced to care about the state (and the para-state party) and to be constantly anxious about what it will offer or withhold from them.

We have only to look back to the local scene at the border during the repatriations of the early 1950s to Greece to grasp the strange competition between parties, states and kin over parental functions (cf. Salecl 1994). The depth of suspicion against repatriated exiles and the extent to which children were seen as the bearers of an ideological virus is very clear in International Red Cross accounts of the first repatriated convoys of children from Yugoslavia. Repatriated children were accused by schoolmasters and others with state authority of having been corrupted by an 'anti-family' (in the report in French, *'contre-familiale'*) upbringing (Lambert 1951:18; see Hart and Vervenioti 2009 and Hart in preparation). The children were under the careful scrutiny of these government-approved locals. Their politics was a problem for family discipline: one appalled stepfather, a village secretary, told the Red Cross envoy that the children loved only Tito, were intent on 'reuniting' an independent Macedonia and ought to be sent to a government re-education camp.

The story I trace here, of a former political refugee who returned from Hungary to live in Thessaloniki and Prespa in the early 1980s, is, like all life histories, unique. I focus on his life-story as paradigmatic nevertheless, because the difficulties that he has experienced in reintegrating into Greece expose the practical and affective results of ethno-political stigma in the context of the totalizing assimilation that Papataxiarchis notes as characteristic of Greek nationalism[37] (Papataxiarchis 2006). The cold-war frames that dominated the childhood of former exiles continue to matter in daily life in Greece, and perhaps most intensely in the micro-universes of its rural borderlands (cf. Close 2004). Former child political refugees who returned to Greece after decades abroad had lived not only through world war and civil war, but also through the dismantling of the socialist states and the globalization of neo-liberalism and the withdrawal of the state from social provision (Harvey 2005:3).[38] The shock of the market ethic has compounded the returned exile's sense of political insecurity given long habituation to forms of socialist life support.[39]

6

Petros was born in Prespa to Macedonian-speaking parents. He was five years old at the time of his removal to Hungary in a convoy with his mother in the spring of 1948. He returned to live in Greece in 1984 with his wife Katerina after thirty-five years in Hungary. They divided their time between Thessaloniki, where they sought work and where their children attended school, and Petros's former village. In 1991, Petros sustained the injuries described in the opening paragraphs of this chapter.

Petros's conscious memory of his childhood village was indistinct ('like a dream', he said) when he was abroad, but when he returned to the site as an adult he felt a deep shock of recognition. Although the village had been entirely destroyed and abandoned, he retained a bodily memory of the layout, and could locate the foundations of his parents' village house instinctively. He remembered isolated details of ordinary life such as the sound of lake water against the break-wall his father had built, and he remembered traumatic incidents of war. Returning to his house one afternoon from a swim in the lake, he had watched his mother, left alone in the hamlet and then pregnant with his sister, encircled and beaten by soldiers looking for information on the location of the partisans. 'I remember it well, it's not the kind of thing you forget...'

The *andártes* (guerrillas), Petros recollected, hid in the mountains while the government army made its rounds, and the double occupation confused

Figure 2   Abandoned house in the Prespa area. Photograph by Laurie K. Hart.

him: 'During the day the army would come. At night came the *andártes.* You could not know how to adapt.' Petros's father had joined the guerrillas. When his father came down from the mountains to visit his family, Petros remembered, he was frightened of him too, in part because he knew that children with fathers in the D.S.E. were more likely to join the convoys sent abroad. 'I didn't want [my mother] to tell me that he was my father ... Only children were leaving. And it was the children whose fathers were in the mountains who had to leave. I held my mother around the neck, I didn't want to go ... that's all I remember of my father in Greece. Otherwise I wouldn't remember him at all.'

Petros remembers hiding in caves from aerial bombardment by the army. He was terrified of the planes: 'they bombed a lot, they killed a lot of people in our village.' The fear, he said, 'stayed with us a long time, inside of us.' He describes how 'many, many, people' were killed hiding in the reeds at the lake, trying to get away. Petros's father was traumatically injured by a grenade and evacuated to a field hospital in Albania, and Petros and his mother left Greece without him. As Petros discovered later, his father lost some of his hearing and his ability to speak for a year after the detonation. Petros commented several times on his father's loss of speech (*eíkhe khásei tin omilía tou*) from the trauma, and later describes the way he, Petros, also lost his normal powers of speech under the stress of repatriation.

Petros's story of the flight is both formulaic and punctuated with sensory, personal, detail.[40] The children set out in boats, each boat with its 'mother', as the leaders were called, to cross the lake to the south side, and they then walked or were carried into the steep hills across the 'Serbian' (Yugoslavian) border. 'We were walking and I heard cries; a child had fallen off a cliff, a little child. "Don't shout, they'll get wind of us," they said, and we got scared, we didn't know who it was who fell ...' Petros's mother was one of the guides that night, but he was not with her group of children. From this point on throughout his childhood and adolescence, he lived with or apart from his parents according to the logics of the system of education and housing controlled by the party and based on age-graded cohorts. He remembers the journey, in open trucks, then the train, then arriving in Hungary. He remembers a 'lot of blood' as they passed convoys of the wounded: 'A lot of blood: the wounded, amputated hands, feet ...'

As a child leaving his village for the first time, Petros was in a state of excitement wavering between fear and pleasure. 'We saw the first automobile of our lives on the road that night in Serbia' – terrified by the sound, they mistook it for a wild cat. Above all, he says, the children wanted to show they had courage, to play at being *andártes*. Later, in school, they watched Russian war films: Petros bought a cap gun at a fair and wore it out shooting at Germans on the cinema screen. He wanted to make sure I understood how children get caught up in the war culture of the adults: 'What do you think the children do in countries where they have war now?', he said, waving his arm towards the recent conflicts and aerial bombardments in Kosovo not far to the north.

He arrived in Hungary and was transferred from one holding station to the next until he was settled in school with a group of children of the same age. It was summer, and they lived, he explained, near the beautiful Lake Balaton, 'in the palaces of the rich' given to them by the Hungarian state. There were vast gardens, and balustrades of marble, 'that we, little vandals, broke up to make balls to play with – imagine!'. At school they learned four languages:

> We had lessons in Hungarian, in mathematics, in geography, history,
> writing, Greek. We had Greek books. And those who were 'locals' [i.e.
> Macedonian-speaking] learned Slavic (Sláviki), Macedonian as we call it,
> the Macedonian language. And Russian. Three languages. Russian was easy
> for us because we speak *ta dópia* and Slavic is the same. And we were very
> good students of Russian because the Hungarian teachers we had didn't
> know it too well.

Petros gratefully remembers the food, housing and education that he received from the Hungarian state. He explains that while, in his early childhood, his parents lived nearby, his home was with the other children at the school. All of the children called his mother (and the other women caretakers) 'mama', and like the other children, he called his own father not 'Papa', but 'Teacher': 'so that I wouldn't remind the others that I had my father there and they did not. And if he scolded me and I wanted to bug him when we were in the room he and my mother shared with my sister, I'd call him "Teacher".

The children did not know when they would go 'back'. They focused on the opportunity to study and to go to university. The idea, as Petros put it, was to become 'a human being' (*ánthropos*), a person of value (implicitly, not a mere labourer). Petros did not in fact go to university, but did receive a good technical training. It is very clear that he recognized the privilege that was accorded by the socialist states to these paradigmatic and most public war refugees during this critical moment of competition between the Eastern and Western bloc.

> In the beginning, until 1956, the Greeks had priority everywhere. [The Hungarians] had a different way with us [political refugees], that is. If you wanted to go to university – easy. After 8 years of gymnasium – no matter how you finished up, you finished it. And then you could go to university. They took you whether your grades were good or not. That's how it was – That was the politics of Hungary, from '48 when they adopted a socialist government, when the communists were in power. And all of those children who were farm kids, who were working-class, they took those kids and sent them to university without any criteria. It was more difficult for the kids from well-placed families, doctors ... They had to be really good students to go to university. That was the way it was until '56. After '56, the counter-revolution as we call it, as they told us to call it (and I still do) changed things. You had to be a good student even if you were Greek. We then had only the same opportunities as the Hungarians.

In 1961 Petros moved to the Greek town of Beloyiannis (Beloiannisz) in Hungary where his father had been living since 1957. He married a fellow Greek political refugee who was not of slavophone descent. They had children, and lived what Petros calls a 'satisfactory life'. Petros repeatedly emphasizes in his account how lucky (*tykheros*) he was to have gone to Hungary.

> The state took care of us. You know, it brought us up; gave us clothes, shoes, everything. It was there to give you food, to teach you a trade, to find work for you and so on. And you could marry, and have a house. These were very fine things. Because of this, I tell you we were lucky [*ticheroí*].

His reference to 'luck' reflects the positive feelings and even the sense of liberation experienced, and nurtured years later in retrospect, by many refugee children. As a striking example of this kind of loyalty, there is the fact that Petros's father volunteered for the security police in reprisals against the 1956 Hungarian uprising against Soviet hegemony. This gratitude did not, however, solve the question of their national belonging. The short-term and shifting reciprocities of the Hungarian state stood out in contrast to the more long-term, and more inexorable, determinations of 'real' kinship, or what could be called, transposing Althusser (1972), kinship in the last instance and in the last analysis. Petros applies the language of luck (*tikhí*) to the intervention and fostering of the Hungarian state and the Greek communist party-in-exile. But this de-mobilization from Greece was in some sense provisional – a matter of being liberated from one's fate (*moíra*) in anticipation of a better inscription within it. Life in Hungary was construed as luck but also as a diversion.

Petros and others in Hungary were acutely aware of continuing political and economic problems in Greece generally and in the rural borderlands especially. In 1958 some exiles returned from Beloyiannis to Prespa but, Petros said, 'all they found there was sheep' and they tried to return to Hungary. His uncles, who had stayed in the village in Greece and had never joined the guerrillas, were nevertheless, he reports, 'hunted down' by the government and interned in detention camps in the islands.

Petros explains that his father, like others in the village, had at the time of the war no particular political orientation and knew nothing about socialism or communism, but joined the guerrillas only because of the relentless harassment he had experienced in the government army as a *dópios*.[41] He had been a government soldier during the Second World War until the army was dissolved and its recruits abandoned to make their way home through German-occupied territory. He was conscripted again during the Civil War, but this time deserted to fight with the rebels.

Given Petros's pragmatic assessment that exile had been an escape from marginality, poverty and persecution, and that his life in Hungary was 'lucky', one might have expected that he would have little desire to return to Greece. Nevertheless, when the opportunity arose in 1982 under a Greek government amnesty, he seized it. He refers to his return in a puzzled way, as if he were still trying to explain it to himself. 'It's a long story', he says. What was most significant, he explains, was the constant invocation of the project of repatriation by his parents and others of their generation. It was the adults, he said, who propagated this desire for return, constantly talking about 'next year in Greece', and celebrating Greek holidays. In one of our conversations, Petros and Katerina speak simultaneously, each reinforcing what the other says:

— Although in retrospect you can say that we did go [to Hungary] for a lifetime,

— It was supposed to be for only forty days. They said it was only going to be for a little time.

— And every year, we'd say, 'Here's to next year in Greece' ... We'd toast in the New Year and say, 'Next year in Greece.'

— For our whole lives.

— That's how our parents put it to us. Forty years we were like this.

— It was our parents who put us up to it. Not from us. Our parents put us up to it.

— All of them, all.

— [raising a glass] '*Aïde*, next year in Greece!'

Petros is surprised that as a 'young kid' he would make such powerful declarations as he did then – that he'd be happy to die if he could only see his village again, and so on. 'We left,' he repeated, 'because we already had one foot on the road ... that's the way we were for a whole lifetime; we married, we settled down and had families and we kept at it. Here's to next year in Greece. Until it finally happened.' The exiles had rosy expectations:

Our parents said to us, 'Let Greece allow us to come back, and the socialists, if we need it, will build houses for us.' Hot air, lies, lies. But really that's what they said – I heard that many times, in meetings and the like. It was propaganda, nothing else.

There was another, geopolitical, reason for returning: the Hungarian authorities had announced that the identity status of Greek Civil War 'political refugee' had been abolished. Petros could choose to become Hungarian, or he could repatriate to Greece.[42] 'They gave us a white piece of paper as a passport,' he explained: 'You couldn't come back with this once you had left. There wasn't any going back.' Petros could not resign himself to a purely Hungarian future.[43] The exiles were distressed by their increasing marginalization as foreign-born refugees in Hungary during a period of the dismantling of citizenship rights for the most socially vulnerable. Cornered by the 'national order of things' (Malkki 1992), the possibility of returning forced their hand. Furthermore, the community in Beloyiannis was beginning to fall apart: as some refugees left their state-owned houses, the state re-distributed them to people Petros saw as 'useless in life, gypsies, ex-convicts', and the villagers had, for the first time, to 'lock their doors'. Petros felt vulnerable as a foreigner, caught in the final phase of socialist national consolidation before the dissolution of communist rule. 'When you are abroad, you feel more Greek.

You miss your *patrída*.' For Petros, his claim in the long term to a *patrída* is a defence against being assimilated into the category of Greek domestic pariahs that includes immigrants, orphans and itinerant gypsies. This is the fear that situates the concept of *patrída* not in amorphous sentimentality, but in the context of a kind of working-class social insurance that revolves around the state's recognition of the claim to territorial belonging and prerogative.

In their excitement, Petros and his friends, all in their early forties, pored over maps of Greece, pointing at random to the names of unknown towns, trying to imagine where they might settle. In the end he resolved to return to the north, where his village, now non-existent, had been located.

The spirit of the Greek Socialist Party's proclamation of amnesty that had precipitated the return did not trickle down to the level of real life in the provinces. The Greek state, Petros said, 'had struck us off the registers' (*mas ekheí xegráfei*) . 'Greece did not accept us ... They had burned everything. We were not registered anywhere; that is, we were recorded with a red pen.' He was at first refused and then granted his re-entry visa (applications for re-entry are selective: political refugees who testify to or are suspected of Macedonian national identification are excluded).[44] Petros was acutely aware, in reflecting on his own history, of the preferential rights to citizenship[45] enjoyed in the 1990s by Russian citizens who were deemed to be *omoyeneís* – that is, of Greek 'descent', in other words, presumed to embody the correct combination of ethnonational and political consciousness and 'blood'. Petros, like many former child exiles from western Macedonia, bases the legitimacy of his claim to return and to belonging on a right of birth, a *ius natalis*,[46] which substitutes for the state's emphasis on blood and allegiance an emphasis on place: hence the intensity of his attachment to the paternal territory itself. To the disappointment of the refugees, neither the Greek communist party (KKE) nor the socialist government (PASOK) celebrated or supported them. There was no greeting party, no provisional housing or work. His petitions to procure a birth certificate produced nothing until a well-placed cousin-in-law of his wife intervened. It was evident, Petros said, that 'We were your [the Greeks'] enemies [*ímastan ekthroí sas, emeís*].'

Petros's father's attempt to recoup his former property in Prespa was unsuccessful. He was told by the ministry that he needed his own father's (Petros's grandfather's) death certificate. But Petros's grandfather had left in 1936 for Argentina, had remarried there, and had died there. In the end Petros's father got nothing, and Petros bought the remains of an old house from an unrelated family who had moved to Australia.

In Thessaloniki, where Petros tried to secure work , he was ridiculed for what he called his 'kitchen Greek'. His linguistic formation had been complex, and his poor Greek marked him as a returnee:

I met my wife in Beloyiannis. Until then I had been mostly with Hungarians (at work). I'd almost forgotten Greek. I understood some but had trouble speaking. Because we were just five Greek kids there and the others were Hungarian and we forgot Hunga... I mean, Greek. And of course we spoke *dópia*. But then I started to speak Greek with my wife, and *dópia* with others, and she spoke Greek to me.

His wife found a job in a small factory. Petros recollected that she had to ask permission for a glass of water or a visit to the toilet. It was, Petros said, not 'democratic' in Greece as it was in Hungary: 'We worked hard in Hungary but it wasn't like here, with the knife at your throat.'

To tell you the truth we were a little frightened. Because there [in Hungary], everything belonged to the state; and here everything was private, and the state is very different from a private owner. To an owner you can't complain ... well, that's what we think. That's what they told us. That's what we heard from the old people how it was with private owners and how they worked. So I bent my head and I worked and things came to a head after a week. I couldn't drink water, I couldn't take pleasure in anything. We'd go home and sit on the balcony, we didn't have anyone, we didn't know anyone ... tears, my wife cried, we cried ...

After his car accident, and his encounter with the bureaucrats at the disability offices, Petros saw things differently. He reduced, as it were, his expectations. He cultivated his garden; the fortunes of his children and grandchildren became the focus of his concern. The injury to his sense of himself remained; it fostered his compassion for the new immigrants in crisis in Greece in the 2010s. He remembered the sting of this rejection:

I wasn't that kind of a person before. I was a social person, I had, I had, how can I tell you? I had children, I had my own work team in Hungary, everything, the whole lot – joys and sorrows. And after ...So that is why I am telling you this, I don't want to complain because I don't like that, I don't want to have a bad opinion of my country (*patrída*). It's just that my country does not love me. And let me ask you something, what am I guilty of? From 1948 to the present, what exactly have I done wrong? From 1948 to the present, what am I guilty of? Because I had the parents I had and I left? Because I became who I became? The government knew me at five years old, it only knew me at five years of age, and all this still follows me.

7

Petros's decision to return to Greece was the result of many factors: of the deeply ingrained injunction to prove his patriotism (not to 'betray' Greece – for example, in becoming Hungarian); of his own dreamlike images of a paternal village home; of his educational formation in the hands of the Greek Communist Party; of the romantic vision of thriving capitalism across the border from the socialist bloc; of his cultural and economic aspirations for his children; of a historical moment in which there were high expectations for the socialist party newly in power in Greece. At the same time, by his own testimony, his return was a fulfilment of the elder generation's repetition of claims and acts of attachment and of Greece's refusal to accept them. And while the object of this desire for return was intimately known to his parents, it was more abstractly known to the next generation. In the transgenerational communication of desires, children adopt and act out solutions that are inevitable even as they are dissonant with their own chronology.[47]

We could describe Petros's odyssey to his homeland as the fate (*moíra*) inscribed in his structural circumstances, if what we understand by 'fate' is not only political-historical determination but also the imaginary and intimate inertia that is captured in *habitus* and in the psyche. Anthropology needs to account more fully for the emotional, social and biographically idiosyncratic texture of relations to the state: as Gillette argues in an article on memories of the Maoist state in urban China,

> If individuals experience national belonging as a significant personal
> relationship then nationalism is subject to the same unconscious psychic
> processes that characterize all of an individual's meaningful relationships.
> Our anthropological understandings of nationalism or other collective
> identities would be enriched if we also explored their psychic dimensions.
>
> (Gillette 2004)

In Petros's narrative, involuntary exile and a subsequent life are construed in a dialectical language not of 'agency' and structural determination but of fatality and digression or rescue, of fate (*moíra*) and luck (*tikhí*). On the side of *moíra* lie both the limitations of the local village and the security of the *patrída*; on the side of luck lie the opportunities of the larger world and the fragility of a provisional citizenship. It was *moíra* that made it impossible for Petros not to return to his country. Relations with the state were precisely not to be conceptualized in the form of contract: it is not a question of 'rights' but of moral commitments. Having committed himself to his *patrída* (and been committed by his fate to it), Petros suffers from an unreciprocated love.

Petros and his family embarked, on their return, on a project of re-Hellenization and everyday re-socialization, as well as critical reflection on the terms of their ethnonational realignment. For Petros this project entails recuperating the value of a Greek identity from his own experience of personal abuses at the hands of Greeks. When he talks about the 'Greeks' (*Éllines*) in Hungary, referring to his (multi-ethnic) refugee community, he freely includes himself in the category. When he uses *Éllinas* in the context of his experience as a refugee *dópios* in Greece with monolingual Greek nationals, he is outside the category. If this inconsistency looks like a contradiction, 'truth', as Jacques Lacan puts it, 'grabs error by the scruff of the neck in the mistake' (Lacan 1988:265). Petros tells a story about his return to the homeland that clarifies what kind of truth he is getting at:

> When I first arrived back to Greece from Hungary I only had the paper currency that I had been given by the consulate in Hungary. I didn't understand that I needed coins for a bus fare and I handed the ticket collector the large drachma bill I had. The ticket collector wouldn't take it and told us to get off the bus. But another passenger got up and paid our fares for us, understanding that we were confused. And I said, well look at that. A Greek, a Greek.

Petros explained what he means by 'a Greek':

> You know what it is? The one guy was power, the ticket collector, but the other was a Greek. And from this experience I understood from the Greek, that a Greek should not take power. Because – this is the way a Greek assumes power? Enough!

If Petros's political identity as Greek is inescapable, he has found a way to live with it, separating state power from civic virtue.[48]

The truth that this expresses – the 'ultimate inconsistency of society' that is hidden, in nationalist ideology, by the fantasy of the ethnically pure homeland (Salecl 1994:15) – is also inherent in local conceptualizations of the 'native' at the border between Greece and the Republic of Macedonia. Repeatedly, I was told by local residents: 'We natives [*mialó*/Slavic speakers], we don't have a brain [*den ékhoume mialó*].' To have a *mialó* is to be clever (*ponirós*), to know how to engage in schemes. It is to be able to 'forecast', as Bourdieu (1968) calls the projective skill and new *habitus* former subsistence farmers needed to acquire to survive as wage labourers in 'modernizing' Algeria. In a context where getting ahead is understood to be the result of the extralegal if not illegal use of patronage networks, this way of being in the world called 'not having a head for things' is also a claim to goodness. It expresses both the structural impediments to and ambivalence towards assimilation. It reflects the strain of a fragmented set of dispositions produced by movement from one social and political field to another in contradiction to it. As Athena, another former child exile and local farmer, explained to me:

> Alexander the Great – whatever they may say – was a Macedonian [*Makhedonas*]. He went all the way to the Euphrates, to India. Then his best friend poisoned him. Before he died, Megalexandros uttered this prophecy: Macedonians will always be slaves. They will never have a state [*krátos*]. Because we are neither Greek nor Macedonian.

Athena claims Alexander as a true (i.e. local) 'Macedonian' (*dopios – Makhedonas*) who travelled away from his native territory and, paradigmatically, was betrayed. The triumph of the Greek and Macedonian states has erased the local Macedonian, who is destined to suffer a double oppression. Athena and Alexander are Macedonians but not Macedonians. Their emperor is also a slave; there is no name left for Athena to use to describe her identity because the state has appropriated all of the alternatives. Petros's story of Greeks and Athena's story of Macedonians expose the deep psychic impasse created by the multiple demands of political exile, ethnic stigma and a half-century of anxiety and surveillance. In breaching the law of identity and contradiction, they refuse the misrecognitions of nationalism.

Political refugees from the Greek Civil War inherited a training in loyalty to 'Hellenism' that was (and is) as inescapable as it was filled with denial and broken promises. They were subjected, in childhood and adolescence, to war and the splits and reformulations of families; in adulthood, to the collapse of socialism and the schisms and deaths of parties and ideologies; and now in old age, to the escalation of neoliberal economic triage. Not all of them harbour a romance of Hellenism or Hellenic identity, or a desire for their own children who have remained abroad to be Greeks. Their life accounts and complex family histories are infused with irreconcilable discourses of nurturance and patriotism, cold-war politics and ethnic resistance. Former child-exiles in Greece are disillusioned, in late middle age, in different ways according to their particular formations and trajectories, that is, variously disillusioned with socialism, ethnonationalism, the free market state, capitalism and the capricious alternation of 'luck' and 'fate' in their politically vulnerable lives. They have all paid, in intimate ways, the multidimensional costs of the stigma of their exile and brutally inconstant moment in history.

Acknowledgments

An early draft of this paper was presented at the Symposium 'State: Ancient and Modern' at Monte Verità, Ascona, Switzerland, 8–11 May 2003. I thank Angela Hobart for the collegial spirit of the Centro Incontri Umani and her encouragement on this project. Later versions have been presented in the Departments of Anthropology at Stanford University and at the University of the Aegean at Mytilene; I thank the participants at those seminars for their critical insights. It goes without saying that my greatest thanks go to Petros, Katerina and others who have been willing to speak about this difficult subject. I thank Tasoula Vervenioti for her infinite scholarly generosity, collaboration and sharing of her archives over the years. She accompanied me to Prespa in 2003 and we first interviewed Petros together. I also thank Jane Cowan and Maria Couroucli for helpful comments, and Stephan Feuchtwang and Maris Gillette for their work and suggestions on memory and cross-generational transfers. Thanks also to counsel from Alex Kitroeff and Karen Van Dyck. I thank George Koumaridis for transcription and indexing of the interview tapes into written Greek. Finally, I thank Philippe Bourgois for his endlessly patient and wise critical insight and editing. A related analysis of this case study will appear in Greek in Papataxiarchis, ed., in press. Fieldwork and writing were supported in part by the National Endowment for the Humanities, the Edmund and Margiana Stinnes endowment, and the Haverford College Faculty Research Fund, and NIH Grant R01 DA 10164.

NOTES

1   An excellent new and comprehensive history and analysis of the evacuation of children by Loring Danforth and Riki von Boeschoten, *Childen of the Greek Civil War: Refugees and the Politics of Memory* (University of Chicago Press, 2012) appeared in 2012 after this chapter had gone to press.

2   Petros refers to his natal language as *'dopia'* or 'Macedonian' according to context. The question of what Slavophone locals in this region have called and call themselves is an ongoing ideological debate that is often out of touch with the reality on the ground. Historically, Slavic speakers in this region have called themselves, variously, Bulgarians, Macedonians, Greeks or simply 'natives', and have organized for political strategies ranging from political autonomy, to cultural and linguistic minority rights, to assimilation (see Aarbake 2003). For historical accounts of the past and present politics of ethnonational allegiances in north-west Macedonia, see Kostopoulos 2008; Kofos 2008; Gounaris 2003; Koliopoulos 1999; see also Agelopoulos 1997 and Cowan 1990.

3   Petros used the English term. On the international significance of the term 'stress' see Ferzacca 2001.

4   The TEVE is the 'Tameío Epangelmatón, Viotekhnón, Émboron', the insurance for
     independent contractors and businesses. The IKA (Ídrima Koinonikón Asfalíseon)
     is the insurance for workers.

5   '*Patrída*' can be rendered into English a variety of ways: as 'fatherland' – which
     preserves the resonance of '*patéras*', father, inherent in the word – as 'homeland'
     and as 'country' in the patriotic sense.

6   The roots of the Civil War reach back much earlier to the period of the Nazi
     occupation and conflicts among ideologically opposed resistance factions over
     control of the resistance and of Greece's political future.

7   Spain, too, is experiencing a period of critical reassessment of its civil-war legacy
     (see, e.g., Ferrandiz 2005). There are important parallels between the Greek and
     Spanish civil wars, including questions of the displacement of children and use of
     child soldiers, to be explored. This chapter is intended as a contribution to that
     developing scholarship.

8   See recent work on detention camps of the 1940s–1970s: Vervenioti 2009b; Voglis
     2002; see Offner 2002 and Stathakis 2004 on the Truman Doctrine and Marshall
     Plan in Greece.

9   The conference that finally initiated a reappraisal ('Greece and the decade of the
     1940s') took place in 1978 in Washington, DC. Combining the study of the Axis
     occupation, the resistance and the Civil War, the conference made it clear that the
     three subjects were inextricably intertwined (see Iatrides 1981).

10   As Engsberg wrote in the preface to the groundbreaking volume by Baerentzen:
     'In Greece the history of the Civil War has, for a number of reasons, been out of
     the range of scholars for many years, and it has been non-existent in that version
     of national self-interpretation which is passed on to the younger generation. And
     since the historical developments that followed the Civil War depended entirely
     on the deep internal conflict underlying the war, this also had to be left out. Thus
     a 40 year span of national history was simply omitted from the schoolbooks and
     the main attention [was] given to Antiquity and to the struggle for independence
     in 1821 instead of modern history.' (1987: 7).

11   In 2000, the network for the study of the Civil War organized its first meeting in
     Thessaloniki. The establishment of a network of scholars in Greece has resulted in
     a significant number of monographs, seminars and research projects on memories
     and events of the 1940s and beyond. In July 2009, the network commemorated
     a decade of systematic and often collaborative scholarship. The bibliography on
     the Civil War from anthropology and oral history is now much enriched: for
     an impressive recent volume and a review of scholarship on the war, see Van
     Boeschoten *et al.* 2008. A significant body of work is emerging on the experiences,
     and the social and political networks, of former child exiles from the Greek Civil
     War (e.g. Danforth 2003, 1995; Voutira and Brouskou 2000; Van Boeschoten 1998,
     2000; Vervenioti 2005; see also Couroucli 2009 and Collard 1990).

12 In 2009, the scholarly presentation in Athens of the publication of a Greek-Macedonian dictionary was attacked by armed thugs from the neo-fascist 'Golden Dawn' organization, opposed to the use of the term 'Macedonian' in a non-Greek context.

13 It is 67 km by road to the nearest official entry into FY Republic of Macedonia, and 40 km to the nearest entry into Albania.

14 Despite a general preference in the 2000s for recognizing some sort of *dopia/*Makedhonas ethnic/minority identity, some locals reject any identification but Greek, and at the other end of the spectrum one resolutely communist-internationalist Prespan friend insisted that he was happy to accept *'Bulgarika'* as a linguistic designation given the kinship among South Slav languages and his solidarity with the former socialist states.

15 Internal Macedonian Revolutionary Organization, also referred to as VMRO. See Aarbakke 2003 for an account of the regional struggles until 1913.

16 Under the Ottoman Empire Prespa was part of the province (*vilayet*) of Monastir (modern-day Bitola in the Republic of Macedonia). The province was ruled by Muslim political functionaries and tax farmers. Reforms in the mid nineteenth century liberalized the conditions for non-Muslim subjects: beginning in the late nineteenth century Muslim (Albanian and Turkish) hegemony fractured under the pressure of nationalization. The Balkan Wars (1912–13) and First World War exacted a high toll, as the borders of Greece, Serbia and Albania were configured and imposed (cf. Hart 1999). The remaining local Muslim population was ultimately expelled under the compulsory 'exchange of populations' between Greece and Turkey (the Treaty of Lausanne, ratified by the League of Nations in 1923), following violent conflict in Anatolia after an unsuccessful Greek irredentist campaign.

17 Most Greeks refer to the current Republic of Macedonia as 'Fyrom' (the acronym for the Former Yugoslav Republic of Macedonia), and to the citizens of that republic as 'Skopjans', that is belonging to the Macedonian capital city of Skopje. The actual situation of the name is unresolved, with inconsistent use internationally.

18 For the past twenty years contemporary self-identification has reflected the general hegemony of a modern, hyphenated sense of identity: most locals I know refer to themselves as Greek (in the sense of national political citizenship and common public culture), and are offended by the term 'Bulgarian' (which they understand as a slur). They identify their ethnolinguistic heritage and immediate cultural community and kin network as *'dopia'* (local) or Macedonian (*Makedónas/Makedónika*). Greece does not officially recognize the existence of any minority groups on grounds other than religious difference: 'non-Muslim groups, principally the Slavophones' are excluded from designation as minorities (Greek Helsinki Report 1999.) See also Cowan 1990 and Agelopoulos 1997.

19 *Politikoí prósfiges.* To refer to the location of their exile, Greek political exiles/
    refugees use the term *yperória,* which means 'outside the borders', or *mésa* (inside),
    or simply 'the countries' (*oi khóres*).

20 Reflecting on the break up of Yugoslavia, Salecl writes: 'the fantasy of the
    homeland is the way society deals with the fundamental impossibility of it being a
    closed harmonious totality' (Salecl 1994:15).

21 Subjectivation or subjectivication has the sense of submission to the social
    order but also of the constitution of the self through the available social,
    cultural and historical categories of being. On the term 'subjectivation' see, for
    example, Judith Butler 2005 and Michel Foucault (e.g. 1977). This approach to
    understanding personhood draws on Althusser's development of a theory of
    subjectivity combining Marxism, structuralism and psychoanalysis (1972) as well
    as generally on Foucault and Bourdieu. See Studer *et al.* (2002) on personhood
    and the Stalinist regime. The state enrolls us in its projects: by 'enroll' I mean what
    Althusser means by 'interpellate' – that is, the person is 'hailed' and called into a
    form of social personhood that is dependent upon the way he or she is recognized
    by institutional power.

22 See Koliopoulos 1999:34–5 on deportations from the 1920s on. In the period
    between the World Wars, questions of loyalty and identity were intensified
    by tensions with the newly settled Pontian refugees from Anatolia, who were
    encouraged to think of themselves as Hellenic *akrítes* or border guards.

23 As noted below, with US material and logistical support.

24 The figures are notoriously unreliable. See Vervenioti 2005. Christophe Chiclet
    offers the figure of 23,700: 10,000 in Yugoslavia, 3,800 in Romania, 3,000 in
    Hungary, 2,600 in Bulgaria, 2,300 in Czechoslovakia and 2,000 in Albania (Chiclet
    1990: 214; these are the numbers given by Bartziotas (1950), a member of the KKE
    Political Bureaucracy).

25 To put this in context, it is helpful to keep in mind that the evacuation of children
    for their safety was common in various parts of Europe in the Second World
    War, and in the post-war period was also well known to have played a part in
    the survival of some Jews in occupied territories. At the same time, there have
    been numerous scandals concerning the post Second World War deportation of
    'orphans' and 'baby-selling' schemes in diverse countries, including Britain and
    Greece (see *The New York Times* 1996 and Wallis 2010.)

26 The Greek government moved Aromani agro-pastoralists from other parts of
    Greece and the Balkans to the area to restock emptied villages in the 1950s and
    1960s.

27 The distinction between 'children' and 'youth' was polemically charged because of
    military conscription and imprisonment of minors on both sides. Some 'children'
    who were evacuated were trained and returned as rebel 'youth' combatants, or
    held and sent to national prison-reform camps.

28   At Orjiokastron near Thessaloniki.

29   One such enduring stalemate has been, for example, Greece's refusal to recognize as legitimate (and not merely de facto) the border between Greece and Albania.

30   See, for example, this caricature in a recent webpost: 'In 1948, Cominform, the first official forum of the international communist movement since the dissolution of the Comintern, put into action a plan to take hostage to communist countries children from Greece during the Greek Civil War. The aim was to re-educate the children as well as blackmail the populace and the Greek government towards reaching a settlement leading to a partition of Greece and the subsequent creation of an internationalist "Macedonian" Republic', *American Chronicle* 2009.

31   It should be noted that the newsletter in 1993 was the product of a post-socialist era, which distinguishes it from the publications of prior periods in the Eastern bloc, where socialism vs. capitalism would have figured explicitly in the interpretation.

32   Cf. Fortes 1970 and Bloch 1973 on the morality of kinship. Key to their analysis is the contrast between short-term reciprocities that require periodic reinforcement through exchange of services and long-term reciprocities that tolerate outstanding imbalances of exchange: the later characterize 'kinship' and require, by definition, apparently altruistic loyalties.

33   Renamed Royal Welfare, Vasilikí Prónoia, in 1956; see Vervenioti 2002.

34   One of these Royal Welfare pamphlets describes a woman who, as a young girl, led a convoy of children from her village across the border. She was heroically profiled in its pages for her role in returning the children to Greece, but she is, in fact, not critical of the evacuation. She proudly remembers how she offered to lead the children, and praises the good care the children received abroad.

35   The story of the mother Eleni Gatzoyiannis, who was tragically tortured and executed for sending her children to the West is well known (Gage 1983).

36   I thank Stephan Feuchtwang for this encompassing term; see Feuchtwang 2011 for important insights into the nature of the transmission of 'grievous loss'.

37   As Papataxiarchis notes, the Greek state conceives of the integration of newcomers in terms of assimilation into this theoretically homogenous body of citizens (Papataxiarchis 2005).

38   Greece's relatively recent apparatuses of social democracy developed only after 1974 within the frame of a party 'spoils system' and have faced continuing crises of both legitimacy and solvency (Close 2004).

39   See also Voutira and Brouskou 2000 on the fates of children evacuated during the war.

40   On the formulaic nature of these flight narratives, compare Brown 2003: 24; Danforth 2003.

41   Such retrospective assessments about political consciousness are made in the present and generally for the purposes of the present: on the question of national

and political sentiment in the area, and the history of grievances against the state, see Koliopoulos 1999:33–45, 68–9 and especially 210–20.

42   Refugees who were refused entry by the Greek government, could then, and only then, re-qualify, individually, as 'political refugees'.

43   In fact, he had sent his daughters to Greece on free summer camp programmes operated by the Greek government after 1979. His older daughter wanted to return to Greece; his younger daughter did not.

44   'The PASOK government rehabilitated the left in [a number of] ways. One was a measure of 1982 to provide official recognition to the national resistance, followed in 1983 by a ministerial decree annulling many past decrees which had deprived left wingers of the 1940s of their political rights and prevented the return of thousands of political refugees and their offspring. By 1988 about 45,000 refugees or their children had returned to settle, of whom only 7,872 had returned before 1975 ... The government's measures were, however, confined to "Greeks by race" so excluding large numbers of former Greek citizens who spoke Slav Macedonian...' (Close 2004). It is worth pointing out that while at the national level left-wingers may have been rehabilitated politically after 1982, this was not the case at the local level through the 1990s.

45   Article 15 of the Greek Citizenship Code; article 4, paragraph 3 of the Greek Constitution of 1986. Article 19 of the Greek Citizenship Code (Law 3370 of 1955) stipulated that: 'A person of non-Greek ethnic origin leaving Greece without the intention of returning may be declared as having lost Greek citizenship ... His minor children living abroad may be declared as having lost Greek citizenship if both their parents or the surviving parent have lost it as well'. Article 19 was abolished by a parliamentary voice vote on 11 June 1998. The new law was not applied retroactively (Greek Helsinki 1999; Boll 2007:69–70; Sitaropoulos 2006:107).

46   A law of birth, that is, rights to citizenship based in birth, i.e. *'patrída'*. It is important to note that in Greece rights to citizenship are also based in *ius sanguinis*, or membership in the Greek 'ethnos' by heredity, on which basis citizens of other states may claim Greek citizenship.

47   Following Lacan one could say that 'signifiers form networks to which we have little conscious access but which will affect our lives completely. They organize our world, the very texture of which is symbolic'. (Leader and Groves 2005:40–1). On the distinction between the signifier and the signified and the independent action of each, see Freud 1960; Saussure 1969. For a different approach to 'transgenerational haunting' in the Hungarian psychoanalytic tradition, see Abraham and Tovok 1994.

48   The complexities of a Slavophone identity that have been managed under one set of conditions in Hungary (a non-Slavophone state), where Petros married a Grecophone descendent of refugees from Asia Minor and worked with

Hungarians in a settlement founded by the Greek communist party, cannot be easily or publicly managed in post-war Greece itself. The negotiation of a Slavophone Macedonian or Greek identity in exile abroad varied with the different ethnopolitical conditions of each country of exile as well as with the personal and political histories of exiles. The case of Hungary, as a non-Slavic speaking country, is arguably exceptional in several respects, particularly vis-à-vis the 'Greek' orientation of the community in exile.

References

Aarbakke, Vermund, 2003, *Ethnic Rivalry and the Quest for Macedonia, 1870–1913*. Boulder, CO: East European Monographs; New York : Distributed by Columbia University Press.

Agelopoulos, Giorgos, 1997, 'From Bulgarievo to Nea Krasia, from 'two settlements' to 'one village': community formation, collective identities, and the role of the individual.' In *Ourselves and Others: The Development of a Greek Macedonian Cultural Identity since 1912*, eds. Peter Mackridge and Eleni Yannakakis. Oxford, New York: Berg.

Abraham, Nicholas and Maria Torok, 1994, *The Shell and the Kernel. Renewals of Psychoanalysis, Volume 1*, ed., trans. and with an introduction by Nicholas T. Rand. Chicago and London: University of Chicago Press. [Original French: L'écorce et le noyau, Flammarion 1987.]

Althusser, Louis, 1972, *Lenin and Philosophy, and Other Essays*, trans. Ben Brewster. New York: Monthly Review Press.

American Chronicle, 2009, 'Tragedies of the abducted Greek children of 1948: the reality of the FYROM claims (Macedonia, Greece).' November 16, 2009. http://www.americanchronicle.com/articles/view/128838. Accessed 3 May 2010.

Anderson, Benedict, 1983, *Imagined Communities: Reflections on the Origin and Spread of Nationalism*. London: Verso.

Baerentzen, L., John O. Iatrides and Ole Smith, 1987, *Studies in the History of the Greek Civil War*. Copenhagen: Museum/Tusculanum Press.

Bartziotas, V., 1950, Μπαρτζιώτας, Β. 'Εισήγηση στην IIIη Συνδιάσκεψη του ΚΚΕ πάνω στο 2ο θέμα. Η κατάσταση και τα προβλήματα των πολιτικών προσφύγων στις Λαϊκές Δημοκρατίες', in ΚΚΕ, n.d. *Επίσημα Κείμενα*. Vol. VI, Athens: 480–537. [Report on the Third Conference of the KKE on the second topic. The situation and the problems of the refugees in the Peoples' Democracies. In KKE, *Important texts*.]

Bloch, Maurice, 1973, 'The long term and the short term: the economic and political significance of the morality of kinship'. In *The Character of Kinship*, ed., Jack Goody. Cambridge: Cambridge University Press.

Boll, Alfred Michael, 2007, 'Multiple nationality and international law', *Developments in International Law*. Leiden: Brill.

Brown, Keith, 2003, *Macedonia's Child-Grandfathers: The Transnational Politics of Memory, Exile and Return 1948–1998*. Donald W. Treadgold Papers series, No. 38. Seattle, Washington: University of Washington.

Bulter, Judith, 2005, *Giving an Account of Oneself*. New York: Fordham University Press.

Carabott, Philip, 1997, 'The politics of integration and assimilation vis-a-vis the Slavo-Macedonian minority of inter-war Greece: from parliamentary inertia to Metaxist repression'. In *Ourselves And Others: The Development of a Greek Macedonian Cultural Identity since 1912*, eds. Peter Mackridge and E. Yannakakis. Oxford and New York: Berg.

Chiclet, Christophe, 1990, 'The Greek Civil War'. In *Background to Contemporary Greece*, eds. Marion Sarafis and Martin Eve. London: Merlin Books; Savage MD., Barnes and Nobles Books.

Close, David H., 2004, The road to reconciliation? The Greek Civil War and the politics of memory in the 1980s. In *The Greek Civil War. Essays on a Conflict of Exceptionalism and Silences*, eds. Philip Carabott and T.D. Sfikas. Centre for Hellenic Studies, King's College: Ashgate.

——— 1995, *The Origins of the Greek Civil War*. London and New York: Longman.

Collard, Anna, 1990, 'The experience of Civil War in the mountain villages of central Greece'. In *Background to Contemporary Greece*, eds. Marion Sarafis and Martin Eve . London: Merlin Books; Savage MD., Barnes and Nobles Books.

Courcoucli, Maria, 2009, *Remembering and Forgetting Civil War: Event(s) and Narrative(s). Pour une Anthropologie de la Grece Moderne*. Travaux présentés en vue de l'habilitation à diriger des recherches: Université Paris Ouest Nanterre-La Défense.

Cowan, Jane K., 1990, *Dance and the body politic in northern Greece*. Princeton, N.J.: Princeton University Press.

——— ed., 2000, *Macedonia: The Politics of Identity and Difference*. London; Sterling, Va.: Pluto Press.

Danforth, Loring, 1995, *The Macedonian Conflict: Ethnic Nationalism in a Transnational World*. Princeton: Princeton University Press.

——— 2003, '"We crossed a lot of borders:" Refugee children of the Greek Civil War', *Diaspora* 12(2).

Ferrandiz, Francisco, 2005, 'The return of Civil War ghosts: the ethnography of exhumations in contemporary Spain', *Anthropology Today* 22(3):7–12.

Ferzacca, Steve, 2001, *Healing the Modern in a Central Javanese city.* Ethnographies in medical anthropology. Carolina Academic Press.

Feuchtwang, Stephan, 2011, *After the Event. The Transmission of Grievous Loss in Germany, China and Taiwan.* New York: Berghahn Books.

Fortes, Meyer, 1970, 'Kinship and the axiom of amity'. In *Kinship and the Social Order: The Legacy of Lewis Henry Morgan,* ed. Meyer Fortes. Chicago: Aldine.

Foucault, Michel, 1977, *Discipline and Punish: The Birth of the Prison,* trans. A. Sheridan. New York: Pantheon Books.

Freud, Sigmund, 1960 (1953), *The Interpretation of Dreams,* trans. J. Strachey. New York: Basic Books.

Gage, Nicholas, 1983, *Eleni.* New York: Random House.

Gillette, Maris, 2004, 'Exploring personal meanings of state-society relations in China', draft paper. [Published version in *The Journal of Urban Anthropology* 33 (2–4):283–320.]

Gounaris, Vasilis, 2003, [Βασίλης Γούναρης]. *Εγνωσμένων Κοινωνικών Φρονημάτων.* Επίκεντρο, Αθήνα.

Gouvernement démocratique provisoire de la Grèce, ed., 1949, *Pour la paix et la démocratie en Grèce: deuxième livre bleu. Sur l'intervention americain-anglaise; Sur la régime monarcho-fasciste; Sur la lutte libératrice du people.* Paris.

Greek Helsinki Monitor and Minority Rights Group, 1999, *Report on Greece to the 1999 OSCE Implementation Meeting, Greece's Stateless Persons, September 21, 1999 Report about Compliance with the Principles of the Framework Convention for the Protection of National Minorities (along guidelines for state reports according to Article 25.1 of the Convention)* http://www.greekhelsinki.gr/bhr/english/special_issues.html (access verified 1 July 2010).

Hart, Laurie Kain, 1999, 'Culture, civilization, and demarcation at the north-west borders of Greece', *American Ethnologist* 26(1):196–220.

——— 2004, 'How to do things with things: architecture and ritual in Northwest Greece'. In *Greek Ritual Poetics,* eds. Dimitrios Yiatromanolakis and Pangiotis Roilos. Washington, DC and Cambridge, MA and London: Centre for Hellenic Studies and Harvard University Press.

——— 2006, 'Provincial anthropology, circumlocution, and the copious use of everything ', *Journal of Modern Greek Studies: Special issue: Ethnographying Greece in late modernity,* eds. Anastasia Karakasidou and Fotini Tsimbiridou, vol. 24(2):307–46.

preserve

Hart, Laurie Kain and Tasoula Vervenioti, 2009,'Ταξίδι στις Πρέσπες, Ιούνιος 2009' και 'Προφορική Μαρτυρία.' *Αναπαραστάσεις της Ιστορίας. Η δεκαετία του 1940 μέσα από τα αρχεία του Διεθνούς Ερυθρού Σταυρού.* Αθήνα, Εκδόσεις Μέλισσα. [Voyage to Prespa, June 2009; and Personal Testimony]

Hart, Laurie Kain, in press, (in Greek) Εθνικό στίγμα και επώδυνες ατομικές πορείες στην παραμεθόριο, μετά τον Ψυχρό Πόλεμο. Η επιστροφή των 'ντόπιων' στη Βορειοδυτική Ελλάδα. ['National stigma and the production of personal suffering at post cold-war ethnopolitical boundaries.'] In Papataxiarchis, ed., *Αναθεωρήσεις του πολιτικού: Ανθρωπολογική και ιστορική έρευνα στην ελληνική κοινωνία.*

Hart, Laurie Kain, in preparation, 'Photography and the recuperation of life after civil war'. Paper presented at the conference: Greek (Hi)stories through the lens, 9–11 June 2011, King's College, London.

Harvey, David, 2005, *A Brief History of Neoliberalism.* New York: Oxford University Press.

Human Rights Watch, 1994, *The Macedonians of Greece.* http://www.hrw.org/en/reports/1994/05/01/macedonians-greece. Access verified 1 July 2007.

Hirschon, Renée, 2003, *Crossing the Aegean: An Appraisal of the 1923 Compulsory Population Exchange Between Greece and Turkey.* New York: Berghahn Books.

Iatrides, John O., 1981, 'Civil War, 1945–1949'. In *Greece in the 1940s: A Nation in Crisis,* ed. John O. Iatrides. Hanover, New Hampshire: University of New England Press.

Iatrides, John O. and Linda Wrigley, eds., 1995. *Greece at the Crossroads. The Civil War and its Legacy.* University Park, Pennsylvania: The Pennsylvania State University Press.

Karakasidou, Anastasia, 1993, 'Politicizing culture: negating ethnic identity in Greek Macedonia,' *Journal of Modern Greek Studies* 11(1).

——— 1997, *Fields of Wheat, Hills of Blood: Passages to Nationhood in Greek Macedonia, 1870–1990.* Chicago and London: University of Chicago Press.

——— 2000, 'Protocol and pageantry: celebrating the nation in Northern Greece'. In *After the War Was Over: Reconstructing the Family, Nation, and State in Greece, 1943–1960,* ed. M. Mazower. Princeton, N.J.: Princeton University Press.

Khlalidi, Rashid, 2009, *American Dominance and the Cold War in the Middle East.* Boston: Beacon Press.

Kofos, Evangelos, 2008, [Κωφός, Ευάγγελος] Ελληνικό Κράτος και Μακεδονικές Ταυτότητες (1950–2005): Εισαγωγικές Επισημάνσεις.' Στο: Ευάγγελος Κωφός, επ. *Μακεδονικές Ταυτότητες στό Χρόνο- Διεπιστημονικές Προσεγγίσεις.* Θεσσαλονίκη: Ίδρυμα Μουσείου Μακεδονικού Αγώνα. [The Greek State and Macedonian Identities 1950–2005: Introductory Notes.]

Koliopoulos, John S., 1999 (1995), *Plundered Loyalties. Axis Occupation and Civil Strife in Greek West Macedonia 1941–1949.* London: C. Hurst & Co., Ltd.

Kostopoulos, Tassos, 2008, Η απαγορευμένη γλωσσα. [The Forbidden Language.] Viviolarama, Athens.

Ladas, Stephen Pericles, 1932, *The Exchange of Minorities; Bulgaria, Greece and Turkey.* New York: The Macmillan company.

Lambert, A., 1951, *Voyage d'Athènes à Salonique et dans la région du Lac Prespa (Florina) en Macédoine Occidentale du 22 mai au 3 juin 1951 effectué par Mr. A. Lambert, Délégué du C.I.C.R (Comité Internationale du Croix Rouge) en Grèce.* (Author's pagination beginning with cover sheet), Vol. ACICR, B AG 239 084 – 030. Genève: ACICR = Archive of Comité International de la Croix Rouge, Geneve.

Leader, Darian and Judy Groves, 2005 (1995), *Introducing Lacan.* Thriplow: Icon ; New York: Totem; Lanham, Md.

Malkki, Liisa H., 1992, 'National geographic: The rooting of peoples and the territorialization of national identity among scholars and refugees', *Cultural Anthropology* 7(1):24–44.

Mignolo, Walter D. and Madina V. Tlostanova, 2006, 'Theorizing from the borders: Shifting geo- and body-politics of knowledge', *European Journal of Social Theory* 9(2):205–21.

New York Times, The, 1996, 'Tales of stolen babies and stolen identities: Greek scandal echoes in New York', *New York Times,* Sat., 13 April 1996: 23, 27.

Offner, Arnold, 2002, *Another Such Victory: President Truman and the Cold War 1945–1953.* Stanford, CA: Stanford University Press.

Omada. (Ομάδα των Ελληνίδων βορείου Ελλάδος: The Committee of Greek Women of Northern Greece), 1948, *Pamphlet,* last in a series published beginning in 1948, summarizing the 'drama of the paidomazoma.' Supported by Queen Frederika's Welfare Committee. Author's collection. Title page missing.

Oungarias, Politistikou Syllogou Ellinon, 1993, *Ellinismos: Organo tou politistikou syllogou Ellinon Oungarias.* Budapest, Hungary. [Hellenism: Newsletter of the Cultural Centre of the Greeks of Hungary.]

Papanicolaou, Lilika S. 1994, *Frederica, Queen of the Hellenes: Mission of a Modern Queen.* Malta: Publishers Enterprise Group (PEG) Ltd.

Papataxiarchis, Efthimios, 2006, Περιπέτειες της ετερότητας. Η παραγωγή της πολιτισμικής διαφοράς στη σημερινή Ελλάδα. Αθηνα: Αλεξάνδρεια. [The Vicissitudes of Otherness: The Produciton of Difference in Contemporary Greece.]

————, ed., in press, (in Greek) *Αναθεωρήσεις του πολιτικού: Ανθρωπολογική και ιστορική έρευνα στην ελληνική κοινωνία.* [Reconsidering the Political: Anthropological and Historical Research on Greek Society.] Athens: Alexandreia.

Pentzopoulos, D., 1962, *The Balkan Exchange of Minorities and its Impact on Greece.* Paris and The Hague.

Premier Rapport, 1949, *Premier rapport général d'activité du CICR et de la Ligue des CR. Rapport adressé a Mr. Trygve Lie le 6 octobre 1949.* ACICR, B AG 239 084-001.01.

Rombou-Levidi, Marica, 2008, Dancing Beyond the 'Barre': Cultural Practices of the Processes of Identification in Eastern Macedonia. Brighton: University of Sussex. Ph.D. Thesis.

Salecl, Renata, 1994, *The Spoils of Freedom: Psychoanalysis and Feminism after the Fall of Socialism.* London and New York: Routledge.

Saussure, Ferdinand de, 1969, *Cours de Linguistique Generale.* Paris: Payot.

Sitaropoulos, Nicholas, 2006. 'Discriminatory denationalisations based on ethnic origin: the dark legacy of Ex Art 19 of the Greek Nationality Code'. In *Migration, Disaporas, and Legal Systems in Europe,* eds. P. Shah and W.F. Menski. London: Routledge-Cavendish.

Stathakis, Giorgos, 2004, [Σταθάκης Γιώργος] *Το Δόγμα Τρούμαν και το Σχέδιο Μάρσαλ. Η Ιστορία της Αμερικάνικης Βοήθειας στην Ελλάδα. Αθήνα: Βιβλιόραμα.* [The Truman Doctrine and the Marshall Plan. The History of American Aid to Greece.] Athens: Vivliorama.

Studer, Brigitte, Bertholde Unfried and Irène Hermann, eds., 2002, *Parler de soi sous Staline: La construction identitaire dans le communisme des années trente.* Paris: Éditions de la Maison des sciences de l'homme.

Taussig, Michael, 1984, 'Culture of terror—space of death: Roger Casement's Putumayo report and the explanation of torture', *Comparative Studies in Society and History* 26:467–97.

———— 1987, *Shamanism, Colonialism, and the Wild Man: A Study in Terror and Healing.* Chicago: University of Chicago Press.

United Nations, Special Committee on the Balkans, 1948, *Annex 2. Report on the Child Refugees.* Geneva.

Van Boeschoten, Riki, 1998, Περάσαμε πολλές μπόρες, κορίτσι μου. Athens, Greece: Ekdoseis Plethron. [We Crossed a Lot of Borders, My Dear Girl.]

———— 1999, 'Politicized borders: the case of Greek Macedonia'. In *Nationalising and De-Nationalising European Border Regions, 1800–2000,* eds. H. Knippenberg and J. Markusse. The Netherlands: Kluwer Academic Publishing.

———— 2000, 'The impossible return: coping with separation in the wake of the Greek Civil War'. In *After the War was Over*, ed. Mark Mazower. Princeton: Princeton University Press.

Van Boeschoten, Riki , Tasoula Vervenioti, Eftichia Voutira, Vasilis Dalkavoukis, Konstantina Bada, eds., 2008, *Μνήμες και Λήθη του Ελληνικού Εμφυλίου Πολέμου*. Thessaloniki: Epikentro. [Memory, Oblivion and the Greek Civil War.]

Vervenioti, Tasoula (Τασούλα Βερβενιώτη) 2002, 'Charity and nationalism: the Greek Civil War and the entrance of right-wing women into politics'. In *Right-Wing Women: from Conservatives to Extremists Throughout the World*, eds. P. Bacchettai and M. Power. New York and London: Routledge.

———— 2005, 'Περί 'παιδομαζώματος' και 'παιδοφυλάγματος' ο Λόγος ή τα παιδιά στη δίνη της εμφύλιας διαμάχης' Στο *Το όπλο παρά πόδα. Οι πολιτικοί πρόσφυγες του ελληνικού εμφυλίου πολέμου στην Ανατολική Ευρώπη*. Ευτυχία Βουτυρά κ.ά. (επιμ.), pp. 101–23. Θεσσαλονίκη: Εκδόσεις Πανεπιστημίου Μακεδονίας. [Concerning 'child Levy' and 'Child Protection': Language and the Children in the Vortex of the Civil War.]

———— 2009a, 'Interview' [in Greek], *Avgi*, 27 April 2009.

———— 2009b, Αναπαραστάσεις της Ιστορίας. Η δεκαετία του 1940 μέσα από τα αρχεία του Διεθνούς Ερυθρού Σταυρού, Εκδόσεις Μέλισσα, Αθήνα 2009, σελ. pp. 199–201. [Representations of History. The Decade of the 1940s in the Archives of the International Red Cross.]

Voglis, Polymeris, 2002, *Becoming a Subject: Political Prisoners in the Greek Civil War*. New York: Berghahn Books.

Voutira, Eftihia, and Aigli Brouskou, 2000, '"Borrowed children" in the Greek Civil War'. In *Abandoned Children,* eds. Catherine Panter-Brick and M.T. Smith. Cambridge: Cambridge University Press.

Wallis, Lynne, 2010, 'British orphans: "It broke our hearts to see them go away"', *The Independent*, Tuesday, 2 March, 2010 (http://www.independent.co.uk/life-style/health-and-families/features/british-orphans-it-broke-our-hearts-to-see-them-go-away-1914210.html). Accessed 15 June 2010.

CHAPTER 9

Diametric to concentric dualism

Cosmopolitan intellectuals and the

re-configuration of the state[*]

JONATHAN FRIEDMAN

The past decades have witnessed a significant transformation of the identity space of the global arena. Intellectuals have played a crucial role in this process as elaborators upon, if not originators of, a series of discourses that have played a central role in a reconfiguration of state power. I shall argue that the actual content of these discourses of cosmopolitanization, globalization, multiculturalism and hybridity, is not the creation of intellectuals, but the spontaneous expression of an experience related to a particular position within the global system of states and inter-state relations. In order to understand the emergence of this particular position it is necessary to recapitulate certain properties of the contemporary world system and its current transformation. The framework of analysis is thus not one that focuses on oppositional intellectuals, but one which concentrates on those intellectuals who partake in the formation of global elites, their discourses and practices.

A widespread discourse focused on the term 'globalization' itself has gained in strength over the past decade. It had much of its origins in business economics, but contributions have also been made by the disciplines to which it spread over the years: cultural geography, sociology (especially cultural sociology), cultural studies (especially post-colonial studies) and even social anthropology (gaining much of its impetus from the cultural studies literature). Some fields, such as sociology, and especially economic

---

* The larger part of this chapter was published as 'Cosmopolitan elites, organic intellectuals and the re-configuration of the state' in A. Kouvouama, A. Gueye, A. Piriou and A.-C. Wagner (ed.), 2007, *Figures croisées d'intellectuels. Trajectoires, modes d'action, productions*. Karthala: Paris.

and cultural geography, were quite empirically focused on the demonstration
of the facts of globalization: processes such as time-space compression; the
transnationalization of capital accumulation; the formation of global cities
in which global centre/periphery relations were collapsed into urban zones;
or the formation of what Castells (2000) calls 'network society', in which the
nation-state declines as a major world operator, leaving only the state itself
and a series of more or less outsourced networks within which a number of
major trades and traffics are relocated. The more culturally based approaches
to globalization were primarily influenced by what was called the 'cultural
turn' in the social sciences, in which culture itself, became the subject matter
of globalization studies (e.g. Appadurai 1993, Hannerz 1992). Virtually all of
these approaches have a common starting point based on intellectuals' sense,
or even experience, that the world is becoming smaller, with travel now
essential (not least to conferences), in opposition to a former situation that
was more localized. Thus the conviction that 'once we were local but now we
are global' became the basis of a variety of representations of this apparently
new world. The situating of this discourse and its experiential foundation is
the subject of this paper, but here it is necessary to demonstrate the degree to
which 'globalization' discourse is a misrepresentation of the world, that is, an
ideology with hegemonic pretensions.

The most prominent and common assumption of this discourse, is its
evolutionary bias, one that is usually couched in terms of technological
development. For both Castells and to a lesser degree Harvey, it is the internet
revolution and the entire technology of the modern computer that is the major
driving force in this development. It is this technology that has allowed for the
speeding up of transaction time, the movement and flexibility of both capital
and its products. This evolutionary assumption is contrary to the one we put
forward here which is closer to the Braudelian framework of world-systems

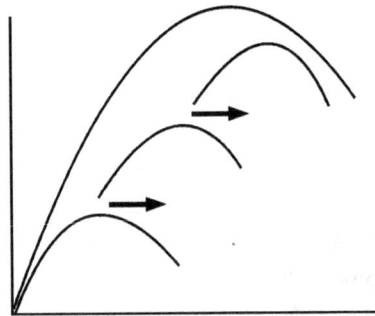

*Figure 1   Hegemonic cycles and globalization in global systems. Arrows indicate
the transfer of capital (globalization).*

analysis. For the latter, globalization is not an evolutionary but an historical process, one that prevails in periods of hegemonic decline, in which the declining zones export capital to newly rising areas within the same system. This is a common phenomenon within the history of a world system and can be represented as follows:

Here globalization is a phenomenon linking hegemonic cycles rather than an evolutionary stage. This interpretation renders comparison, for example between the past century and the present, a real possibility. Between 1870 and 1920 a number of phenomena comparable to today's situation are clear expressions of an important parallel development. This is the period during which Britain declined as world hegemon; having been the 'world's workshop' at mid-century, it produced only 14 per cent of the world's manufactured goods in 1914. At the same time it became the world's major exporter of capital, while the internal economy not only stagnated in production terms but became increasingly a financially dominated economy in ways that some were to describe as decadent, and which is comparable to the current domination of world finance. This trajectory from world workshop to world banker has been experienced by many hegemonic powers. Figure 1 depicts a series of expanding hegemonic powers, each replacing the other in the centre of a world system. It includes the history of displacement from the Mediterranean to Iberia, then to Holland and then England, followed in this century by the United States and perhaps today China, which is fast becoming a world workshop. For those who have assumed that globalization is a stage of history, one in which the state system is replaced by global capital in the form of transnational companies and their accompanying institutions such as the World Bank and the World Trade Organization, the following statistics must be considered seriously:

Chinese Industrial production as percentage of world production
tractors: 83%
clocks/watches: 75%
toys: 70%
penicillin: 60%
cameras: 55%
vitamin C: 50%
laptop computers: 50%
telephones: 50%
air conditioners: 30%
TVs: 29%
washing machines: 24%
refrigerators: 16%

furniture: 16%

steel: 15%

Diaspora – 30 million; 75% of all foreign investment in China. Control of
60–70% of the GDP of Indonesia.

This is in a period when US production, which had been over 40 per
cent of the world's manufactured goods following the Second World War,
dropped to 12 per cent in the 1980s. This development supports a model
of shifting accumulation rather than evolution. If there is a trend in the
process, it is toward a general expansion of the entire system. And here, of
course, technology plays a significant role, even if it is one that is essentially
quantitative. There is also an envelope curve in the graphic that signifies the
limits, also technologically determined, of the expansion process as a whole.
Most processes of cyclical expansion end with general declines, and even
the emergence of a so-called dark age in which institutions disappear; the
economy becomes more localized and even subsistence-based, and the urban
structures collapse. There are not many documented cases, but the examples
of the end of the Bronze Age and the end of the Roman Empire provide clues
for understanding the process. Today, while there is a clear shift in hegemony
toward East Asia, it is also commonly asserted that if China were to attain
the same standards of consumption as Western Europe the world ecosystem
would collapse. The approaching limits of oil production are an indicator of
this potential crisis.

Cosmopolitanism as a constituent of the state arena: double polarization

Global elite formation refers to a process of identification in which a
cosmopolitan identity is core. The study of elites is of course not new, and
their definition is not reducible to a question of class. Rather, they have two
essential characteristics: the function of leadership and the establishment of
ideological hegemony. The formation of national identity, for example, is very
much orchestrated historically by elites, for whom such identity made perfect
sense. This making sense is the operative basis of such identity. It creates a
certain resonance among a wider group, if not an entire population, that is
the triggering mechanism for the emergence of ideological hegemony. The
following simple model is an attempt to grasp two processes that are typical
in central hegemonic states in periods of decline, periods that are also eras of
globalization. I have referred to this process in terms of double polarization.

In periods of decline the paradigm of modernism loses its purchase on
populations primarily because of the fading of any experience of development,
one that was part of the doxa of the previous period of expansion. The future

fades and there is a scramble after new forms of more tangible identity: roots, religion, ethnicity. These tangible identities are what can be called cultural identity in that their core characteristics are not based on identification with a particular social position (as in class) but with an autonomous set of specific elements, including language, history, modes of life, 'beliefs' etc. The adaptive advantage of such identities is that they are independent of the social success or failure of the individuals who partake of them, and each harbours their own quite particular (i.e. cultural) project. This process of re-identification which took off in the mid-seventies is still a powerful force, one that leads to growing fragmentation generated by the formation of sub-national sodalities and movements, with gangs and gated communities (in both the literal and the figurative senses) increasing segregation.

In periods of hegemonic expansion organic elites tend to identify with the state and with the idea of a developmental future. In the history of the nation-state, intellectuals largely formulated the myths of the state, its history, as well as its cultural content. They were also active in the making of national citizens in their roles as teachers and public intellectuals. There were those who identified as cosmopolitan or internationalist in such periods, but they are of marginal significance. Categories such as cosmopolitanism have a *longue durée* as do other categories of the territorial state. The absolutist state, while different in its organization, contained the same kinds of categories: immigrants, ethnicity, nationality, foreigner, diasporas and cosmopolitans. The salience of the categories varies with time, of course, and the articulation between state organization and position in the larger arena determines the nature of this salience. There are cosmopolitan elites throughout the history of Early Modern and Modern Europe who have developed a discourse of world governance, of the parochial nature of the local state, and whose distrust of 'the people' is associated with the notion that the wise of the world should rule. The Rosicrucians, the Freemasons and other cosmopolitan 'clubs' are old phenomena, and while their place was rarely at the centre of state politics, the French revolution, for example, was certainly a target for their engagement, as were the humanist and anti-clerical ideas of the eighteenth century. Freemasonry really came into its own within the British empire, where it had a function in the production of 'public school' recruits for the ruling cadre and where a certain universalist humanism was cultivated as the ideological core of the imperial project itself. This was a general trend within the cosmopolitan bourgeoisie that emerged in the eighteenth and nineteenth centuries.

> The cosmopolitan bourgeoisie in the eighteenth century came to adopt
> a perspective on its own society as if it were a foreign one a target for
> 'colonial' exploitation. Freemasonry provided a cover for developing the new

identity on which the exploitation of members of one's own community is
premised. By entering the masonic lodges, merchants and those otherwise
involved in the long-distance money economy such as lawyers and
accountants, realised the primordial alienation from the community which
is the precondition for market relations, exploitation of wage labour, and
abstract citizenship.

(Van der Pijl 1998:99)

But this was also the age of emerging national identities, so the strategy
whereby the population of a country was seen as a mass of subjects and
not citizens was increasingly inappropriate, and became challenged by the
development of working-class politics in the nineteenth century. The elite
organizations were not so much against working-class goals as against
working-class politics and autonomy, claiming that they knew what was best
for ordinary people. Caroll Quigley (1981) has documented how the British
upper class at the end of the nineteenth century can be understood as a
family affair in which a very few intermarried aristocrats filled most of the
important positions in the imperial and national governments. Cecil Rhodes,
governor of South Africa, headed a real secret society, 'The Society of the
Elect', and a subgroup headed by his associate Alfred Milner, 'The Association
of Helpers', did much to work out the plans for the League of Nations and the
Commonwealth. Sensing already that the empire would not last forever they
envisioned a world of nation-states dominated by responsible leadership, such
as that of the British. This was the model that was inherited by the United
States following the Second World War. Towards the end of British hegemony,
at the beginning of the twentieth century, there is a significant increase in the
salience of cosmopolitanism within the various forms of internationalism. It
is important not to conflate the two. Internationalism, associated with the
socialist international, never gave up the national as the basis of political action,
but saw the political field as a set of states in interaction and the international
field as a political field within which the world might be transformed.
Conversely, cosmopolitanism denies the significance of the nation-state
and seeks to replace it with a single world social and political space, one in
which the national is seen as a stumbling block rather than a constituent of
world order (Mauss 1969; Nairn and James 2005). Mauss distinguished the
two terms on the grounds suggested above, and his differentiation throws
light on the way the terms are used today. The currently popular notion of
transnationalism is equivalent to Mauss's cosmopolitanism, in that it sets out
to supersede the nation as such. Much of the post-colonial discourse of what
is today called 'occidentalism' (Buruma and Margalit 2003) represents such an
onslaught. The power of this ideology today is related to the phenomenon of

hegemonic decline, but is also the expression of a larger and more substantial transformation of the intellectual field of the West, one that has been referred to in terms of ideological inversion (Jacoby 1994, Friedman 2004), in which a former critique of Western imperialism has become a critique of Western culture in general. Now this inversion is also an expression of decline and it takes on various forms. However, among leftist intellectuals one might envisage it in the terms described in Figure 2:

1968	1998
the national	the postnational
the local	the global
collective	individual
social(ist)	liberal
homogenous	heterogenous
monocultural	multicultural
equality (sameness)	hierarchy (difference)

Figure 2   The inversion of 'progressive' ideology.

These two lists compare what was assumed to be progressive in 1968 and today. The left of 40 years ago was oriented to a core notion of collective sovereignty, of which the local and the national were logical extensions. Homogeneity meant primarily the maintenance of a single social project to which all were supposed to assimilate themselves. This also implied both monoculturalism and equality, not in the sense that cultural difference was not tolerated, but that it was irrelevant or unmarked in relation to the social project. Equality was the self-evident character of these projects and, in the sense that equality implies sameness, it depended on the sharing of common goals. This 'New Left' schema declined from the 80s onwards and was transformed into an ideology of culture by those who either replaced the older group or radically changed their own positions once in their new-found upwardly mobile positions as well-paid academics and members of the culture industries. The emergence of this group is captured, however superficially, in the literature on the 'Bobos', or bourgeois bohemians, children of the 60s who transformed the radical into radical chic, and whose political agenda moved rapidly towards one or another form of liberalism.

The occidentalism implicated in this transformation is one which, interestingly enough, maintains an imperialist position with respect to the 'other', in so far as the latter is still seen as an object and as totally lacking in intentionality in the positive sense. Thus terrorism in its various guises is not seen as a true project directed against an 'us'. It is merely the extension or translation of our imperialist behaviour into their reactive violence. Thus it would in fact be 'us' who are the instrumentalizers of terrorism, as Islamism, for instance, would hardly be said to exist on its own, but as no more than a righteous reaction or resistance to oppression. While this inversion exists in differing degrees among intellectuals, it is an increasingly prevalent mentality. This also accounts for the identification with the cosmopolitan among members of this group, one that opposes the nation-state on the grounds that it is the essentializing basis of racism. This unites both liberal intellectuals and those who claim a more radical left-wing identity. Thus Appadurai has as his project, normative more than scientific, the demise of the nation-state, or at least the 'nation' half of it – 'We need to think ourselves beyond the nation.' (Appadurai 1993:411); while Hardt and Negri say in their explicitly progressive version,

> Nomadism and miscegenation appear here as figures of virtue, as the first ethical practices on the terrain of Empire.

And this is followed by a violent attack on the local and especially the indigenous:

> Today's celebrations of the local can be regressive and even fascistic when they oppose circulations and mixture, and thus reinforce the walls of nation, ethnicity, race people and the like.
>
> (Hardt and Negri 2000:362)

Thus the nomadic is the future, a future of hybridity, which is somehow opposed to the homogeneity of the national. In an interview in France, Negri criticized the French Left for its (nationalist) opposition to the proposed European constitution. While he agreed that the constitution was basically liberal and therefore reprehensible, he still encouraged a yes vote for one reason only, 'Oui, pour faire disparaître cette merde d'Etat-nation [to get rid of the damn nation-state]' (*Libération*, 13 May 2005).

It is noteworthy that *Empire* (2000) was pubished by none other than Harvard University Press and that it received favourable reviews in such journals as *Foreign Affairs*, a publication of the U.S. Council on Foreign Relations, as well as in the *New York Times*. It was positively praised by the post-colonial studies elite, but the old New Left did not fall for its message (Balakrishnan 2003), which was that we, including the authors, are at the beginning of a new and final age of empire, one which is governed by no particular country, but which is embedded in global networks that control our lives. In this new era, the figure of the nomad is also one of the revolutionary, and replaces that of the aristocrat of former times, who was always and everywhere 'at home.'

The post-colonial vision of a former left is the foundation for the not-so-new variant of cosmopolitanism that has become the identity of the new global elite. It is shared by transnational capitalist, media, diplomatic, United Nations (especially UNESCO) and other global institutional complexes, such as the World Trade Organization, World Bank and more traditional clubs (such as the Bilderberg), where global governance is often on the agenda. The role of intellectuals in this is not terribly creative, but they function to elaborate on the cosmopolitan vision that has produced a serious contender for global, or at least Western, ideological hegemony. This hegemony is of course mediated by the media and has turned 'the global' into a kind of doxa. That 'we live in a globalized world', that globalization forces the government to make certain cuts, that globalization is a new form of cultural enrichment (via migration) – in all of these common-place expressions and understandings globalization is converted into a progressive force of nature to which must adapt or perish. This is the evolutionary bias of the discourse that we have argued against above.

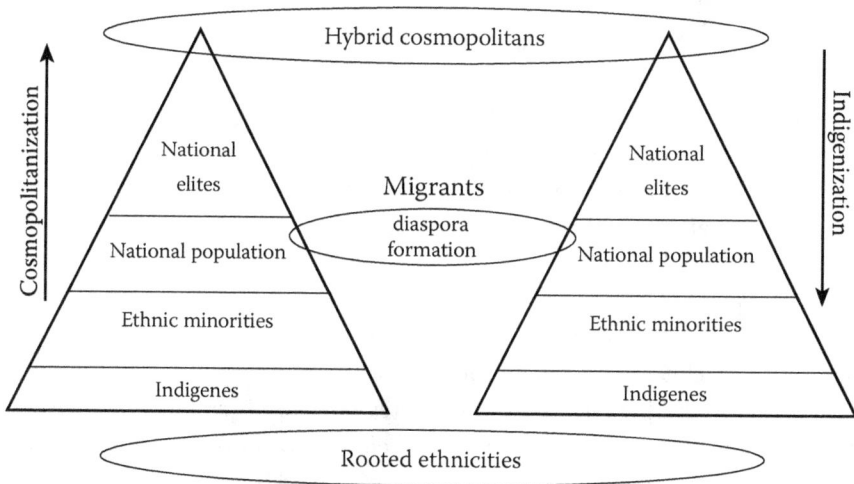

Figure 3   The dialectic of cosmopolitanization and indigenization.

Figure 3 represents the location of cosmopolitan elite identity within the larger context of the nation-state. It is the cosmopolitan space itself that defines the contours of elite identity and which is the locus of production of cosmopolitan discourse. Intellectuals elaborate their discourses from within this space but are not its originators. The positionality of cosmopolitan intellectual identification has been critically assessed by Dirlik (1997) in a work whose title is itself revealing. *Postcolonial Aura* deals with various aspects of the relation between the transformations of global capitalism and the rise of post-colonial elites from the upper echelons of the Third World.

> The current global condition appears in the discourse only as a projection
> of the subjectivities and epistemologies of First World intellectuals of Third
> World origin: the discourse constitutes the world in the self-image of these
> intellectuals, which makes it an expression not of powerlessness but of
> newfound power.
>
> (Dirlik 1994:344)

Perhaps overdrawing the relation between position and ideological content, but clearly on the right track, he suggests:

> To insist on hybridity against one's own language, it seems to me, is to
> disguise not only ideological location but also the differences of power that
> go with different locations. Postcolonial intellectuals in their First World
> institutional location are ensconced in positions of power not only vis-à-vis
> 'the native' intellectuals back at home, but also vis-à-vis their First World
> neighbors here. My neighbors in Farmville, Virginia, are no match in power
> for the highly paid, highly prestigious postcolonial intellectuals at Columbia,
> Princeton, or Duke; some of them might even be willing to swap positions
> and take the anguish that comes with hybridity so long as it brings with it
> the power and the prestige it seems to command.
>
> (ibid.: 343)

Figure 3 also represents the double polarization characteristic of periods of hegemonic decline. It is not applicable to East Asia, where an inverse process of integration is occurring and where elites tend to be national rather than cosmopolitan. Horizontal fragmentation, referred to above, based on cultural identification related to ethnic, gender, territorial and other cultural categories is accompanied by a vertical polarization in which class distance increases and new elites as well as new lumpenized underclasses emerge. These are complementary processes and are inconceivable as autonomous phenomena. Thus the cosmopolitanization of elites in a process of upward mobility occurs simultaneously with the indigenization of downwardly mobile sectors of the population that, with no hope of future mobility, search for roots. Here the horizontal and vertical become co-terminal. Nationalist fundamentalism is equivalent if not identical, in structural terms, to Islamic fundamentalism, and the two confront one another in the multicultural street. In the nation-state context it is a confrontation between the national (native) and the transnational (diasporic, Islamic); but both are fundamentalist in content.

The cosmopolitan is also more than a mere representation of the world. Its strategy of encompassment hides a separation from the masses, the creation not only of a segregated world of schools, hotels, restaurants, but also one of interaction and even of intermarriage. There is, then, an equivalent ethnicization of the elite so that class position is consolidated by cultural identity. Here again there is evidence from elites, if not necessarily from intellectual elites. Thus, while the latter describe themselves as open, tolerant and even encompassing with respect to the world's diversity, they tend to transform that diversity into a relation of consanguinity.

'j'ai le sang ex-patrié' … Je suis américain, de passeport et de nationalité mais ma famille et celle de ma femme aussi, ont un grand nombre de ramificationsdans beaucoup de pays, ce qui fait qu'on a toujours eu en peid aux Ètats-Unis un peid à l'étranger.

['I have ex-patriot blood' … I'm American by passport and nationality, but my family as that of my wife, have a great number of branches in many countries, which means that we always have a foot in the United States and one abroad.]

Mon père était un peu vagabond, et on avait ca dans les veines. Mes frères, c'est pareil: j'ai un frère en Autriche, un en Finlande, une soeur en Espagne. Mon père se déplacait beaucoup, et j'ai dû prendre ca.

[My father was a bit of a vagabond. He had it in his veins. My brothers are similar: I have a brother in Austria, one in Finland, a sister in Spain. My father moved a lot and I seemed to have followed suit.]

(Wagner 1999:116)

And the opposition with respect to the 'other', the plebeian, also manifests the complementary of this double process. They are referred to by these elite subjects as 'terrestrials' in contradistinction to themselves. The verticality of the representation is clearly a question of social difference:

Alors le terrien, c'est quelqu'un qui a un espace limité. Son activité se concentre sur la terre qu'il possède. Si l'autre va sur sa terre, il ne l'acceptera pas. Il est attaché à sa famille, à ses enfants, qu'il veut garder chez lui, parce que sa famille cultive sa terre.

[The earthling, then, is someone who lives in a limited space. His activities
are concentrated on the land that he inhabits. He would never accept
someone trespassing. He is attached to his family, to his children whom he
tries to keep at home because his family needs to cultivate its land.]

(ibid.:204)

Here openness is at the same time the expression of a specific biologized/
racialized identity. This is also conveyed by the fact that cosmopolitan identity
hovers above the nation-state, the transcendence of which is its very definition.
And at the bottom of this polarized social order, already classified as local,
stuck in the ground, closed and xenophobic, it can be suggested that there
are real indigenous groups that in some cases seek to exit the nation-state via
the bottom, forming international alliances. Some racist groups, giving up
on the multicultural nation-state, have their own international organizations
based on race rather than 'nation'. The Washitaw Indians are Black self-
identified Indians occupying three southern states of the U.S, and may be
said to combine these two tendencies. They have a homepage, an empress,
their own licence plates, and an arsenal of weapons that keeps the authorities
at bay. They combine Black and American Indian identity, claiming to have
come to the New World when it was still joined to the continent of Africa. It
is noteworthy that they are allied to the white militia group 'The republic of
Texas' in a paradoxical union that pits them both against the main enemies:
Washington, the Vatican, the Jews and all others who have an agenda of world
domination. In this sense, cosmopolitan representations of the social order are
quite complementary to those of the indigenized bottom of that order. They
find themselves at opposite ends of a shared semantic space.

Both identities are part of an oppositional praxis that can only be
understood in terms of a broader process of double polarization. The
cosmopolitan space has been a zone of attraction for a great number of
intellectuals. We have argued that it is the intellectuals that are the primary
producers and bearers of the discourses of cultural globalization within which
hybridity has come to play such a prominent role. The examples supplied
above suggest that this identity is one that cuts across previous left-right
divisions; it might be further suggested that there is a merging of the centre
left and right in the contemporary transformation of such elites, one that is
implied in the inversion of the content of the notion of the 'progressive'.

The logic of post-colonial cosmopolitanism

The formation of cosmopolitan elites is a product of the conjuncture of the
wider inversion of ideology with a process of upward mobility that produces
a distance to 'the people'. This is a process of ideological ranking as well as

class differentiation. If there is a logic to this positioning, it seems to have the following schematic structure:

Positioning 'above' the world generates a reconfiguration of the world's actual fragmentation in terms of a vision of 'diversification' or (in more static terms) simply 'diversity' and (in common policy parlance) 'multiculturalism'. This diversity includes the national population with which one might at one time have been identified, in an earlier period of stronger national identity. The result is the fracture of the relation between the state as container and a nationally defined population. The latter becomes just another ethnic group similar to the other ethnic groups that have come to occupy the territory as immigrants. In this way the state is separated from the former nation and becomes redefined as a multi-ethnic or multicultural polity. Hybridity expresses the idea of the mixedness of this identity, but it is often the product of the consumption of diversity rather than any participation in it. Consumption is the practical expression of what in identity terms is encompassment of the world's differences. Real difference is often frightening and far too vulgar for the new sophisticates, who prefer to objectify , or rather commoditize, it so as to be suitable for furnishing the space of elite living rooms and salons. In this sense hybridity is the encompassment of diversity within the life space of the cosmopolitan. 'We are the world', it is said; but not the real world of social experience, only the object world.

This logic generates an enemy, that part of the population that is either indigenizing or really indigenous in the sense defined by the United Nations. Both of these populations are oriented to local territory and tend to stress the necessity of homogenization, either by exclusion or by assimilation. The latter are, in these terms, closed against globalization, and probably racist, a term that has come to be conflated with nationalism and localism (see Hardt and Negri above). The logic of cosmopolitanism is a positional logic, but it is internally coherent and for its participants quite authentic as a form of identity. It is in this context that we can understand the way the same arguments are replicated repeatedly across different domains and why the discourse creates a resonant sense of familiarity for those who partake in it.

It is important to note that we are arguing against the idea that discourses of globalization are either the product of scientific activity or of intellectuals as such. Rather, the bases of the latter are in a certain position within the world of the nation-state, the global arena and the kinds of experience they generate. The examples of self-identified cosmopolitans are not taken from interviews with intellectuals. The spontaneity of the cosmopolitan imaginary is perfectly resonant with the discourse of consultants who often have their laptops as their only offices. In interviews with such higher end

consultants at the transnational corporation Cap Gemini, the following kinds
of statements are made: 'J'avais 30 ans et j'aspirais à m'ouvrir sur le monde…
Je suis pour l'évolution: le décloisonnement est très enrichissant. On s'apporte
mutuellement beaucoup. [I was 30 and I wished to open myself to the wider
world. I am for evolution: opening up oneself is very enriching. We have so
much to give one another.]' (Chemin 2001:22).Openness to the wider world,
seen in evolutionary terms, is a process of enrichment. These are the kinds of
terms that can be found in the pages of *Public Culture*. The parallels are not
the product of diffusion, but of spontaneous recognition or interpretation of
the world.

> Awareness of global interconnectedness is the key. Most globally aware
> individuals can tell you about the gradual process they experienced or the
> 'ahha' moment when they suddenly realised 'its all one world'. From Earth
> Day to the Amazonian rainforest, it may have been their interest in ecology
> and the environment; for others it may have been actual travels, or exposure
> to international organizations like the United Nations or humanitarian relief
> agencies, even the Peace Corps. Space exploration has also contributed to
> the 'one world' realization … Whatever the source, being able to think and
> feel interconnected on a global level is what's causing the paradigm shift
> here. The world is borderless when seen from a high enough perspective,
> and this has all kinds of implications: socially, politically, economically
> and even spiritually … Regardless of how the awareness began, it generally
> culminates in a sense of global citizenship … The best approach is to
> develop a sense that 'I belong anywhere I am, no matter who I am.'
>
> (Barnum 1992:142)

Thus, while intellectuals may indeed be engaged in elaborating on a
cosmopolitan identity, there is a core of representations that are more
generally accessible and which is the basis of their writings.

Cosmopolitan governance

In a once strongly homogenizing Sweden a new multicultural state has been
declared, following the logic outlined above. This is not a mere change in
strategy, although such change is the overriding factor. It is declared that the
once homogeneous country not longer has a common history. In the well-
known government 'Integration proposition' of 1997/98, which went on to
become the *Integration Act* we find the following preface:

> A country's history often serves to integrate individuals in a larger unity.
> As a large group of people originate from other countries, the Swedish

population now lacks a shared history. Contemporary membership in Sweden and support for the society's basic values has, therefore, greater significance for integration than a common historical origin.

(1997/98:23)

The state relocates itself above the various 'peoples' that inhabit it, and declares a neutral *primus inter pares* policy, in which Swedes and 'other immigrant populations' are defined as equally ethnic (note the confusion of ethnic, national and religious identity).

Further, the government has decided that a person's ethnic background or ethnicity can be Swedish as well as Sami, Finnish, Kurdish, Muslim, etc. (1997/98:33)

Finally, the new constitution of society is redefined as plural rather than national:

The point of departure for a new politics according to the government: society's ethnic and cultural plurality should be the basis of the formulation of general policy and its implementation in all the domains and levels of society.

(1997/98:19)

Policy-oriented intellectuals have argued for the necessity of immigration in order to create and maintain diversity, which is seen as a goal in itself:

Diversity is linked with immigration. If immigration is stopped, diversity is jeopardized. Policy-makers should reassess immigration policy. Diversity should not be seen as a means to handle what is perceived as 'problematic immigration'. Rather, immigration needs to be seen as the positive means to achieve the goal of diversity. All Western countries have ageing populations. If welfare systems are to be maintained immigration of labour power will soon become an economic demographic necessity.

(Westin 2000:734)

This implies that if immigrants decided to return home, or if life became bearable at home and they felt disinclined to leave in the first place, then we would have to force them to emigrate. The relation between this increasingly implemented policy and the self-identification of the government elites reinforces the distancing of the latter from anything resembling 'peoplehood'. When asked in a television interview if he were Swedish or not, the minister of integration (SVT, 21 April 1998) replied tersely, 'No! Definitely not!' and then proceeded to recount a mixed, that is, hybrid, genealogy that included

Scots, Germans and Danes. This is comparable to the hybrid blood referred to above, and can be understood as the same kind of identification except that it is not clear whether the minister feels at home anywhere in the world. In this transformation the question of class, once the major social question, is replaced by the question of identity, especially ethnic identity, and the major problem becomes racism itself. Many 'organic' intellectuals become instrumental actors in this transformation in which globalization is combined with immigration in a single scheme.

It is also perhaps not a mere coincidence that in this period political salaries have increased faster than all other salaries, or that there has been a plethora of scandals concerning abuse of credit cards and of state aeroplanes for private desires; that is, that there is an increasing lack of trust between the political class (a term that has only recently appeared in Swedish) and their constituencies. The social democratic prime minister has, unlike any minister before him, built a mansion during his period of office. The construction firm belongs to his brother. There is increasing evidence of political class (i.e. party) endogamy, and one commentator has referred to this as the 'political aristocracy' (Isaksson 2006). The prime minister is married to the director of the State Wine Monopoly, an employment that provides her a salary of 26,000€ per month. When the prime minister was asked how he could afford such a house he replied that he was married to a wealthy woman. Needless to say, it was he who had appointed his wife to her current position. All this appears as quite new to average citizens, not least those social democrats who had a very different kind of political culture in mind. Only a couple of decades ago Sweden was one of the most egalitarian democracies in the world. Politicians usually thought of themselves as servants of the people. They lived modestly and had modest salaries.

This transformation is not unique to Sweden, even if it represents an extreme example. In France a similar analysis has emerged of what a recent title calls *Le gouvernement invisible: Naissance d'une démocratie sans le peuple* (Jaffres 2001) which followed the book *La faute des élites* (Juilliard 1997). While these are quasi-journalistic works, they reflect an understanding that something has changed. While there has always been a political class of graduates from the ENA (Ecole nationale d'administration) and the Polytechnique, there has been, in this strongly republican country, a strong sense of the identification of that class with a popular project. But this is no longer the case.

Le constat de l'épuisement du modèle social-démocrate a transformé les militants de la révolution, puis de la réforme, en militants du libéralisme culturel.

> [The understanding that social democracy had run out of steam
> transformed these militants of the revolution, then of reform into militants
> of cultural liberalism.]
>
> (Juilliard 1997:201)

Here there is the same move from socialist or social democratic ideology toward cultural liberalism. This is echoed in the transformation of class to cultural politics more generally, leaving what is left of the working class to find its own identity and project (which it has done in its move to nationalism).

> Aux ouvriers elles ont substitué les immigrés et ont reporté sur ceux-ci le
> double sentiment de crainte et de compassion qu'inspire généralement le
> prolétaire. Or l'immigré n'est pas seulement victime de l'exclusion sociale,
> mais aussi de l'exclusion ethnique, autrement dit du racisme.

> [Immigrants have replaced workers and they are the object of a double
> feeling of fear and compassion that the proletarian once inspired. But
> the immigrant is not merely victim of social exclusion but also of ethnic
> exclusion, in other words, racism.]
>
> (ibid.:105)

This leaves the former class, the so-called *français de souche* or 'ethnic French' (another new term, generated by the ethnic fragmentation and ethnicization discussed above) in a position of being red-necked, backward-looking, closed, populist and, of course, potentially or actually racist or even fascist.

> Fallait-il aller plus loin et se demander....si le peuple n'est pas un ennemi
> naturel de la démocratie, séduit par l'autoritarisme, complice des tyrans et
> enclin à la violence.

> [Should we go further and ask... if the people are not the natural enemy
> of democracy, seduced by authoritarian and accomplice of tyrants and
> violence.]
>
> (ibid.:204)

These parallels are indicative of powerful forces at work in the social and political transformation of the state. The globalization of the elites, the separation of the state from the nation and a combination of structural changes in political strategy that empty politics of its former ideological content. Instead, the goal is simply to maintain power and even to increase it.

This is evident in the emergence of New Public Management as an eventual replacement for democratic rule, one that appears easiest to apply at the local or the global/regional level, since it can go unnoticed by the majority of citizens who care increasingly little about politics.

> NPM discourse is constantly confronted with a powerful counter-discourse
> of 'public sector values' stressing democracy, equality, accountability,
> participation etc. In NPM discourse, the contradiction does not exist;
> management techniques are said to provide the same benefits as classical
> democratic institutions: to be responsive to customers is equivalent to
> democratic control, measuring performance is the essence of accountability,
> choice is pluralism, etc.
>
> (Bislev, Hansen and Salskov-Iversen 2000:27)

This is the discourse that informs what is called, in various guises, *la voie unique*, or in Swedish, *den enda vägen*, the former expression from the left, the latter from the right. And it is this strategy that is the core of the 'new socialism', including that of the American New Democrats, the British Third Way and the more revealing German Neue Mitte. This strategy, following NPM, is simply economic liberalism combined with a minimal welfare policy. It is the definition of a new centre of political power, one that defines itself as progressive, but not necessarily in the traditional sense. Anthony Giddens, the major theorist of the Third Way, puts it as follows:

> 'Radicalism' cannot any longer be equated with 'being on the left'. On the
> contrary, it often means breaking with established leftist doctrines where
> they have lost their purchase on the world.
>
> (Giddens 2000:39)

That is, sometimes radicalism implies its opposite, which is why Blair is sometimes referred to as 'Thatcher without the handbag'.

NPM discourse is an essential part of the politics of global institutions, not least in the European Union, where a green paper on 'organic democracy' stresses that the true actors in the new form of governance are governments, multinationals, ethnic corporations and the like. The role of the demos is reduced to the legitimation of the real governance that is projected as the future of European politics (Burns *et al.* 2000). It is interesting to consider the logic involved here. NPM implies that the best solutions to political problems that can be arrived at by experts. They are thus removed from the political sphere and become issues of organization. Now, if there is only one way to run a governmental process, then the question of political differences disappears in the equifinality of strategic choices. All parties use more or less the same experts, so political difference is reduced to the minimum. So why vote at all. What can people, already defined as basically ignorant and potentially dangerous have to say in such an important process? That people have already understood this in some sense is reflected in the declining participation in electoral politics, as well as in the increasing populism that is an expression of precisely the fact that the people are no longer consulted on issues concerning their existence.

This transformation creates a serious problem for politicians, and does much to account for the practically hysterical use of the word 'democracy' in global and national politics. Democratization of the world has become the major goal of Western states. And since it is no longer the democratic process that is essential, as there are no longer any choices, the word itself has become transmuted. It no longer refers to the political arena but to the attributes of persons. It is now embodied and represents the notion of respectability. This the product of the transformation of a diametrical dualism into a concentric dualism.

In a seminal article, Lévi-Strauss (1963) argued that there is a common distinction to be found amongst kinship-based societies. There are those based on reciprocal relations, best expressed in what is called moiety organization, where the entire society is divided into two parts that marry one another and which, following the logic of reciprocity, are more or less egalitarian, at least in the long run. This is apparent in the spatial organization of villages in which there are two halves separated by central structures or a public space, or even a men's house. This is contrasted to another village form in which there is also a kind of dualism, but one that is expressed in the relation between a central zone and a periphery. In this the centre is associated with seniority, males, chiefs; the periphery with youth, females and commoners. This structure is also open, in so far as it can extend out to the world so as to express a more general oppositions between culture and nature, cultivated and savage, cooked and raw. This mode of organization is referred to as concentric dualism. It is dualist, but it is also hierarchical or asymmetrical, in so far as the two halves of the opposition are unequal. And while it may express itself in dualist terms, it also expansion to a third term or even a continuum of terms. Lévi-Strauss argued that social dualism in general is ambivalent and that the truly diametric form does not exist in reality, being always complicated by the existence of asymmetrical relations. There is also a suggestion that this ambivalence has a historical significance, in so far as diametric and concentric dualisms are historically related. Diametric dualism can thus become concentric in the process of hierarchization, though the reverse process is also possible.

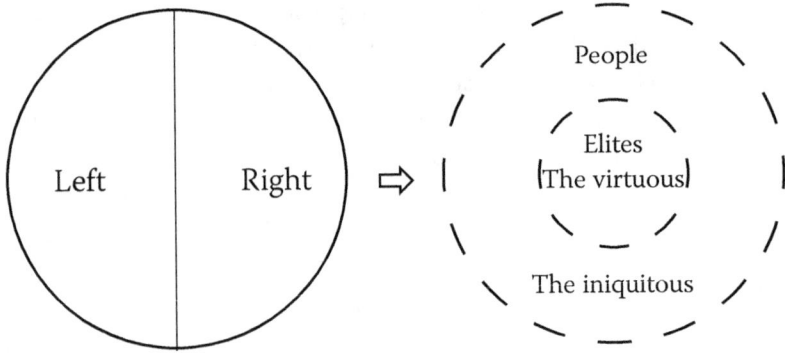

Figure 4   Diametric to concentric dualism.

One can apply this kind of dualist analysis to the transformation of the Western political sphere, even if neither the form nor the process is identical. The left/right opposition dominated politics throughout the 'modern' era, even if there was also a continuum with respect to the extreme parties of the left and the right. The left/right polarity however was dominant, in that it organized the discourse around a pro-socialist versus a pro-capitalist opposition. This was also, of course, the era of class conflict, upon which the opposition of left and right was founded. This diametrical dualism has today been transformed into a concentric dualism, for the reasons we have outlined. The unitary solution of the *voie unique* and the Third Way is best expressed in the spatial notion of the Neue Mitte, the 'New Centre', a fusion of right-centre and left-centre that defines a new kind of politics, one that is self-defined as simply practical and effective, i.e. New Public Management. It renders democratic politics irrelevant by obviating the issue of political alternatives. The new centre represents respectability; those who implement the best engineered solution to whatever social problem should arise. Those who still maintain ideologies and are, by definition, to the right and left of this centre are re-categorized as the non-respectable, the undemocratic, the iniquitous. They are sometimes reduced to populism, fascism, left and right, and they are associated with a population that is redefined as the dangerous classes. Concentric dualism opens towards various other categories and represents a continuum of respectability rather than an opposition between discrete complementary categories. Mayor Livingstone of London, too far to the left for Blair, was attacked as undemocratic in the same kind of language used to attack the right-wing Haider in Austria. The embodiment of the notion of democracy (referred to above) is clear in these examples. It is now people that are democratic or not, rather than the political arenas within which they operate. This embodiment and reconfiguration of the term is a significant aspect of the transformation of the political sphere. The process also entails the moralization of the political. 'Democratic' is not only equated to respectable in the social sense, but even more so in the moral sense. It implies that one is able to carry out the strategy of the dominant party, to maintain political power, to mystify really serious problems so that people 'don't get upset'.

The concentric structure is not entirely separate from the diametric structure. The two are interwoven in an ambivalent reality within which one or the other forms can become dominant. Changing dominance is, of course, a question of historical context, and we suggest that it is part of the larger process of declining hegemony, even if it can also arise in other circumstances. A Swedish social democrat expressed this by saying, openly, that a conservative–liberal party victory was the equivalent of a *coup d'état* for her. The openness of concentric dualism applies both to the top and bottom. Thus the elites need not belong exclusively to the territorial state, but can hover in the higher realm of the transnational, whether regional (EU) or global. If the latter is conceived as a conical, rather then two–dimensional, concentric form this becomes easily apparent. In this way the upward mobility of elites is also their outward mobility, just as depicted in the pyramidal structure in Figure 3. It is also expressive of the transformation of governance we have outlined. Here the cosmopolitan content of the new political discourses are clearly identical with cosmopolitan identity in general, so that the discourse of globalization can already be said to contain a certain form of governance within itself. In the green paper on the future of democracy proposed for the European Commission we find an entirely new system of governance. The diagnosis involved in the promotion of the new governance is as follows:

First, the causes of the need for a new governance are:

- *Increasing scientification of politics*, particularly the use of expertise. In the politics of knowledge and technology, scientific and technical experts advise policy-makers. However, experts do not speak with a single voice or authority. As a result, effective monitoring, deliberation, and decision-making about many, if not most, policy areas today are far beyond the capacity of a typical parliament. The sovereignty of experts complements as well as competes with parliamentary or popular sovereignty.
- *Expanding role of organizations as vehicles of collective decision-making.* Governance is diffused beyond parliament and its government, resulting in participation by groups – which the paper describes as organizational citizens rather than individual citizens. Although such groups expand the

issue agenda, many major processes of governance escape the reach of the nation-state.

- *Changing international environment*, which is characterized by globalization, transnationalism, and regionalization. A particular problem is the twofold phenomenon of globalization and the sectoral specialization of the agencies of governance, which reduces policy options and shifts problems towards an international/supranational space not governed by the traditional forms of democracy. (Burns *et al.* 2000:2)

The political has been reduced to expertise or even science (NPM). Instead of citizens we now have collective actors unaccountable to the nation-state. Globalization has transformed the entire field of decision-making in relation to traditional democracy. The solution is a new 'organic' democracy:

- *Representation.* Representation in the new governance arrangements is highly heterogeneous, specialized, and distributed. Diverse interest groups represent themselves, which contrasts sharply with territorial representation in parliamentary democracy.
- *Sovereignty and authority.* A new dispersed sovereignty is emerging, which is layered, segmented, diffused, and increasingly non-territorial.
- *Responsibility* and accountability — for policy-making and regulation formally reside in the system of parliamentary democracy. In practice, other agents have assumed much of this power and reduced parliamentary government's practical authority. Most of those exercising influence over policy-making are not accountable to the larger public but to their specialized organizations and interests as well as to themselves. Public expectations about responsibility are misplaced, in large part because they are grounded in political mythology of national sovereignty and parliamentary democracy.
- *The transformation of 'law' and public policy-making.* In the past, one distinguished between laws, which were determined through legislative processes, and norms and contracts, which emerged through interactions in civil society. Today we have a wide variety of collectively determined rules and regulations as well as regulative forms, in addition to other social control mechanisms. (Burns *et al.* 2000:3)

The solution proposed by Burns *et al.* is to simply ride the wave and adapt governance to the changing conditions of power. Thus the political process is dominated by various interest groups, be they transnational firms or ethnic corporations, rather than by a 'people', who may also be redefined as a special interest group. Rather than having parliamentary democracy, the rules of the game are now such that accountability is not to a public but to specific publics, a plurality of 'peoples', organizations, firms, NGOs, etc. Finally, law is transcended by a complex system of rules and regulations that emerge in the new interactions among new dominant actors. The true organic democracy is the order that is worked out among these actors. What is missing in all of this is the demos. Their function is reduced to precisely that of legitimating the rest of the process. This fascinating scenario, democracy without the demos, is implicit in NPM and sometimes explicit in policy statements. Organic democracy is a variant of the general logics that we have discussed, one which is not as new as it at first appears. It is close to the kinds of rule found in absolutist states and in previous imperial structures. In this transition it can be seen that sovereignty, which, formally at least, passed from the state (as royalty) to the people throughout the nineteenth and twentieth centuries, is on its way back to the state (again as a class itself, a new aristocracy).

Sweden has for several years had a minister of democracy, a minister whose function is unclear according to the person who was appointed. Her new salary was high, especially for Sweden, and she was very happy with it. She also admitted to having gotten the appointment via her mother, a former minister. Several questions are pertinent here. If Sweden is a democracy, why does one need a minister of democracy? What does it imply for democracy when such a minister has received her position via family connections and influence? The idea of such a ministerial position is related to the obvious decline in citizen participation in elections and the documented growing lack of respect for politicians. A ministry of democracy would provide remedies for this situation. Efforts at spreading more information to 'the people' and the usual slogans concerning the equal worth all people did not succeed in eliciting scepticism. An enormous number of reports were published during this period, but there is no indication that they were taken seriously. The secretary of the committee on democracy complained that the government was reluctant to accept increased citizen power. The government proposition presented by the new minister in 2002 was attacked by four of the country's leading political scientists, who complained that the government apparently thinks that it is the citizenry itself that is the greatest problem for democracy, not those who govern (Petersson *et al.* 2002). Another commentator (Jonsson 2002) discussed the language used in attempting to improve democracy, the avowed function of a minister of democracy. One of the most common terms dealt with what is called 'anchoring' or grounding of government policy among the people. The methods are well known and include an array of techniques taken from the advertising industry. But the direction is clearly top-down rather than bottom-up. Given precisely the 'legitimation crisis' occurring in the country, it seems the primary purpose of the new ministry is to re-legitimate governance as it now functions, rather than to change its structure. It is interesting that this is precisely the function designated to the European Parliament in the vision of organic democracy, that is, the legitimation of the functioning of the real governmental process.

Conclusion: cosmopolitanism and the absolutist state

We have traced the relation between intellectuals and globalization to the transformation of the political order of the Western state. The argument we propose runs as follows:

1. The process of globalization is a concomitant of hegemonic decline and a major shift in the locus of world accumulation.

2. In this process the forces of integration that existed previously, and as expressed in the international order of nation-states under Western hegemony, begins to unravel.

3. This leads to the breakdown of imperial order and to political and cultural fragmentation in the geopolitical arena, a process that is primarily intra-state rather than inter-state, as it is the state that is increasingly weakened by the export of capital and the resultant indebtedness.

4. In terms of identity, the transformation involves the decline of modernism and the rise of processes of cultural identification: ethnic, indigenous, national, regional. In some parts of the system, especially its weaker links, these processes lead to conflicts among the cultural fragments, or between the fragments and the state. Political instability in these zones leads to mass migration toward the declining centre.

5. There is also a real fragmentation of the economic process under the pressure of decline: flexible accumulation, outsourcing, flexible labour, lumpenization and marginalization. Fordism is replaced by networks of outsourced production and globalized circulation of people and goods within such networks. Guns, drugs and people are among the major economic sectors in the world economy today.

6. These networks, not least the illicit ones, link up with the fragmentation process itself, arming gangs, militias and mafias for the increasingly violent hunt for wealth and power.

7. There is also massive vertical polarization within the state order itself. The upwardly mobile become both wealthier and globalized, and numerous groups are drawn into this process of elite formation. Finance capital, media elites, political classes and cultural elites, including intellectuals, all interact within a process of cosmopolitanization; simultaneously, the lumpenized bottom fragments ethnically and the former national population indigenizes.

We are primarily concerned with the upper echelons of the global order, but one cannot understand them outside of the larger context sketched here. The role of the intellectuals is, of course, variable, depending on the way they are distributed within the social order itself. We have argued that there is a strong tendency for the formation of a cosmopolitan intellectual elite that contributes significantly to the development of a coherent ideology that is exhibited in the field of discourses referred to as globalization. But globalization is not their invention. It is, to the contrary, the spontaneously derived experience of occupying a particular social position (such as frequent flying). When this organic representation of the world is elaborated upon it becomes the foundation not only for globalization discourses and concepts such as multiculturalism and hybridity, but also for democratization, human rights and the like.

1. The emergence of elite globalization discourses, a product of the social mobility of a certain segment of the intellectuals, occurs in a situation of ideological inversion in which a former critique of Western imperialism is transformed into a purely cultural critique of Western culture, values, science and rationality. This is expressed in the form of occidentalism. All things culturally dangerous and bad are associated with those who still identify with the social field of national identity, those who have not elevated themselves to a post-national position.

2. This generates in its turn a tendency (one among others) to a division in the political elite, pitting national against cosmopolitan factions. In Sweden, where the latter are dominant, the state moves from the nation-state format to that of the multicultural state. In this most extreme form, the population inhabiting the state is redefined as a set of ethnic groups of nationals, indigenous populations and immigrant ethnic minorities. All are defined as ethnic groups, including the national population, and the political class re-situates itself in cosmopolitan space: identifying with Europe or with the world. In France there are similar tendencies but globalization discourse has not (yet) become dominant. There is there a significant political tendency that identifies as 'left republicanism', an impossibility for the Swedish elite, for whom republicanism equals nationalism equals essentialism and racism and therefore cannot be associated with the left. On the European scale, cosmopolitan ideology has made much headway and it is here, as in international organs such as UNESCO and the World Bank, that a particular pluralist notion of global governance has become increasingly dominant.

3. This development seems to imply a number of related tendencies:
   a. The separation of the state from the nation. What might be referred to as the lift-off of the state implies the transformation of the people into

a set of 'peoples' or ethnic populations, including the former national
population.

b.   In this process the state is also transformed from within, with a transfer
of a sovereignty from people to a governing body. This accounts for
the increasing power allocated to state institutions, the tendency
to represent a set of abstract principles embodied in the idea of
democracy, and the inversion of the relation of representativity itself.
The state now represents the higher principles of democratic rule vis a
vis the people, rather than being itself the representative *of* the people.

c.   Rulers participate in a higher cosmopolitan sphere, the regional or
the global, where they discuss solutions to issues of governance and
formulate plans that are not the product of grass-roots initiatives but
which must at most be made acceptable to those roots. This is the gist
of NPM methodology, one that occurs (as in the situation above) when
real political choices are replaced by a praxeology of rational rule, itself
an ideology of absolute power.

d.   These processes provide the basis for the transition from diametric to
concentric dualism. The function of respectability in this transition is
that it fixes the status of political leaders in an absolutist way. They
become independent of the usual democratic process, embodying
democracy in themselves. They embody as well the *voie unique* of a
new governance that is independent of any 'people's will'. They are
no longer representatives of the people but representatives of higher
principles. This new absolutism is cosmic, in so far as it derives from
a higher order; and it is also cosmopolitical, in so far as it unites the
rulers of the world in a potential network of morally exemplary actors
(except for those rogues and rogue states that are not allowed into the
fold). The conjunction of power and morality in this concentric order
has, increasingly, the character of theocracy, of absolutist rule based on
cosmic principles of 'the good'.

The fact that there is an implicit logic linking cosmopolitan ideology
and global governance of a particular kind ought not to be particularly
shocking, but the intuitively obvious character of the connection is not clear
and I have endeavoured to map this out for the reader. I have also argued
that intellectuals, who are the fellow travellers as well as script writers for
this historical tendency in regime change, have, therefore, a central role in
the process. I have not argued that intellectuals are to be seen as a unitary
phenomenon. On the contrary, there is a broad continuum of intellectual
positions within the historical process. But in order to account for the
formation of new positions, both with regard to social identity and to power,

it is crucial to keep in mind the fact that this history occurs within a broader logic of social re-configuration and re-identification that is its true explanatory context. This accounts for the complementary character of some of the texts that deal with the other end of this transformation, by those who might perhaps be classified as 'left republicans'.

> The *Neue Mitte* manipulates the Rightist scare the better to hegemonize the 'democratic' field, i.e. to define the terrain and discipline its real adversary, the radical Left. Therein resides the ultimate rationale of the Third Way: that is, a social democracy purged of its minimal subversive sting, extinguishing even the faintest memory of anti-capitalism and class struggle. The result is what one would expect. The populist Right moves to occupy the terrain evacuated by the Left, as the only 'serious' political force that still employs an anti-capitalist rhetoric—if thickly coated with a nationalist/ racist/religious veneer (international corporations are 'betraying' the decent working people of our nation). At the congress of the Front National a couple of years ago, Jean-Marie Le Pen brought on stage an Algerian, an African and a Jew, embraced them all and told his audience: 'They are no less French than I am—it is the representatives of big multinational capital, ignoring their duty to France, who are the true danger to our identity!' In New York, Pat Buchanan and Black activist Leonora Fulani can proclaim a common hostility to unrestricted free trade, and both (pretend to) speak on behalf of the legendary *desaparecidos* of our time, the proverbially vanished proletariat. While multicultural tolerance becomes the motto of the new and privileged 'symbolic' classes, the far Right seeks to address and to mobilize whatever remains of the mainstream 'working class' in our Western societies ... In this uniform spectrum, political differences are more and more reduced to merely cultural attitudes: multicultural/sexual (etc.) 'openness' versus traditional/natural (etc.) 'family values'.
>
> (Zizek 2000:37–8)

Cosmopolitanization and celestialization: a final note

Is there a general process involved in the transformation of political power? This discussion outlines a process of centralization and hierarchization that seems to have broad anthropological and historical parallels. In an analysis of the latter process among the Kachin of upper Burma, as it related to the formation of early Chinese states (Friedman 1998 [1979]), I argued that there were two components: one an invariant structure of the cosmos in which social seniority stretched from the living to the dead to the gods (Friedman 1998). This cosmos was not one in which the dead and the gods were simply the past generations of the living, but very much living intentional beings who did crucial work, providing society with fertility and life force in return for sacrifices. The other process was of political hierarchization, not necessarily an evolutionary but rather a historical process, in which prestige was converted into rank via marriage alliance and competitive feasting. Ability to provide larger distributions was immediately expressed as a better and therefore closer relation to ancestors and thus gods and the only possible form that this 'closer relation' could take was genealogical proximity. The capacity and activity of large-scale wealth distribution was defined and experienced as the product of kinship-structured seniority, so that prosperous lineages were immediately understood as socially elder, closer to the ancestors. Thus chiefship took form within a pre-established cosmic hierarchy.

Interesting in this respect is that there is a gradual inversion of the content of relations involved in this transition. At the start, a potential chief sacrifices to the ancestors on behalf of either his lineage or the larger village. In this relation, the chief represents the 'people' to the ancestors. At the end of the process, the acknowledged chief represents the ancestors vis a vis the 'people.' In this sense, the democratic is transformed into the autocratic. Early states were often theocratic in character, not because of the advent of a priesthood that ruled, or because after attaining power kings claimed sacred status, but because the logic of power was a logic of relations between the gods and the people. Political position was thus, by definition, 'religious' in character, though this notion of religion is ours and not theirs. Nor can the power of the ancestors, gods and sacred kings be understood as *'supernatural'* since in this cosmology that realm is clearly a part of nature. The formation of theocratic chiefdoms and states is not one that occurs locally and then spreads. On the contrary, as it is based on expanding exchange relations, it can be said that chiefly power is part of the formation of an inter-chiefly network. Thus local hierarchization is part of a regional (global) process and not an isolated phenomenon. The results are significant for our discussion. They link this smaller scale development with the logic of Chinese 'celestial bureaucracies' (Balasz 1968). While the processes involved are vastly different, there is a certain logic of hierarchy that links different forms of absolutism in which sovereignty always belongs to the top of the hierarchy.

NOTE

1   Those against the European constitution in France, discussed above, were referred to as reactionary and even racist, as were Swedes, whether nationalist or communist, who voted against accepting the common European currency.

REFERENCES

Appadurai, A., 1993, 'Patriotism and its futures', *Public Culture* 5: 415–40.

Balakrishnan, G. and S. Aronowitz, 2003, *Debating Empire*. London, New York: Verso.

Barnum, C., 1992, 'Effective membership in the global business community'. In *New Traditions in Business. Spirit and Leadership in the 21st Century*, ed. J. Renesch. San Francisco: Berrett-Koehler.

Salskov-Iversen, Dorte, Hansen, Hans Krause, and Bislev, Sven, 2000, 'Governmentality, globalization and local practice: transformations of a hegemonic discourse', *Alternatives* 25(2): 183–222.

Burns, Tom, Carlo Jaeger, Angelo Liberatore, Yves Meny and Patrizia Nanz, 2000, 'The future of parliamentary democracy: tradition and challenge in European governance', Green paper prepared for the Conference of the European Union Speakers of Parliament. European Commission, Secretariat General: European governance team, November, Brussels.

Buruma, Ian and Avishai Margalit, 2004, *Occidentalism: A Short History of Anti-Westernism*. London: Atlantic Books.

Castells, M., 2000, *The Rise of Network Society*. Oxford: Blackwell.

Chemin, C., 2001, 'Rhétoriques mondialisantes, rhétoriques de la mondialisation et production des champs sociaux en enterprise', *Mémoire DEA en Anthropologie Sociale*. Paris: EHESS.

Dirlik, A., 1994, 'The postcolonial aura: third world criticism in the age of global capitalism', *Critical Inquiry*, Winter: 328–56

——— 1997, *The Postcolonial Aura : Third World Criticism in the Age of Global Capitalism*. Boulder, Colo.: Westview Press.

Friedman, J., 1998 [first edition 1979], *System, Structure and Contradiction in the Evolution of "Asiatic" Social Formations* (2nd edition). Walnut Creek; Altamira: Westview Press.

——— 1998, 'Transnationalization, socio-political disorder and ethnification as expressions of declining global hegemony', *International Political Science Review* 19(3).

——— 2004, 'Globalization'. In *The Blackwell Companion to the Anthropology of Politics*, eds D. Nugent and J. Vincent. Oxford: Blackwell.

Giddens, A., 2000, *The Third Way and its Critics*. Cambridge: Polity Press.

Hannerz, U. (1992). *Cultural Complexity: Studies in the Social Organization of Meaning*. New York, Columbia University Press.

Hardt, M. and A. Negri, 2000, *Empire*. Cambridge: Harvard University Press.

Isaksson, A., 2006, *Den politiska adeln*. Stockholm: Bonnier.

Jacoby, R., 1994, *Dogmatic Wisdom: How the Culture Wars Divert Education and Distract America*, New York : Doubleday.

Jaffres, L. 2001, *Le gouvernement invisible: Naissance d'une démocratie sans le people*. Paris: Arlea.

Jonsson, A., 2002, 'Att legitimera makten', *Dagens Insustri* (28 January).

Juillard, Jacques, 1997, *La Faute des élites*. Paris: Gallimard.

Lévi-Strauss, C., 1963, 'Do dual organizations exist'. In *Structural Anthropology*. New York: Basic Books.

Mauss, M., 1969 [1920], 'La nation et l'internationalisme'. In Marcel Mauss, *Oeuvres*, vol. 3 : *Cohésion sociale et division de la sociologie*. Paris: Les Éditions de Minuit.

Nairn, T. and P. James, 2005, *Global Matrix : Nationalism, Globalism and State-Terrorism*. London. Ann Arbor, MI: Pluto Press.

Petersson, O., Holmberg, S., Lewin, L. and H.M. Narud, 2002, 'Statsvetare kritiserar demokratipropositionen: "Lejon glömmer politikernas ansvar"', *Dagens Nyheter* (22 January):4.

Pijl, K. van der, 1998, *Transnational Classes and International Relations*. London: Routledge.

Regeringens proposition 1997/98, *Sverige, framtiden och mångfalden – från invandrarpolitik till integrationspolitik*. Stockholm.

Quigley, C., 1981, *The Anglo-American Establishment: From Rhodes To Cliveden*. New York: Books in Focus.

Wagner, A.C. 1999 *Les nouvelles élites de la mondialisation: une immigration dorée en France*. Paris: Presses Universitaires de France.

Westin, Charles, 2000, '"A view from continental Europe", review symposium on report on the future of multi-ethnic Britain', *Journal of Ethnic and Migration Studies* 26(4):719–38.

Zizek. S., 2000, 'Why we all love to hate Haider', *New Left Review* 2.

INDEX

Abrams, Philip   1, 125–6, 142
acephalous organization   23–5
adoption   24, 39, 52
aesthetics   v, 13, 55, 57–8, 65, 72, 89, 161, 163–4, 174, 171
Agamben,Giorgio   9, 23, 41–2, 44, 49, 51–2, 127, 131, 142, 157, 159
agnatic, agnation   24–30, 33–4, 36–8, 40, 44, 47, 50, 118
Albania   225, 237, 249–51
Albu Nasir   103–5, 108, 119
ambiguity   26, 29, 32, 40–1, 44–7, 72–3, 76, 150, 174, 189–90, 234
Anderson, Benedict   164, 187, 235
anthropology, anthropologists   1–4, 9–10, 12–14, 23, 41, 46–8, 51, 55, 57, 61, 67,
        69, 81, 87, 89, 112, 115–17, 125, 244, 248, 261, 287
Arendt, Hannah   12, 23, 30, 38–9, 42, 46, 51
authority   4, 7–8, 23, 25, 29–34, 39–40, 47–9, 51–2, 59, 61, 92, 98, 105, 108–9,
        113, 116, 128, 156, 159, 164, 168–9, 188, 195, 204–5, 209, 211–12, 235, 277,
        281–2
autocracy   7–8, 16, 77, 133, 137, 195–6, 206, 288

Ba'ath Party   87, 94, 102–5, 109–10, 117–19
Badie, Bertrand   97–8
Baghdad   90–1, 94, 112, 114, 116, 119
Bali   15–16, 161–93 passim
Baratayuda   see Great War, the
'bare life'   41–2, 127, 129, 131, 140, 142–3, 157
bayt (house)   93, 96, 98–100, 102–3
Bedouin   95–6, 100
Bima   167, 173, 183, 185, 190
Bloch, Maurice   129, 251
body   2, 39, 98, 129–30, 138, 140–2, 174, 177
Bourdieu, Pierre   9, 15, 245, 250
bourgeoisie   91–2, 116, 197, 210, 265, 267
Buddhism, Buddhists   16, 148, 151–2, 155, 158, 163
bureaucracy   1, 5–6, 9, 14, 56, 68, 94, 158, 164, 166, 225, 243, 250, 288
buth   27, 31, 37

Cassirer, Ernst   v, 149–50
caste   9, 16, 25–6, 28, 30, 49, 51, 166, 168, 176, 190, 196–8, 200, 202, 208–9, 212,
        214, 216, 220, 262
chiefs, chieftanship   22, 36–7, 39, 49–51, 58–60, 68, 87, 91, 94, 98–9, 106–8, 111,
        118, 197, 199, 279, 288
China   6, 11, 88, 154, 157, 159, 210, 244, 263–4
chorus   64, 67–8, 76–7, 80, 82

www.ingramcontent.com/pod-product-compliance
Lightning Source LLC
Chambersburg PA
CBHW060149280326
41932CB00012B/1698